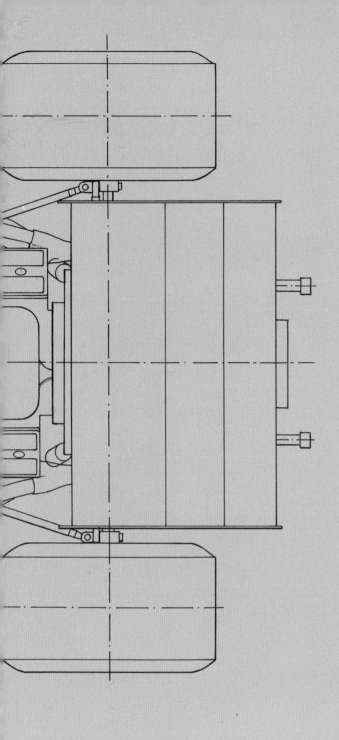

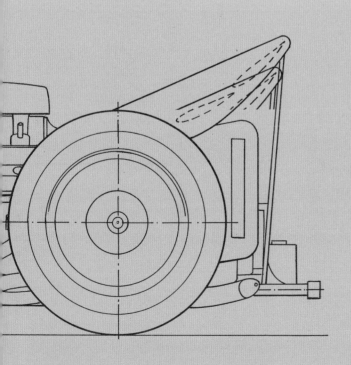

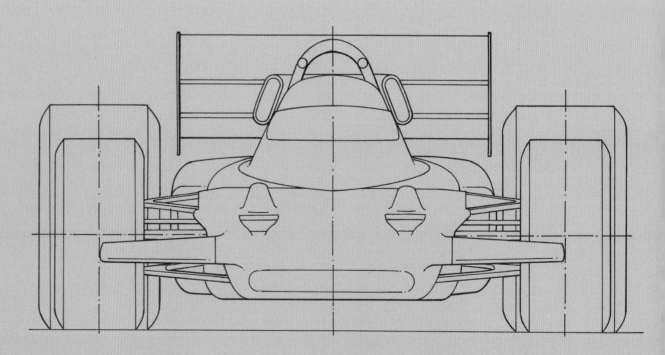

Item	PART No.	ASSY No.	No. OFF.	DESCRIPTION		

TEAM LOTUS
NORWICH NORFOLK NOR 92 W ENG

THIS DRAWING IS THE COPYRIGHT OF TEAM LOTUS LTD. IT IS PRIVATE
SUPPLIED ON THE EXPRESS CONDITION THAT IT IS NOT USED FOR
COMMUNICATED TO ANY OTHER PARTY WITHOUT THE WRITTEN
TEAM LOTUS LIMITED

SCALE	ONE TENTH FULL SIZE					P
LIMITS						

LAYOUT No.	WEIGHT	ESTIMATED:		ACTUAL.		VED
ISSUE	FINISH				DATE	
					TRACED	JGH
DATE	MATERIAL		SPECIFICATION	CONDITION	REMARKS	
FINISH						
	TITLE	TYPE 72 FORMULA ONE LOTUS GENERAL ARRANGEMENT				
APPROVED	GA No.			PART No.	72-2000	
MOD. No.	ASSY No.					

LOTUS 72

FORMULA ONE ICON

Michael Oliver

Coterie Press Limited

Lotus 72
FORMULA ONE ICON

A COTERIE PRESS BOOK

First British Edition July 2003
Published in the UK by Coterie Press Limited
6 Forest Hill Industrial Estate, Perry Vale,
Forest Hill, London SE23 2LX
Tel: +44 (0)20 8699 5111
Fax: +44 (0)20 8291 6463
coterieltd@aol.com

For other excellent books by Coterie Press have a look at our website:
www.coteriepress.com

Copyright © 2003 Coterie Press Limited
Text Copyright © Michael Oliver
Commissioned Photography Copyright © William Taylor
Other Photography Copyright © Individual Artist where applicable

All Rights Reserved
No part of this book covered by the Copyrights hereon may be reproduced, stored in a database or retrieval system or
copied in any manner whatsoever without written permission, except in the case of brief quotations embodied in articles
or reviews. For information on this please contact the publishers.

ISBN: 1 902351 06 1

The Publishers extend their special thanks for help in the preparation of this book to: Clive Chapman, Eddie Dennis and
everyone at Classic Team Lotus, Emerson Fittipaldi, Simon Hadfield, Michael Schryver, Fred Bushell, Eric Walitsch, David
McLaughlin, Hugh Edgley.

AUTHOR: MICHAEL OLIVER
CREATIVE DIRECTOR: WILLIAM TAYLOR
EDITOR: GILL OLIVER
DESIGN: PAUL COOPER DESIGN
PRINTED BY: COLORPRINT HONG KONG
ORIGINATION BY: MTA LONDON

ALL COMMISSIONED PHOTOGRAPHY IS BY WILLIAM TAYLOR
Other images courtesy of The Classic Team Lotus Archive, Ian Catt, Pete Lyons, Ford Image Library, Eric Walitsch, Dr
Milan Schijatschky, The GP Library, LAT Photographic, Ferret Photographic, Michael Keyser, Norman Hayes, Alex and
Miguel Soler-Roig, Michael Schryver, Jerry Booen, Ben van Rensburg, Aldo Zana, Joakim Thedin-ChampionCards, Dave
Sims, Stevie May, John Hostler, Brian Kreisky, Nigel Snowdon, Gary Critcher, Gianni Cancelliere-Actual Foto, Tony
Matthews, Paddy Driver, Allan Trim.

The 'IAN CATT COLLECTION' of over 10,000 motor racing images is managed under licence by Coterie Press and is
available to other publishers, at the above address.

The 'CLASSIC TEAM LOTUS' photo library and archive is also managed by Coterie Press and available for use.

The General Arrangement drawings that appear at the front and rear of the book were supplied by Classic Team Lotus.
Full size reproductions are available to purchase at **www.classicteamlotus.co.uk**

Contents

Foreword
by Emerson Fittipaldi

The first time I drove a Lotus 72, during practice at Monza in 1970, I had a huge crash and I was very lucky to escape without injury. The walk back to the pits was very difficult because I knew that, when I got there, I'd have to explain to Colin [Chapman] what I had done to his brand new car, which I was supposed to be running in for Jochen [Rindt]… I told him that it was completely my fault. Although he was not pleased at all, I think he respected the fact that I was honest.

I only had one other big accident in a 72 and, incredibly, that was in the same car, 72/5, nearly three years later at Zandvoort! That time it was a wheel failure, so there was nothing I could do about it. It probably cost me the World Championship in 1973, as I hurt my ankle and it was a long time before I felt comfortable in the car again.

To win the Championship in 1972 was something very special. We had such a difficult time in 1971 but we made some big improvements to the car at the end of the year so we knew we'd be in good shape for the next season. Everything just came good and the car was superb. When it was right you could drive hard and still keep the tyres in good condition. At Monza, when I had the chance to take the title, the weekend started badly – the transporter crashed, then I had a fuel leak just before the start – but we still won the race and the Championship!

I was very lucky in my career to join Lotus when I did, to work with Colin, Maurice Phillippe and Peter Warr and to drive what was, to me, one of the greatest Grand Prix cars ever, if not the best. It looked good too, particularly in black and gold and I still keep a model of my Championship-winning car in my office.

The 72 stayed competitive for so long and the reason for this was that we were constantly making improvements to it. If you look at the car in 1973 and compare it with how it started in 1970, the only thing that was similar was the monocoque and the basic style of the body. All the wings, wishbones, drive-shafts, pull-rods, gearbox layout, oil tank, were completely different. The basis of the car was the same but we were constantly modifying the suspension geometry, roll-centres and so on.

I am so pleased that someone has finally written a book about the 72. Michael has obviously made a big effort to track down the people who drove and worked with the cars and he has uncovered many interesting facts and stories that I'm sure you won't have heard before.

For me, it was a very special moment when I got back behind the wheel of my favourite chassis, 72/5, at the 2002 Goodwood Festival of Speed. The car is still owned by the Chapman family and Colin's son Clive was there to see it run, while my former Chief Mechanic, Eddie Dennis, was looking after it. It was 32 years since our disastrous start together at Monza but I felt like I had never been away from it. That is the sign of a truly great racing car.

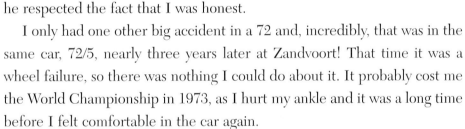

EMERSON FITTIPALDI MARCH 2003

INTRODUCTION

Colin Chapman once told Doug Nye: "The 72 went through unbelievable variations. By the end of its six seasons it was a totally different car to what had begun; you could write a book about that one alone…" Seeing as Doug has a lot on his plate these days and since I had already written a book about the Lotus 49, it seemed a natural progression for me to write one about its successor. Chapman was right – I've had no problem finding enough material!

The Lotus 72 is, in my opinion, one of the most striking Formula 1 cars ever to have graced the track, particularly in its menacing black-and-gold John Player Special livery. It and Emerson Fittipaldi are inextricably linked, for the Brazilian raced a 72 from October 1970 until October 1973 and even won a Championship in one. Emerson was my boyhood hero, so you can imagine what a pleasure it was to talk to him about his days driving the car. I was even more pleased when he agreed to provide the foreword for this book.

The 72 was a triumph of technical excellence, and therefore I have tried to give this aspect appropriate consideration. However, I am not an overtly technical person and I don't find page after page of complex terms and detailed specifications very appealing when I read books myself so I have tried to keep things straightforward and, where possible, explain technical language in layman's terms.

For me, the most interesting side of the story is the fact that its success was achieved because of the brilliance, determination and dedication of people, whether it was designers, draughtsmen, fabricators, mechanics, team managers, drivers or their wives. It is this story that I have tried to tell and to do so I have spoken to many people, for whose co-operation I am very grateful.

Although many of the key players such as Colin Chapman, Maurice Phillippe, Jochen Rindt and Ronnie Peterson are sadly no longer with us to contribute their side of the story, I am greatly indebted to those who have given their time so freely to assist in the compilation of this book. I think I can say with confidence that I have spoken to every surviving driver of a Lotus 72 – my only regret is that I didn't manage to make contact with Jim Crawford before his untimely death in 2002.

ACKNOWLEDGEMENTS

I would particularly like to thank the following:

Geoff Aldridge, Ralph Bellamy, Uta Blignaut, Sir Jack Brabham, Dougie Bridge, Allen Brown, Rory Brown, Manning Buckle, Peter Burroughs, Ian Campbell, Clive Chapman, Dave Charlton, Dave Clapham, Gary Critcher, Jabby Crombac, Bob Dance, Eddie Dennis, Paddy Driver, Hugh Edgley, Peter Elleray, Spencer Elton, Robin Emslie, Emerson Fittipaldi, Jim Fowler, Dougie Garner, Simon Hadfield, Adrian Hamilton, Gavin Hards, Rex Hart, Brian Henton, Dave Hill, Ken Howes, Gordon Huckle, Jacky Ickx, Mike Jacklin, Eddie Keizan, Stevie May, Vic McCarthy, Peter McIntosh, David McLaughlin, John McLoughlin, John Miles, Derek Mower, Gordon Murray, Doug Nye, Patrick O'Brien, Jim Pickles, Eddie Pinto, Dieter Rencken, John Robins, Tony Rudd, Dick Scammell, Ian Scheckter, Jody Scheckter, Michael Schryver, Trevor Seaman, Mary Seldon, Dave Sims, Alex Soler-Roig, Miguel Soler-Roig, Tony Southgate, Barry Sullivan, Norman Thersby, Andrew Thompson, Allan Trim, Tony Trimmer, Jannie van Aswegen, Dave Walker, Dave Walton, Peter Warr, John Watson and Reine Wisell.

Once again, I couldn't have written this book without the unerring support and encouragement of my wife Gill, whose sagacious editing has transformed my rambling prose into something more readable! I'd also like to say 'sorry' to my two boys, Matthew and Dominic, who once again have had to put up with me not being around in the evenings and weekends as much as they would have liked. Finally, a big 'thank you' to my father, Robert, for giving me access to his library at all hours of the day and night!

Michael Oliver
Witney, April 2003

CHAPTER 1 BACK TO THE DRAWING BOARD

The Lotus 72 was a car way ahead of its time, so much so that it was still winning races four years after it was first introduced. Indeed, some characteristics of its basic design concept, such as side radiators and torsion bar suspension, are still found on present-day Grand Prix cars. Its simple two-wheel drive 'back to basics' design carried forward some of the best facets of the Lotus 49, while at the same time tackling its weaknesses and embracing the latest thinking on aerodynamics.

The catalyst for its development came mid-way through the 1969 season, when it became clear to the Lotus boss Colin Chapman and his Chief Designer Maurice Phillippe that they were going to have to admit defeat with the innovative but troublesome Type 63 four-wheel drive Formula 1 car and literally and metaphorically go back to the drawing board. While the 49, in B specification, was still more than capable of winning races, it could not reasonably be expected to remain a competitive proposition for too much longer.

Failure was not a word which existed in Colin Chapman's vocabulary. However, a test with the 63 held at Oulton Park, the day after Jochen Rindt had driven it into second place in the Gold Cup race, convinced him that there were no significant benefits to be had from its complex four-wheel drive system. Former Team Lotus Chief Mechanic Bob Dance remembers the occasion well. 'What we found was that the more torque we transferred to the rear wheels, the better the car handled. Originally, we started off with the torque split as 60% to the rear wheels and 40% to the front but it ended up at 80:20. It was at that point that we decided we might as well revert to two-wheel drive without all the weight and friction penalties associated with the four-wheel drive car!'

Before designer Phillippe's untimely death, he explained the way in which the 72 came about to journalist Jabby Crombac: 'Colin said: "I am going to write down a series of requirements for the new car and I'd like you to do the same." We then went away and independently produced our lists. That made it possible to come up with individual ideas and then discuss them together. It was a

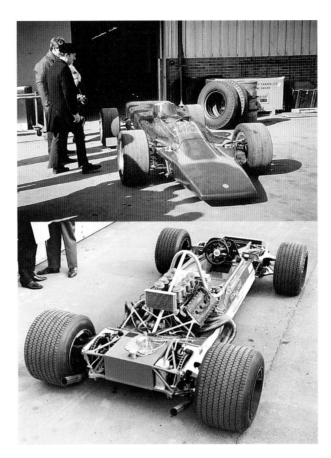

Top: With Colin Chapman looking on, the Type 56 emerges into the daylight for the first time at Hethel early in 1968. **Middle and Bottom:** The failure of the Lotus 63 was the catalyst for the development of the 72.

real challenge and you felt that you had to come up with good ideas. He insisted that he wanted a rising rate suspension. I wasn't convinced but he was the boss. On the other hand, the idea of inboard front brakes came from me.'

Former BRM Chief Engineer Tony Rudd remembers that the design process was already well underway by September 3rd 1969, which was the date he joined Group Lotus, after being unceremoniously sacked by BRM. He remembers this time very clearly: 'Colin always had a drawing board in the living room. In those days he lived in Keswick Road, Cringleford, before he moved into East Carleton Manor. I'd just joined Lotus and he was very good to me. I lived in a holiday home on the coast and Hazel Chapman used to invite me over to supper one, maybe two

nights a week. We used to have a meal and then he and I would retire to long sessions at his drawing board where the 72 layout was. He'd got a pretty good GA [General Arrangement] drawing on the board when we started to talk.'

In the period since the design of the Lotus 49, aerodynamics and tyres had become dramatically more important influences on Formula 1 car design and Chapman sought to exploit his great knowledge of the former area from his work at Indianapolis, and the latter via his close relationship with tyre company Firestone.

At Indianapolis in 1967, Team Lotus had carried out extensive tests with a Type 38 Indy car into the effects of lift (which could be generated both by the shape of the body and also the gyroscopic effects of the wheels spinning at high speed) on a car's position on the track and specifically its ride height. They were amazed to find that, far from being pushed down at high speeds, the car actually rose up on its suspension due to the lift induced by the body shape. The result was the striking wedge-shaped Type 56, which ran at Indy in 1968 and would have won the race but for a small failure in the turbine close to the finish. The car's 'doorstop' body shape countered the effects of lift and actually produced negative lift (more commonly known as downforce) in the same way that the nose fins and rear wings on a Formula 1 car did. The Type 57/58, designed as a dual Formula 1 and 2 car, also appeared with a wedge body shape in 1968 but was shelved following the death of

GOLD LEAF
TEAM LOTUS
RACING FOR BRITAIN

LOTUS 72 GRAND PRIX CAR

Above, Below & Opposite Page Far Right: Wedge profiles of Types 70 (Formula 5000/A), 57/58 (Formula 2/1), and 56 (Indy car), which pre-dated the 72. **Opposite Page Left:** The assembled audience of journalists, Team Lotus mechanics and office staff listen as Colin Chapman explains the thinking behind his new design.

Jim Clark and then abandoned when it was found that its De Dion suspension seemed to offer no tangible benefits over existing arrangements.

When the Type 63 four-wheel drive car failed in 1969, Chapman and Phillippe returned to the wedge profile used in those earlier designs and made it the basis for their 1970 Formula 1 challenger. By doing so, they would be using the shape of the body to produce downforce. This, allied with the adoption of a new design of rear wing, meant that they could achieve more overall downforce for less drag than rival cars. Weight distribution was another key factor, since it was a considerable influence on traction out of corners. Consequently, the decision was taken to try to achieve a bias towards the rear which, when allied to the large amount of downforce from the rear wing, would give the required levels of grip.

A common complaint from the drivers of the Lotus 49 was that they got roasted by heat from the front-mounted radiator. Their feet often got very hot or even burnt and the hot air sometimes made the drivers feel nauseous. The wedge shape of the 56 was achievable because no water radiators were required for the turbine engine but with a DFV they were a necessity, so instead of following normal practice of putting a single radiator at the front, Chapman and Phillippe decided to site two smaller radiators at the sides, by the driver's shoulders, which also helped achieve the stated aim of moving weight towards the rear of the car.

Chapman wanted to use the 72 to exploit his strong relationship with Firestone to maximum advantage. He and Phillippe decided that the best way they could do this was to run inboard brakes. This meant that the car had a low unsprung weight, the advantage of which was that the tyres the 72 ran could be softer, with less rigid sidewalls than those of its rivals and it could run a steering geometry that put less work into the tyres. It also meant that the uprights, wishbones etc could be much smaller and lighter because

they didn't have to carry the weight of brake discs and calipers. The only possible disadvantage of this arrangement was that it required a shaft to run from the inboard disc to the front wheel to perform the braking function and if these failed then the ability of the car to retard itself from high speeds would be severely compromised.

The two Lotus designers also concluded that suspension was another area in which they could gain an advantage. Instead of the traditional coil-spring and damper set-up, they opted for a layout utilising torsion bars, attached to the wheel upright by a complex linkage. This linkage was designed to give rising rate characteristics, so that it was soft under normal conditions but stiffened near the limits of its travel. What this gave was not only a car with a tremendously comfortable ride but, more importantly, it was designed to enable the handling of the car to remain

constant, regardless of the fuel load – although subsequently this turned out to be one area where the car had problems in races.

In addition, as Chapman once laughingly related to journalist and historian Doug Nye, it would prevent drivers (Graham Hill being the most notable example) from spending hours and hours lapping a circuit in practice, trying to sort out their car's bump-stops: 'My big dream of a car for Graham was one with rising-rate suspension, so he could never ever get on a bump stop! Then he couldn't play around with it, and that alone would have made my season…' Peter Warr, who was Competitions Manager of Team Lotus throughout the Lotus 72 period, recalls that a novel alternative to bump stops was adopted. 'The car was designed right from the word go with skid blocks front and rear. What would happen would be that, before the suspension got metal to metal on the dampers, or metal to metal on the torsion bar operators, the chassis would hit the ground. The drawback of that was that the piece that hit the road was the bottom of the front frame, because that was where the skid blocks were. And as soon as you had a damaged front frame the whole thing had to come out of the front of the car, get re-jigged, re-built and riveted back in. It was an absolute nightmare from the maintenance point of view.'

The other aspect of the suspension design of the 72 that was intended to allow it to make best use of its softer Firestones and aerodynamic characteristics, was the incorporation of anti-dive and anti-squat geometry. Anti-dive was used at the front to stop the car dipping under braking, and anti-squat at the rear, to prevent it from sitting down on its haunches under acceleration. This was achieved through angling the top and bottom front wishbones downwards at the front, and the rear radius rod

downwards towards the back of the car at the rear. Once these basic design parameters had been established by Chapman and Phillippe, work could begin in earnest on detailed design of the car. The earliest finished drawing of an individual component dates back to December 19th 1969, so it was clear from the start that the new car was not going to be ready for the season opener in South Africa on March 7th 1970, since this was less than three months away.

Work on the new car was carried out in great secrecy, according to Warr. 'We were still based in the main office of

Lotus designers concluded that suspension was an area in which they could gain an advantage

Lotus Cars, the big open plan office in the area that led through to the middle workshop which housed Team Lotus at the time. Beyond Colin's office there was a flat, which was accessible down a corridor from the director's garage, so that you could drive into the director's garage behind closed doors. So we set Maurice [Phillippe] up in the flat, with a drawing board. The idea was to keep things pretty much to ourselves. 'The workshop was self-contained in the sense that no-one else had access to it unless we said so. Secondly, all the elements of Team Lotus were in there – the fabricators, a couple of machines, the stores, and the bays for the race cars. But what it meant was that we could actually build things like the bucks and jigs, and then the first car out of the public eye. The car was sufficiently radical that we really wanted to be able to do it like that.'

It was so radical that Team Lotus found itself working with many outside component suppliers it had never previously used. This led to a number of problems due to them not being

used to the short time-frame demands of racing teams, as Warr recounts. 'The whole gestation period, the drawings, getting bits made and getting sub-contractors to deliver as well as finding parts that were different to any other parts that had ever been used was absolutely horrendous. Once they came together, the thing actually went together quite quickly – the final build of that car was probably only six weeks. But the gestation period was enormous.'

One particular component which caused headaches were the torsion bars, according to Warr. 'These were compound torsion bars with a solid shaft up the middle of a hollow one and couplings on either end, and they had to be gun-drilled. So you go to a company that does gun-drilling and they are used to saying "What is it, January? Oh well, would April be alright?" And you say "No, no, no, we want them by next week." And their reply is "Next week, guv? You've got to be bloody joking!" So we had to educate a whole new array of suppliers and contractors which made it all more complex from that point of view.'

No April Fool

On April 1st 1970 – April Fool's Day in the United Kingdom, traditionally a day for playing practical jokes – the world's press were invited up to the Lotus factory in Potash Lane, Hethel in deepest Norfolk, for the launch of the long-awaited 72. In those days there were no glitzy central London new car launches with music and scantily clad girls. Instead, the doors of the workshop were thrown open and journalists, team personnel and

photographers gathered around the car in a circle to listen attentively while Chapman briefed them on the key characteristics of the new car.

The most visually obvious aspect of the 72 was its sleek aerodynamic profile compared with other Formula 1 cars of its era. The low, chiselled nose at the front was facilitated by the decision to replace the traditional single front-mounted water radiator with the two smaller radiators slung either side of the tub. The whole top surface of the chassis sloped gently down towards the nose to generate downforce from the airflow across the car with the aerodynamic package completed by a distinctive three-tier rear wing balanced out by nose fins at the front.

The tub itself was a complex construction, since its manufacture involved double curvature, a job that had been entrusted to long-time Team Lotus sheet metalworker, Frank Cubitt. It not only bulged out in the middle where the majority of the fuel would be held in side tanks but the tub was also waisted in at the bottom. It was an exquisite job, with flush-riveting used to keep the external surfaces of the car as smooth as possible. It was not such an all-enveloping monocoque as the Lotus 49, being more of a bath-tub style of construction, with the driver being shielded from the airflow by a large Perspex windshield. The outer skins of the tub were made of 18 gauge NS-4 alloy sheet wrapped around steel bulkheads, while the inner skins for the cockpit and fuel cell cavities were mainly 20 gauge L-72 Alclad aluminium sheet. Fuel was housed in three separate FPT rubber tanks –two side tanks feeding a seat tank with a collector pot behind the driver's back. Total fuel capacity was 45 gallons.

At the front of the tub was the footbox housing the

throttle, brake and clutch pedals, which were hinged at the bottom, this also provided the mounting points for the solid inboard front brake discs and pads. An integral part of the footbox was an incredibly complex sub-frame made out of square tubing which supported the uprights and suspension, while the anti-roll bar was mounted in front of the footbox. The wishbones sloped sharply downwards, to provide the anti-dive characteristics sought by Chapman and Phillippe.

A thin tubular structure extended forwards from the footbox, which provided the locating point for the front nosecone as well as being home to the battery and fire extinguisher. Broad, 'A-shape' wishbones fabricated out of argon arc welded nickel-chrome-molybdenum were used top and bottom, onto which were mounted cast magnesium

alloy uprights, with a hollow brake-shaft joining the hub to the brake discs on either side. Thirteen-inch wheels shod with the latest Firestone rubber, held on with safety bolts, completed the package.

The front torsion bar ran alongside the tank bay area next to the driver's legs, with the end protruding from the front bulkhead. The usual length of bar necessary to achieve the required springing had been halved by the use of compound torsion bars, which consisted of an inner solid bar attached to an outer hollow bar through a splined connection. A lever (known as the torque arm) was mounted on the inner part of the bar, which provided the spring through a link attached to the top wishbone. Damping was via inboard-mounted Armstrong shock absorbers. The whole front footbox/subframe part of the

Inboard solid Girling disc brakes and Armstrong dampers were also employed at the rear, with the discs connected to the fabricated steel uprights by standard Hardy Spicer drive-shafts. Fifteen-inch wheels fitted with Firestone tyres held on with safety bolts provided the grip at the rear. Extensive use of lightweight alloys and magnesium ensured that the car was close to the minimum weight limit of 530 kilograms, distributed 65% to the rear, 35% to the front. The key dimensions of the car were that it had a wheelbase of 8ft 4ins and a track of 4ft 9ins.

After being allowed to give it a brief examination, make notes and take photographs, the assembled throng of journalists were then ushered to the side of the Hethel test track to watch as Jochen Rindt put the car through its paces. However, it was a very short-lived demonstration, as Peter Warr recounts. 'We'd tested it before the launch to make sure the wheels went round and when you put your foot on the brakes it slowed down, the gear-change selected and so-forth. After that, Colin wanted everything looked at, because the first time you run a racing car you've got to see that everything is working the way it should be. The car was basically stripped out overnight, as it would be the night before a race. I don't think we took the engine out but we certainly had the gearbox off and looked inside it and took the suspension and the brakes apart and all the rest of it. The mechanics working on the car very carefully disassembled the rear suspension, took the inner torsion bars out and then put them back and reset the ride height.

'No-one had told them that because of the nature of the beast, they take a 'set'. So they put them in on the other side – not their fault at all, no-one had told them – set the ride height of the car, got everything done, painted the Firestone on the tyres and so on. We wheeled it out for Jochen to drive on the launch day and he did two and a half laps, came past the journalists and stopped beside me – I was away from where they were standing. He jumped out of the car and said "We'd better put it away." I said "What's

car was clothed in the wedge nose-cone, which featured two NACA-ducts to direct air to the brake discs and two corresponding air-exit chimneys positioned above each disc.

The rear of the car saw the 3-litre Cosworth DFV being utilised as a stressed member, just as with the Lotus 49. At the top, an alloy plate from the cam covers was bolted to ear-like brackets on the upper corners of the tub, while at the bottom the engine was held on by two large bolts. A 'C-shaped' subframe was attached to the rear of the engine at several points, onto which the single upper wishbone mountings and rear anti-roll bar located. This wishbone also provided the locating point for the linkage down to the rear compound torsion bar, which ran longitudinally and actually extended out of the back of the car on either side of the gearbox. A wider spread 'A-shaped' tubular lower wishbone was adopted, located on the back of the engine to

the front and on a sandwich plate fitted to the Hewland transaxle. The forward mounting points for the rear suspension were much higher than the aft ones, to achieve the required amount of anti-squat geometry. Because of the absence of braking loads on the suspension and the wide-based lower wishbone, only a single rear radius rod was deemed necessary, this locating on the top of the upright and on the side of the DFV engine near to its forward face. It was also angled upwards, again in accordance with the requirement for anti-squat geometry. Slung over the five-speed Hewland DG300 gearbox was a 'saddle' oil tank with a small cooler mounted on top of it, very similar to the arrangement which had proved so successful on the Lotus 49Bs.

Opposite Page Top Left: Original oil tank arrangement mirrored that of the Lotus 49B/C, while the torsion bars can be seen protruding at the bottom. Note 'tri-plane' rear wing design. **Opposite Page Top Right:** NACA ducts in nose fed air to inboard front discs. **Left:** Rindt managed to grab a few wet laps of Hethel in his new mount prior to its launch. **Above:** The battery and fire extinguisher started off located inside the nosecone. This shot clearly illustrates the complex front frame, solid inboard discs, brake-shafts running to hubs and steep forward raking of front wishbones. **Right:** This low angle shot taken at the launch, shows off the sleek wedge profile of the 72.

up Jochen?" and he said "Well, it started out fine and it's just been going down and it's now on its belly." What had happened was that the set that had been taken in the torsion bars the first day it ran had unwound and it had taken the set the other way. So that was the end of the running on the press day. Any journalists who didn't have their cameras out bloody quick, probably missed the whole affair!

'I remember Maurice Phillippe – who was a fairly even-natured person, it took quite a lot to get him revved up – losing his cool about the torsion bars and there being a big set-to. But he ended up with quite a bit of egg on his face because the mechanics said "Well, if we're not supposed to put them in the wrong way round, where's the piece of paper which tells us not to? Where's the build sheet which says these are left- and right-handed?" And Maurice went "Oh…"'

Top Left: Rindt's brief test at Snetterton, proved inconclusive although it revealed overheating problems requiring the side radiator ducts to be widened. **Above Top:** For 1970, tobacco firm John Player continued its sponsorship of Team Lotus with the cars resplendent in the red, white and golf of its Gold Leaf brand. **Above:** The Lotus number one gives his initial verdict to mechanic Eddie Dennis and Racing Manager Dick Scammell. **Bottom Left:** Rindt giving the 72 its first – very brief – run in front of the press at Hethel. **Opposite Page Top Left:** Single rear radius rod, which located on the cam cover, was angled sharply upwards to provide anti-squat characteristics. **Opposite Page Top Right:** Side radiators on the 72 were not a new idea but it was the first Formula 1 car to successfully adopt this format. Drivers were happier too because they no longer got roasted by rads in nose. **Opposite Page Bottom:** Graham Hill also got behind the wheel of the 72 at the launch. Doug Nye recalls him climbing out of the car and in his distinctive voice, saying to Chief Designer Maurice Phillippe "vewy nice Maurice, vewy nice".

Rindt's mechanic Eddie Dennis remembers that it was actually down to a mistake by the manufacturers. 'They had some arrows on them to note the way they were supposed to be tensioned. They were actually marked up wrongly by the people who made them.' Dennis also recalls another minor drama. 'It was all a panic to get it out as always and the tyres had all been left with about 30-40lbs psi in them, so poor Jochen went out with tyres which were much too over-inflated. They were something like half as hard again as they should have been! By the time Graham [Hill] went out in it, it had come to somebody's attention and they had been pressured down to 18 or 20psi.' The fact that Hill also drove later that day indicates that a 'quick fix' was found to raise the ride height of the car temporarily.

The press launch though was not the first time the 72 had run at Hethel, as Jabby Crombac (then editor of the French magazine Sport-Auto) recalls: 'It was late March. I came to Hethel with my assistant editor, Claude Savoye, who was a bit of a road test man. We were doing a story on the Lotus Seven Series 4 and we said we'd like to go round the track at Hethel with it. We were driving round when suddenly we were asked to stop because another car wanted to use the track. It was the 72, so we had quite a scoop!' Although Jabby took a photo of the car (being driven by Jochen Rindt) that day, the negatives have long since been mislaid, although one picture, did appear in the May issue of Sport-Auto, together with a report of the subsequent press launch which Crombac did not attend.

The first person ever to drive a 72 was chief mechanic Gordon Huckle, who remembers the occasion well. 'I drove the thing the very first time it ever turned a wheel, at the Lotus test track, I did about 10 laps. We were using safety bolts to hold the tyres on, a thing that came about because of Jimmy Clark's accident. I remember I was going round the track and I thought "I don't know, that left front's looking a bit funny" and it had gone flat on me! That was the first-ever shakedown run of the car, before a race driver had even got in it.' Interestingly, Emerson Fittipaldi tells a story of how he was present the very first time the 72 ran

and says that the bottom engine mounts broke. Either way, it is apparent that the first few runs for the 72 weren't exactly auspicious!

Further, limited testing was carried out at Snetterton by Rindt, at which point it was discovered that not enough air was getting to the radiators through the narrow-waisted ducts in the side pods, causing the engine to run hot. Consequently, the pods were pointed outwards into the airstream a bit more and the resultant gap had to be crudely filled in with an additional strip of fibreglass. However, all too soon it was time to load the cars onto the transporter and head off for the first race, the Spanish Grand Prix. The moment of truth had arrived.

All too soon it was time to load up the cars and head off for the first race, the Spanish Grand Prix

CHAPTER 2 A FALTERING START

The team faced the Spanish race with a mixture of anticipation and apprehension. Since testing up to that point had been very limited and therefore inconclusive, this would be the first true measure of the competitiveness of the new car. A second 72, chassis 72/2, was nearing completion and this was assigned to Rindt, with Miles being entrusted with the prototype, 72/1.

The race was held at the tight and twisty Jarama circuit near Madrid, a venue last used in 1968, when Graham Hill had scored a morale-boosting win for Gold Leaf Team Lotus in the aftermath of the death of his team-mate Jim Clark. The intervening race, at Barcelona in 1969, proved somewhat less successful, resulting in spectacular accidents involving both Rindt and Hill when the tall rear wings on their Lotus 49s collapsed over one of the high-speed humps of the Montjuich Park circuit.

The weekend did not start well, when the team's transporter was held up at the Spanish border by over-zealous and uncooperative border officials – a not uncommon experience for racing teams in those days. Chief Mechanic Gordon Huckle takes up the story. 'That trip was horrendous because we were still building one of the 72s in the back of the transporter! We got stuck at the Customs on the Spanish border, so we got the car out of the back of the truck – we were stranded there for three days – and worked on it then. Ken Tyrrell's son was there as well and fortunately he could speak a bit of Spanish so we used him as an interpreter.'

Meanwhile, John Miles flew down with Chapman and Phillippe and was already thinking about the apparent frailty of the car. 'I was sitting next to Maurice and I remember asking him about the strength of the rear wishbones because they looked so weak. He looked through his calculations again and he assured me that they wouldn't fall apart. In fact, they didn't fall apart but almost everything else did!'

The intention had been for the team to arrive at Jarama in enough time to allow a few days of private testing. With the border delays, they managed only to get the car out on Thursday but this turned out to be an unmitigated disaster. As Rindt braked heavily for the tight right-hander at the end of the start/finish straight, the bolts attaching the solid front disc to the brake-shaft CV joint sheared, causing the car to spin violently. The problem had been caused by heat build-up in the insulation spacer (made of a material called Tufnol) between the disc and the shaft, which caused it to disintegrate. This allowed play in the retaining bolts, causing them to break, as Warr explains. 'We knew right from the word go that the heat from the brakes would have to be insulated from the surrounding components.

'I don't know whether it was Maurice or Colin who

Top: On the 72's debut at Jarama, Miles failed to qualify. **Bottom:** At the Spanish GP a disgruntled Rindt retired with electrical problems but more worrying was the poor handling of the car.

came up with the idea of using Tufnol. Effectively, it is a sort of compressed resin plastic and we had these rings of Tufnol between the brake bell and the inner end of the CV joint that was connected to the brake-shaft. That was supposed to insulate the CV joint from the heat of the disc. But what we didn't have in those days because they weren't developed until later, were floating discs. The original car had solid disc bells and the disc was bolted hard up to the bell. On later cars, the bell had pegs in it, the discs had slots, and the discs actually floated so that there wasn't a direct heat path. What happened was that the Tufnol blocks had never been subjected to this sort of heat, it was way over their design capability and they started to break up.'

Although the car spun to a halt virtually unscathed, Rindt was not amused at having been the unwitting victim of another component failure. However, it wasn't just the

breakage that upset him, as Peter Warr explains. 'The real reason Jochen was upset was that the car handled like shit! There are cars that have had anti-dive and there are cars which have had anti-squat but I don't think any car had ever had anti-squat and anti-dive together, and so exaggeratedly. What happened was, if you turned into a corner, it picked up the front wheel and as you accelerated out, it picked up the rear wheel.' Overnight modifications were made to Rindt's car in an effort to overcome the problem with heat build-up. This was done through the adoption of ventilated brake discs, which were heavier than the solid ones but would not generate such high temperatures, as well as the replacement of the Tufnol spacers with metal ones.

Apart from the difficulties with the brakes, the 72 was suffering the usual new car troubles. The car was rolling badly in the corners, due to the suspension settings being

too soft. Added to this, the Cosworth DFV engines were experiencing electrical problems, which were limiting the amount of track time the drivers were able to get. On the first day of practice, the Friday, Rindt got the car running reasonably well, ending up in fifth place only seven-tenths of a second away from fastest man Denny Hulme.

For Miles, the whole experience was frustrating and bewildering in equal measure. 'The main thing was that the car really didn't handle at all well because of the horrendous amount of anti-dive and anti-squat it had. I think the front wishbone had an inclination of 12 degrees. Now the actual percentage anti-dive that must have given was probably 100%! The result is that you have no braking feel because the car won't dive at all. The first thing you know about the brakes locking is that you see smoke coming off the tyres, you don't have any sensation at all, and the car is not slowing down quickly. That was the first thing and then of course they found all the anti-squat on the rear was producing a lot of jacking effect. A little anti-squat can work but they put a hell of a lot on the back. It didn't actually lift the rear wheels, you just got appalling traction.'

The following day saw further frustrating niggles, with gear selection maladies hampering Rindt's efforts and he was one of the few drivers not to go faster than the previous day, ending up eighth fastest on the third row of the grid. Further problems with the electrics kept the mechanics on their toes, while a switch to 17-inch wide rims at the rear did not help, by causing extreme understeer, so the Austrian reverted to the standard 15-inch versions. The luckless Miles though did not even manage to qualify, his

72 developing ignition trouble just before the final qualifying session, forcing him to revert back to a 49. 'There are four pictures I've got of me going into one of my extreme moods, more and more despairing of the whole situation. I wanted to shoot myself to be honest with you!'

The combination of the rush to build the second car, the long (apart from the enforced delay at Customs) journey down from Hethel to Jarama and the sheer volume of work at the track took its toll on the hard-working mechanics, as Eddie Dennis recalls. 'We got there and kept on working and we had a period where we just didn't sleep. Herbie was the first one to go. We just lifted him into the truck. He hadn't collapsed but he just went to sleep, passed out really. Later in the meeting, I'd gone somewhere just to get a bite to eat, sat down for a sandwich and the next thing I knew I was back in the garage again, I'd been helped back there – I'd partly passed out.' Chief Mechanic Gordon Huckle agrees that it was one of the toughest weeks of his time with Team Lotus. 'We worked out that over a seven day period, from the time we left the factory to the time we got back, we'd had a total of something like eight hours sleep each. We were zombies, there's no other way of describing it.'

Further drama was to come on race day as the organisers dithered over whether to allow the four non-

qualifiers to start, in addition to the 16 cars they had agreed to pay start money to. After the 20 cars had lined up on the grid (including Miles), the race officials had a last-minute change of heart and the police were ordered onto the grid to 'escort' the drivers out of their cars – a ridiculously heavy-handed approach which did nothing to endear the organisers to the drivers and teams. As the remaining cars set off on their warm-up lap, Rindt's 72 refused to start and there were anxious moments as the mechanics tried to coax it into life. It finally fired up and Rindt was able to take his place on the grid. His race was rather short-lived though, with a recurrence of the ignition troubles that had bugged the team all weekend bringing his 72 to a halt after only nine of the 90 scheduled laps.

It had been an uninspiring start to the 72's racing career. Expectations for the car, both within Team Lotus and among the Formula 1 world at large, had been high and this dose of reality had brought them back down to earth with a bump. The team returned home to prepare for their next

Opposite Page Top: For Rindt early mechanical failures and teething problems dented his confidence in the 72. **Opposite Page Bottom Left:** This must have been a brief moment of respite for Lotus number two John Miles in an otherwise very trying year. **Opposite Page Bottom Right:** Miles on the grid before the start of the International Trophy. **Left:** The 72's performance at Silverstone confirmed the drivers' worst fears about its 'spooky' handling. This is Rindt before the start of heat 1. **Below:** Rindt's comments sum up the predicament: "Driveable in wet. Very bad in the dry. No feel to car."

race, the International Trophy at Silverstone, which would take place exactly a week after the Spanish Grand Prix. By the time the transporter reached Hethel, there was barely time for the exhausted mechanics to strip down and rebuild the cars before they had to leave for Silverstone. In fact, due to their hectic schedule, they did not arrive until late on Friday afternoon and therefore missed the morning session and most of the afternoon's practice too.

Despite the limited time available, the team had still managed to make a few changes to the cars, including thicker anti-roll bars, larger front nose fins and modifications to the brake disc carriers, following Rindt's troubles at Jarama. Although Rindt's car still sported ventilated discs in practice, these were replaced with solid ones for the race on Sunday.

In the handful of laps that he managed on Friday, Rindt had turned in a time some 11 seconds slower than pole-sitter Chris Amon. Things went from bad to worse on Saturday, when practice was a wash-out with constant heavy rain showers meaning that the grid would be decided from Friday's times. This did not stop drivers going out though, for there was £100 for the fastest time in each of the 30 minute periods that went to make up the two-hour practice session. The 72 went quite well in the wet, Rindt trading fastest laps with Jackie Stewart's March and ending up with £200 to show for his efforts. Miles, who had not got out at all in the dry Friday session, was reasonably quick on the day but his wet-weather time was only good enough to put him on the back row of the grid for the race.

Race day was dry and the fact that the 72s had experienced virtually no dry-weather track-time at Silverstone looked likely to count against them. This proved

to be the case, with Rindt struggling with his car's unpredictable handling – particularly under braking – and unable to keep up with the other Formula 1 cars in the mixed field. He eventually finished a distant fifth in the first of the 26-lap heats, while Miles trailed home 11th, hampered by a broken rear roll bar. In the second heat, Rindt lasted only seven laps before ignition trouble forced him out for the second consecutive weekend, while Miles' throttle pedal broke at half-distance and he retired. It was clear that further dry-weather running was necessary in order to fully evaluate the car and try and identify where the problems with its handling lay.

Tony Rudd accompanied Chapman to this race and clearly remembers a rather awkward atmosphere on the flight home. 'We flew back together from Silverstone in the Navaho, we were very nearly back to Hethel and hadn't spoken since take-off – Colin was obviously in a very black mood – and he turned to me and said "What do you think is wrong with the bloody thing?" And I said "Well, the only thing I can put my finger on is the anti-squat and anti-dive". He didn't agree with that but I reminded him that when I was at BRM we too thought it was a wonderful idea. At the time, we'd tried it on Jackie Stewart's car first, at Silverstone and he'd thought it was good. It was wet, or not quite dry, so the lap times weren't quite comparable. Then we'd tried it on Graham at Snetterton and he'd thought it was good and the lap times were, I think, comparable. So we'd converted both cars and had gone to Brands Hatch and both drivers had thought they were dreadful!

'They said they couldn't race them, they couldn't mix it. They didn't get a feel from the car as to what it was doing, that's what we'd taken away. It didn't understeer, it didn't

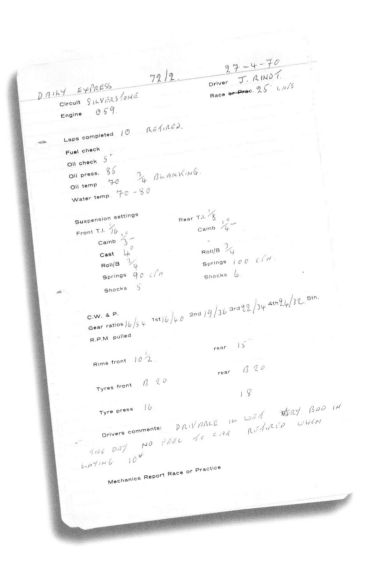

First Person

Gordon Huckle on his year as Chief Mechanic in 1970

"We used to come away from a race meeting and I'd have a list of about 30 items that the Old Man wanted done, plus what the drivers wanted done, plus what we'd decided we wanted to do as well and you just worked and worked and worked. Over the year, every one of the mechanics on the team collapsed at one point or another with fatigue."

roll, it didn't twitch, it didn't do any of the bad things but the drivers couldn't put their finger on quite why they couldn't tell what it was doing. Of course that was what anti-squat and anti-dive does, it puts artificial sensations in. We made up our mind that was what it was and put the cars back the way they were before and then all the feeling came back so we knew where we were with that. Colin and I had quite a discussion for the rest of the flight. We sat in the aeroplane after we landed for quite a while and talked about it but he didn't agree with me then'.

Gold Leaf Team Lotus stayed on at Silverstone for an extra day of testing to give the cars a thorough evaluation. The conclusion was that the main issues were the car's lack of feel, particularly on long, fast corners and under braking. Graham Hill also drove, doing more than 50 laps and he concurred with the works drivers' feedback, saying that while roadholding, braking and straight-line speed were good, the lack of feel made the 72 difficult to drive on the limit. This, combined with his conversation with Rudd, obviously convinced Chapman that the anti-dive and anti-squat could be responsible for at least some of the shortcomings in the car's behaviour, as Rudd recalls. 'A little while later, he said, "Come and have a talk" and I went into his office. He'd got some drawings laid out on his desk [to remove the anti-squat and anti-dive] and we talked a bit more about it. And he said, "Well, I'm going to try".'

While removing the anti-squat at the rear only entailed the construction of new sub-frames and relocating the forward mounting points for the radius arms, the modifications required to eliminate the anti-dive geometry at the front of the car were far more complex. This was because it involved substantial re-working of the front sub-frame, which then did not fit into the existing skins of the tub. The result was that the tub of Rindt's car, 72/2, had to

be unstitched and completely rebuilt using new skins as well as additional stiffening, since the team suspected that chassis flexing may also have been contributing to the car's problems.

These modifications weren't exactly the work of a moment, as Peter Warr explains. 'I can't even begin to tell you the number of hours that we worked, to get all that done, I mean it was just horrendous. It was also a by-product of the fact that this was an integral design, if you wanted to change it, and I mean we were changing big lumps of it, the whole of the front suspension mounting, the whole of the rear suspension mounting, just absolutely horrific.' The team calculated that it would take five weeks to convert Rindt's car alone: if they started immediately there was a chance they might be able to complete the work in time for the next-but-one race, the Belgian Grand Prix.

There simply wasn't enough time to convert Miles' car and instead the revisions were to be incorporated into a third tub already under construction. For the time being, he would have to make do with a partially converted car, as Warr explains. 'You couldn't do it. I mean we were working shifts through the night. The same people were working night and day. Colin Knight had a group of blokes who I reckon, rivet for rivet, shutline for shutline, weld for weld, would outperform any other race team by a long way and were used to doing it consistently, and this programme was

Opposite Page Top Right: Rindt's
Monaco GP win, would serve to
kick-start his Championship
challenge. **Opposit Page Middle:**
72/1 with anti-squat removed was
tested by Rindt at Silverstone in
the week prior to the Belgian
Grand Prix. **Opposite Page Bottom:**
Miles retired from the International
Trophy with a broken throttle
pedal. **Right:** Rindt doesn't look too
convinced by Colin Chapman's
explanation of the peculiar
handling of his car. **Below Right:**
72/1 was taken to the Monaco GP
as a spare car and practised briefly
by Miles.

too much for them. They just couldn't cope with the volume of work that was required.'

On Rindt's car, an extra stiffening baffle was added on either side in the middle of the tub, which resulted in the side fuel tanks having to be split in two. Consequently, a filler was added to the left side of the tub to serve the two forward tanks. In addition, the inner cockpit skin was strengthened and the rear surface of the cockpit was moved forward slightly to give a more robust box section area around the driver's shoulders. All this work was immensely time-consuming, both for the fabricators and the mechanics, who were trying to cope with stripping and rebuilding the cars at the same time as preparing the old 49s for the forthcoming races.

Only a fortnight separated the International Trophy from the prestigious Monaco Grand Prix, so the decision was made to take two 49Cs to the principality, with 72/1 – yet to be modified – as a spare 'just in case'. Miles did try the car on Saturday afternoon but was some three seconds off his pace in 49/R10, so concentrated on the older car. Unfortunately, on his first visit to Monaco, he failed to qualify, the second successive Grand Prix that this had happened, even though his time in regular qualifying had been faster than one of the graded drivers with a guaranteed start. With Rindt qualifying way down the order, morale in the Team Lotus camp was not exactly high. However, as the history books relate, the Austrian turned the situation around on race day to score a sensational last-lap, last corner victory to kick-start his 1970 World Championship challenge.

After the hectic schedule of races in late April and early May, there was now a welcome four-week interlude before

the Belgian Grand Prix. This gave Team Lotus a chance to re-group and undertake the rebuild programme on both 72s. The prototype chassis, 72/1 was modified with the anti-squat characteristics removed but retaining the anti-dive geometry at the front and without the extra strengthening baffle in the forward part of the tub, while the more extensive work on 72/2 continued. On the Monday prior to the Belgian race, Gold Leaf Team Lotus went down to Silverstone, ostensibly to enable Rindt to try out 72/1 in its revised form but also to give a young up-and-coming Brazilian driver by the name of Emerson Fittipaldi a try-out in a Formula 1 car by putting him in a 49. He acquitted himself very well, impressing both Chapman and Rindt and

marking himself out as a driver to be watched, although there was no immediate prospect of a race seat.

With the work on 72/1 completed, it travelled to the Belgian GP, to be held at the fearsomely fast Spa-Francorchamps road circuit, along with a single 49. Meanwhile, Dave 'Beaky' Sims and Dougie Garner stayed behind at Hethel to finish off the work on 72/2. The intention was for Rindt to drive the 72 and Miles 49C/R6 or one of the 72s, depending on whether the work on 72/2 was completed in time. The original nose fins had been refitted on the car, the larger fins used at the International Trophy meeting resulting in no overall improvement in performance. In addition to the two regular works cars, there was once again a third entry for the Spaniard Alex Soler-Roig, who had tried and failed to qualify a 49 at Jarama. Even in those days, a pay driver could bring much-needed top-up funding, as Peter Warr explains. 'I think it was after Jarama, that we realised that we were going to spend the budget for the whole year by April or May and we needed some more wedge (money). So Colin sent me off to Spain to talk to Soler-Roig and we had meetings with Calvo Sotelo, the fuel company putting together a package for him to drive a third car. But in the circumstances, he was always going to get whatever was left and he was pretty miffed, as you can imagine! We managed to patch it up because I think it was just pretty heroic for him, a Spaniard, to be in Formula 1 at all, and driving for a works team was pretty special.'

Soler-Roig's deal had come about because of his friendship with Rindt, as he explains 'I asked Jochen to drive with me in the Six Hours of Madrid at Jarama and we won the race [in Soler-Roig's Porsche 908]. In practice I was faster than him, and he said "You are fast – why don't you drive Formula 1?" So he helped me set up a deal with Lotus.' In addition to the support he received from Calvo Sotelo, the Spaniard had also managed to attract government funding for his drive through a novel source – the Ministry of Sport!

Rindt went out in 72/1 on Friday afternoon and, before he had a chance to record a time, his right rear hub seized braking the lower wishbone mounting. A manufacturing fault in the upright was to blame, as Eddie Dennis explains. 'They hadn't been drilled for a breather hole in manufacture and the pressure built up and blew the seal out'. The subsequent loss of lubricant caused the bearings to seize, breaking the wishbone mounting. The Austrian abandoned his car in disgust at the side of the road and, from that point on, drove the 49 in which Miles had been practising.

At this point in time, it is apparent that Rindt was still quite disillusioned at the apparent lack of performance of his new car and he was also troubled by certain aspects of its build, as Gordon Huckle recounts. 'Rindt was very concerned about the size of the bolts holding the suspension on the car. I think we were down to 5/16" or a quarter inch diameter bolts. In fact, I was looking in my tool box just the other day and I found some spacers in there that we used to make the bolts fit the rose-joints because the rose-joint holes were too big! He made so much fuss that we went up one size on the bolts on the suspension because he wouldn't drive it. The Old Man was convinced that they would be OK but Rindt was concerned about them breaking. We never had one go, though.' John Miles also remembers Rindt's concerns – as well as his own – about the fragility of the car at such a high-speed circuit. 'I had a left-rear wheel fall off at the hairpin at Spa – it just dropped off! Jochen said to me "I wouldn't drive that car if I were you".'

Rindt's concern about the bolts led to Alex Soler-Roig being given the opportunity to drive the 72 intended for Rindt, 72/2, although this was against the advice of his friend, as he explains: 'Jochen refused to drive the 72 any more that weekend because he was very worried about the size of the bolts – he said they were too thin: he wanted bolts the size of his finger! Colin said to him "Look, I'm the engineer, I'll worry about that, you're the driver". But he still wouldn't drive it. So I said that I would drive the car. Jochen said to me "Are you crazy, this is the fastest circuit of all" but I said that I might not get another chance to drive a 72, so I did.' However, he would have to wait for his chance, because the car was still being built!

Work on 72/2 was not finished until the early hours of Friday morning and it was rushed out on a trailer in true Team Lotus style, reaching Spa on Saturday afternoon, as 'Beaky' Sims explains. 'The rest of the team went on to Spa and left Dougie and I behind to finish the latest car with all the mods for Jochen. We ended up doing three all-nighters. They left us with a Thames van and trailer and we eventually finished at something like four in the morning and set off for Harwich to get the ferry to Zeebrugge. We'd had five days with no sleep and there were just the two of us. We were completely finished!

'When we got to Spa we had no tickets, no passes, no windscreen sticker and we didn't know where we were going because somehow or other we approached from the other side of the circuit to where you would go for the paddock. We saw this gate to what looked like the track, so we lifted this barrier up and got in, and then got lost on the inside of the circuit. Eventually a marshal led us into the paddock. When we finally arrived, the Old Man saw us and said "Get it off the trailer, come on quick, quick, we've got to get it out". Well, we'd only briefly started it up at Hethel, warmed the engine, and checked all the systems were working. It hadn't turned a wheel! And the Old Man said, "You've got to change the ratios, it's got the wrong ratios". The last thing I can remember is trying to take the lay shaft off the gearbox and that was it, I don't remember anything else, I just passed out. Fellow mechanic Derek Mower remembers that Chapman was keen that no word of the

exhausted state of his employee should leak out. 'The Old Man said to me "Put him in the truck, don't let anybody see him" and we stuck Beaky in the sleeper in the transporter and he slept there all day!' Eddie Dennis took over work on the car but, as a result of the extra time required to change

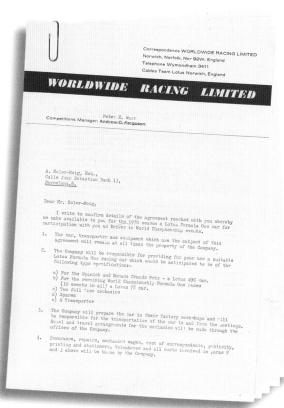

the ratios, it still missed the first Saturday afternoon session.

Dennis was another suffering from the effects of sleep deprivation that weekend, as a story told by Mower [known in the team as Joe 90] amply illustrates. 'We were staying at Stavelot and working in a garage there and we never used to get any sleep. After practice you used to have to load the truck up, take it round to Stavelot, unload it and start working on the cars and you wouldn't start working on them until maybe eight or nine o'clock at night. Beaky, Jake [Eddie Dennis] and I were staying in this house and there were two beds. Beaky and I were in the double bed and Jake was in the single. One night Beaky woke me up and said "90, 90, look at Jake" and there was Jake on his knees at the bottom of the bed. We said "Jake, what are you doing?" and he said, "I'm adjusting the roll bar!" The poor sod was still asleep.'

Meanwhile, 72/1 had been repaired and was given to Miles who, on another circuit completely new to him, managed to put in a respectable performance to qualify on the outside of the fifth row, albeit nearly four seconds slower than Rindt's front-row qualifying performance in the ageing 49C. Soler-Roig finally got behind the wheel of 72/2 in the one-hour Saturday evening session but unfamiliarity with the car and the fact that he only managed three laps of the track meant that his time was some fifteen seconds adrift of the slowest qualifier.

This came as a great disappointment to the Spaniard, as he recalls: 'I only did three laps of the circuit because the car was late arriving. It was out of this world – like a Formula 2 car with a Formula 1 engine! On my third lap, Jack Brabham passed me before the corner leading onto the Masta straight. But I found that I was able to stay with him and could have passed him but I had to take my foot off the throttle because fifth gear was too short and I didn't want to over-rev the engine. Going up the hill on the last part of the lap a pin broke on the gear lever and the car went into neutral and I stopped out on the circuit. When I got back to the pits, I told Chapman that fifth gear was too low and he said that it was not possible. But I said "Look, I had to take my foot off [the throttle] on the straight, so it must be short" so he said that he would change the ratios for the race.

He did not get the opportunity to find out if this resulted in an improvement, for the organisers decreed that, because the Spaniard did not complete the required

minimum number of five practice laps he would not be allowed to start the race. Miles' car was therefore the sole 72 in the race but at least he'd made it, having suffered the ignominy of non-qualification in the previous two Grand Prix, and that after his promising points-scoring debut in South Africa. In the race, thankfully run in warm, dry conditions, Miles barely reached half-distance and was running last on the road when he retired. He had spun at the Les Combes left-hander and when he reached the pits it was found that both rear tyres had hardly any pressure in them. In addition, the car had been experiencing gear selection problems and the fuel breather on the roll-over bar was pressurising and blowing fuel through into the trumpets and making it run rich, causing the engine to misfire, all of which had conspired to make the car a pig to drive.

The limited running that Soler-Roig had done in 72/2 had proved inconclusive and it was very clear that what was required was a prolonged session of testing away from the glare of a race weekend, in which the car could be fully sorted. The decision was taken to travel to the venue for the next race, the Dutch circuit of Zandvoort early and spend a day prior to the Grand Prix testing. The Saturday after the Belgian race, 72/2 was taken down to Silverstone for Miles to drive, so that the car could be set up after its limited running at Spa, in preparation for the main test at Zandvoort.

Opposite Page Top: Confronted with a car he'd never sat in and a circuit he'd never driven, Soler-Roig understandably struggled to set a decent time in the newly-revised 72/2 at Spa. **Opposite Page Bottom Left:** An anticipated 10 events in a 72 proved a somewhat optimistic pledge to Soler-Roig. **Opposite Page Bottom Right:** Wheel bearing failure in practice for the Belgian GP did little to help Rindt's confidence in the 72. **Left:** Rindt was instumental in helping his friend Soler-Roig to get a drive with Lotus in Formula 1 for 1970.

First person
Tony Rudd on Jochen Rindt

"He was very difficult, he was not objective. If you changed the car and it was better, Graham [Hill] would produce a lap time and tell you what was better and Jackie [Stewart] would produce a lap time and tell you it was better although he couldn't always tell you what was better. But with Rindt, if he didn't like it he wouldn't go faster, despite the fact that the car might be a lot faster! The rows that Chunky [Chapman] and Rindt had, they were not one-sided. Chunky used to grumble like hell about Rindt and say he didn't know why he put up with him and so on. His version of it was that Rindt was a right pain in the arse. I must say that on the rare occasions I went to a race and listened in on the discussions, I don't know whether I was on Chunky's side but I certainly wasn't on Rindt's!"

Prior to the Dutch Grand Prix it had been decided that the team would not run a car for Soler-Roig at this race. Everyone at Hethel had their work cut out modifying the 72s and building new cars – the last thing they needed was the distraction of running a third car and a different one at that. In addition, the team's original commitment to run the Spaniard in a 72 when one was ready for him could not be fulfilled, as Warr explains. 'The situation within the team was really very difficult. At the time we did the deal it was done in good faith and we didn't know we were going to have the dramatic problems with the early anti-squat, anti-dive 72s, which would take so much modification. Jochen elected to drive the 49 at Spa, so Soler-Roig had a go in the 72 there. The 72 wasn't up to snuff even for Jochen, so it could hardly be expected to be for Soler-Roig. And so, by the time we got to Zandvoort, and had two modified cars, there was only the 49 left as it were'. The test at Zandvoort proved to be a turning point, not just in the performance of the 72 but also in Rindt's attitude towards it. His change of heart meant he and Chapman had been able to swap their atmosphere of belligerent confrontation for a spirit of co-operation and it reaped immediate dividends, according to Peter Warr. 'I think what Colin said, in one of their heart-to-hearts, was "Listen Jochen, you've got to pull your weight as well, so when I want you to come testing, and you get the call from Peter, you turn up, you don't say that you are too busy or can't be bothered". At Zandvoort he came back with a smile on his face every time he drove the car!' With 72/2's new stiffer tub and more feel being transmitted to the driver

following the removal of anti-dive and anti-squat, Rindt found he was able to consistently lap the windblown, sandy Dutch circuit well inside the existing record.

Team Lotus testing records for June 16th 1970, the Tuesday before the Dutch Grand Prix, show that Rindt completed 75 laps in 72/2. Pulling maximum revs of 9,500, he set a best time of 1m17.6s compared to the official lap record at the time of 1m21.8s. Under driver comments is recorded the simple statement 'Car handling better.' The test was not entirely trouble-free, as Eddie Dennis explains. 'We had a problem with a bit of a failure on the rear sub-frame. When we found it we got the Old Man [Chapman] and Maurice to look at it. The Old Man was saying "Hopefully we can get it to run". I used to apply a safety-type code where if you don't think it was safe you say so. They were going to try to keep on running with it and I didn't agree with them, so I went off and I said to Jochen "Look I haven't told you anything but just go and stick your head underneath the back of the car and have a look at it on a casual basis. Then they've got to do something about it."

Which he did.'

Also present that day was 72/1 – still in the same anti-dive/no anti-squat configuration it had run at Spa – and Rindt did 14 laps in it for a back-to-back comparison. Interestingly, he was quick in that too, recording a 1m18.8s best lap but preferred the revised car, as Gordon Huckle explains. '72/1 worked but the drivers hadn't got the confidence in it. What they were saying was that there was no feel in the car, under braking into the corners and they couldn't really judge their braking distances properly. They weren't getting the feedback off the car, it just felt very neutral.' John Miles also did a handful of laps in 72/2, recording a fastest time of 1m23.2s, some way off the pace, although he later set a 1m21.5s in 72/1. For the purposes of comparison, it is worth noting that Championship contender Jack Brabham was also testing at Zandvoort that day and his best lap in the BT33 was a 1m20.7s, underlining just how much pace Rindt and the 72 had found following the modifications.

The fact that the car was finally beginning to fulfil some of its promise came as an immense relief for the team and its boss, according to Warr. 'After the huge excitement that the announcement of the car generated because it was so different to anything else at the time and the great expectations that everyone had for it, I think Colin was mortally wounded that it really didn't work at all. He therefore applied himself to the degree and level needed to produce a bloody brilliant car. And he came up with a set of modifications which just transformed the car and made it unbeatable.'

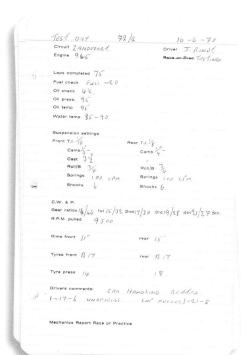

Above & Left: Pre-race testing at Zandvoort proved encouraging, as engineering records and lap time records show... **Right:** Rindt blitzed the opposition in practice for the 1970 Dutch Grand Prix, easily taking pole.

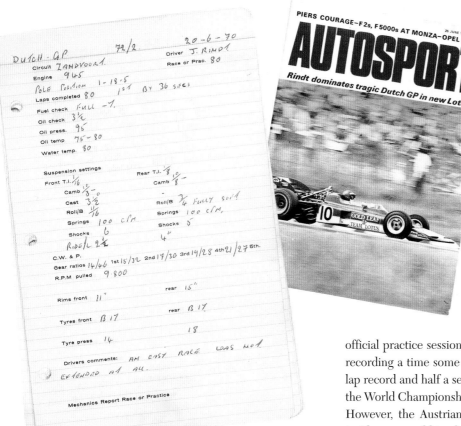

The other main change to the specification of the car had been a switch to the lighter Hewland FG400 gearbox, which was an amalgam of the FT200 gear set put on to the final drive section of a DG300 box, saving some 20lbs in weight over the DG300s used by most of the rest of the field. This modification was only done to Rindt's car and Miles' 72/1 continued to use the DG300 box. The only other change which had been made to the 72s were two little winglets which had been attached to the side plates of the rear wing in an effort to gain a little extra downforce.

The form shown in testing was continued in the first official practice session on the Friday morning, with Rindt recording a time some three-and-a-half seconds inside the lap record and half a second clear of his nearest challenger, the World Championship leader at the time, Jackie Stewart. However, the Austrian's practice session was not without incident – a grabbing brake causing him to spin off into the sand at the Tarzan hairpin. Although damage initially appeared to be superficial and confined to the nose-cone, it transpired upon closer inspection that the spin had actually bent the tub, as Derek Mower explains. 'We had to work all night to straighten the thing and rivet doublers on. Where the engine bolted on, it had just rippled the tub. It was quite a big job because all the radiators had to come off, the fuel tank had to come out and they were a bugger because they used to leak if you just looked at them!'

Engine problems restricted Rindt's efforts in the two-hour session on Saturday morning but come the afternoon session the dominance of the 72 was plain for all to see. On full tanks and new tyres, he recorded a time, which was only ever bettered by Stewart's March, and Ickx's Ferrari, so it was no surprise when he went out with a light fuel load and scrubbed-in tyres and took an easy pole position. What was more, he achieved this without having to use all the road and driving in a very smooth fashion, which contrasted sharply with the sideways heroics of his rivals. Finally, the 72 was fulfilling the promise which it had so far failed to transfer from the drawing board to the track. To add to the feeling of optimism in the Gold Leaf Team Lotus camp, Miles put in his best qualifying performance of the season so far to place eighth on the grid, on the outside of the third row.

Although Rindt was out-dragged at the start by Ickx's Ferrari, the Belgian's time at the front of the race was short-lived. As they approached Tarzan for the third time, the sleek Lotus dived inside the scarlet Ferrari under braking and took the lead. Rindt began to stretch his advantage in an effortless fashion and was never challenged again, leading the remaining 78 laps. At one point, an already good day for Team Lotus looked likely to get even better. Miles had been running well in fifth place but spun without hitting anything on the 49th lap, dropping back two places. Although he subsequently regained a place when John Surtees spun, the wily former World Champion recovered to catch and pass Miles with five laps to go to secure the final Championship point. However, the shine of Rindt's dominant victory was well and truly removed when it became clear that his close friend, Piers Courage, had died in a fiery accident at around quarter-distance. Therefore, there was sorrow rather than joy on his face when he received his victor's garland and he did not take the customary lap of honour in deference to his friend's memory. Similarly, the victory dinner planned for that evening was cancelled and it was a sombre Team Lotus equipe, which returned to Hethel the next day.

The next round of the Championship, the French Grand Prix, was to be held that year at the undulating Circuit de Charade, comprised of public roads in the mountains near Clermont-Ferrand. At fractionally over five miles in length, it was something of a cross between Spa-Francorchamps and the Nürburgring, with each lap taking around three minutes. Rindt's victory at Zandvoort had catapulted him up the Championship points standings to second, only one point behind leader Jackie Stewart. Not only that, but the Dutch race had shown that the Austrian's sophisticated Lotus comprehensively had the legs on the reigning World Champion's comparatively crude-looking

CHAMPIONNAT DU MONDE
DES CONDUCTEURS F1
GRAND PRIX DE FRANCE

CLERMONT-FD

BP

5 juillet
1970

PROGRAMME
OFFICIEL 3^F

Far Left: Driver comment says it all: "An easy race – was not extended at all." **Bottom Left:** Rindt's office: rev counter in middle is flanked by combined oil pressure/temperature gauge on left and water temperature gauge on right. **Left & Below:** The 72 was visibly easier to drive at Zandvoort and Rindt revelled in its new-found speed.

March 701. A good run of results mid-season could still enable Rindt to challenge for the Championship title, a hope which had looked positively forlorn after the first three rounds of the series, when he had failed to score any points.

Gold Leaf Team Lotus had not sat on their laurels in the wake of their superiority in Holland. Chief Mechanic Gordon Huckle's notebook shows a job-list of 28 items for the cars, a general job-list of 12 items, seven development items and 10 things to chase up. A few pages on are listed a further 10 items under 'Development work for French Grand Prix', so clearly there was no let-up in the workload for the mechanics. More modifications had been made to the chassis of both cars in an effort to make them more robust. Additional reinforcement was added behind the drivers' shoulders to try and improve torsional rigidity, while the engine mounts which had failed during practice at Zandvoort had also been strengthened on a more permanent basis than had been possible 'in the field'. At the rear of the car, the Armstrong dampers had been repositioned at an angle of 45 degrees, which put them out in the airflow. This solved the problem experienced when they had been mounted vertically and had been roasted by the exhaust, causing them to fade to almost nothing,

something which had afflicted Miles from very early on in the Dutch race.

Smaller aerodynamic revisions saw the removal of the extra 'ear-fins' on the rear wing and the revival of the larger front nose-fins. Eddie Dennis recalls that the 'ear-fins' were probably deemed to have been outside the regulations, although he doubted they made much difference to the performance of the car. 'I don't think they made much difference anyway. I think if they'd proved to be a big advantage there would have been some reason for them to stay.' Another change for this race was the addition of rear wing stays, which ran from the rear torsion bar mounting points to the rearmost inside edge of the wing end-plate. On a related note, and something which is of particular relevance to future events is an entry in Huckle's notebook, dated June 29th 1970 (the Monday before the French race). Under longer term 'Chase Up' items, it reads 'Rear wing stays drawn half an inch above FIA rules'. Additionally, the battery had also been moved from its original position in the nose, to the back of the car and mounted on a tray behind the gearbox in an effort to increase rearward weight bias.

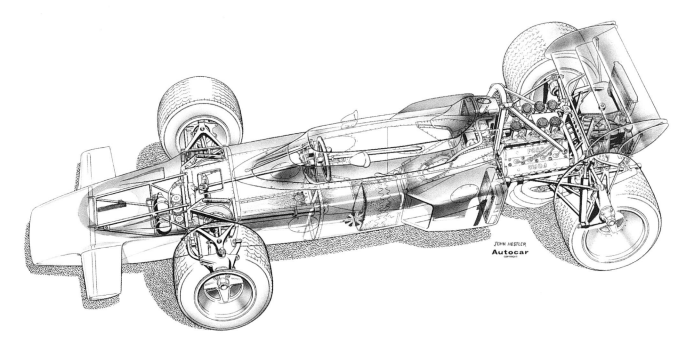

JOHN HOSTLER
Autocar
COPYRIGHT

Rindt had not been looking forward to racing at Clermont-Ferrand, since he had previously experienced problems with nausea induced by the roller-coaster nature of the circuit's undulating curves combined with relatively few straights. However, after starting the weekend with his white full-face Bell helmet, he switched to his black open-face version which allowed more air to reach his face and did not experience any problems thereafter. Ironically, shortly after making the switch, a stone flew up from the wheels of Jean-Pierre Beltoise's Matra and cut Rindt's lip quite badly, requiring four stitches – had he been wearing a full-face helmet he would have escaped unscathed.

The Lotus 72 wasn't the dominant package it had been at Zandvoort. The tighter bends induced excessive understeer and the torque of the Cosworth DFV V8 engine could not match that of the 12-cylinder units in the back of the Ferraris and Matras on the long pull back up the hill on the return leg from Clermont-Ferrand. Rindt's understeer was solved by alterations to the camber on the front wheels but Miles' car didn't seem to respond to this change and

The final innovation was a rather odd-looking device which was placed over the brake disc exit vents as soon as the cars came into the pits, which blew cold air into the area around the discs helping prevent heat build-up problems, as Huckle explains. 'We found that a lot of that problem [with heat build-up] was caused by the car being stationary rather than when it was running. So we cobbled up something a bit quick, to stick on the front disc vents. It was just a reverse moulding of the top of the nose of the car, to which we had added a couple of blowers.'

Huckle remembers that Clermont-Ferrand was another exhausting weekend. 'We had a bit of wheel trouble – we were getting cracks on the wheels. I got a right bollocking from the Old Man. He was panicking for wheels to go on the cars and I told him that we were crack-testing them. We were using R Drops in those days, it's a red dye that you spray on, then you put a chalk secondary coat on, and if there is a crack it shows up like a red line. So we were crack-testing them as fast as we could and I was saying to the mechanics "Right, just do the test and let's have them" and I left them still with the red dye on them. The Old Man went berserk! He was saying "What are the drivers going to do when they see that on the wheels?" And I said, "Well, they'll probably be bloody pleased because they can see we've been doing something about it" but he made me take the wheels back and paint them before I could put them on the car!' The huge workload continued to take its toll on the mechanics. This time it was Dougie Garner who collapsed, the night before the race, and he had to be carried back to the team's hotel and put to bed.

The nine points for a win at Clermont-Ferrand transformed Rindt's championship chances

was some way off the pace. In the final practice session, Rindt joined an elite group of six drivers who had cracked the three-minute barrier but was still only sixth on the grid and on the third row (a two-by-two grid formation was adopted at Clermont due to the narrow track) alongside 'Black' Jack Brabham. Ickx and Beltoise had produced an all-12-cylinder front row, with the fastest DFV runners being the Marches of Amon and Stewart, which seemed well suited to the circuit despite their more primitive design. Miles continued to struggle and his cause was not helped when he ran out of fuel during the final Saturday session, which proved to be the faster of the two held that day. As a result, while others around him improved considerably, he had to be content with a similar lap-time to the one he had set in the morning (when he was 9th quickest), dropping him right down to the penultimate row of the grid.

In the race, the Ferrari and Matra streaked away from the rest of the field, opening up a sizeable gap over the best of the Cosworth runners, Stewart. Amon came next, while Rindt had got the drop on Brabham and was pushing the March hard. When Stewart was forced to pit with ignition trouble after five laps, the Austrian was elevated to fourth and two laps later he forced his way past Amon to claim third. For a time this looked to be the best finish he could hope for, since he was not making any impression on the flying 12-cylinder machines at the head of the race. However, at the end of the 15th lap, the Matra came round in the lead, the Ferrari now mortally wounded with a burnt valve. Ickx retired during the next lap, promoting Rindt to second place.

By half-distance, Beltoise comfortably led Rindt by 16.3 seconds and was extending his advantage by around a second a lap. Shortly after this though, the Matra started to handle strangely, as a result of a slow puncture, and Rindt and Amon closed in for the kill. At the end of the 26th of 38 laps and to the dismay of the partisan French crowd, who had been hoping for a Matra victory, Rindt came by in the lead. From this point on, the Austrian drove a text-book race, never extending himself but just doing enough to keep Amon at bay, coming home just under eight seconds clear.

Meanwhile, Miles had been troubled by a clutch that wouldn't disengage at the start as well as low oil pressure. However, he persevered and, as others fell out, he moved up the order, even managing to pass Francois Cevert's March at half-distance as the Frenchman struggled with gear selection woes. At the finish, Miles was eighth, completing a satisfactory day for the team. Certainly, a win was more than they could have hoped for after practice, or even mid-way through the race. Lady Luck had smiled on them once again.

Dougie Garner had enjoyed an unusually relaxing day, as he explains. 'When I woke up, I looked round and everybody had gone to the race. They had decided to leave me there because I was too knocked out. My initial thought was 'Oh God, first duty: must get there.' So I got changed into my gear, rushed downstairs and, of course, Clermont-Ferrand was shut! I asked the receptionist for a taxi to get to the track but she said there was no chance. I had got all the passes and could get in easily but getting there was the problem. I was just thinking 'What the hell do I do?' – and it was getting on a bit because I'd slept quite a long time – when I looked up at the TV in the bar and they were on the start-line! I thought 'Well, there's absolutely nothing I can do now, anyway'. So I sat and watched the race and we won. That was the satisfying part. There I was drinking a beer watching the other guys work their socks off! It didn't happen like that very often…'

The win at Clermont-Ferrand transformed Rindt's Championship chances. While he took a maximum nine points to take his tally to 27, the Championship leader going into the race, Stewart failed to score. Jack Brabham kept his hopes alive by finishing third to join the Scot on 19 points but the Austrian's lead of eight points was looking good. A fortnight after the French race, the Grand Prix circus moved to Team Lotus's home ground for the British Grand Prix at Brands Hatch. After Piers Courage's fatal accident at Zandvoort, Frank Williams had tried to sign up Emerson Fittipaldi, with the result that Lotus had to move quickly to secure his services. This was done with the promise of a Grand Prix debut at the Kent circuit aboard one of the team's trusty Type 49s, Soler-Roig having turned down the chance to drive the car again, as he explains: 'After France Chapman offered me a 49 for the British Grand Prix. I said that I wanted a 72 but he said he couldn't give me one and that if I didn't drive the

First Person

Derek Mower on John Miles and Jochen Rindt

"John wouldn't commit to the kind of driving that Jochen would. Graham [Hill] used to have to work hard to go quick but when he did, he was very quick. But Jochen could do it naturally. His actual words were "You should be able to do a split-arse lap in five laps". And he used to laugh, he used to take the mick out of John because he'd go round as long as the track was open and he'd have to do loads of laps to get up to speed, whereas Jochen would go out, do five laps and come and sit on the pit wall. Then as soon as Ickx or somebody went faster, he just hopped in the car and he'd go out and go a bit quicker. But I suppose that's the difference between World Champions and the others."

Opposite Page Top: John Hostler's cutaway drawing reveals the bare bones of the 72. **Opposite Page Bottom:** For the French Grand Prix, the rear dampers were moved outboard to prevent a repetition of overheating problems experienced in the previous race. Miles, shown, came home eighth. **Left:** Rindt and the 72 were not as dominant in France around the undulating Clermont-Ferrand circuit as they had been at Zandvoort but still came away with a win due to rivals dropping out.

First Person

Derek Mower (below left) on working for Colin Chapman

"I can remember the Old Man coming in to the garage and starting a job list. Beginning at the front of the car, he got to the rollover bar and he'd got 100 jobs already, for that night! Then he'd come back in the morning and we'd all be knackered from another all-nighter and he'd say 'I can't see what there is on that list to keep you boys up all night!' He was a bastard, he was! But you used to work hard for him. You'd pull your finger out because you knew if you did, you stood a good chance of winning."

49, he would give it to Emerson Fittipaldi. I said I didn't want to drive the 49, so that was the end of it.'.

Rindt's 72 showed further evidence of the ongoing programme of development being applied to the cars by appearing with an airbox that had scoops either side of the driver's head feeding air into the intake trumpets of the DFV engine. This change required modifications to the roll-over bar braces, which had previously been mounted on the engine cam covers but which were now forward-facing and located on the monocoque. As there hadn't been time to convert both cars, Miles' 72/1 was still in the old configuration minus the airbox. The other change was to the positioning of the oil cooler. As with the later specification 49s, this had been located atop the oil tank which saddled the gearbox but it was not getting enough airflow due to being positioned behind the three-tier wing and probably wasn't helping the wing to be at its most effective, either. Consequently, it was moved to the left-hand side of the tank on both cars, positioned in the airflow behind the rear suspension. Finally, the larger front nose fins used in France were retained for the British race.

With the race as usual in England being held on a Saturday, practice sessions took place on the Thursday and Friday. On Thursday Rindt was quickly into the groove after some adjustments to the ride height to stop the car bottoming on the bumpy track. He set a time one second faster than Stewart's pole time for the Race of Champions in March and Brabham's lap record in the same race. No one else could get within eight-tenths of a second of his pace. Miles was ninth fastest, topping off a good start to the meeting for the team. On Friday, things went all wrong for Rindt when, early in the session, his car developed a fuel

leak and the rest of the session was spent changing the bag tank. Miles was really getting into the swing of things though, revelling in being able to drive on a circuit he knew. The Englishman knocked another nine-tenths of a second off his Thursday time, putting him well up the grid, ahead of reigning World Champion Stewart and Clermont-Ferrand pacesetter Jean-Pierre Beltoise. Despite his problems, nobody bettered Rindt's Thursday time, although Jack Brabham equalled it. Thus, he would start from pole position, with team-mate Miles in the middle of the third row.

At the start, Rindt failed to capitalise on his pole position and had to slot into third place behind fellow front-row men Ickx and Brabham. On lap seven, there was drama as simultaneously Ickx slowed with a broken limited slip differential and Rindt dived up the inside of Brabham under braking for Paddock, the swooping downhill right-hander at the end of the

start/finish straight. For a moment, it looked as if the two cars were going to touch, for Brabham was not going to give way without a fight, but as they came upon the slowing Ickx, the Austrian forced his way ahead. Meanwhile, Miles had also made a poor start and dropped back a couple of places on the first lap. He was running steadily behind Stewart and Beltoise when, after only 13 laps, he was forced to pit with an engine problem. After several more slow tours, he retired with a suspected broken camshaft. 'That pissed me off big time because that was one place I wanted to do well. I knew it and I'd qualified reasonably high up, I couldn't believe it.'

Brabham tracked Rindt's 72 for the next 63 laps, there being little to separate them. With only 11 laps to go, Rindt appeared to miss a gearchange coming out of South Bank corner and Brabham was through, although the latter remembers it slightly differently today. 'He admitted to me afterwards that I was pressing him so hard, right on his tail all the time that he eventually gave up and let me go by'. Either way, in only four laps Brabham pulled out a 10-second advantage over the Austrian and looked certain to avenge his embarrassing last corner defeat at the Monaco

Grand Prix. As he went out onto his last lap, his lead of 14 seconds seemed unassailable. However, in a final incredible twist of fate, the Brabham ran out of petrol at Stirlings bend (the penultimate corner on the circuit) and Rindt shot past him coming into Clearways, rounded the last bend and took the chequered flag, to the astonishment of Chapman, his crew and the rest of the crowd. Half a minute later, Brabham coasted slowly across the line, his momentum plus the downhill run from Clearways being just enough to carry him along the straight and across the finish line, before anybody else could deprive him of second place, at least.

But this was not the end of the drama. In post-race scrutineering, it was found that the stays supporting the rear wing on Rindt's car were bent and when Racing Manager Dick Scammell refused to bend them straight without first consulting Chapman or Warr, the car was disqualified from the race by the RAC's Clerk of the Course, Dean Delamont. Team Lotus immediately launched a protest. Subsequently, the stays were straightened out and re-fitted and every possible permutation of mounting hole and adjustment was tried and the car was, apparently, still found to be legal. The whole situation hadn't been helped by the uneven surface of the scrutineering bay at Brands and doubts among the scrutineers as to where to accurately measure the height of the wing! It left a sour taste in everybody's mouths but the outcome was that three and a half hours after the finish, Rindt was re-instated as the winner of the race.

More than thirty years on, it emerges that Chapman and his mechanics were all too aware that the wing was illegal and the struts had been bent deliberately when the car was on its victory parade lap on the back of the trailer to conceal this. 'It was too high and the Old Man knew it' explains

Eddie Dennis, one of the mechanics on Rindt's car. 'He actually said at the time "Don't worry about it, they'll never disqualify us." It was quarter to three-eighths of an inch too high. For some reason during the meeting the car went from very good one day to the next where he couldn't match the times. The Old Man was mystified, so he told us to drill a couple more holes in the wing to make it higher, which then made it illegal. It used to be measured from the undertray, the lowest point of the car. The wing was supported by some tubular struts and when it went off on the trailer we bent them, we did it off our own backs really.' The incompetence of the scrutineers was further underlined by what happened when they weighed the winning car, according to Dennis. 'What they didn't realise was that Dick Scammell's briefcase was still in the cockpit. So they were carefully weighing the car and there's this big

old-style briefcase plonked in the cockpit, that had just been left in there by mistake!'

Dennis's version of events is backed up by Chief Mechanic Gordon Huckle, who confirms that the decision to raise the wing was Chapman's. 'I said to the Old Man at the time "If we win this race, we're going to be in the crap". He said "Oh, we'll worry about that after the race". Typical! When we got onto the trailer to go round I'd armed myself with a couple of allen keys ready to drop the wing down but of course the two mechanics had beaten me to it and leaned on the stays and bent them!' In the drama of the finish and post-race protests and disqualifications, the performance of young Fittipaldi could easily have been overlooked. He had acquitted himself well, driving sensibly to qualify on the last row of the grid and then coping admirably with gear selection troubles and a broken exhaust in the race to come home in a creditable eighth place.

Rindt had now won three successive Grand Prix and had further stretched his lead in the Championship over the luckless Brabham to a comfortable 11 points. Jackie Stewart's title challenge looked to be fading after he

Opposite Page Top & Bottom: Rindt qualified on pole for the British Grand Prix at Brands Hatch and led for much of the race. **Above:** After a near race-long battle with Jack Brabham, Rindt inherited victory in the dying moments when his rival faltered. **Below:** The British race marked the first appearance of an engine airbox on Rindt's 72/2, necessitating repositioning of the rollover bar stays. In contrast, Miles' 72/1 ran without these modifications.

followed on from his non-finish in France with a retirement at Brands. Jacky Ickx, who had led and retired from both of these races, languished in 12th position in the table at this stage with only four points.

A final amusing postscript to the wing story comes from Dougie Garner. 'After we had got back from the race, the Old Man was looking at the cars that were stood in the workshop and he said 'Cor, look at this! The rear wing must have been touching the oil tank. Let's see how many sand bags it takes to force that down onto the tank.' So we were lobbing these bags onto the rear wing and we got to this tremendous weight and he was saying 'Cor, that's fantastic, this means the wing is shifting that much weight.' What we didn't have the guts to tell him is that we used to pull the rear stays out and drop the wing down and it sat on the oil tank so that it would go in the truck. That was what made the mark on the wing, not the fact that it was being pushed down by aerodynamics! It was very embarrassing and nobody would tell him. He used to get upset about the

bodywork being damaged and things like that, so it was a bit of a double-edged sword that one!'

Despite the good form of the Lotus 72 and his strong position in the Championship, Rindt was a troubled man. The death of his close friend Courage, on top of numerous other fatalities in recent years, had increasingly led him to contemplate retirement, as Jabby Crombac explains. 'At the July meeting, the opening of Paul Ricard for a Formula 2 race [the Trophées de France], all the press and the drivers were invited to a very nice hotel on the island just outside Bordeaux which belonged to Mr Paul Ricard. We were all waiting for dinner time, lying on the grass in front of the hotel and I had a 'soul-to-soul' with Jochen. He asked me "Do you think I should retire?" And I said "Jochen, if you don't enjoy it any more, retire". He said, "If I was to do that, I would not race tomorrow". He was a very, very unhappy man.'

Crombac believes that it was Rindt's desire to become World Champion and the economic and publicity benefits that would accrue from that, which kept him going in 1970. 'He was a great businessman. He had this racing car show going and he was thinking of doing a line of sports clothes. I think he would have done that and he would have succeeded because he was so good in business. I'm pretty sure that's what he had in mind. But he really wanted to finish as a World Champion. That would have given him a fantastic start, that's why he was trying very hard. So, even though he wasn't enjoying himself any more, he wanted to succeed.'

The next race, the German Grand Prix, was traditionally held at the daunting Nürburgring circuit but Rindt had been instrumental in campaigning for the race to be switched to the featureless Hockenheim track. This consisted of two flat-out blasts through the forest, each punctuated mid-way by a chicane, the two legs being linked

by the daunting Ostkurve at one end and a twisty infield section, where the majority of the spectators were housed in giant stadium-style grandstands, at the other.

A new car, chassis 72/3, had finally been completed for this race and was destined for Miles to use. This was a full parallel suspension car to replace the hybrid machine the Englishman had been forced to drive so far and it also featured the lighter FG400 gearbox and airbox as used for the first time at Brands by Rindt. The only change evident on the Austrian's 72 was that the suspension had been chrome-plated. Meanwhile Emerson Fittipaldi had impressed Chapman sufficiently to have earned himself another drive in the ageing 49C.

As soon as practice began on Friday morning, it was apparent that the biggest opposition to Rindt was going to come from the two flat-12 Ferraris of Ickx and Reggazoni. They were both fast in a straight line and stable through the crucial 'stadium' section, which surrounded the pits and start/finish area. Reggazoni was fastest in 1m 59.8s – the only driver to break the two minute barrier – in the one-and-a-half-hour session on Friday afternoon, held in warm, dry conditions, with Ickx second and Rindt third but two seconds off the leading Ferrari's pace. Miles was playing himself in, becoming accustomed to his new mount. He finished up just over two seconds adrift of his team-mate, mid-way down the order, although he probably would have narrowed this gap had he not suffered a blown engine towards the end of the session.

The Saturday morning session, again held over two hours, was probably the best of the weekend, with conditions being hot and overcast. Rindt came out on top, picking up an excellent tow to just dip below two minutes on 1m 59.7s, while Miles pulled himself up to end the session sixth-quickest with 2m 01.6s, still two seconds off

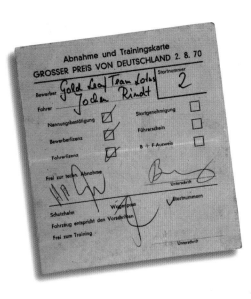

Above: While Rindt takes the plaudits of the crowd at Brands Hatch, his mechanics get to work 're-positioning' the rear wing to make it legal… **Right & Opposite Top:** The combination of a low downforce set-up and excellent traction out of corners meant that Rindt could win the German Grand Prix as he pleased, prompting his famous "a monkey could have won in this car" comment. **Opposite Bottom:** Rindt was dominant once more on the high-speed blast through the forest at Hockenheim. In the early stages, Amon's March made it a four-way battle for the lead along with the two Ferraris of Ickx and Reggazoni.

the Austrian's pace. In the afternoon, the hot, dry conditions were generally acknowledged to be slower but Ickx pulled out all the stops to take pole with a stunning 1m 59.5s lap. Rindt could only manage seventh quickest, while Miles sat out most of the session while his engine was changed. When he did get out the new unit was misfiring, so he was unable to improve on his morning time and would start from 10th on the grid. Fittipaldi had continued to impress, setting 13th fastest time, ahead of some much more modern machinery and a full second faster than Graham Hill could manage in Rob Walker's 49C.

Race-day was again hot, sunny and dry. Miles' frustrating weekend continued when he blew yet another engine in the one hour morning warm-up and it was only by dint of super-fast work by the Team Lotus mechanics that he was able to take up his position on the grid. The start brought instant good news for Rindt. While he slotted into second position at the first corner behind Ickx, the Austrian's nearest Championship challenger Jack Brabham, already in a lowly 12th position on the grid stalled and got away some time after the rest of the field had departed. Within five laps, he had retired, due to a split oil union.

The race developed into a classic slipstreaming battle between the two Ferraris, the Lotus and the March of Chris Amon. For the first few laps, Rindt shadowed the Ferrari closely, keeping up with apparent ease. On lap seven, he passed Ickx on the approach to the first chicane and held the lead for three more laps before the Belgian nosed ahead again. This pattern continued for the duration of the event, with Ickx's team-mate Reggazoni even reaching the front for several laps. Further down the order, Miles was having a good race and had moved up to seventh before he suffered his third engine failure of the weekend at half-distance. The odds were evened up a little on lap 31 of 50 when Reggazoni spun off coming into the start/finish straight as a result of gearbox troubles with his Ferrari and was unable to restart. Then it narrowed down to a two-horse race when the engine in Amon's March expired in a

cloud of smoke on lap 35. Much to Ickx's frustration, the low frontal area of the Lotus 72 and its superior traction out of the corners meant that Rindt was able to pass him almost at will. However, the tenacious Belgian did not go down without a fight and, when Rindt ran wide onto the grass two laps from the finish, he took his chance and forced his way though. However, by the end of that lap Rindt was back in front, a position he held to the chequered flag, taking the win by a margin of 0.7 seconds after 210 miles of thrilling wheel-to-wheel racing.

That evening, Rindt was fulsome in his praise for Chapman and the Lotus 72, as his close friend Jabby Crombac recalls. 'He said to me "It's so good, so easy to drive, a monkey could have won in this car." It was his main theme that night.' While the Austrian was undoubtedly supremely talented, this comment reflected the fact that he

finally had a car with which he could demonstrate his skills, as Crombac points out. 'His success came because, at last, he had the right car. When he was driving the Type 49, the car was a little bit outdated by then and also his 1969 season was spoilt by his crash in Barcelona and it took him a long time to get 100% fit again.'

This had been Rindt's fourth consecutive Grand Prix win, a feat last matched by Jim Clark in 1965 and the World Championship position was now looking very strong. Of the five closest contenders in the points, only one – Denny Hulme – managed to score any points in Germany. Following Brabham's early demise, Stewart blew his engine after a miserable weekend, Amon's engine blew and Rodriguez's ignition cut out. Ickx's second place promoted him to joint sixth place with Rodriguez on 10 points but this was still 35 behind Rindt, meaning that he would have to win four more Grand Prix without Rindt scoring any further points to have a chance of overhauling the Austrian. Gold Leaf Team Lotus's excellent day was completed by the fact that Fittipaldi had driven a storming race to finish fourth and score his first-ever World Championship points.

CHAPTER 4 THE PRESSURE BUILDS

Two weeks after Hockenheim, the Grand Prix circus reconvened in Austria for the first Grand Prix to be held at the high-speed Österreichring circuit at Zeltweg. Based on his form in Germany, Rindt seemed certain to be in contention for another victory, one which would put the World Championship result virtually beyond doubt. Similarly, it seemed likely that the strongest opposition would once again come from the Ferraris. The Maranello concern was out in force, fielding three cars for Ickx, Reggazoni and new boy Ignazio Giunti, who had made an impressive debut earlier in the year at Spa.

The 72s of Rindt and Miles were unaltered, there being little point in changing a successful formula, while Fittipaldi was now a permanent fixture in the third car. While this was again an aging 49C, he was looking forward with relish to the prospect of getting his hands on a 72, which was expected to materialise in time for the Italian Grand Prix.

The organisers had laid on a massive 11 hours of timed practice, starting with a three hour session on the Thursday, followed by four hours on both Friday and Saturday. Thursday's session was hot and dry and the timesheets were topped by the two Ferraris of Reggazoni and Giunti, Ickx not taking part as he was apparently finishing his honeymoon in the South of France! Rindt was third quickest, while Miles was ninth, 1.3 seconds behind his team-mate.

After this session, there was a little drama which created a lot of work for the team and its mechanics: Ken Tyrrell had 'pointed out' to the organisers – without going so far as lodging an official protest – that the bodywork housing the side-mounted radiators did not conform to the regulations. Following the problems with overheating experienced in the car's early outings, the pods had been widened with the addition of some rather crude-looking fibreglass spacers and this had taken it 2.5cm over the legal limit on either side. Consequently, the organisers raised this with Lotus and the mechanics had to set to work carrying out the necessary revisions. After making some changes for Friday, they had to spend most of Saturday in the garage carrying out further modifications to satisfy the scrutineers. As Eddie Dennis explains, there was quite a lot of work involved: 'We had to beat in the side of the monocoque to move the radiators inwards. But we did it anyway and it didn't stop us or the performance of the car.'

The ramifications of this are interesting, since it meant that, technically, the car had not complied with the regulations when it had won at Zandvoort, Clermont-Ferrand, Brands Hatch (in addition to the illegal-height wing!) and Hockenheim. Nowadays, a team of lawyers from a rival constructor would probably have set to work trying

Left: In front of an expectant Austrian audience Rindt's car is wheeled through the paddock by Eddie Dennis. **Below:** Miles rolls out of the paddock at the start of another frustrating weekend for the Englishman.

to get the car's victories annulled and Rindt's championship points taken away but in 1970 this wasn't 'the done thing' and a quiet word in the ear of the stewards was deemed more appropriate. It appeared that the last laugh was had

by Lotus, for when they completed these revisions, the car's frontal area was marginally reduced and it picked up an extra couple of hundred revs on the straights, increasing straight line speed! This was something that Eddie Dennis

The 72's were unaltered, there being little point in changing a successful formula

reported back, with some glee, to Tyrrell. 'I said to Ken "Good idea, thanks for that, it gave us a few more revs!" You've got to take the mick when you can!'

Friday's afternoon session was also hot and dry and this proved to be decisive for grid positions. Just as at Hockenheim, it was Rindt, Reggazoni and Ickx who dominated proceedings, these three being the only drivers to dip below the 1m 40s barrier. Just when it seemed that a Ferrari would secure pole, Rindt came up trumps with a 1m 39.23s lap to snatch it. Meanwhile, Miles had to sit out the session, as he had spun earlier on and damaged the rear-end of the car. Saturday's session was spoilt by rain, which began to fall mid-way through the afternoon. However, before this, Miles had managed to get out and record a 1m 41.46s, good enough for fifth quickest in the session and 10th on the grid. Rindt did not venture out until the rain had thoroughly soaked the track and so did not set a representative time. The only obvious changes made to the cars during practice were the substitution of stiffer torsion bars, but since this did not appear to improve the handling, the team reverted back to the original models.

An Austrian leading the World Championship, on pole position and with a pretty good chance of winning the race was enough to attract spectators in their droves to the

picturesque circuit. When the flag fell, all Rindt's hard work in securing pole position was wasted when he was out-dragged by Reggazoni while Ickx also managed to pass him on the opening tour. By lap two, Reggazoni had dutifully let his team leader by, a position the Belgian was to hold until the finish. On the third lap, the leading group came across a huge oil slick laid down by Francois Cevert's March, which had blown its engine in spectacular fashion on the preceding lap. The resulting skirmish saw Rindt lose three places as he got his car back under control, dropping him behind Beltoise, Giunti and Amon. On lap seven he re-passed Amon and by lap 10 he was ahead of Giunti but by this stage he was 10 seconds adrift of the leading 12-cylinder trio of Ickx, Reggazoni and Beltoise. Gradually, lap-by-lap, he inched closer to them, closing the gap to 8.5 seconds after 13 laps, 6.8 seconds by lap 18 and to 5.8 seconds by lap 21. However, just starting lap 22 of 60, he threw his hands up in the air in a gesture of disgruntlement as his Cosworth DFV expired and he pulled off the track, drove round the back of the pits and into retirement.

In fact, it was not surprising that the engine blew, since it was DFV 901 the unit that Rindt had used to win the German Grand Prix and that had also done all the practice sessions in Austria prior to the race. With the dire Cosworth

Left: Rindt and Chapman look confident and relaxed as they chat in the paddock at the Österreichring. **Middle:** After the furore at Brands Hatch over the height of Rindt's rear wing and Ken Tyrrell's 'unofficial protest' about the width of the 72s, great care was taken to ensure that they conformed fully with the regulations. **Right:** Dave Sims, Graeme Bartels and March mechanic Bob Sparshott ponder the rear-end of Miles' 72/3. The Englishman was forced to sit out the vital Friday practice session as a result of an 'off'.

First Person:

John Miles on Jochen Rindt and the 72

"I always found that Jochen was driven on by his pursuit of a World Championship, if you like, but at the same time he was always having severe concerns about the car. He was almost schizophrenic about it. I don't think he was happy in the 72. It was almost like he was dashing for a Championship. Once the car started to go, to really fly, he just wanted to get that Championship. He understood the situation he was in but he was prepared to overlook it because his drive to win this Championship was all-consuming, that's how it seemed to me. Whereas I got more and more depressed by it, more and more concerned about the way the whole thing was going, how it was run. There was no caution there. Perhaps I am just over-cautious, and that's why I never made a very successful Formula 1 driver. I thought too much! But that probably kept me alive…"

engine shortage at the time, Chief Mechanic Gordon Huckle remembers that they had agonised over whether or not to install a fresh engine for the race. 'It was going so well, it was one of those searching situations: do we leave it in or do we take it out? Rindt was quite happy with it and the Old Man was saying, "Well, if it's all right, leave it". It is easy to look back with hindsight: if we'd have changed it we might have been alright. It had certainly done a fair bit of mileage, that engine.'

Miles' race had been even shorter for, on the third lap, when running in ninth position, his car had veered violently to the right under braking for the penultimate corner and he had been forced to muster all his strength and experience to keep the car on the road. 'Prior to that, every time I braked there had been an awful lot of vibration from the front of the car which was making me brake early, thank God – I mean 25 yards early. I was lining up for this left-hander and when I put the brakes on the car jumped from the left to the right side of the road. Fortunately, I was only knocking off 30-40mph, it wasn't like braking from 200mph down to whatever.' The cause of this sudden deviation was a broken left front brake-shaft, leaving the Englishman to

Top Right: Dave Sims (left) and Derek Mower (right) look on as Miles pulls into the paddock after his left front brake-shaft broke. The fracture is not visible, as it occurred at the outboard end, obscured by the rubber seal over the CV joint. **Right:** Rindt's car in the paddock at the Österreichring. Chief Mechanic Gordon Huckle is in the foreground, Eddie Dennis leans over the car, Dave Sims watches as Graeme Bartels emerges from the transporter.

Right: Rindt had to play second fiddle to John Surtees in the Oulton Park Gold Cup, after a first-heat miscalculation on gear ratios left him with too much time to make up on aggregate in the second leg. Here he leads Jackie Stewart, making his debut in Tyrrell 001.

Opposite Page: Farewell, the Gold Cup was the last time British fans would see Rindt in action.

cruise around the rest of the lap and into the pits to retire. The only Lotus finisher was Fittipaldi, giving the Lotus 49 its Grand Prix swansong. He struggled with fuel mixture problems to finish last, five laps down on winner Ickx.

What promised to be a good weekend and an opportunity to virtually sew up the World Championship had rather disintegrated for Team Lotus. Amazingly, neither Brabham, Hulme, Stewart nor Amon had been able to capitalise on the Austrian's plight by scoring points, so his Championship lead was maintained. The only significant change in the standings was that Ickx had leapfrogged up the order by virtue of his win, to join Stewart in fourth place with 19 points, while Rindt was still at the head of the table with 45.

Rindt and Lotus would now have to wait three weeks

before they could have another crack at securing the title in the Italian Grand Prix at Monza. Mathematically, eight other drivers could still take the Championship if one of them were to win most of the remaining four Grand Prix and Rindt were not to score any more points. Realistically, that seemed pretty unlikely to happen based on the evidence of the preceding races and it appeared that only Brabham, Hulme and possibly Stewart and Ickx had any true chance of victory. Given the poor form of the first three, that too seemed unlikely, to the point where the Belgian was emerging as the person most likely to be Rindt's strongest challenger in the final few races.

Before Monza, there were plenty of things to keep the team occupied. Firstly, they had to investigate what had caused the brake-shaft to break on Miles' car. The team concluded that the failure had been caused by drilling imperfections, where the hollow shaft had been drilled from both ends and the two holes didn't quite meet. A stress fracture had developed at this point and spread outwards, causing the shaft to break near the outboard end beneath the rubber boot of the CV joint.

The non-Championship Gold Cup race at Oulton Park in Cheshire, England, took place just six days after the Austrian Grand Prix, ensuring that there was no time to relax after the long journey home from the Osterreichring. A single car, 72/2, had been entered for Rindt to drive and this was fitted with solid brake-shafts as a precaution while the investigations into Miles' brake-shaft failure were ongoing.

There was also the small matter of finishing off the construction of chassis 72/4 for the Rob Walker team, which had been promised to them for some time now. The build could not begin until a new car had been completed for Miles to use at Hockenheim. It had not been possible to finish 72/4, which was being built up from what could be salvaged from 72/1, in time for Austria and in fact Rob Walker had scratched his entry from the race, feeling that his 49C was no longer competitive enough to warrant the long journey down to the Osterreichring. The team finally took delivery of the car on the Tuesday after the Austrian race and, bar what they described as "a few laps of Hethel in the dark", had not had any opportunity to test the car prior to arriving at Oulton Park on Friday.

The two one-hour practice sessions on Friday were blighted by rain. In the first, no one set a representative dry-weather time, while in the second just the opening few minutes were dry with only John Surtees and Jackie Oliver managing to complete a flying lap before the rains came down once more. Consequently, the grid had a rather odd look to it, with Rindt languishing down on the fourth row in 10th place and Hill in 12th, both of them well in amongst the F5000 runners.

In the race, which was dry, Rindt quickly worked his way though the field to third place, but could not make an impression on the flying Surtees, having only his fourth race in his eponymous chassis, and Oliver's BRM. The reason for this was that the Austrian's top gear was too low and he was losing out to the other two on the straights. He was also suffering clutch problems due to a union having come undone early in the race, causing the clutch fluid to leak out, and he finished the first 20 lap heat 12.8 seconds behind winner Surtees. Hill had a miserable race in his new 72, experiencing stiffening throttle slides almost as soon as he started the race, then on lap three the oil pressure in his DFV dropped and he was forced to retire. As there was not enough time to change the engine before the second heat, this ended a rather disappointing debut for the new chassis.

For the second 20-lap heat, Rindt had a higher top gear fitted and the clutch union was repaired. From third on the grid this time, he was able to keep in touch with leader Oliver, who made a tremendous start, and second-placed man Surtees. On the third lap, Rindt slipped past Surtees and two laps later he was through into the lead. At half distance, his advantage was 5.5 seconds but with only six laps to go it became apparent that Surtees was in trouble, the ignition cut-out kicking in at a lower rev limit than it should and a failing crown wheel and pinion causing excessive vibration. Rindt was given the signal to speed up as there was a chance he could wipe out his first heat deficit and take overall victory on aggregate. As they went into the final lap he led Surtees by 10 seconds. However, the determined Englishman put in a final flourish to actually reduce the gap on his rival and emerged the victor on aggregate by 3.4 seconds, with Rindt in second place overall and Oliver third.

As soon as he had taken the chequered flag, Rindt parked his car at the first corner, Old Hall, crossed the track to collect his suitcase which he had left at a marshal's post before the race and was into his plane and flying off to Vienna, where he was reported to be attending a hill-climb. Meanwhile, it was left to one of his mechanics to get behind the wheel of the 72, complete the slowing down lap and acknowledge the plaudits of the crowd.

Rindt and Lotus would now have to wait three weeks before they could have another crack at securing the title at Monza

CHAPTER 5 DISASTER AT MONZA

The Italian Grand Prix weekend started well for Gold Leaf Team Lotus, since Peter Warr finally managed to get Fittipaldi's signature on a contract that would keep him with the team for the following season, as he explains. 'We were not disenchanted with John Miles but we felt that he hadn't really fulfilled the expectations we had of him from his Formula 3 days and there were some thoughts that we were probably going to have to think about a replacement driver. Then, as Jochen went through his year and it became more and more likely that he was going to win the Championship, he was making noises that, if he did, he was going to retire, so we immediately needed not only one, but possibly two drivers. Therefore we were very keen to keep Emerson on board.'

Although Fittipaldi later built a reputation as an astute, tactically-minded driver, Warr remembers it was the Brazilian's forceful style behind the wheel, which initially won him over. 'He was a very different animal in those early days. He was not only very fast but he was aggressive in his driving and looked like a real hard charger. Certainly, he had done well enough in the lesser categories to be someone you looked out for. I actually signed him for 1971

in one of the rooms of the Hotel de Ville in Monza, before practice'. Only later that weekend would the true significance of securing that signature become apparent.

After their disappointing start with 72/4, the Rob Walker team were determined to get some serious running in and made their way down to Monza early so that they could test at the track in the days before the meeting. By contrast, Gold Leaf Team Lotus once again arrived late, having been working day and night to finish a new chassis, 72/5. In fact, the new car still wasn't fully completed, the mechanics having to finish off the job at the circuit on the Friday morning. This followed a gruelling journey from Hethel which saw them arrive at Monza at 10am as a result of being held up at the Italian border. Everyone chipped in to get the car finished, with Fittipaldi even doing his bit by helping the mechanics to put the numbers on!

Chief Mechanic Gordon Huckle didn't even make it to Monza, becoming another victim of the gruelling 1970 work schedule. 'What I remember about Monza weekend is being flat on my back in bed. I had collapsed. We were getting ready to go to Monza and the night before we were going off, I was taken home and put to bed. I'd got low blood pressure, low temperature, I was just absolutely out.

The doctor told me I had to have two weeks in bed.' It was a sign of his dedication to duty that, when the team needed some new parts made and shipped out, Huckle got off his sick-bed and went into the workshop to oversee things. However, a rare compassionate side to Chapman was revealed as a result of this, since he showed himself to be concerned about the health of his mechanic, despite being in the midst of a hectic race weekend. 'They wanted them shipped out there a bit quick. I remember getting them sorted and the Old Man phoned me up and threatened me with all sorts of mayhem if I didn't go back to bed. I got a right rollicking for going into the factory to sort it out.'

According to Fittipaldi, the plan had been for Rindt to take over the new car after the young Brazilian had shaken it down. 'Colin asked me to run the car in on the Friday and

Above Left: Calm before the storm: Rindt gets a few quiet words of advice from Chapman prior to the first practice session. **Above Right:** Lotus finally confirmed the existence of its turbine Formula 1 car when a Press Release announced it would not be taking the 56B to Monza.

then on Saturday I was going to go back to Jochen's car.' Despite having done a fair bit of Formula 2 and 3 in Europe, Fittipaldi had never actually raced at Monza. His only prior experience of the circuit had been a lap in a hire car on the Thursday! When he got out in the second session on Friday, Fittipaldi ran in 72/5 with a rear wing but no nose fins. After a few laps, he came into the pits and Chapman told the mechanics to take the wings off his car, as they had done earlier with Rindt's. Fittipaldi was unsure about this, having seen that Hill, who had been testing for much of that week at the circuit, had kept his wings on. However, being a 'new boy' he felt obliged to bow to Chapman's experience and out he went, sans wings.

The car was still very new and Fittipaldi was concentrating on bedding in the brakes and learning the braking points for each corner. Eventually, after five or six laps he started to speed up but was still keeping a watchful eye on his mirrors, trying to keep out of the way of any faster cars coming up behind him. On one lap, Ignazio Giunti's Ferrari passed the Lotus on the run down to the Parabolica. Fittipaldi takes up the story: 'I looked in the mirror and I saw Jack Brabham coming. I didn't want to be in his way and I looked again in the mirror for a fraction of a second. When I looked back at the track I was already 100 metres inside the braking area, completely beyond the limit! I flew over Giunti's rear wheel, went through the sand, over the bank and into the trees!'

'It was not a pleasant walk back to the pits to face Colin. The first thing he said was "What happened?" I said, "I screwed up. I looked in the mirror and missed the braking point completely". It was difficult for me to say but I had to tell the truth because it could have been a mechanical

failure or something that could be a compromise for the future. It was completely my fault. Colin was not very pleased with that, the first time I ever drove a Lotus 72!' Although the mechanics struggled valiantly to repair the car in time for the Saturday session, it was a hopeless task, and Fittipaldi's weekend was over.

Meanwhile, Rindt and Miles had been getting on with the task of setting up their cars for the ultra fast track. When he had arrived, Miles had observed the set-up of Hill's Rob Walker car, with its wings set at a very shallow angle of incidence and it was in this form that the two works cars practised in the first Friday session, although they went out very late in the session and ran just a few laps due to the late arrival of the transporter. They were anything but impressive: Miles was 19th in 1m 28.54s, nearly four seconds off the pace and Rindt was even further down the order in 22nd, his 1m 29.97s one and half seconds

adrift of his team-mate. However, it was Hill who showed the potential of the car by registering the eighth-quickest lap, a 1m 26.38s compared to Ickx's fastest time of 1m 24.61s. For the second afternoon session, Rindt's car was shorn of its wings and he returned the fifth-fastest time of 1m 25.71s compared to Ickx's best of 1m 24.14s, while Miles – still using the wings on his car – was only eight-tenths slower than his team-mate on 1m 26.51s. Fittipaldi had set a 1m 28.39s before his accident, while Hill suffered from a number of new car troubles and could not get anywhere near his earlier times.

Towards the end of the day, Miles was ordered to take the wings off his car. 'We had never, ever done any work with the car without wings. I was surprised how well I had been running on the first day because I'd never been to Monza before. I had come to the same wing settings as Graham – the centre plane knocked out on the rear wing and the front fins very flat – and that seemed to work. I wasn't happy but I could drive the car. I was trundling round and then in the mirror I saw this red thing coming up behind me, luridly sliding round the Lesmos. I thought that as it was near the end of practice, I'd let him by. And it was Jochen. He came past under the bridge towards Ascari and the car looked absolutely dreadful, it was all over the road.

Opposite Page: After its brief appearance at Oulton Park, Rob Walker's 72/4 arrived early in order to get in some much-needed testing. Driver Graham Hill had already settled on a low-downforce configuration for Monza by the time the Gold Leaf Team Lotus transporter rolled into the paddock. **This Page:** All hands to the pumps: Chapman joins Rindt, Eddie Dennis and Dick Scammell in mopping up a spillage on 72/2 in the paddock at Monza.

And I was shocked, probably thinking "Shit, no wings!"

'Anyway, he blasted down the straight and drew away from me a little bit but I caught him up again quite a lot under braking. I came into the pits and Chapman said, "Take the wings off John's car" and I said to Beaky [Dave Sims] "I don't want to take the wings off" and he said, "The Old Man has told me to". So they took the wings off and I got to the Curva Grande and I wasn't going quickly or anything and the car just snapped into oversteer. At those sorts of speeds you don't go into serious oversteer but I got into one of those 'whooahh...I don't want to be here' moments, I just cruised around and came back into the pits and said, "I can't drive this thing, I've got no time to sort it out".

'The car just had a huge amount of rear lift. It felt like it had downforce at the front and lift at the back, which is what it probably did have, otherwise it wouldn't have had such a bloody big wing at the back. If you then chuck the wing away, the fronts really are just trim tabs, they do quite a lot of work but in surface area they do relatively nothing compared with the rear. Frankly, I don't think the car was sortable without wings, because the shape was so different from a normal racing car. It looked as if it was designed to have downforce at the front without wings and you needed very little front wing to balance the rear downforce.

'We finished practice and Colin and I were sitting in the truck and I said, "That was the most awful race car I've ever driven". He said "We're going to leave the wings off your

car tomorrow" and I said, "I don't want to take the wings off". He said "Well it's the only way you are going to go quick" and I said "Maybe it is, if we had time to sort the car out".'

This disagreement between Miles and Chapman was probably the final straw that ended their relationship. Miles was distressed that this man whom he had always looked up to and held in such high esteem could show such callous disregard for the wishes of his driver, to the point where he overruled him. Chapman probably felt disappointed that his driver appeared not to trust him and would not bow to his judgement and instincts that this was the route to go.

Miles' pessimism after the Friday afternoon session was in stark contrast to his team-mate Rindt's optimism, as

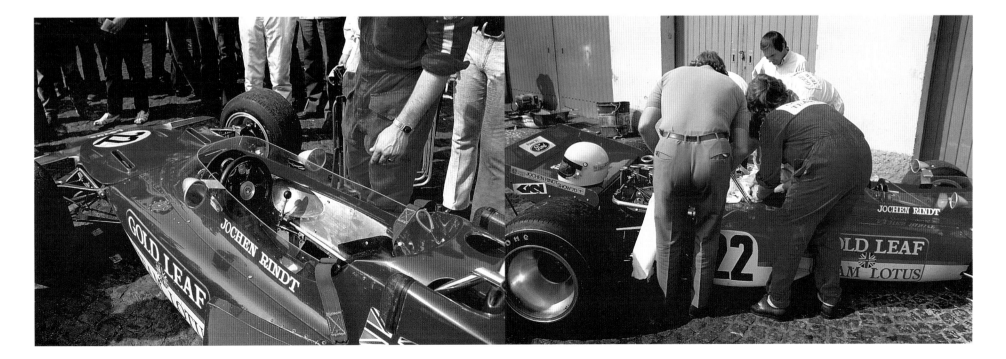

Competitions Manager Warr remembers. 'Jochen was full of himself about how he was going to blow everyone away'. Taking the wings off had made his 72 more slippery through the air, which, as his mechanic Eddie Dennis points out, was vital at Monza. 'Jochen said "Running without wings, I'm picking up 600 or 800 revs", or something phenomenal like that. The previous year, most people ran without wings. The circuit was such that with wings you would just fall back from the main group on the straights and you could not make all that up on the bends.'

With the gain in straight-line speed, Rindt found that his car was also under-geared. The team also had a special Cosworth development engine, which they planned to install for Saturday's final qualifying session, as Dennis explains. 'Cosworth had done us a couple of really quick engines, ones they did for us when the season was critical and it was between us and Ferrari. I suppose they gave us slightly preferential treatment. They were certainly up on horsepower to what we were normally running.' Combined with a higher top gear ratio, this would give the car a maximum speed of around 205mph and Rindt a fighting chance of landing a front row grid position.

Miles remembers the events of Saturday very clearly. 'I had yet another sleepless night, came into the circuit the next day and there were no wings on my car. Beaky was very apologetic but he said he couldn't do anything about it, he'd been told to take the wings off. I was a bit late out for practice, the car wasn't quite ready, they were still fuelling it up and adjusting the mirrors while I was sitting in it but Jochen was out on the button.' Before Miles could make it out onto the track, a spooky silence descended over the circuit as all the cars that had been practising slowly filed back into the pits. Denny Hulme, who had been following

Rindt very closely, came in and stopped by the Lotus pit to report that the Austrian had crashed heavily on the entrance to the Parabolica. By this time Miles was ready to go out onto the track. 'I saw Chapman and a couple of other guys in the team coming towards me walking through the crowd. They pounced on me and Chapman said, "Jochen's had an accident, go out and see what's happened". Fortunately, the marshalls wouldn't let me out.'

From Hulme's account, and from those of eyewitnesses at that point on the circuit, it appears that Rindt had begun

Above Left & Opposite Page: Miles began the Italian Grand Prix weekend running with nose fins and rear wing. **Above Right:** Emerson Fittipaldi was entrusted to run in the brand new chassis 72/5 on Friday before Rindt would take it over on Saturday but crashed, damaging the car beyond immediate repair. **Right:** Hill was more comfortable with the Rob Walker 72 at Monza and found a low downforce set-up that retained the rear wing and front nose fins.

braking heavily for the Parabolica, just past the 200 metre board. His car veered slightly to the right, then left, then right again and finally speared sharp left and hit the barrier. Ordinarily, the car would have simply glanced off the barrier and probably ended up in the sand on the outside of the corner, with Rindt able to climb out and dust himself down, perhaps with no more than a few cuts and bruises. However, the barrier had not been properly secured and the wedge nose of his car went under the guardrail. On impact, the left-front wheel flew back across the track,

almost hitting Hulme, while the front of the car, including the right front wheel, went under the barrier, chopping off one of the supporting posts. The next post it came to did not yield, with the result that the whole front section of the car – including the right front wheel, suspension and footbox containing the pedals – was ripped off, while the steering wheel was pulled through the dashboard bulkhead. The remains of the car rebounded violently away from the barrier, spinning like a top and coming to rest in the sand.

Poor Rindt was pulled down into the cockpit, because his feet were tangled up in the section that was ripped off. He never wore his crotch strap due to fear of fire and it was this that enabled him to be pulled down so that the lap belts cut his throat. Although the Austrian was not officially certified dead until he reached the hospital in Milan, this was purely a legal procedure to avoid the meeting being cancelled, since Italian law would have required this if it were found he had died at the circuit. The plain truth is that he was probably killed instantly or certainly within seconds of the accident taking place.

Worse still, had he been fighting for his life, Rindt would probably still have died on the way to hospital, due to an astonishing display of bureaucracy and incompetence, which saw the on-site facilities of the Grand Prix Medical Unit mobile hospital ignored (for the aforementioned legal reason) and the police escort for the ambulance taking it to Monza hospital in error, meaning that it was a full hour before the Austrian got to Milan's Niguarda hospital.

On hearing of the crash, Dick Scammell, Eddie Dennis and Bernie Ecclestone ran off towards the site of the accident, as Dennis describes. 'Bernie and myself just legged it off to the Parabolica. It's amazing how far it is down there, it's a lot further than you think from the pits.

Before Miles could make it out onto the track, a spooky silence descended over the circuit as all the cars that had been practising slowly filed back into the pits

By the time we got there, he'd gone, they'd taken him away in an ambulance.' Scammell made it just in time to see Rindt in the ambulance and clearly recalls that the Austrian was already dead at this point. When Dennis and Ecclestone arrived a few moments later, a marshal made a cutting motion across his throat to them, to signal that there was little chance of their driver surviving. Stunned, Dennis resorted to picking up pieces of the wreckage, something he remembers vividly to this day: 'I picked up some bits of brake and burnt myself – they were still hot'.

Meanwhile, Jabby Crombac, who had spent the weekend in negotiations with Chris Amon trying to get him to sign to drive in Formula 1 for Matra in 1971, stepped in to offer transport to the hospital. 'I had my rental car and I took Colin, Hazel and Nina and, I think, Bette Hill to the Niguarda hospital. And of course, when we arrived there, we were told that it was finished [that Rindt was dead].'

The wreckage of Rindt's car was hung rather unceremoniously on the back of a lorry and brought back into the pits, where it was placed in a garage pending further investigation. Miles, Hill and Rob Walker were able to make a cursory examination of the car in the gloom, at which point Miles recalls that Hill made a remark which summed up the slightly callous attitude that drivers had to adopt in the face of their colleagues dying on a regular basis. 'Graham looked at the car and said, "Let's face it, he's dead, isn't he? When does practice start, Rob?"'

However, there was to be no more practice for the remaining Lotus 72s. As the severity of the accident became apparent and news of Rindt's death spread, the order was given for Gold Leaf Team Lotus to pack up their things. The works 72 of Miles and the Rob Walker car of Hill were withdrawn and quickly loaded into their transporters. From the von Trips/Clark accident of 1961 Lotus had plenty of experience of the Italian justice system and they were anxious that their remaining cars and equipment should not be impounded so within a matter of hours they were on their way and heading for the border. There was nothing left for Miles to do other than to return to his hotel, have something to eat, phone home and then return to England the next day. His telephone call was particularly welcome because it cleared up some confusion about who had been killed that day. 'I had dinner that night with Emerson and phoned my wife. My parents were frantic because they had been driving along and turned the radio on and heard the tail-end of a broadcast saying something about a Lotus driver having been killed at Monza.'

The Italian Grand Prix went ahead the next day as planned, without any Lotus participation. After 243 miles of manic slipstreaming, Clay Reggazoni emerged victorious to score a popular victory on Ferrari's home soil. With Stewart coming home the runner-up he moved up to tie for second in the points standings with Jack Brabham on 25 points but Rindt was still 20 points ahead. Hulme kept in contention with fourth place, to put him on 23 points, while Reggazoni leapfrogged team-mate Ickx, who had retired, to take fifth spot in the standings with 21 points.

Everyone at Team Lotus was naturally devastated by the shocking turn of events at Monza. Just when they had seemed on the brink of a joyous World Championship victory, their star driver had been cruelly snatched from them. Eddie Dennis sums it up when he says: 'The upsetting thing is you talked to him, strapped him in and then you didn't see him any more, he was gone. It was like losing a member of your family really. You build up that sort of partnership with somebody.' Colin Chapman flew Rindt's widow Nina home to Switzerland in his plane, where she was joined by Sally Courage, widow of Piers. Meanwhile, one of Rindt's mechanics, Herbie Blash, took the Austrian's road car home and Peter Warr stayed behind to make arrangements for the funeral and to engage a firm of lawyers for the court proceedings that would inevitably follow.

The funeral took place in Graz, Austria, five days after his death. Mechanic Eddie Dennis, who had worked with Blash on Rindt's car, was dreading the occasion as he did

Below Left: This shot shows the late 1970 specification of the 72, with battery mounted behind the gearbox, wing stays supporting the trailing edge and side-mounted oil cooler. **Below:** Relaxing in the pits, Rindt ponders how he might extract some more speed from his car after languishing down the order in early practice runs. **Opposite Page:** Hill and Rindt venture out onto the circuit for practice on Friday. At this stage, the Austrian's car was still running noticeably more wing than the Rob Walker team's car.

not know how Nina would react, this being the first time she had seen him since the accident. However, his fears were unfounded: 'She came up and hugged me – that was a massive relief, I can tell you'.

Tony Rudd was to become a central figure in the investigations into the cause of Rindt's accident, representing Team Lotus in a technical capacity. However, the initial inquiry, and criminal charges relating to it, were short-lived. 'There was an inquiry and the Automobile Club of Milan, who organised the Italian Grand Prix, retained an Italian lawyer. He was a very nice chap who could speak a certain amount of English. He was, I think, brilliant. He got the case against Chunky [Chapman] thrown out – I think

the indictment was improperly drawn up. So the whole thing was thrown out and that was that. Chunky was livid. He said, "I didn't want to get off because I'd got a clever lawyer. I wanted to get off because I didn't design a dangerous car." He was very cross about that.'

Just when it seemed that Chapman would not be given the opportunity to defend himself, the shock news came through that the case was to be reopened, as Rudd explains. 'The mayor or whoever it was, the prefect of the commune of Monza, was trying to close racing down in the park and he was using the accident as a reason. The whole thing was driven by Italian politics. Whoever he was, he got the case reopened, quite a bit later on. The way it was done was that they got an engineer who worked for Marelli and then Ferrari, called Colombo, sworn in as a magistrate. He had a home in Monza, from his Marelli days and he was put in charge of the investigation. He was a very competent engineer and knew a bit about racing cars from the work he'd done with Ferrari but I think he was principally an ignition man. Colin only found out what was going on virtually at the conclusion of his investigation. Of course, being a magistrate, if Colombo found that there was a case to answer, Colin would have been arrested. So it was quite a critical event.

'Colin contacted me and said he wanted me to go with Peter Jowitt from the RAC, to meet Colombo. Peter and I talked the same language, we'd never worked together but I got on quite well with him. We flew to Milan in the company aeroplane and went, quite late in the evening, to see Colombo. He was about to close the investigation but he said some of the statements we'd brought him, helped fill in some of the things he didn't understand. He asked if we could get them supported by notarised statements from the various witnesses. One of the things we'd got was a photograph of a picture on the cover of an Italian magazine, showing that the guardrail had not been bolted back in place. All the negatives had disappeared and we had to get the magazines re-photographed, which was quite a business.

'The other key element was Denny Hulme's statement, because he said that Rindt went by and was fishtailing out of control. He believed it was an aerodynamic effect, it wasn't a case of put the brakes on and only one wheel locked, the car was fishtailing. So we'd got to get that statement notarised. And that got quite tricky because, to find a notary public in the paddock at Silverstone is quite difficult! My eldest daughter had a school friend whose father was a notary and he mustered an armful of other notaries around the country and we took one to Silverstone with us and got Denny to notarise his statement. Then I'd got to get all this to Colombo in Milan on the Monday morning because he was completing his report and sending it in that day, so I was tight for time. I went to London to see John Miles at his home and got his statement notarised. Then I took some of the other stuff, including all the photographic evidence, and got that notarised in Norwich on Saturday night.

'I got it all together and I flew to Milan on the Sunday night. I met Colombo in his office at Marelli, early on the Monday morning and gave him all the other statements and stuff. What we had told him made sense, but this evidence filled in the gaps. So that was fine and I could go home. Chunky objected because I hadn't brought a copy of Colombo's report with me! It was a week or so before the report arrived. It was all very diplomatic but it said that part of the trouble was that Rindt didn't wear his crotch strap and the car was aerodynamically unstable and the front wheel went under the guardrail because the barrier hadn't been bolted back when they'd dug a drainage ditch. It also said that there was 400 metres of gravel run-off area and, even if the brakes had failed, the car could still have gone into the run-off and slowed down. The drive-shaft may have failed but that wasn't a life-threatening influence.

'We were pretty sure that was a separate incident, the brake-shaft failing. It failed because Team Lotus hadn't got the facilities to crack-test the shaft themselves. There was quite a lot of technology round this part of Norfolk, what with the North Sea rigs and all the rest of it and they sent the shaft to a specialist firm in Norwich or Yarmouth. It was made of a special material and, to increase the fatigue strength, you shot-peened it. To crack-test it, you needed to have it polished and that's when they scratched it. The scratch was in a radius. I don't see why it broke there, actually, the stressing shouldn't have been that critical but it

Above: Eddie Dennis makes final preparations as Rindt gets ready to climb aboard. **Opposite Page Top Right:** Shorn of nose fins and rear wing, Rindt's car looks naked as he edges forward out of the Lotus pit. **Opposite Page Bottom Right:** As the clock ticks towards 3pm, Nina Rindt enjoys a last-minute ice-cream as her husband prepares himself for Saturday's practice session.

wasn't really relevant and it had probably been on the way to failing at the same time. I could have had quite a party with the crack-testing people. They tested them and certified them as OK. I think they used to do it periodically as a matter of routine. I could have said "Are you sure that the crack wasn't under way the last time you had the shafts?" I didn't know whether they shot-peened them again after they tested them…they should have done. But anyway, I believe that the shaft didn't cause the crash. He was out of control aerodynamically.'

In truth, the reason why Rindt lost control of his car will probably never be known. It is a strangely bizarre twist of fate that the causes of each of the accidents which have claimed the lives of three World Champion drivers – Jim Clark, Jochen Rindt and Ayrton Senna – remain a mystery to this day and will probably never be pinpointed. Certainly, plenty of people have opinions on the subject of Rindt's crash, each convinced that their explanation is the correct one.

An examination of the facts throws up several clues. The tyres produced by Firestone for this event were, in the words of Peter Warr, 'brick shithouse jobs', meaning that they were exceptionally hard. 'It took eight laps to bring them up to temperature! But we couldn't run the softer compound, they were too soft. So we decided to run hard tyres on the left and softs on the right.' This is confirmed by Rindt's mechanic, Eddie Dennis, who adds: 'He was out scrubbing tyres on the left-hand side because the right-hand side tyres didn't take a lot of wear. He was scrubbing a set of race tyres, left front and left rear and bedding race pads in at the same time. So there was a little bit of unevenness, if you like, in the tyres and their grip.'

Finally, the decision to remove the wings had implications for both the aerodynamic balance of the car (greater download was generated by the three-tier rear wing than by the two front nose fins) and the brake balance of the car, since there was now considerably less grip at the rear end. As Peter Warr points out: 'If you have too much brake balance to the rear, when you apply the brakes the car will start to fishtail.' This is precisely what the car did in the initial stages of the accident. Dennis also agrees that this may have contributed to the accident. 'You'd have to change the balance bar accordingly because with any braking the weight transfers heavily to the front and the back end can go lighter. It certainly could have unbalanced the back end of the car because we'd only just taken the wings off the previous day.'

Warr recalls that Rindt had only done a handful of laps

(he had completed four) before he went for it. Therefore, it seems likely that his tyres (or the left-side hard compound ones, at least) would not yet have been fully up to their optimum temperature. Warr believes that this, combined with the incorrect brake balance and aerodynamic instability, created the conditions under which Rindt's car spun out of control. For what it is worth, Warr believes to this day that the brake-shaft did not break: 'I think he came hammering down to the Parabolica, got on to the brakes and the car fishtailed. It went to the right and he caught it, then to the left and he caught it, then to the right and he caught it again and then the softer right-side tyres gripped and sent him off to the left. No-one ever proved to me that the shaft broke through a torsional failure. It was broken off like a piece of cheese.'

Others are not so sure. Tony Rudd admits to being perplexed as to why the car veered left so sharply when there was still braking effect on three of the four wheels, which he believed should have allowed the Austrian to slow the car down and just go off into the run-off area. Again this lends credence to the theory that this sudden veering left was caused by the aerodynamic and braking instability and was not attributable (or not solely attributable) to the shaft breaking. A lack of appropriate tyre-marks also perplexed him. 'There were no tyre-marks of locking the left-front tyre. He should have locked the left front, because it was the right brake-shaft that broke and there weren't any marks of that.'

John Miles also believes that the brake-shaft broke but

that the aerodynamic instability of the car must have contributed to the accident. 'Chapman's whole correct philosophy was that, if you could extract downforce from the body – not wings, just from the shape of the car – that was downforce for free. Subsequently, when the car started to go well, it proved to be the case, because the car was very fast down the straight and it was bloody good round the corners as well. So, case proved. But you can't have it both ways. You can't have a car like that and then dump the wings and expect it to suddenly work.

'But I do have trouble in believing that the car would suddenly snap left. Jochen was such a fantastic driver. OK, it fishtailed, as I understand it from Denny Hulme, the car did a little wriggle. It was as if Jochen had put the brakes on, the shaft snapped and he knew instinctively that he had to take away the thing that was causing the instability but then he had to stop, so he had to reapply the brakes and the car just snapped left. It turned left so dramatically, in much the same way as mine had turned right in Austria. If it had been a fishtailing accident, it would have been more like a tank-slapper, it would have kept going more or less in the same direction. But I still don't believe the difference in grip would cause such a violent deviation. It might make the car move around or you'd lock a brake on the side with less grip. But you can lock a brake on one side when you are doing 180mph and you don't suddenly spear off the road, because a locked brake is still a lot of grip. It may not be the same as the unlocked side but it is not 50% less.

'People conjectured that the aerodynamics were the

reason. I thought they were a contributory factor, undoubtedly I'm sure, the car was unstable, or far less stable. It hit the barrier before the corner, going at 180-200mph. To lose control in that distance and hit the barrier and spin to a stop, there has to be something that sent the car out of control. Absolutely, positively, sent the car out of control. I suppose I always have my broken brake-shaft incident in the back of my mind, although the failure was different.'

Chapman himself, in a letter to Autosport several weeks after the tragedy, claimed that photos of the car at the point of impact clearly showed black marks on the track and across the grass verge from the effect of heavy braking, although he did not say whether it was possible to determine which wheels these were from. However, what he did point out was that the nature of the failure of the brake-shaft was quite different to that experienced three weeks earlier by Miles at Österreichring. That one had arisen from inside the hollow shaft and was believed to be due to an imperfection during the drilling process. All remaining shafts had been given a thorough and detailed examination and no such similar flaws had been found on them, so they had been refitted for Monza.

The break in the shaft at Monza was different, according to Chapman's letter. 'The fracture of this shaft was…a jagged 'birds-mouth' type of fracture, more

consistent with torsional failure due to extreme overload rather than fatigue. Whether this shaft broke under heavy braking, which seems unlikely because it had only completed 15 laps' running since the detailed inspections previously described, or whether with the brakes locked on, it received an additional to normal maximum torque on impact with the barrier, it is impossible to say'. Certainly, pictures exist of the broken shaft but whether it could be described as having a jagged 'birds mouth' type of fracture is open to interpretation.

Tony Rudd says that another possible cause occurred to him several years later but that he dismissed it. 'I had a long talk with Chunky later on, about the 77, the car that was fully adjustable in all directions! That was the one where, if you put the front brakes on, the universal joints locked up and stopped the suspension working because there was brake torque going through the universal joints, they locked and then the suspension wouldn't flex, which was a common failure. I did wonder whether that could have broken, or added to the loads on the 72's brake-shafts. That would have been like a Borra test, a German gentleman who devised a fatigue test where you bent it while the shaft was rotating. I hadn't thought of it until the 77 but there was no evidence of that either.'

It is also interesting to consider the opinion Emerson Fittipaldi expressed in his autobiography, Flying on the Ground. 'Something went wrong with the car, I am quite sure of that, but there is one odd thing that most people don't know. In 1971, we tried the car at Silverstone without wings, and I nearly crashed on braking. It was terrible on braking; I braked and the car started weaving. Perhaps the crash had something to do with the wings. I have seen many films and pictures, and there was no way Jochen could crash just there unless something went wrong with the car.'

Irrespective of what caused the car to crash, it is important to remember that it was the incorrectly fitted guardrail which caused Jochen Rindt's death, in that it allowed the front of his car to go under it, rather than deflecting it, causing such a violent impact which ultimately proved fatal. It was not until May 1976 that this was finally, rather grudgingly acknowledged by the Italian authorities, and Chapman cleared of all charges in connection with Rindt's death.

Above: Road to disaster: Rindt leaves the pitlane for the final time. **Left:** Eddie Dennis looks over the remains of Rindt's car. Clearly visible is the broken right-front brake-shaft, while the shaft on the left-front wheel is intact. **Opposite Page:** Critical moment: Rindt brakes for the Parabolica on the lap of his accident. After taking this shot photographer Thomas Rohracher turned to see the aftermath of the crash.

CHAPTER 6 PICKING UP THE PIECES

old Leaf Team Lotus decided not to take any cars to the next round of the World Championship, the Canadian Grand Prix, since it needed time to regroup. In the meantime, a team of mechanics was sent back down to Monza, having been given permission to remove the engine from the car by the Italian authorities. In fact, what happened was that the whole rear end, virtually undamaged in the accident, was removed and brought back to England. Among the mechanics, in a disguise, was chief designer Maurice Phillippe, who wanted to have a more thorough look over the car than had been possible in the immediate aftermath of the crash.

Although the works cars didn't travel to Canada, Rob Walker took the decision to enter his 72 for Graham Hill. The only change to the specification of the car was that solid brake-shafts had been fitted, as a precaution pending the outcome of the investigation into Rindt's accident. The only other change from the standard 72C specification was that, to facilitate improved rearward vision, Hill had his wing mirrors mounted on rather ugly-looking stalks which did nothing for the overall attractiveness of the car.

It was a pretty disastrous weekend for the Rob Walker team. The car did not practice on the Thursday since they were still waiting for the solid brake-shafts to arrive, while on the Friday, a variety of new car niggles restricted Hill's time on the track and he ended up slowest in the session. Saturday's session was even worse, for a fuel union came loose, then the distributor cap came off and before long the inevitable spark met fuel and the car was on fire. Fortunately, the on-board extinguisher sensed the fire and put out the flames, without too much damage being done. Hill had been unable to record a representative time, so his best lap from Friday counted for the grid, putting him right at the back of the field. Further angst was caused during the race morning warm-up, when his clutch exploded, but this was repaired by the mechanics in time for the race.

The Grand Prix itself was no less eventful. Just before one third distance, having worked his way up to 15th position, Hill pitted with a loose rear wishbone mounting as well as being unable to select fourth gear. His stop cost him 11 laps and put him right out of contention. He continued to circulate but the car was still handling very strangely and he eventually finished 12th but unclassified, 13 laps behind the winner. Closer inspection after the race found that the extra loading caused by the loose wishbone had caused the sub-frame on which the rear suspension was mounted, to break, hence the decidedly spooky handling.

The winner of the race was Jacky Ickx, after pole-sitter Jackie Stewart, having his first race in the new Tyrrell, retired from the lead at one-thirds distance with a broken stub-axle. With Brabham and Hulme joining Stewart in retirement, this meant that only Ickx could now overhaul Rindt's points total to become World Champion. His team-mate Reggazoni, who finished second behind him in Canada, could equal Rindt's total but on count back would lose out because he could not match the Austrian's number of race wins.

At the end of September, Gold Leaf Team Lotus made two announcements. Firstly, that it would be rejoining the

Right: Graham Hill in Rob Walker's 72/4 was the sole Lotus representative in the 1970 Canadian Grand Prix after the works team's decision to withdraw its entries.

GOLD LEAF TEAM LOTUS

RACING FOR BRITAIN

REINE WISELL

At the age of 29, Reine Wisell fulfilled one of his ambitions in motor racing when in October 1970 he became a full works Formula One driver for Gold Leaf Team Lotus. That he finished third in his first Grand Prix is justification of the talent he possesses but never giving up in his often having to make do with uncompetitive cars but never giving up in his struggle to reach the top in motor racing.

Since 1968, when he finally made his mark in International competition with 11 outright wins, 2 second places, 1 third and nine lap records in Formula Three, his progress has been somewhat easier with many Formula Two and Sports car rides to keep him busy and the promise of a McLaren Grand Prix car at Silverstone in May, but took over the Sid Taylor F.5000 car after Peter Gethin for 1970. In fact he had only one outing in a McLaren Grand Prix car at four races. In fact he had only one outing in a McLaren Grand Prix car at was promoted to the Formula One race late in the season he equalled Jackie Stewart's new Formula One lap record at the circuit.

After five or six years experience in Formula Junior and Formula Three where he often had to simply drive faster than everybody else because his car is used power due to the elderly nature of his machinery, he has tempered his will to win with a sound knowledge of tactics and his very professional approach to his race and test driver.

In Sweden, where he was born, Reine is fast becoming a national hero and his fame is much already that he is simply known by his christian name and he returns to Motala, his home town, whenever his motor racing commitments allow, to relax and keep fit with plenty of exercise. Like his Gold Leaf Team Lotus team mate Emerson Fittipaldi, he is neither smokes nor drinks, but unlike Emerson and much to the delight of his female fans, Reine, blonde and good looking, is not married.

In 1971 in addition to his Formula One commitments, Reine will be driving a Lotus Formula Two car in the European non-graded Drivers Championship, something he would not have been able to do if he had finished in the first six in Mexico, as he would have become a graded driver after only two Grande Prix.

That he will become a graded driver in 1971 is almost certain if the style and nature of his debut in Grand Prix racing is continued in the new season.

March, 1971.
WORLD CHAMPION CAR CONSTRUCTORS 1963, 1965, 1968, 1970

fray for the next race, the US Grand Prix at Watkins Glen and, secondly, that John Miles would be replaced by Swedish driver, Reine Wisell. Despite his turbulent weekend in Monza, his ousting still came as a shock to Miles: 'I felt like a fighter pilot who was the only one to come back alive. The fact that Chapman sacked me at that time I was really, really broken up about it. But actually I think, from his point of view it was the right thing to do and actually from my point of view it was the right thing to do. I had much better fun racing in 1971. I knew by that time that I wasn't going to set the world alight'.

Looking back on it today, Peter Warr insists Miles' sacking was a necessary decision after the traumas of Monza. 'When Colin asked me to phone John and tell him we didn't want him, it wasn't to do with John's ability or non-ability as a race driver, it wasn't to do with his attitude, it wasn't to do with the fact that he perhaps thought about it too much, that he was too intelligent to be a race driver, nor that he should go out there and give it more welly. Colin just felt that we needed a completely fresh sheet of paper.'

Wisell had made his name as a rapid driver in Formula 3 between 1967 and 1969. He had progressed to driving a Chevron in Formula 2 in 1970 and then the semi-works

Formula 5000 McLaren run by Sid Taylor, following Peter Gethin's promotion to the McLaren Formula 1 team in the wake of Bruce McLaren's death. Even before his arrival in Formula 5000, Wisell had already attracted the attention of McLaren, who had given him a singleton Formula 1 outing in the 1970 International Trophy, when he finished a creditable fifth at the wheel of an ageing M7A.

Peter Warr felt that Wisell was just the kind of driver Gold Leaf Team Lotus needed. 'Wisell and Peterson were the two Swedes of the moment and Reine came highly recommended by the people we spoke to. He seemed like a very sensible lad and certainly a quiet enough personality that we felt he would fit in and get on with the job. I think we still saw Emerson as the future but Wisell was the ideal one to back him up, a good steady journeyman Formula 1 driver.'

When he discovered that he had been promoted to team leader in the wake of Rindt's death, Fittipaldi – still reeling from the loss of a team-mate and friend – assumed a tremendous burden of responsibility, that he had not felt driving the number three car. 'Jochen's death was devastating to me and my wife. I think it was the first time a team-mate of mine had died like that in a crash. Jochen

had been extremely good to me when I first tested the Lotus 49 at Silverstone. He did a few laps in the car before me and then while I was doing my first flying laps, he came to the pit wall and held out the lap-board to show me the times! He was very enthusiastic about my career and suddenly he was gone.

Then Colin called me and said "I would like you to be the number one driver" and that was another shock to me because I was not expecting it in only my fourth race. With Jochen still having the chance to win the Championship, I mean there was tremendous pressure on me.'

Wisell's only experience of the 72 was a brief test session prior to the US race, where he was reported to have lapped less than half a second slower than the Brazilian. 'They took Fittipaldi and me to Snetterton just a few days before the cars were flying out to America. But it was a few laps only.' The next time he would sit in one would be for the start of official practice at Watkins Glen.

The main changes to the three cars which arrived in America were, unsurprisingly, to the brake-shafts, which were solid on both of the works cars and the Rob Walker car, thicker in fact than the ones that Hill had used in Canada. The newest car, 72/5, had been repaired following its high-flying antics at Monza, and was given to Fittipaldi while Wisell had taken over Miles' former car, 72/3.

Opposite Page: Watkins Glen saw the re-appearance of 72/5 after Fittipaldi's practice shunt at Monza. **Above:** Ugly duckling: the Rob Walker 72 sprouted mirrors mounted on stalks to try and improve Hill's rearward vision, which spoiled the car's clean lines. **Left:** Reine Wisell had impressed in Formula 3 and Formula 5000 and was given his chance at Team Lotus after the sacking of John Miles.

First Person

Reine Wisell on joining Gold Leaf Team Lotus

"I never thought about it [whether or not to take the drive after Rindt's accident]. It was the way to go, I was hoping for Formula 1 and I went to, at that time, the best and quickest team. But it was more fun to drive other cars like Formula 3s and 2s because, at that time, you could have some influence on what to do to the cars. Coming to

Lotus was different, they just told the drivers to go home and do something else while the mechanics were doing the job during the evening. I liked to be involved, look at the work and talk to the mechanics, so it was tough."

In the first practice session, the 72s were well to the fore, with Fittipaldi ending up fifth and Hill finally finding some pace from his car, a much improved sixth, while Wisell played himself in gently to set the 15th fastest time. Since neither driver had spent much time behind the wheel of a 72, they were both allowed to complete a large number of laps. In total during the whole two days of practice, Fittipaldi completed 220 laps, which is more than double the actual race distance, while Wisell did a similar number.

Shortly after the beginning of the final session on Saturday, the skies darkened and the heavens opened. At first it seemed that there would be no opportunity for drivers to improve their times from the previous day but right at the end of the session the circuit dried out and there was a rush to set a good time. Fittipaldi excelled himself by setting the second-fastest time of the session, putting him third on the grid behind pole-man Ickx and Stewart in the Tyrrell. Wisell acquitted himself well too, ending up ninth, just over a second slower than his team-mate, while Hill was two-hundredths shy of the Swede's time and lined up alongside him to make an all-Lotus 72 fifth row.

On the eve of the race, the engine in Fittipaldi's car was changed. The unit which was installed was, rather fittingly, the development Cosworth DFV, number 901, which had been removed from Rindt's car following his accident. Eddie Dennis takes up the story. 'The engine returned [from Italy] and went back to Cosworth and that's the one that went into Emerson's car for Watkins Glen as well. I remember him saying when we fitted it in his car for the race: "The engine has got a big smile on its face". That was the phrase he used, meaning it was a good engine.'

Fittipaldi approached the race in a resolute mood. 'I said to myself that I had to be extremely careful, I had to finish. I could not afford to make another mistake like Monza.' To make matters worse, he was not feeling well that weekend, either. 'I had a tremendous cold on Saturday night, with a very high fever. Colin called a doctor who came to give me an injection and some medicine. I sweated the whole night! I went to practice for the warm-up in the morning and my eyes were red and I had this extremely high fever but when I sat in the car and I did a few laps with the adrenaline, everything was gone, I felt great.'

Race day had dawned cloudy and cold, with a few spots of rain in the air and at one stage a wet race seemed likely. However, the rain held off and at the start, Stewart streaked off into the lead, a position he held until his retirement on lap 83 with a blown engine. The pace of the Tyrrell was such that by lap 31, the Scot had lapped Wisell, running in eighth place. Meanwhile, Fittipaldi had made a poor start, squandering his good grid position and had come round at the end of the first lap in eighth place. He picked up two places with the retirements of John Surtees and Jackie Oliver both with blown engines and then for the next twenty laps ran in a solid sixth place, just ahead of Hill, who was having his best run yet in the Rob Walker 72. However, the Briton's miserable luck resurfaced on lap 30, when he was forced to pit with his cockpit awash with fuel as a result of another broken fuel union. Two more stops followed as he tried to get rid of the fuel in the seating area and then did a rather comical synchronised striptease in conjunction with John Surtees, who gave him his overalls to replace Hill's fuel-soaked ones. His race finally ended, rather appropriately on lap 72, when his clutch exploded yet again.

Meanwhile Fittipaldi continued to make steady progress. 'At the beginning of the race, the track was half-wet, half-dry, because it was drizzling. It was very difficult to drive the car and then after halfway the track got more grippy, I was gaining more confidence and I started running

faster and faster towards the end.' The retirements of Reggazoni and Amon lifted the Brazilian a further two places to fourth position by lap 48 of 108. However, six laps later, he too was lapped by the flying Tyrrell. Just three laps later came the decisive moment at which the 1970 World Championship was, effectively, secured for Jochen Rindt. His only possible challenger for the title, Jacky Ickx, had been running in a comfortable second place, ready to pick up the win should anything happen to Stewart's car (as indeed it did). However, he did not benefit from this since, on lap 57, the Ferrari headed for the pits with a broken fuel breather spraying petrol everywhere and promoting Fittipaldi to third place. The subsequent repairs saw Ickx

drop right down the order and out of contention, although he would stage a fighting recovery to storm back through the field to finish fourth.

Twenty tours after having been lapped, Fittipaldi was able to un-lap himself by virtue of the fact that Stewart's car had been smoking heavily and since his engine was on the

Opposite Page & Below: Fittipaldi's mature drive in the 1970 US Grand Prix at Watkins Glen provided Team Lotus with the lift it needed after the tragic events of Monza.

verge of expiring and the Scot had slowed his lap times in an effort to coax his car to the finish. The inevitable demise of the Tyrrell saw Pedro Rodriguez's BRM assume the lead of the race. With 25 laps to go, he was a comfortable 17 seconds ahead of Fittipaldi and there was a gap of a further half minute back to third-placed man Wisell who, like Fittipaldi, had found himself climbing steadily up the order as a result of the high attrition rate. Just as it seemed that the diminutive Mexican would score his second victory of the season, he dived into the pits with only seven laps remaining, his car in need of more fuel. The BRM's stop was more than long enough to enable Fittipaldi to slip by into the lead and almost allowed Wisell to sneak through as well.

The Brazilian calmly reeled off the remaining laps to take the chequered flag, greeted by an ecstatic Chapman who hurled his cap in the air with delight, a sight which Fittipaldi still remembers fondly to this day. 'That was one of the most fantastic views from the cockpit, to see Colin

jump up in the air and throw his hat to me, not to Jim Clark, to Graham Hill or Jochen.' Chief Mechanic Gordon Huckle also recalls the hat-throwing but for a different reason. 'I'll always remember that: the Old Man threw his hat up in the air and jumped up and down and the car went past and then he said to me "Hey Gordon, get my hat, get my hat" and I said "No, you go and get it, I'm not going out there." That

was typical of him! He could have afforded a new hat anyway!'

In winning the race, Fittipaldi had ensured that Rindt's points tally could not be overhauled and he was now officially the 1970 World Champion, the first ever posthumous winner of the title. The development DFV, as used by Rindt at Monza that fateful Saturday, never missed

Left: New boy Wisell makes a point to Lotus boss Chapman and Racing Manager Dick Scammell. **Above:** Fittipaldi's victory in the USGP secured the World Championship title for Rindt.

a beat. It was a fitting way to settle the outcome of the Championship, as Fittipaldi says. 'To have won my fourth Grand Prix, been Team Leader for Lotus, Jochen winning the Championship, I mean coming from the tragic weekend [at Monza], it was a complete turnaround, a fantastic turnaround.'

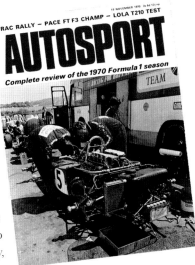

The final round of the Championship, the Mexican Grand Prix at the Autodromo Ricardo Rodriguez on the outskirts of Mexico City, became an irrelevance, in terms of the Championship at least. As it turned out, this was a good job, because Lotus had a torrid time and Ickx once again led a resounding Ferrari 1-2. The only changes to the 72s for this race were that they had reverted to the smaller diameter solid brake-shafts as used by Hill in Canada, as the larger diameter models had apparently damaged fourth and fifth gears. The 72 would continue to use these solid shafts for the rest of their racing career.

In practice, Fittipaldi blew up two DFVs, leaving him 18th and last on the grid, while Wisell had a torrid time with a bout of sickness leaving him weak, although he at least managed to qualify 12th. Fastest Lotus 72 was Graham Hill, his time good enough to put him eighth on the grid, although there was some doubt over whether he actually did go this fast.

The start of the race was delayed by the huge and very enthusiastic 200,000 strong crowd spilling over the fences and onto the grass verges at the side of the track. Numerous appeals for them to get back behind the grass banks were ignored, including those from local hero Rodriguez as well as Fittipaldi, the latter roped in because he spoke Spanish. 'One hour before the race started, I went out on a car with Pedro to ask the spectators to move. They were sitting on the guardrails alongside the track, like bull-fighters! But it was no use…' Eventually, with the organisers fearing a riot if it was abandoned, the race got underway. Fittipaldi's appalling run of bad luck that weekend continued when he blew a third engine on only the second lap and three tours later Hill was also out with an overheating engine. Meanwhile, Wisell, running firmly in last place, pitted with gearbox problems and later stopped twice with a broken oil pressure line, eventually continuing after it was blanked off to finish 10th, nine laps behind the winning Ferrari.

On this curiously uncompetitive note, Gold Leaf Team Lotus ended their 1970 season. A year that had promised so much, had indeed delivered a World Championship for the Lotus 72 in its debut year but there was no World Champion to collect his trophy. With the deaths of Bruce McLaren and Piers Courage as well, it had been a brutal year for Formula 1. However, with their two young chargers having made such a dramatic impact on their debuts in the 72 at Watkins Glen, the team had every reason to be optimistic about the 1971 season.

WORLD CHAMPIONSHIP TABLE 1970

Pos	Driver	Race	S.Africa	Spain	Monaco	Belgium	Netherlands	France	Great Britain	Germany	Austria	Italy	Canada	USA	Mexico	Total	(dropped)
1	Jochen Rindt				9		9	9	9	9						45	
2	Jacky Ickx						4			6	9			9	3	9	40	
3	Clay Regazzoni						3		3		6	9	6			6	33	
4	Denny Hulme		6		3			3	4	4			3		4	27	
5	Jack Brabham		9		6			4	6							25	
5	Jackie Stewart		4	9			6					6				25	
7	Pedro Rodriguez				1	9					3		3	6	1	23	
7	Chris Amon					6		6	2				4	2	3	23	
9	Jean-Pierre Beltoise		3			4	2				1	4			2	16	
10	Emerson Fittipaldi									3				9		12	
11	Rolf Stommelen					2				2	4	2				10	
12	Henri Pescarolo				4	1		2		1						8	
13	Graham Hill		1	3	2				1							7	
14	Bruce McLaren			6												6	
15	Mario Andretti			4												4	
15	Reine Wisell													4		4	
17	Ignazio Giunti					3										3	
17	John Surtees						1						2			3	
19	John Miles		2													2	
19	Johnny Servoz-Gavin			2												2	
19	Jackie Oliver										2					2	
22	Dan Gurney							1								1	
22	Francois Cevert											1				1	
22	Peter Gethin												1			1	
24	Derek Bell													1		1	

Pos	Constructor	Race	S.Africa	Spain	Monaco	Belgium	Netherlands	France	Great Britain	Germany	Austria	Italy	Canada	USA	Mexico	Total	(dropped)
1	Lotus-Cosworth		2	3	9		9	9	9	9				9		59	
2	Ferrari					3	4		3	6	9	9	9	3	9	52	(3)
3	March-Cosworth		4	9		6	6	6	2			6	4	2	3	48	
4	Brabham-Cosworth		9		6	2		4	6	2	4	2				35	
4	McLaren-Cosworth		6	6	3		1	3	4	4		3	1		4	35	
6	B.R.M.				1	9					3		3	6	1	23	
6	Matra-Simca		3		4	4	2	2		1	1	4			2	23	
8	Surtees-Cosworth												2	1		3	

CHAPTER 7 LOSING DIRECTION

Although it had little in common with the 72 apart from its wedge body shape, it is important to understand the significance of the four-wheel drive Lotus 56B turbine Formula 1 car to the story of the 72. This is because it could be said to have acted as a distraction for both Gold Leaf Team Lotus, and its drivers, as well as a drain on its financial and logistical resources. Its existence is one factor that contributed to the difficult year Lotus endured in 1971, although there were many others at work as well.

The performance of the Lotus 56 turbines at Indianapolis in 1968, together with positive remarks from Graham Hill about their smooth handling after he drove one at the Mosport Park circuit, encouraged Chapman to develop a Grand Prix car with a turbine engine. Work had begun in August 1968, using a spare 56 tub, which was given the type number 56B. Just one chassis was completed, whereupon the project was temporarily shelved, as Chapman's attention was focused on the ultimately unsuccessful four-wheel drive Type 63 Formula 1 car for the 1969 season.

It was not until the middle of 1970, when the Lotus 72 had been sorted into a race winner, that Chapman's interest in the project was rekindled. John Miles remembers another factor that had stirred Chapman into action at that point: 'I think Colin was a bit fed up with the Cosworth repair bill! I blew up loads of engines in the 72 for no known reason, I didn't over-rev them or anything. He still had quite a strong belief in four wheel drive and he wanted a reliable power plant. Theoretically, that engine should have been good for 1,000 hours.'

The existence of the car was known to several motor racing journalists but they had been asked to treat it as a secret and had abided by Chapman's wishes. However, in mid-August, a daily newspaper blew the whistle on the story, saying that the car was going to appear for the first time at the Italian Grand Prix. In the end, it was not taken to Monza, since quite naturally the team was focusing on trying to win the Championship with Rindt. However, the car's existence indicated the seriousness of their desire to

continue to innovate even when they were at the top of their game. Intensive testing was undertaken during the winter of 1970/71 with a view to racing the car during the 1971 season. This was carried out by Fittipaldi and Wisell as well as the team's Formula 3 driver, the Australian Dave Walker.

As with the Indianapolis cars, power was transmitted from the engine to the main drive line by a two-inch wide

Above: Turbine exposed: this shot clearly shows the bulky bath-tub monocoque of the 56B, reflecting the fact that it had first been designed back in 1967. Note inboard front brakes, which pre-dated those on the 72.
Top Right: Ancestry of 72 is clearly evident from this press launch shot of the turbine car. **Right:** Promising Australian Dave Walker was entrusted with much of the testing of the 56B, shown here at Silverstone.

Morse Hy-vo chain. Changing gear ratios involved taking the magnesium casing enclosing the chain apart and changing the sprockets, as on a bicycle or motorbike. The brakes had to be considerably more effective than on most other Grand Prix cars, and deficiencies in this area were one reason why the car did not race sooner. Miles explains: 'with the turbine you had no engine braking, quite the reverse. At idle you'd got something like 70hp going through the transmission, so you needed a massive amount of braking power to absorb that energy.'

The engine ran on aviation kerosene and due to high consumption, the car had to carry a lot of fuel, relative to conventional cars. Total capacity was around 350 litres (75 gallons) to enable it to get through a full Grand Prix,

compared to the 45 gallon capacity of the 72. The apparent danger of carrying so much fuel was tempered by the fact that kerosene was much less flammable than petrol. However, it made the car heavy which, combined with the weight of the four wheel drive system, took it way over the minimum weight limit.

The car made its debut at the non-Championship Race of Champions at Brands Hatch in March 1971, driven by Fittipaldi. It qualified a respectable 7th, albeit four seconds off pole. It had also been impressive in the wet practice session, where Fittipaldi posted the second fastest time: 'The car was superb in the rain, incredible with the four wheel drive'. In the (dry) race the car suffered from bottoming out on the bumpy track and eventually, at two-thirds distance, the right rear suspension broke. Wisell took the wheel in April for the Rothmans International Trophy at Oulton Park, where the car ran as high as fifth before the suspension broke yet again, this time due to a puncture.

Fittipaldi was back in the car for another non-Championship race, the International Trophy in May, at Silverstone. Its excellent traction and stability in low torque situations was more suited to Silverstone because in those days it was a series of straights linked by fast corners. As a result, Fittipaldi put the car on the front row, qualifying third, ahead of many more illustrious drivers and cars. After a good start he was forced to retire at the end of the second lap when a wishbone bearing seized, tearing the pick-up point out of the monocoque. The car was repaired and re-appeared at the back of the grid for the second leg. What ensued was a storming drive through the field from Fittipaldi and he eventually finished a very creditable third

Below Left: The Turbine was entered in the 1971 Italian Grand Prix by Worldwide Racing in place of 72s in anticipation of legal problems associated with Rindt's death the previous year. Note bulges in side of tub to accommodate enough fuel to last a Grand Prix distance. The car is shown in the form it ran in its final race at Hockenheim, with wings and nose fins. **Below Right:** Emerson Fittipaldi gave the 56B its debut in the 1971 Race of Champions. **Opposite Page Left:** 'Rene Whistle' as Reine Wisell was sometimes called, appropriately drove the turbine at the 1971 British Grand Prix but finished way down after throttle problems. **Opposite Page Right:** 'Pioneer' Fittipaldi was prepared to give the turbine a chance, despite the fact that driving it detracted from his programme with the 72.

GOLD LEAF TEAM LOTUS

RACING FOR BRITAIN

Managed by Team Lotus Ltd.
Norwich/Norfolk
NOR 92W ENGLAND
Team Manager/Colin Chapman BSc Eng.
Competitions Manager/Peter E. Warr
Telex 97401
Racing Manager/Richard J. Scammell
Cables/Team Lotus/Norwich

DAVID WALKER

Lombank Formula Three Champion in 1970, runner-up in the Forward Trust Formula Three Championship and third in the Motorsport/Shell Championship, David Walker is an established front-runner in International single-seater racing. David will once more be representing Gold Leaf Team Lotus in the Formula Three category in 1971, driving the single works car in the Shell Super Oil and Forward Trust Championships.

Born in Sydney, Austria, David Walker joined Gold Leaf Team Lotus in 1970, after a very successful season in Lotus single seaters in 1969 during the course of which he clinched the British Formula Ford Championship with 13 wins, 7 second places, 7 third places and 8 lap records. To add to this impressive list he had fastest lap no fewer than 16 times.

However, this one season reveals little of the background to a driver who has 6 years of competition experience behind him. Aged twenty nine, David's sporting career started with many successes in a variety of athletic endeavours whilst still at school in Australia.

After leaving school, he was an active member of the Palm Beach Surf Life Saving Club and his interest in motor-racing was aroused only in 1960 when he visited England on a working holiday. Such was his enthusiasm that he spent 3 months at Jim Russell Racing Drivers School before returning to Australia overland, practice which was to prove valuable when he took park in the London-Sydney Marathon 1968.

1963 saw the delivery of a new Formula Junior Brabham and a third place in his first race with the car, and later the same season he was signed as a members of the Scuderia Veloce joining other Australian "big name" in this Shell-sponsored team. In the remainder of 1963 and during 1964 David Walker notched up 14 firsts, 6 second and 12 third places in Australian National races to finish 2nd in both the 1½ litre and Formula Two Championship as well as winning a Formula Junior Championship.

In 1965, there was to have been a European season but family matters kept David at home and apart from some long distance saloon car races, he had to wait until June, 1966 for his next single seater drive. This was at last in England but the season was not as rewarding as it might have been as his sponsor withdrew from racing before the end of the year, following government financial restrictions.

A Formula Three season in Europe followed in 1967 in a Merlyn and resulted in a win at the Adriatic Grand Prix with one second and three fourth places. By this time the name David Walker was being talked about for he appeared in pole positions, took lap records and generally got in amongst the fastest Formula Three works car but unreliability kept the name out of the results. As a result of a last minute change, 1968 found David Walker in Formula Ford and after a slow start he joined the Jim Russell Team and gained 12 wins, 4 second and one third place and took 5 lap records on the way. Aided as he had been by the Jim Russell Racing Drivers School, he elected to stay in Lotus cars in Formula Ford for 1969 with the results already quoted, and graduated to full works driver status in 1970 when he was first home no fewer that 16 times.

In addition to driving the Gold Leaf Team Lotus Formula Three car in 1971, he will almost certainly be seen from time to time in a Gold Leaf Formula One car.

March, 1971.

WORLD CHAMPION CAR CONSTRUCTORS 1963, 1965, 1968, 1970

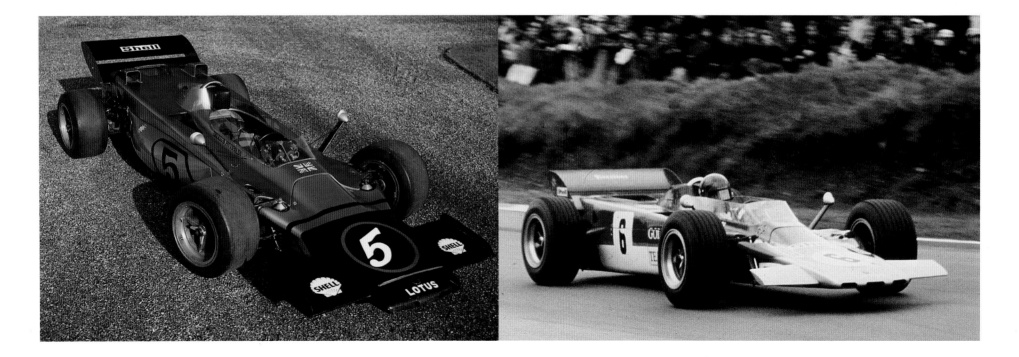

behind Hill – now driving for Brabham – and Amon's Matra.

Another non-Championship event, the Jochen Rindt Memorial race, at Hockenheim in June, was the venue for the car's next outing. This time it was driven by Walker, although his weekend proved to be short when, early in the second practice session, the turbine started cutting out and hesitating and flames began to appear out of the exhaust "funnel". The car was withdrawn and the engine had to be returned to Pratt & Whitney for a full rebuild.

A week later at Zandvoort, the car made its first appearance in a World Championship round for the Dutch Grand Prix, with Walker at the wheel. It did not arrive until the Friday evening and, with a wet morning session on the Saturday and adverse winds on the main straight in the afternoon, times were generally slower than the day before. Given these factors he qualified down in 22nd place, more than four seconds off the pace of Jacky Ickx's pole-sitting Ferrari.

Race day dawned wet and, with the advantages of four-wheel drive, its smooth torque curve and vastly superior Firestone tyres, the car looked to have a really good chance of causing an upset. Walker was briefed to take it easy, with team manager Peter Warr instructing him not to race anybody for the first 25 laps. In spite of this warning, his progress through the field was meteoric: at the end of lap one he was 19th and by lap five he was 10th, lapping faster than the leaders, Ickx and Pedro Rodriguez (BRM).

However, on lap six disaster struck going into the Tarzan hairpin at the end of the main straight. After his initial rapid progress through the field, Walker was finding it increasingly difficult to pass people and keep them behind him as they were outbraking him at Tarzan: 'I hit the brakes trying to take an inside line to prevent someone going inside me and I started locking things up. The car had an idling speed of 70-odd miles an hour so, as I was getting down towards the corner and freeing the brakes up and braking and freeing and braking, every time I took my foot off the brake it started accelerating again for 25 or 30 metres! Once I got to the corner I tried to spin the car but again, being four-wheel drive, it didn't want to spin and it just quietly went off the edge of the road and about 10 feet into the sand! And with no reverse gear or anything that was it.'

Chapman, who believed the car had a great chance of winning the race, was not amused, as Walker clearly remembers: 'He went through the roof. I think he felt that from my point of view I could have been one of the few people in history to have won a Grand Prix at their first attempt and it was potentially a first ever win for a turbine car, so a lot of history went out the door that day!'

The 56B's second Grand Prix was Gold Leaf Team Lotus's 'home' race, at Silverstone in July. Reine Wisell was assigned to drive the car but, in typical Chapman fashion, it seems the first the Swede knew about this was when he arrived at the circuit on the Friday morning. 'Just when I was expecting my 72 to come out of the trailer, there was the turbine! I was not very happy...' Although Wisell set a lap time faster than Fittipaldi had managed in practice for the International Trophy race, he was only 19th on the grid.

In the race, problems with an incorrectly adjusted throttle resulted in the car finishing a lowly 13th, 11 laps behind the winner.

Fittipaldi returned to the wheel for the Italian Grand Prix at Monza in September. As a result of legal problems associated with Rindt's fatal accident the previous year the car was entered by Lotus subsidiary Worldwide Racing and repainted in an eye-catching gold colour scheme with black trim lines. In addition the large rear wing had been replaced by a smaller lip at the rear of the wedge in order to obtain a low downforce set-up. After qualifying 18th, the turbine was adversely affected by high ambient temperatures in the race, which reduced its power output, as well as two cracked brake discs and chronic understeer. Fittipaldi finally finished 8th, one lap down on winner Peter Gethin's BRM.

The car's final race of the season (and of its short career) was in the Preis der Nationen at Hockenheim, a week after Monza. Driven by Fittipaldi once more, it was still in the same gold and black livery but had regained its rear wing. In practice, Emerson qualified second, albeit nearly two seconds slower than Frank Gardner's Lola F5000 car on pole. The race format – two 15 lap heats – enabled the 56B to perform better due to its lighter fuel load. In the first, although quick on the straights, Fittipaldi lost out heavily in the twisty stadium section and was unable to find a way past Gardner, eventually finishing second, four seconds back. The second heat was more or less a repeat. Although he upped his pace, setting the fastest lap (and only 0.7 seconds off Jacky Ickx's outright record), Fittipaldi was unable to pass Gardner and finished 1.4 seconds behind, to claim second overall in the event on aggregate: 'I remember Colin put the maximum boost, maximum injection of fuel and we nearly burned all the blades from the engine! But that was the best race we had with that car.'

By this stage, it had become clear that a turbine car could not be made into a competitive proposition in Formula 1. A decision was taken to end the experiment. Differing theories have been put forward as to why the car was not successful. Chapman himself told journalist Jabby Crombac that he thought that it wasn't the engine that killed off the turbine Grand Prix car but the four-wheel drive. John Miles does not subscribe to that theory: 'I think it was a number of things, the adjustability, the weight and no compensatory advantages'.

Walker felt the main obstacle lay in the driving technique required, which made wheel-to-wheel racing particularly difficult: 'I always said that the problem was going to be when you got into traffic and were trying to hit a braking area, back off and then re-accelerate while still on the brakes, it was an extra thing to think about when you were trying to outbrake someone else, or with people diving inside and around you.'

Turbines and four-wheel drive were subsequently banned from Grand Prix racing so it is unlikely that Lotus would have had much of an opportunity to persevere with the concept anyway. Although it was a car of tremendous technical interest at the time, it will ultimately be remembered as one of the few Chapman Lotus Formula 1 cars that failed to live up to expectations.

Left: The 72s started the year virtually unchanged from 1970 apart from some changes to suspension geometry to accommodate new low-profile Firestones. Fittipaldi is shown here in South Africa at the wheel of 72/5 where he retired after an engine blow-up. **Below:** Missed opportunity: Walker had the chance of an upset in the 1971 Dutch Grand Prix, where the turbine's smooth power delivery, four-wheel drive and Firestone wet-weather tyres gave him a distinct advantage over the rest of the field. His crash on lap six was not well-received in the Lotus pit... **Right:** While Fittipaldi drove the turbine at the 1971 Race of Champions, Wisell took the wheel of 72/3, which was to become his regular car in the first part of the 1971 season.

The team's focus on testing and developing the turbine car, allied with a chronic shortage of engines caused by the three blow-ups experienced by Fittipaldi in Mexico, meant that a bare minimum of testing was done with the 72s during the winter of 1970 and early 1971. Only minor modifications were made to the cars over this time, as Fittipaldi explains. 'We did very little testing between 1970

fastest time, while Wisell only completed a few laps before his engine, which had been popping and banging, cut out. By the time the mechanics had traced the problem to an electrical fault, the first day's practice session was over. Both drivers managed to improve their times on Saturday, with the Swede just pipping the Brazilian to take third place on the grid. Fittipaldi had his car at some amazing angles as he struggled with oversteer but he was barely able to better his previous day's performance and looked distinctly unhappy. One thing which did cheer him up was that the last part of the session was blighted by rain, and he took the opportunity to go out and sample his car in the wet. Proving the adage that a bad car is often good in the rain, he comfortably set fastest time in the conditions.

Come race day, things were little better. In the first 50-lap heat, Fittipaldi lost a nose fin early on, which further upset the already unpredictable handling of his car. After dropping down the order to ninth, he eventually pitted and lost three laps having it replaced. Meanwhile, Wisell drove a good race to finish fifth despite a top-end misfire and was credited with the fastest lap, nearly a second quicker than he had managed in practice. Before the second heat had even got under way, Fittipaldi was out, his engine having lost oil pressure on the warm-up lap, while Wisell's car was still misfiring and he was complaining about the handling before they'd even started. During the race, he made several stops to try and rectify the problem and eventually began to circulate quite rapidly, but on the 35th lap he missed fourth gear on the approach to the fast right-hander after the pits and spun off into the Armco, fortunately without doing significant damage to the car. It transpired that the Swede had been experiencing gear selection problems for several laps before his accident.

The team now had nearly six weeks to prepare for the first round of the World Championship, to be held at the Kyalami circuit in South Africa. However, the focus of development continued to be the turbine car, with the result that, when they appeared in South Africa, the cars were pretty much as they had been in the Argentine and the races at the end of the 1970 season. Shortly before the South African race, it was announced that Dick Scammell, Team Lotus Racing Manager since 1968, had left to take up a position working for Tom Wheatcroft, meaning that at Kyalami, the team was quite thin on the ground, with its two drivers, just four mechanics and Colin Chapman. The

and 1971. But they did a lot of work to make sure the brake-shafts would be stronger for the next season.'

The winter had seen the departure of Chief Mechanic Gordon Huckle, along with Herbie Blash (who in fact had quit in the wake of Rindt's accident but resurfaced at Brabham) with Eddie Dennis taking over Huckle's job. Derek Mower and Dave Sims continued into 1971 – although they would leave after the second Grand Prix of the year to be replaced on Fittipaldi's car by Steve Gooda and Jim Pickles – while Rex Hart and Mike Coughtree were assigned to Wisell. Later on, in July, Stevie May bolstered the depleted ranks when he joined from the production side of Lotus Cars (although he had been working for the Formula 3 team in his spare time). Finally, Vic McCarthy was a popular addition to the ranks as he was given the job of driving the transporter, allowing the mechanics to get some much-needed rest on the way to races.

The team's first appearance of 1971 was a non-Championship race, the Argentine Grand Prix, held at the Buenos Aires Autodrome and this was intended as a dress-rehearsal for a full round of the World Championship in 1972. There had been rumours that Lotus would take the turbine car but they turned out to be false and instead the team arrived with the two regular cars, 72/5 for Fittipaldi and 72/3 for Wisell, plus a 49, which was hired out to

Emerson's brother, Wilson.

The cars themselves had been tidied up with small detail changes (e.g. improved mountings for the mirrors to enhance rearward vision) but were basically unchanged, with two major exceptions. Firstly, Firestone had produced some new low profile tyres, which required different diameter wheel rims and minor revisions to the suspension geometry. Secondly an alternative design of nose, with vents in the side to channel air to the inboard brakes rather than the two NACA ducts on the top of the original design

The first time Fittipaldi drove the car in its new form, he could not believe it was the same Lotus he'd raced to victory at Watkins Glen, as he explained in his biography Flying on the Ground: 'I was trying like hell in Argentina to do a quick time, but it was just impossible. I could not do one lap the same as the lap before in the same place. Sometimes I would brake at one point and the car would start to lock up under braking, then I would get too wide a line. Sometimes when I turned the steering the car kept oversteering and I was too much on the inside…one of the few times I spun a car was in Argentina. I had never spun a Formula 2 or Formula 1 since I started racing, and this was the first time because I was trying too hard to drive the car quickly, and it just didn't handle.'

Despite these problems, he managed to set the third-

plan was that Competitions Manager Peter Warr, who did not go to South Africa, would do Scammell's job in the team as well as his own, fulfilling more of a Team Manager's role.

Fittipaldi was in his regular chassis, 72/5, while Wisell was once more at the wheel of 72/3. Their race numbers were 2 and 3, there being no number one in deference to the posthumous World Champion. Official practice took place on the Wednesday, Thursday and Friday afternoons, with the race scheduled for the Saturday. Both drivers were well down the order on Wednesday but on Thursday Fittipaldi set the third-fastest time with the aid of some experimental Firestone tyres. This was ultimately good enough for fifth on the grid and placed him on the second row due to the 3-2-3 formation adopted at this wide track. Wisell was 10th quickest on Thursday and then improved his time on Friday, even though he was only 13th fastest on the day – to secure 14th place on the grid. Fittipaldi's session was spoilt by yet another engine blow-up, shortly after he had equalled his time from the previous day.

At the start, Fittipaldi capitalised on the slow getaways of two of the front-row men, Stewart and Amon, to grab second place on the long run down the straight to Crowthorne and, for the first three laps, he maintained this position behind leader Reggazoni in the Ferrari. However, the handling of his car was very unpredictable – he was unable to use the same experimental Firestone tyres he had used in practice – and he quickly began to drop down the order. By lap 10 he was seventh and by lap 30 he was ninth,

having even been overhauled by his team-mate who had started nine places further back on the grid. Wisell was making impressive progress and, by lap 33, he was up into sixth place. The sight of Wisell ahead of him seemed to halt the loss of places on the part of Fittipaldi and, apart from a few laps where he was usurped by Francois Cevert in the Tyrrell, the cars ran in sixth and seventh places for some time until the retirement of John Surtees promoted them each a place.

The prospect of having both cars in the points at the finish was just beginning to seem a possibility when, just before three-quarters distance, Fittipaldi's engine let go again as he flashed down the main straight in front of the pits. Wisell continued in fifth place until, two laps from the finish, he was able to nip past the ailing McLaren of long-time race leader Denny Hulme to steal fourth place.

The week after the South African race, Gold Leaf Team Lotus announced plans to run a third car "from time to time" in Formula 1 races, the drive being split between two up-and-coming Formula 3 pilots, Dave Walker and Tony Trimmer, starting with Trimmer at the Race of Champions.

Since a third 72 chassis was still under construction, this would initially be at the wheel of the now nearly veteran 49C but the intention was to field a third 72 chassis as soon as was practical.

Two weeks after South Africa, most of the major Formula 1 teams were back in the UK for the non-Championship Race of Champions, to be held at the undulating and twisty Brands Hatch circuit in Kent. An analysis of the 10 Cosworth DFVs that Gold Leaf Team Lotus possessed, revealed that only one of them was ready to race. To make matters worse that engine, in Wisell's car, had done practice and races in both Argentina and South Africa and had therefore run for around 800 miles since its last rebuild!

Although an engine came back from Cosworth in the week before the Race of Champions, this was put in Fittipaldi's car ready for the following week's big-money Questor Grand Prix. A second engine was expected back at the end of the week and this was to be put into the old faithful 49C for Tony Trimmer to drive. Consequently, it seemed a logical time to give the turbine car its first

I remember asking Colin Chapman "How do you get these things off the line?" and he just put his arm around me and said "You're driving it boy, not me"

competitive outing, and this was entered for Fittipaldi to drive. Wisell's car sported revised uprights, which changed the geometry to suit the latest ultra-low profile Firestone tyres. Friday's practice was ruined by torrential rain, and Wisell recorded the sixth-fastest time despite the tired engine in his car. When the engine destined for Trimmer's 49C was found by Cosworth to be down on power and blowing out oil, a late decision was made to bring Fittipaldi's 72 down from Hethel overnight for the young Englishman's first taste of Formula 1 power.

Saturday's weather was better. Before going out, Trimmer's car was hastily converted to the latest specification with the new uprights and he did a relatively slow time just to put himself on the grid, before the car was wheeled away to have its routine pre-race check, something it had not been possible to do before it left Norfolk due to the last-minute decision to run it. This meant that he missed the afternoon session, which proved to be the fastest of the weekend. Wisell posted the eighth-quickest time,

complaining of handling problems in addition to his tawdry DFV and in fact was pipped by Fittipaldi in the turbine, who set a time 0.3s quicker. Trimmer's time from the morning session was the slowest of all the runners who practised, with the result that he lined up on the last row alongside Peterson, whose March arrived too late to take part in official practice. 'We managed to squeeze a couple of laps in the last practice and started at the back. I had no experience at all. Actually I'd never driven a Formula 1 car until those couple of laps. I remember asking Colin Chapman "How do you take these off the line?" and he just put his arm around me and said "You're driving it boy, not me" and that was all the advice he gave me!'

The race started in wet and slippery conditions but rain was no longer falling and in fact the surface dried out quite quickly. Trimmer's race was over virtually before it had begun, for at the end of the first lap he pitted, apparently with fuel pressure problems. 'I was on the inside of the back row with Ronnie Peterson and everybody moved left going

up to Paddock and I got the most incredible start, passed car after car and stayed on the inside in the run-up to Druids, came out of the corner and the thing just cut out on me. It was probably just as well, I'd have probably killed myself!' Although he rejoined after having lost seven laps, he only did another few tours before pulling into the pits once again, this time to retire, the cause being given as a faulty electrical fuel pump.

In fact, as mechanic Dave Sims explains, there was a much more simple explanation for the car's early demise. 'It was Emerson's car and he didn't want Trimmer to drive it. It had a new engine. The Old Man told me he didn't want the car to finish, he didn't want any mileage on it. He said, "I want it sensibly done, so that you can bring it in [to the pits] to actually say it's got a problem." We disconnected the alternator wire out of the spark box and, of course, gradually the battery went down, the misfire got heavier and in the end, he came in and we pretended to work on it. It was a joke. We had a bet between ourselves it wouldn't even make the warm-up lap and get on the grid!'

Wisell ran steadily in fifth place for much of the race, only for his engine to begin misfiring as well finally cutting out with seven laps remaining. After the race, when a mechanic went to fetch the car, it started first time, so it appeared that the Swede was the victim of an intermittent electrical problem, possibly caused by all the wet-weather running that weekend.

Two days later, the team was packing its cars up and sending them for transportation to the Questor Grand Prix, to be held at the brand new Ontario Motor Speedway in Ontario, California, USA. The organisers had originally hoped to stage the event as a non-Championship Formula 1 race but when the FIA declined permission, it was switched to a race held under Formula A series rules, which incorporated both stock block 5-litre Formula A/5000 cars and 3-litre Formula 1 cars. They had secured major sponsorship from a firm called Questor, with a total race purse of US$250,000, which in 1971 was a considerable amount of money, hence it was no surprise that some 16 Formula 1 cars made the long trip over from Europe especially for the race.

With three full days of practice, and no Championship points at stake, the race offered Gold Leaf Team Lotus an

Opposite Page Left & Right: Top Formula 3 driver Tony Trimmer drove Fittipaldi's 72 in the 1971 Race of Champions after problems with the 49 he was due to drive. Some subtle 'knobbling' by the mechanics ensured the engine didn't get too much wear and tear in the race… **Left:** The mechanics prepare Fittipaldi's car for Trimmer to drive.

coolers, one on each side of the tank. Both measures were intended to clean up airflow around the back of the car but also at increasing the rearward weight bias of the car with the aim of improving grip. The new wing was said to provide the same amount of downthrust for less drag and was wider than the old three-tier version by virtue of the fact that the low-profile Firestones reduced the risk of the end plates fouling the tyres. In addition, anti-squat on the rear suspension, which had been drastically reduced when the car was revised to C specification in 1970, was further reduced. Because his car was yet to have these modifications completed, Wisell was entrusted with the turbine for this race, while Trimmer was driving a 49C.

The immediate impressions were that the changes had done little to improve the handling of the car, for Fittipaldi was the slowest of the established Grand Prix drivers entered, excepting Wisell in the turbine, who was having to come to terms with driving a relatively unfamiliar car. His seventh place on the grid was a whopping 3.6s slower than pole-man Stewart's Tyrrell, which in Formula 1 racing is a lifetime.

Above Left: Wisell enters the pit lane at the 1971 Race of Champions. Note revised, cleaner nose following removal of NACA ducts. **Above:** First significant update to 72 design for 1971 was seen at the Rothmans International Trophy meeting in April, where Fittipaldi's 72/5 appeared with a revised oil tank and cooler configuration, plus a single-plane rear wing. This was found to provide more downforce for less drag than the original tri-plane design. **Opposite Page:** Trials with Koni dampers instead of Armstrongs proved encouraging at Spain, although a repetition of a rear suspension cross-member breakage caused the Brazilian's retirement and ultimately convinced mechanic Dave 'Beaky' Sims that it was time to move on.

excellent opportunity to try to get to the bottom of the handling problems which had been afflicting the car in the races so far. In Flying on the Ground, Fittipaldi describes that meeting vividly: 'Colin went there specially to test the car. We took everything: different torsion bars, different wings, different size of tyres, 13-inch, 15-inch, different wheels, wide, narrow. We started testing first from the wings and went all through the car, shock absorber settings, torsion bars, everything. When we changed something like torsion bars, the car was easier to drive, but not quicker. We could not do a consistent lap time because the car was changing so much from lap to lap – jumping perhaps one second per lap, both cars. And I was driving really hard.'

After practice, the two cars lined up 9th and 11th, slower than the fastest Formula A/5000 car, a Lola T192 driven by Mark Donohue and, to make matters worse, sandwiching the Formula A Lotus 70, driven by George Follmer which, in comparison to the sophisticated 72, was something of an old-fashioned, agricultural machine, albeit with lots of grunt.

The race was run in two 32-lap heats of just over 100 miles, since the Formula A cars did not have enough fuel tank capacity to do a 200 mile race without stopping. Both

Lotus entries were out before the end of Heat 1, Fittipaldi dropping down the order with a misfire and later retiring with a throttle problem and Wisell being eliminated by a failed ignition. Nonetheless, for his efforts, Fittipaldi still won US$8,350 for the team – not bad for around 30 laps driving!

After Ontario, Fittipaldi had a long chat with Lotus Chief Designer Maurice Phillippe about the 72, urging him to make changes to its design, as he described in his biography. 'I told him the car was impossible. He wanted to know how it could be so good in 1970 and how I, as a new driver, could possibly know. It was considered to be the best car at that time. I couldn't tell him why it was wrong.' Nonetheless, it was obvious that the car was struggling with a major handling imbalance, snapping from understeer to oversteer at the slightest opportunity and something had to be done.

The first evidence of attempts to improve the car came at the Rothmans International Formula 1 Trophy race, held on Good Friday at the Oulton Park circuit in Cheshire, twelve days after the Questor Grand Prix. Fittipaldi's 72 sported a new single-plane rear wing, plus a new cylindrical oil tank mounted on the back of the gearbox, with two oil

session of practice was ruined by rain, it ensured that they would start the race from lowly grid positions, Fittipaldi 14th and on the sixth row and Wisell two places behind him on the seventh row.

In the race, Fittipaldi had moved up to ninth before pitting just after one-third's distance with brake problems. The Brazilian had been troubled by a brake warning light – indicating low fluid level – coming on and, with the Montjuich Park circuit being rather confined and lined with Armco, there wasn't much run-off if anything went wrong. The mechanics bled the system and added more fluid and sent him on his way, but by this stage he had lost six laps. Although he continued, the car was still weaving alarmingly under heavy braking. Another pit stop with twenty laps to go revealed that the cross-member on which the lower rear wishbones are located had broken and he retired.

Wisell had pitted just before his team-mate, complaining of poor handling and a difficult gear change, perhaps linked to the modifications made in practice. He lost 13 laps in the pits and, although he too rejoined, he circulated well off the pace and eventually finished 12th and last of the classified runners, 17 laps behind winner Jackie Stewart in the Tyrrell.

After Ontario, Fittipaldi had a long chat with Lotus Chief Designer Maurice Phillippe about the 72, urging him to make changes to its design. The first evidence of attempts to improve the car came at Oulton Park

In the race, Fittipaldi made a storming start, coming round fourth at the end of the first lap. After running in this position for the next five laps, he stopped out on the circuit. A mechanic was sent to investigate and eventually Emerson was able to rejoin after the transistor box had been repaired. He eventually finished 7th and last, some 13 laps down on winner Pedro Rodriguez in a BRM.

The frenetic pace of the 1971 season continued as, nine days later, the teams reconvened for the start of practice for the second round of the World Championship, the Spanish

Grand Prix at the Montjuich Park road circuit in Barcelona. For this event Wisell's car had been converted to the same specification as Fittipaldi's was at Oulton Park and the two oil coolers on both cars now sported aluminium ducts to help scoop air into them.

Fittipaldi was troubled all weekend by problems with his brakes, while Wisell was uncomfortable in his car and decided to try a new driving position which involved repositioning the gear-lever. Both cars were in the rear half of the field in the first two sessions, so when the final

For Dave 'Beaky' Sims, the breakage on Fittipaldi's car in Barcelona was the final straw and he left for pastures new, frustrated at the team's inability to overcome the same recurring problem. 'My car was breaking the wishbones again and again, always the left lower rear. It was cracking at the pick-up point. The Old Man used to say, "Oh, it's broken again" and I would say "Well, why don't we modify it?" and he'd say, "You're not here to tell us what to do, you're there to be told!" We went to the Questor Grand Prix. I was on Emerson's car then and it broke in exactly the same place. Then it broke again in Barcelona. Emerson said to me "Is it the same bit?" and I said "Exactly the same" and the Old Man went berserk.' Although Sims and Derek Mower left Lotus at the same time with the original intention of starting a Formula 2 team, this didn't work out and Sims went to work for the March Formula 1 team while Mower joined the Vels Parnelli team in the US.

t was clear from the early season races in 1971 that the Lotus 72 in its existing specification was not a match for other Grand Prix cars in the way that it had been the previous year. The competitive edge that it had appeared to enjoy in 1970 had been wiped out, either through other manufacturers introducing new and better cars of their own, or through the 12-cylinder cars enjoying a horsepower advantage.

If it wasn't for the fact that both his drivers were displaying obvious speed in their Lotus 69s in Formula 2, Chapman might have been excused for thinking that the problem lay not with his cars but the men behind the wheel. After all, as Phillippe had said, this was the car which comprehensively blew off its opposition to win the World Championship in 1970! Wisell won the classic street race at Pau the weekend after the Spanish Grand Prix and Fittipaldi had a strong run to second in the Eifelrennen at the Nürburgring, so it began to seem that indeed, they were right when they said the car was difficult to drive in its current form.

Fittipaldi remembers the car's lack of reaction to changes as being the main obstacle. 'We couldn't set up the car, that was our biggest problem. That's what I was telling Colin and Maurice Phillippe, because the car didn't react to changes. That year I was running Formula 2 and I was very sensitive to changes I made. When you change or modify the suspension you should have a reaction and I didn't have any. That was very frustrating for me and I was saying to Colin "I don't understand why the car doesn't react." But the car was reacting – it was getting better or worse according to the amount of bumps and grip on the track. We were really lost, I tell you. The first six months up to July/August we were going round in circles, chasing our tails.'

Additionally, as Reine Wisell points out, the lack of proper testing was hindering both the development of the car and the team's relatively young, inexperienced drivers. 'We had no possibility of testing because they had run out of money, so testing was Friday qualifying. Fittipaldi moved in and lived near Chapman and I was living in Switzerland and that gave more possibilities for Emerson to test but with the limited money they had at that time there was hardly any testing at all. Perhaps a few things but I was not involved, I just came to the races.' A decision was taken to substantially revise the 72s, with the aim of introducing the new specification car, or one of them at least, in time for the Monaco Grand Prix, which was to take place five weeks after the Spanish Grand Prix.

In the meantime, there was the non-Championship

International Trophy race at Silverstone, at which Fittipaldi was entered in the turbine and Wisell in his regular car, 72/3. While Emerson put the turbine on the front row, Wisell endured a miserable practice, missing out on the only true dry session of the weekend on Thursday morning due to continuing gear selection problems. In the showery afternoon session, he spent most of the time in the pits with clutch problems. It was not until final practice on Friday afternoon that he got any serious running, but he still only managed 22nd fastest, slowest of all the Formula 1 cars and behind quite a few of the Formula 5000 entries. In the race, Wisell worked his way up through the field to finish the first 26-lap heat in seventh place. In the second, he was running in a secure fourth when, with three laps remaining his engine just stopped for no obvious reason – yet again.

A continuing shortage of engines and the usual last-minute panic in getting things finished meant that Fittipaldi's car went to Monaco in its new specification without having turned a wheel, while there had not been enough time to convert Wisell's car. The changes – which were focused on the rear suspension – were significant enough to warrant the team designating the revised car a 72D. Twin parallel radius rods at the rear replaced the

single radius rod of the original design, with one locating on the engine and the other attached to the rear bulkhead, while twin parallel lower links were adopted instead of the original wishbones. The objective of all this was to try and prevent toe-steer. Revised top links were also introduced, while the oblong-shaped frame which had been used to mount all the suspension components on had been discarded. In its place was a top cross-member, while at the bottom a space-frame was bolted to the gearbox which carried the lower suspension. The team had also switched from Armstrong to Koni dampers, which they had first tried at Barcelona when the drivers had reported an immediate transformation of their car's handling. The Konis were seen as being superior to the Armstrongs because they offered greater adjustability. Finally, they reverted to the original three-plane rear wings for this meeting, as they could be set to achieve greater downthrust than was possible with the newer single-plane model.

Practice was blighted by unseasonally inclement weather, with rain spoiling the Thursday afternoon session and final practice on Saturday afternoon. This meant that the only opportunity for dry running came in the Friday morning session, which tended to penalise those drivers who had never raced on the circuit before as well as those with unsorted cars. Fittipaldi fell into both these categories, so it was no surprise to find him in 17th position on the grid, with only Schenken's Brabham slower. Wisell on the other

Above: Fittipaldi drifts 72/5 out of Station Hairpin in the Monaco Grand Prix.
Right: Progress at last, Fittipaldi was on the last row of the grid for the Monaco Grand Prix but knew that the near parallel link rear suspension was a big step forward.

LOTUS 72

hand at least had a car that he was familiar with and had driven the circuit as a Formula 3 driver back in 1969, when he narrowly lost out on victory to his countryman Ronnie Peterson. His greater comfort was reflected in his 12th place on the grid, the first time he had outqualified his Brazilian team-mate. Despite his limited dry-weather track-time in the car, Fittipaldi was convinced that the 72D was a different car and told Chapman so, to which the Lotus boss is said to have retorted 'He's on the last row, I don't think he knows for sure!'

The race was run in dry conditions and it was soon apparent that the revised car was much more to Fittipaldi's liking, for he was tigering his way through the field in a way that hadn't really been seen since some of his early Grands Prix. At the end of the first lap he had passed Amon – who had been left on the grid – Cevert and Gethin, then on the third lap he slipped ahead of John Surtees. For the next twenty-odd laps Emerson followed Rolf Stommelen in the number two Surtees until he found a way past on lap 27 of 80. For another 15 laps or so the determined Brazilian tracked the Matra of Beltoise until the Frenchman's fading brakes sent him up the escape road at the chicane and he was through and into the points.

Not long afterwards, the dominance of race-leader Stewart and his Tyrrell car was underlined by the fact that he lapped Fittipaldi. With a long gap up to the next runner, Denny Hulme, the rest of the race was somewhat lonely for the Lotus driver, although he was cheered by the retirement of Siffert at three-quarters distance, which elevated him to fifth place. Meanwhile Wisell had retired just after quarter distance with a collapsed hub bearing. It wasn't clear whether this was the result of a coming-together with the forceful Ferrari driver Reggazoni, just before the tunnel, or whether it had failed of its own accord. Either way, it was a pity, because at the time he had been running in 7th, three places ahead of Fittipaldi, so a good points finish had looked on the cards.

The following week, on Whit Monday, Fittipaldi continued his rich vein of form in Formula 2, which had seen him win round 3 of the European Championship at Jarama the week before Monaco. He scored a comfortable victory in round 4, held at Crystal Palace, at the wheel of his works-supported Lotus 69. After the race, he travelled back to Norwich in the Capri that he had just collected from Ford and the next day, he and his then wife, Maria Helena, set off with their things packed up in the car to move to their new flat in Lausanne, Switzerland. It was on this journey, on a quiet road just outside Dijon, that Fittipaldi had a big accident, seriously injuring both himself and his wife. The whole incident was hushed up at the time but the Brazilian suffered a puncture wound in his chest caused by a broken steering wheel and the accident left him with two

Right: Wisell, a former winner of the Formula 3 race at Monaco, was at home on the streets of the principality, out-qualifying his team-mate. **Below:** Points at last: Fittipaldi drove a good race to come home fifth in the Monaco Grand Prix, his first top-six finish of the year. **Opposite Page Top:** Dave Walker took over 72/5 – originally intended for Trimmer – at Hockenheim in the non-Championship Jochen Rindt Memorial race. He didn't endear himself to Chapman when an oil cooler fell off his car, the consequent engine blow-up adding a DFV to the repair bill. **Opposite Page Bottom:** Wisell had his first outing in 72/3 as a D spec car.

fractures of the sternum and three broken ribs. He also lost a lot of blood and ended up having to have blood transfusions. His wife, who was pregnant at the time, suffered a broken jaw and facial injuries, which called for

bone and skin grafts and was extremely painful for some considerable time afterwards.

Once again, Jabby Crombac's ties with Team Lotus proved invaluable, while the closeness of the Formula 1

community was also underlined. Crombac recalls: 'I remember it vividly because I was asleep and suddenly at five o'clock in the morning the telephone rang. It was Peter Warr and he said, "Get up, take your car and drive down to Dijon because Emerson and Maria Helena are both in hospital there". I had to go and sort out the wreck of the car, the luggage and everything. Meanwhile, Jackie Stewart organised a medical plane so I had to take the luggage to the plane and so on.'

Emerson was out of racing for nearly five weeks as he recovered from his injuries and during this time the team took in the non-Championship Jochen Rindt Memorial Trophy race at Hockenheim. It was announced that Tony Trimmer would have another chance in the 72, driving Emerson's car, while Wisell would drive his regular mount and Walker the 56B turbine. For this low downforce, high speed race, the single plane rear wings were put back on the 72s, while Wisell's regular car, 72/3 had been updated to the full 72D spec raced by Fittipaldi at Monaco.

On the first day of practice, the turbine's engine went off-song and so Walker was put in Trimmer's car, the unlucky Englishman once again pushed onto the sidelines. The thing that the stocky Walker remembers most about that weekend was how awkward it was for him to drive the 72, since it was the first time he had ever sat in one! 'I was extremely uncomfortable because I was all hunched up in the thing and the gearchange was sort of halfway back to my elbow. At that point in time it was very, very difficult to drive, particularly as I wasn't sitting in the car properly.' Wisell was really flying, revelling in the improved handling of his car and was third on the grid, one of only three cars to beat the magic two minute barrier, albeit nearly three seconds slower than poleman Jacky Ickx's Ferrari. Walker was further back down the grid, having failed to notice that he had lost one of his oil coolers somewhere on the circuit, with the result that his engine blew up.

In the race, Wisell ran a strong second behind Ickx and ahead of Ronnie Peterson's March 711 before being forced to stop at the pits complaining of having no brakes. Although the fluid was topped up, it transpired that the problem was due to the rivets holding the front bulkhead having been worn away, causing it to move under pressure. He rejoined two laps behind and continued to circulate to finish a despondent 10th. This was one place behind teammate Walker, who had endured a frustrating race fighting a lack of fuel pressure (he ran on the starting pump) and later the loss of fourth gear, while he also had a big spin at the high-speed Sachs Curve, which must have shaken him up somewhat.

A week later, the Grand Prix circus reconvened among the sand dunes of the Dutch Zandvoort circuit for round four of the World Championship. With Fittipaldi still out of

LOTUS 72

action, the opportunity was taken to give the South African Formula 1 Champion Dave Charlton a chance at the wheel of the Brazilian's car, since he was considering the purchase of a 72 to maintain his superiority in his domestic series. He would drive providing Dave Walker raced the turbine car, which was awaiting a new engine, otherwise the Australian would take over the 72 from Charlton. As it turned out, Charlton never even got a chance to drive the 72 as Walker crashed it on only his second lap on Friday, while waiting for the turbine to be finished. Although he reported back to Chapman that the damage was confined to 'Just a couple of radius rods and dinged at the rear' Peter Warr recalls the damage as being somewhat more extensive. 'He came back and said, "Oh, I've gone off Colin, it's not very bad, just the rear end" and he'd knocked the gearbox off it!' Consequently, the car was a non-starter and the team was down to just the singleton 72 plus the turbine.

Once again, Wisell was right on the pace, his time good enough for sixth, on the third row of the grid. However, he was less comfortable in the wet conditions on Saturday morning, so it was disappointing for the team when race day dawned cold, wet and windy. Nonetheless, on the right tyres to have in the conditions – Firestones – he made a

good start and was running fifth in the early stages when he felt something come loose on the final corner leading onto the pit straight. 'It felt like something had broken at the rear end, a hub or something. The same thing had also

happened to me in Monaco. I just managed to stop the car after the pit exit and I thought I couldn't drive it all the way round for one more lap, so I reversed into the pits.' The problem turned out to be a loose wheel, so it was tightened and Wisell was sent on his way. However, his pit-lane manoeuvre had fallen foul of officialdom and he was black-flagged ten laps later. By this stage, Walker had already put the turbine in the sand, so it was an early end to the weekend for Gold Leaf Team Lotus.

Two weeks later, Fittipaldi's 72 had been rebuilt – the tub was found to have escaped unscathed from Walker's Zandvoort accident – and its regular Brazilian pilot made a brave return to the cockpit, still extremely sore and with his ribs heavily strapped, for the French Grand Prix. The race was being held at the new Circuit Paul Ricard, a flat and relatively featureless track situated between Toulon and Marseilles in the South of the country. Although it was the first time a Grand Prix had been held at the circuit many of the leading teams had tested there, the most notable exception to this being Lotus.

This unfamiliarity with the circuit gave the team and drivers something else to think about, and it was therefore no surprise that both cars were mid-way down the timesheets after the first session. Despite his discomfort, Fittipaldi ended up the quicker of the two drivers, although Wisell's practice was interrupted by a strange problem – the outer tube of a rear torsion bar broke, which was the first time the team had ever experienced such a failure. Wisell asked for his car to be stiffened up for the Saturday morning session and promptly outpaced his team-mate, whose car had an engine change overnight.

Neither had an opportunity to participate in final practice, for Colin Chapman had decreed that they would skip it in order that the mechanics could concentrate on fully race-preparing both cars. Although the drivers were probably quite put out about this decision at the time, it was one that in retrospect turned out to be wise. Wisell would start from the outside of the sixth row, with Fittipaldi sitting squarely in the middle of the seventh row behind him. Before the race, Chapman took his two drivers aside and gave them his own unique brand of pep talk, as Rex Hart explains. 'The problem was that Fittipaldi and Wisell were still relative newcomers. They were very hard on first and second gear. They used to do gearboxes in like there was no tomorrow. Every time we took the gearbox apart the dogrings were knackered! Before the race, we dragged the gearbox out and the Old Man got both of them standing in

front of him like a couple of little schoolboys and just gave them a severe bollocking. He said "Look at this: why do you think its got number 1 on this car? Because it's the best bloody car and you're doing this" and he really gave them shit! And that was the turnaround point – it didn't start to improve until then.'

What Chapman said must have made an impression on his two young drivers! When the starter's flag dropped, Fittipaldi made a tremendous start, blasting past his team-mate and coming through at the end of the first lap in 14th place. On the fourth lap, he despatched with Hulme and on the next lap both Peterson and Surtees became victims. Rolf Stommelen was the prey on the following lap, while a 'double-whammy' on both Matras on lap 15 lifted him above Amon and Beltoise in one fell swoop and into seventh position. Six laps later, the demise of Reggazoni and Hill promoted the Lotus to fifth place. When Pedro Rodriguez retired at half distance, Emerson was up to fourth and already embroiled in a tooth-and-nail battle with the wily Swiss driver Jo Siffert in the other BRM. He trailed the Yardley car from lap 15 and, although he managed to nose ahead, Siffert was not going to give up without a fight and retook third four laps later. It was not until lap 48 that

the scrap was finally resolved in the Brazilian's favour, securing his first rostrum finish and easily his best result of the year. At one stage, even second place had looked a possibility, for second man Cevert's Cosworth engine had gone flat with a broken exhaust and Fittipaldi was closing in on him. At the chequered flag, there were only six seconds in it but the Frenchman held on to secure a Tyrrell 1-2.

Wisell had struggled to keep up with his team-mate's meteoric progress but after 35 of the 55 laps he was up to seventh place. All his hard work was thrown away with a spin on lap 40, which dropped him back to 10th but, undeterred, the Swede stormed back up the order and the retirement of Schenken's Brabham with five laps left promoted him up into sixth to secure the final point and the first double points finish for the team since Watkins Glen the previous year. All in all, it was a good weekend for Gold Leaf Team Lotus, for Dave Walker took on the all-conquering Alpine-Renaults on their home turf in the supporting Formula 3 race and beat them.

A rare test session at Silverstone followed, giving Wisell some grounds for optimism about the forthcoming race there, although it was not without its problems, as he recalls. 'I had two good days testing and I was very quick with the 72, although it broke the rear suspension three times. It did it two times at Woodcote, which was nearly flat out! But I was satisfied, I was very happy because it was going very quickly.'

Eleven days after the French Grand Prix, the teams gathered at Silverstone for the British Grand Prix. With race-day traditionally on a Saturday due to the Sunday Observance law, practice was scheduled for Thursday and Friday, in the form of two one-hour sessions on each day. Wisell was allocated the turbine, since the team was giving Charlton another chance in a 72 to make up for his Zandvoort disappointment prior to his return to South Africa. The fact that he was about to buy a 72 from them was probably an additional consideration.

The only significant modification made to the cars was a revision of the airboxes feeding cold air to the inlet

trumpets. Previously (and since the British Grand Prix the previous year, in fact) these had consisted of two intakes either side of the driver's head but Lotus had now adopted a single airbox above the roll-over bar in much the same fashion as many other leading teams and as pioneered by Matra as long ago as the Mexican Grand Prix in 1970.

Fittipaldi, now feeling much better, was right on the pace from the beginning of the first session, ending up second-fastest, only two-tenths of a second slower than the Tyrrell of Jackie Stewart. In the second session, both drivers went faster but the margin between them was maintained, with Emerson again second on the timesheets. On Friday, the Brazilian closed the gap to one-tenth of a second on the all-conquering Tyrrell but a new contender emerged for pole, with Reggazoni slipping ahead of the Tyrrell by a tenth. However, while the final session was building to a crescendo, Fittipaldi had to sit in the pits, for the high speed cornering vibrations of his Firestone tyres had caused his top left side engine mounting to break and he had to have both sides strengthened before he could go out again.

Opposite Page: Wisell put in his best qualifying performance of the year at the Dutch Grand Prix but was unable to capitalise on it in the race. **Right:** Fittipaldi really began to motor in the second half of the season, qualifying fourth at Silverstone, despite problems with broken engine mountings.

Eddie Dennis recalls that this was a tense operation, with the welding being done 'in situ'. 'I had the bag [fuel] tank folded back and filled with damp rags and I could feel the sweat running down the back of my neck, brazing up near a fuel tank!' Thanks to Dennis's speedy work, the Brazilian managed to get out right at the end of the hour and, although his time was good enough for sixth in that session, it was probably asking a bit much of him to post a quick time in a matter of minutes. To add insult to injury, Siffert suddenly turned in a fast lap out of nowhere in his BRM and Emerson was bumped off the front row. The other 72 of Charlton first suffered a broken oil union and then suffered the same fate as Fittipaldi, except for the fact that this time both top engine mounts had broken. This precluded him from participating in the final session at all, which was a shame, since the South African Champion had begun to display a useful turn of speed, having been 13th quickest on Friday morning.

The day had started well for Lotus with Dave Walker taking victory in a thrilling wheel-to-wheel Formula 3 race. However, it took a rapid turn for the worse when, on the warm-up lap, Charlton's 72 started smoking heavily. When the flag dropped, he struggled away and completed one slow tour before he came into the pits to retire, a piston having broken up inside his DFV engine. Meanwhile at the front of the grid, Fittipaldi had thrown away all his good practice efforts by fluffing his start and being swallowed up by the pack. At the end of lap one, he was down in 11th place.

All was not lost though, for the Brazilian was on fine form, positively scything through the field, passing Cevert, Gethin, Ganley, Hulme and Schenken so that by lap 13 he was up into sixth position and closing on Ronnie Peterson in the slippery March 711. On lap 22, he was past the rapid Swede and giving chase to Ickx in the Ferrari. However, he pulled the March and Schenken's Brabham along with him, making a four-car train disputing fourth place. At exactly half-distance, Peterson got back past the Lotus. Emerson had been experiencing some rather odd handling as a result of having stiffened the torsion bar rate before the race to avoid bottoming on full tanks and he was also bothered by the same tyre-induced vibration, which had caused problems in practice.

A few laps later, Ickx was out, putting Fittipaldi back into fifth but this was a position he held for only four laps because Schenken was putting in a storming race in the old Brabham BT33 and he got the better of the Brazilian on lap 42 out of 68. Lady Luck was on the side of Lotus this time

Above & Right: Dave Charlton agreed to buy 72/3 just before the Dutch Grand Prix and take it back to South Africa to race in the national series there. Much to Wisell's disgust Charlton took his place in 72/3 for the 1971 British Grand Prix as well. Note the new spec 'periscope' airbox. **Opposite Page:** A bitterly-fought battle with Tim Schenken in the British Grand Prix was finally resolved in Fittipaldi's favour, the Brazilian finishing third for the second successive race.

sterile than before but it was still one of the toughest challenges that a Formula 1 car or driver could face.

Emerson was already familiar with the 'Ring but spent the first part of practice on the Friday morning doing full-tank runs. Wisell didn't even get out for a full lap, as the mechanics spent the first part of the session finishing off building the car and he confined himself to a few laps round the start/finish loop. In the afternoon, Fittipaldi began to go faster, knocking ten seconds off his full-tank run times, while Wisell was playing himself in, growing used to his new car. In the final session, Emerson really got into the groove, ending up eighth-fastest, while Wisell's limited practice meant that he was further down the order, in 16th position on the grid.

At the start, Emerson was 'jumped' by Schenken in the Brabham and Andretti's Ferrari passed him by Breidscheid so that he came round 10th at the end of the first lap. Meanwhile, Wisell's car had fuel pressure problems and was left on the line. The mechanics rushed onto the track and squirted fuel down the inlet trumpets and finally got the Swede going, albeit well behind the rest of the field, so he was set for a lonely race. Fittipaldi's car was handling badly on the opening lap and it later transpired that this was because the front anti-roll bar had broken. Nonetheless, on the second tour he re-passed Schenken and the retirement of Ickx's Ferrari promoted him a further place up the order. When Denny Hulme in the McLaren went out it elevated the Brazilian to seventh but this was as high as he got for, at the end of seven of the 12 laps he pulled into the pits, his 72 having lost oil. A further lap following attention from the mechanics was no better so he reluctantly retired. Wisell

though, for on the next lap, Siffert retired his BRM from third place and just five tours later second man Reggazoni was out too, promoting the Brazilian to fourth. Then, with

First Person
Vic McCarthy on Emerson Fittipaldi

"He was just a friendly, modest guy. I remember the story that Jim Russell told Chapman that he'd got this kid at the school and said to him "Hey I can't teach this kid anything, he's so good. Sign him!" He

was very pleasant and polite, very nice. And a brave fella too. He raced with a broken sternum for quite a while. I used to strap him up before the race. He'd come into the transporter before he got in the car and I'd tape him up, with him wincing like crazy."

only five laps remaining, Schenken's gearbox – which had been jamming in fourth and fifth gears – finally gave up the ghost and he coasted to a disgruntled halt. This left Fittipaldi to take his second successive third place, promoting him to fourth place in the World Championship, albeit with little chance of catching runaway leader Stewart, who had won his second successive Grand Prix in the Tyrrell.

A new car, 72/6, was completed in time for the next race, the German Grand Prix, although only just, since the mechanics ended up having to work several all-nighters to complete the car before they left for Germany. Wisell claims he never felt comfortable in this car. 'They sold 'my' 72 to Dave Charlton, then they built another one and I didn't feel like it was really as good. I liked the one I drove first very much. We never got it to feel the same way. When they made a seat for me, I was sitting far too high to get the right feeling. I liked to sit very low and that changed the roll centre for my body, belts and so on.' Fittipaldi was in his usual car, 72/5, the only difference in specification being a return to ventilated discs rather than the solid ones used in Great Britain.

After a one-year hiatus at the characterless Hockenheim circuit, the Formula 1 circus returned to the Nürburgring, which looked very bare and quite different following a massive rebuilding and reprofiling exercise aimed at making it safer. It might have looked a lot more

plugged round at the back of the field but did not manage to catch and overtake anyone, ending the race some six and a half minutes behind the winning Tyrrell of Jackie Stewart who, by this stage in the season, had virtually tied up the World Championship with a run of wins.

A fortnight later, the Austrian Grand Prix took place, at the picturesque Österreichring circuit in the rolling hills of Zeltweg, overlooking the old aerodrome circuit. Both cars were unchanged from Germany and Emerson was immediately on the pace, ending the Thursday afternoon session fourth-fastest, while Wisell took longer to get 'dialled in', ending up in the bottom half of the order. On Friday, things got even better, with Fittipaldi actually topping the timesheets – the first time that he had ever achieved this at a Grand Prix meeting. He was still troubled by his car weaving heavily under braking and when the mechanics investigated this after the Friday session, they found that one of the front calipers had one magnesium and one aluminium side. When this was changed, it seemed to virtually eliminate the problem and, in the third and final session on Saturday afternoon, Emerson fairly scorched round in a time quicker than his previous day's efforts. This though was only good enough for fifth-fastest on the day and the same position on the grid, on row three alongside Jacky Ickx. Wisell circulated for lap after lap and did manage to improve his pace markedly on this final day, setting ninth-best time, to put him two rows behind his team-mate.

In the race, Wisell made a much better start than Fittipaldi and the two came by nose-to-tail in seventh and eighth places, with the Brazilian in front. On the fifth lap, Fittipaldi was past the already ailing Ferrari of Stewart's nearest challenger in the World Championship, Jacky Ickx, and a lap later Wisell followed him through. The retirement of Reggazoni's Ferrari on lap 9 promoted the Lotus twins up a further place, putting them in fifth and sixth, positions they maintained until a charging Graham Hill put his 'lobster-claw' Brabham BT34 between them on lap 17 of the scheduled 54. Twelve laps later, Wisell had reclaimed his sixth place but the team formation was only maintained for another couple of laps before Fittipaldi found his way past his rapidly becoming frequent nemesis, Tim Schenken in the Brabham BT33.

The demise of Jackie Stewart four laps later elevated Fittipaldi into third and then six laps later, Stewart's team-mate Cevert was out with a blown engine. Suddenly the young Brazilian was second and Wisell fourth. Towards the end of the race there was great tension and excitement in the pits when it became apparent that leader Jo Siffert was slowing dramatically and Fittipaldi was catching him at 3-4 seconds per lap. From 24 seconds with ten laps to go, he had whittled the advantage away to only seven seconds as they started their final tour. However, the skilful Siffert hung on grimly to finish with four seconds in hand. It was discovered after the race that he had a slow puncture to his BRM's rear tyre and had done marvellously well to even finish, let alone keep cool and win the race. To complete a fantastic day for Lotus, Wisell managed to put some distance between himself and Hill and hold on to take fourth and three hard-earned Championship points. It had been the team's best showing of the year, without a doubt. What was more, Fittipaldi's second place had pushed him up to fourth position in the World Championship standings, although the outcome of the title was decided in Jackie Stewart's favour with the retirement of Ickx and the failure of anyone else to close the points gap on him.

In the light of their strong showing at the Österreichring, it was perhaps disappointing that Gold Leaf Team Lotus decided not to send any cars to the Italian Grand Prix.

The ongoing legal situation arising from Rindt's fatal accident meant that there was a risk of Chapman being arrested if he entered the country, as well a the team's cars being seized. Consequently, the turbine was sent for Fittipaldi to drive in the name of Worldwide Racing and Wisell was not entered at all. However, a Lotus 72 was entered for the race, this being the ex-Rob Walker car, 72/4, which had been sold to Jo Siffert. Siffert had arranged to rent it out to the sportscar driver, Herbert Muller but in the end it didn't show up for reasons which never became apparent.

Just after the Italian race, it was announced that the Chief Designer of Team Lotus, Maurice Phillippe – who had enjoyed a pivotal role in the design of both the 49 and 72 among others – was to leave the company. He had been tempted by a big-money offer from the Vels-Parnelli team

Above & Opposite Page: The high-speed sweeps of the Österreichring suited the 72 and Wisell equalled his best finish with fourth in the Austrian Grand Prix.

and the prospect of designing cars for both Indy and Formula 1 racing. A successor was not announced at the time.

The next appearance of the 72 was in the Canadian Grand Prix, five weeks after the Austrian race. They were once again unchanged, with Fittipaldi and Wisell in their regular cars. On the Friday, Fittipaldi managed to record the third-best time in the morning session, but unfortunately his clutch centre tore out before he could start setting any fast times in the afternoon. Wisell was quickly in the groove though – perhaps mindful that his contract would soon be up for renewal – and set fifth-fastest time, which was his best performance of the year. On Saturday morning, Fittipaldi was back ahead of his team-mate, setting fourth-fastest time, while Wisell was seventh. In the final session, Fittipaldi was again on form in third, good enough for fourth on the grid, while Wisell was only two-tenths slower to put him on the row behind the Brazilian.

Race day dawned wet and cold. In the warm-up,

First Person

Jabby Crombac on Chapman and Phillippe

"They worked so well together because they started at the same level. Maurice was a special builder too and therefore Colin appreciated that, to build your

own special develops a sense of practicality. Colin soon found out that Maurice was doing a good job. The first task he gave him, Maurice did a bloody good car for him, even before the 72, I mean with the Indy car [Type 42/43 and later the 56]. I think he was appreciative of the outcome.

When Colin said 'I want this car to be like this and like that', Maurice produced an extremely good car following his requirements. When Maurice left to go to Parnelli, Colin was absolutely livid because he produced the Parnelli [Formula 1 car] and Colin said, "This is exactly the car we should have been doing".'

Fittipaldi found his car to be undriveable, and asked for it to be set up full soft. Chapman refused, offering merely to put on more rear wing and go softer on the shock absorbers, another indication that he still didn't trust the instincts of his young Brazilian charge. Wisell, revelling in the conditions, made up a place early on, while Emerson dropped back from his grid position to run in sixth, so that

the two 72s were again running nose-to-tail, as they had done in Austria. The retirement of Beltoise's Matra promoted them to fifth and sixth and another impressive points finish seemed in prospect. Although he looked to be driving more smoothly than his team-mate, Fittipaldi was actually struggling to stay ahead and, shortly after they had both been passed by a charging Denny Hulme, Wisell passed the Brazilian. Not long after this, he also passed Ickx, who was struggling in his Ferrari, a feat Fittipaldi repeated four laps later.

While Wisell cruised on in fifth, Fittipaldi was unable to do anything about the fast-closing Francois Cevert in the Tyrrell and, on lap 57 of the scheduled 80, was demoted to seventh by the Frenchman. By this stage, it was getting decidedly dark and murky and the race organisers took the decision to shorten the race and finish it after 64 laps. Already World Champion, Jackie Stewart emphasised his season-long superiority by taking another victory, with only the second and third-placed cars on the same lap. Wisell must have been delighted to finish in the points again, and particularly to have beaten his team-mate in a straight fight for the first time.

The eleventh and final round of the 1971 World Championship was held in the United States, at the Watkins Glen circuit. The two Gold Leaf Team Lotus cars for Fittipaldi and Wisell were virtually unaltered from Canada, except for the fact that the Brazilian had persuaded Chapman to put bump rubbers on the rear suspension. This was a modification which had resulted in his Formula 2 Lotus 69 suddenly becoming competitive, as he explains. 'We did two things, reinforced the suspension and took away most of the progressive [rising rate]. The original Lotus 72 had progressive suspension, so that the more the car went on bump, the stiffer it would get. It was very, very difficult to set up the car for bumpy circuits. At most of the smooth tracks with not much grip, like Paul Ricard, the car wasn't so bad but everywhere it was bumpy

and grippy, it was a disaster – it was very difficult to drive. I was doing a lot of tests at that time with Koni shock absorbers on my Formula 2 car and I had convinced Colin to try the Konis on the 72. Instead of rising rate we used bump rubbers and it made the car much more driveable.' Although the Lotus boss took some convincing, as the 72 had been designed with its torsion bars to run without

Although the Lotus boss took some convincing, it was a sign of the shifting balance between Fittipaldi and Chapman

bump rubbers, it was a sign of the shifting balance in the relationship between the two that Fittipaldi got his way.

The modification resulted in an immediate improvement in pace. The young Brazilian was quickly in the thick of things, setting the third-fastest time in the Friday sessions, while Wisell was further down the order

grid, he came round at the end of the first lap in a lowly eighth place, with team-mate Wisell once again running in formation right behind him. On lap two, the Brazilian passed Amon's Matra to put some space between himself and the other Lotus but on lap six Wisell's race was all over, his brake pedal having gone to the floor again, the resultant contact with the barrier putting his car out of the race. Fittipaldi's day turned sour only a few laps later, as he pitted with a sticking throttle. Incredibly, this was the first of four stops, for he suffered a flat rear tyre four laps later and after another couple of tours was forced to pit again to replace a left rear lower rose joint, which had rubbed on the ground when the tyre went flat. Finally, the line to the fuel pressure gauge broke and sprayed him in fuel, necessitating a break to sort that out. He eventually resumed, to finish a sorry 19th, ten laps behind the winner.

after running out of fuel on the circuit due to one of the rubber fuel cell's collapsing. Both drivers were also troubled by severe tyre vibrations, which had become a feature of the new-generation slicks, which had been introduced, by Firestone and Goodyear that year. In the Saturday session, Wisell again ran out of fuel, then later on a brake master cylinder failed and his car chunked a tyre. Despite all this, the amiable Swede ended the session tenth-quickest and ninth-quickest overall for a place on the

fourth row. Meanwhile Fittipaldi was vying with Stewart for pole position and the US$2,000 that went with it. Just as Chapman thought they'd won it, the Tyrrell man came along and beat his time, eventually going just seventeen-hundredths faster than the Brazilian.

Fittipaldi's starts weren't the best in 1971 and Watkins Glen was no exception. From second on the

The final Formula 1 appearance for Gold Leaf Team Lotus came three weeks later at the Rothmans World Championship Victory Race, essentially a race staged to celebrate Jackie Stewart's achievement in winning the title. A single-car was entered for Fittipaldi, while Wisell resorted to piloting the Sid Taylor McLaren Formula 5000 car. In practice, Fittipaldi put his car on the outside of the front row, alongside the two BRMs of Gethin and Siffert, having recorded third fastest time.

The Brazilian remembers this event on the bumpy Kent track as really confirming that the Lotus 72 had come good again at last. 'That was the first time that year the car was running really strongly and that was the package for 1972. It was the combination of reinforcing the suspension and changing the progressive rate on the rear suspension and the front. Brands Hatch was the first real test and I was very, very pleased with the way the car ran, because it was a bumpy circuit.'

Above: Jacky Ickx in his Ferrari had a mirror-full of Lotus 72s in the Austrian Grand Prix, as first Fittipaldi and then Wisell passed him. **Left:** Tony Matthews' superb cutaway drawing lays bare the Lotus 72 in mid-1971 specification. **Opposite Page:** A front row grid position and fastest lap in the Rothmans World Championship Victory Race boded well for Fittipaldi's prospects in 1972.

needless death of yet another established Formula 1 star.

Thus ended the 1971 season, the first in which Team Lotus had failed to win a Grand Prix or, indeed, any kind of Formula 1 race, since the late 1950s. While there was little doubt that the car had not been as competitive as in 1970, Eddie Dennis believes that much of the lack of results was attributable to unfamiliarity with the circuits on the part of the two young drivers. 'I think you might have to put some of it down to driver experience because both of them were competing at some circuits they hadn't even been to before.' This would seem to be supported by the fact that, when he got to circuits where he had raced before, such as the Österreichring and Watkins Glen, Fittipaldi was much more competitive.

By contrast, Wisell had no such previous experience to fall back on, plus he also seemed to be second in line for any development parts, a pattern that would be repeated the following year with Dave Walker. Dennis also thinks that the Swede lacked that instant outright speed that differentiated the top drivers from the rest of the field. 'Wisell was a steady driver and in practice he would do the most laps of anybody, grinding round and round and round, but just below what would be a goodish pace and then he might just squeeze in one quick lap. He wasn't a bloke who could turn it on immediately for a really fast lap.'

Fittipaldi ended the year in sixth position in the World Championship, with 16 points to the 62 of title winner Jackie Stewart, while Wisell was 12th, with 9 points. However, the speed and competitiveness of the 72 in the final few practice sessions and races of 1971 gave considerable grounds for optimism for the 1972 season. Before then, there would be a number of major changes, both in the driver line-up and team personnel and, most notably in the livery of the cars. A new era was about to begin.

What should have been a joyous occasion turned into a very sad one, for the event was marred by the tragic death of Jo Siffert in a fiery accident on lap 15, which resulted in the race being stopped. At the time, Fittipaldi had been harrying leader Gethin and had already set the fastest lap of the race, which was also a new lap record for the circuit. So a promising performance was overshadowed by the

WORLD CHAMPIONSHIP TABLE 1971

Pos	Driver	Race S.Africa	Spain	Monaco	Netherlands	France	Great Britain	Germany	Austria	Italy	Canada	USA	Total	(dropped)
1	Jackie Stewart	6	9	9		9	9	9			9	2	62	
2	Ronnie Peterson			6	3		6	2			6	6	4	33	
3	Francois Cevert					6		6			4	1	9	26	
4	Jacky Ickx		6	4	9									19	
4	Jo Siffert					1	3		9			6		19	
6	Emerson Fittipaldi			2		4	4		6					16	
7	Clay Reggazoni	4			4			4				1		13	
8	Mario Andretti	9						3						12	
9	Peter Gethin									9				9	
9	Pedro Rodriguez		3		6									9	
9	Chris Amon	2	4			2				1				9	
12	Reine Wisell	3				1			3		2			9	
12	Denny Hulme	1	2	3							3			9	
14	Tim Schenken						1	4						5	
14	Howden Ganley									2		3		5	
16	Mark Donohue										4			4	
16	Henri Pescarolo					3		1						4	
18	Mike Hailwood								3					3	
18	John Surtees			2		1								3	
18	Rolf Stommelen			1		2								3	
21	Graham Hill							2						2	
22	Jean-Pierre Beltoise		1											1	

Pos	Constructor	Race S.Africa	Spain	Monaco	Netherlands	France	Great Britain	Germany	Austria	Italy	Canada	USA	Total	(dropped)
1	Tyrrell-Cosworth	6	9	9		9	9	9			4	9	9	73	
2	B.R.M.		3		6	3			9		9		6	36	
3	Ferrari	9	6	4	9			4				1		33	
3	March-Cosworth			6	3		6	2	1		6	6	4	33	(1)
5	Lotus-Cosworth	3		2		4	4		6		2			21	
6	McLaren-Cosworth	1	2		3							4		10	
7	Matra-Simca	2	4			2				1				9	
8	Surtees-Cosworth			1	2		2			3				8	
9	Brabham-Cosworth						1	4						5	

CHAPTER 9 EARLY SEASON PROMISE

n November 1971, the Team Lotus Formula 1 plans for the 1972 season were announced. The most significant piece of news was the announcement that Players were to continue their sponsorship of the team for a further three years but that the emphasis would be shifted away from the Gold Leaf brand towards promoting the John Player Special brand. As such, the cars would be liveried in the distinctive black and gold of the cigarettes and would henceforth be referred to as John Player Specials while the team was to be known as John Player Team Lotus.

Fittipaldi recalls his surprise when Chapman called to tell him of the new colour scheme and when he saw it for the first time. 'Colin called me and said, "Well, Emerson, the car is going to be black". I said "Black?" He replied, "Yes, black." And when I saw the Lotus 72 in black with the gold lines I told Colin "Well, it just needs four handles to be a coffin!" But it looked beautiful and it still is. To me, it is one of the top three best-looking Formula 1 cars ever, if not the best.'

A new driver line-up was also revealed. Out went Wisell, who had generally failed to impress in 1971 and had been comprehensively out-driven by team-mate Fittipaldi. In came the 30 year-old Australian driver, Dave Walker, who had totally dominated International Formula 3 racing in 1971, winning 25 races from 32 starts, thereby justifying his

Below: Menacing black-and-gold John Player Special livery was introduced for 1972. Fittipaldi joked that the car only needed four handles and it would look like a coffin! New chief designer Martin Waide's modifications for 1972 included the classic 'anvil' airbox and deep side-plates on the rear wing, although the latter were quickly abandoned.

decision to stay with the formula for a further year after a successful 1970 season. His uncompromising style of racing, plus excellent tactical astuteness which always seemed to see him come to the front of the pack on the final lap, were felt to be the ideal ingredients for a successful Formula 1 driver. His win in front of all the John Player top brass in the thrilling British Grand Prix support race had certainly convinced them both of his worth and the merit of extending their association with Team Lotus.

A replacement for Team Lotus design chief Maurice Phillippe was also announced, this being Martin Waide, a long-standing employee of the company who had designed the Lotus 70 Formula 5000 car. Eddie Dennis stayed on as Chief Mechanic, while Steve Gooda and Jim Pickles continued to look after Fittipaldi's car, assisted by Trevor Seaman, who had re-joined the team at the 1971 US Grand Prix. Rex Hart and Stevie May were assigned to Dave Walker, with Vic McCarthy once again being in charge of the transporter. The winter brought mixed fortunes for Fittipaldi. On a personal level, he suffered a tragedy when his wife Maria-Helena gave birth to a stillborn baby. However, on the racetrack, he managed to win the Formula 2 series held in his native Brazil, the Torneio, at the wheel of his Team Bardahl Lotus 69.

In January, several subsidiary sponsors for John Player Team Lotus were announced. Texaco was to take over from Shell as the official fuel and oil supplier, with its decals prominently displayed on the cars, while Champion succeeded Ford house brand Autolite as the supplier of spark plugs. Meanwhile, Firestone announced that it would once again continue its long-standing relationship with Team Lotus for the supply of tyres.

When the John Player sponsorship extension was

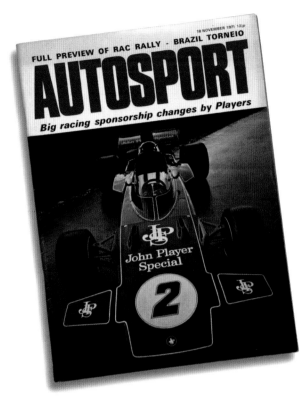

announced in November 1971, the car shown in the new livery was basically in the same form that it ended the season. However, when the announcement of the 1972 secondary sponsors was made, pictures were released which showed that Waide had already made an impact on the way the car looked. He had revised the airbox to a distinctive 'anvil' shape, which was unique to the 72, while the rear wing on the car shown – 72/6 – had sprouted enormous end-plates. Geoff Aldridge, who was working in the Team Lotus drawing office at the time, remembers that the anvil airbox certainly wasn't the result of extensive wind-tunnel testing or anything. 'I think that happened by

accident. Martin drew it and it just seemed to stick, some things do sometimes. He thought that, if he had a space at the back of it and you put some grease in there it might catch some dust that was flying around rather than send it down the engine, which was fairly sensible.'

The 1972 season's opening race was in Argentina, at the Buenos Aires Autodrome which had played host to a non-Championship race the previous year. Fittipaldi was entered in his regular car 72/5, which first appeared at Monza 1970, while Walker was in the more recent 72/6. In the first of the two Friday practice sessions, Fittipaldi was quickly on the pace, while Walker had some problems with his front suspension, which restricted the number of laps he could do. In the second session, Fittipaldi ended up seventh quickest, while Walker was some three and a half seconds adrift of his team-mate. On the Saturday, Emerson improved his times to pull himself up to fifth on the grid, while Walker went faster but was still more than two seconds slower than the Brazilian. On a grid where the gap from the pole-sitter to the slowest qualifier was only 3.5 seconds, this meant that the Australian was on the penultimate row of the grid for his first Grand Prix in a 72.

Fittipaldi made a good start (an area of weakness for him in 1971) when the chequered flag dropped and was up into fourth place by the end of the opening lap. His progress contrasted sharply with that of Walker, who remembers his first Grand Prix only too well. 'Graham Hill was behind me on the grid and he got a run at it and went up the inside into the first corner with a couple of wheels in the dust and gravel. I got showered in rocks and stones and

one of them went down the intake trumpets and jammed the throttle open. I switched off and tried to free it up and then ran back to the pits. No-one was allowed to touch it but a mechanic came back with me and we managed to free the thing up and eventually got the car going.' The Australian restarted on lap 22 but was black-flagged and disqualified shortly afterwards for using tools not carried in the car – an inauspicious start to his season.

Meanwhile Fittipaldi was making good progress. He passed Denny Hulme's McLaren for third on lap three and on lap eight swept past the Brabham of pole-man and local hero Carlos Reutemann to claim second spot. By lap 15, he

was only two seconds adrift of race leader Jackie Stewart, and looked to have a good chance of challenging the Scot for victory. However, all of a sudden, the gap started to grow and it was apparent that the Brazilian was in trouble. It transpired that his car was jumping out of fourth gear and, just after one third's distance, Hulme re-passed the black-and-gold Lotus. Fittipaldi held on gamely to third place for another 25 laps but it was all in vain for, approaching two thirds distance, he came into the pits with a broken rear radius rod and retired. Apparently, after the race Fittipaldi said that he had got so much traction off the line at the start that it had bent both top radius rods at the point where they tapered and this was where the rod had finally broken. More tellingly, he also said that the car had never handled better than when it had the two bent radius rods!

After the Argentinian race, Fittipaldi's car was flown to South Africa, where he conducted tyre testing for Firestone, achieving times well inside the previous year's pole position. This was despite being hampered by a poor choice of compound and construction, which Firestone estimated would allow him to chop a further half a second off when he returned for the Grand Prix.

Walker's car was flown home to Britain, giving the mechanics a valuable opportunity to smuggle in some Argentinian wine they had taken a liking to. The access plate for the forward fuel tanks in the side of the tub were unscrewed and the bottles stowed inside on top of the FPT rubber fuel bags. However, what they didn't realise was that someone else in the team had the same idea. When they got home to the UK, Walker's mechanics duly removed the wine bottles they had placed in there and the car was then sent on its way to South Africa. On the first day of practice at Kyalami, the fuel check didn't come out right and, when

mechanic Stevie May investigated, he found another bottle of very well-travelled wine still languishing in the fuel tank bay!

A month after the tyre-testing at Kyalami, the South African Grand Prix took place. Fittipaldi and Walker drove their regular cars, the only major change being a switch to Magnesium Electron Surtees-style wheels all round. Meanwhile, all the decals on the car were now in black and gold to tie in with the JPS colour scheme. A third 72 was entered, this being the ex-works 72/3 for local hero and South African Champion, Dave Charlton, which had been updated to 1972 specification in terms of the new shape airbox.

In practice, Fittipaldi was once again straight on the

Opposite Page Top: This line-up of 1972 John Player Team Lotus personnel provides a stark contrast to modern-day Formula 1. From left to right: Fittipaldi's mechanics Trevor Seaman, Jim 'High Idle' Pickles, Steve Gooda, Team Manager Peter Warr, Chief Mechanic Eddie Dennis (on monkey bike), transporter driver Vic McCarthy and Walker's mechanics Rex Hart, Stevie May and Mike 'Coughdrop' Coughtrey. **Opposite Page Bottom:** Fittipaldi ran strongly in Argentina before being forced to retire. **Above:** Fittipaldi really came of age towards the end of 1971 and it was clear that he was going to be a Championship challenger in 1972.

pace, reflecting the fact that he was now visiting circuits he had raced on the year before. In the first session he set the fourth-best time, which he improved to second-best the next day. On the final day, he was forced to sit out part of the session when he came in for a tyre change and a crack was found in a top rear wishbone. The car was ready for the last quarter of an hour but unfortunately in the confusion, one of the locks on a front right wheel nut had been left off and, as he sped through the left-handed Jukskei Sweep on a quick lap, the wheel came off and he had to work extremely hard to bring the car to a halt without hitting anything. The suspension was undamaged and the mechanics came over with another wheel, so he was able to resume and managed to put in one more lap before the chequered flag came out to signal the end of the session! All this drama meant that he was able only to match his time of the previous day, which was good enough for third on the grid, on the outside of the front row.

After jettisoning his excess wine baggage, Walker managed to improve on his Argentinian qualifying performance to achieve a mid-grid position, around one and a half seconds slower than Fittipaldi, while Charlton outperformed the second works car by two-tenths of a second. Such was the rate of progress in Formula 1 that his time would have been good enough for the front row of the grid in the 1971 South African Grand Prix but here he was back on the seventh row!

Having maintained his starting position on the first lap, Fittipaldi engaged in a ferocious battle for second place with Denny Hulme and Mike Hailwood, while the winner of the Argentinian race, Jackie Stewart, maintained a slight lead on them. On lap 17, Emerson got past the McLaren of Hulme and started to close in on the Tyrrell but seven laps later Hailwood's Surtees slipped past the Brazilian and began challenging Stewart, even getting alongside him at one point down the main straight. These positions were maintained for another six laps before the Lotus 72 came round in second place, the Surtees having pulled up with broken suspension in an incident which nearly collected Fittipaldi too. Emerson kept up the pressure and was only 1.1 seconds behind Stewart when the Scot suddenly pulled into the pits to retire just after half-distance.

The Brazilian therefore found himself in the lead of a Grand Prix, a position that he had not enjoyed for some considerable time – since Watkins Glen 1970, in fact. However, the handling of his car was deteriorating as the fuel load lightened and it was oversteering wildly, with the result that second man Hulme began closing in again. It was only a matter of time before the Lotus was overhauled, and this happened on lap 57 of 79. Emerson managed to maintain position ahead of third man Peter Revson also in a McLaren for the remaining laps to collect a well-deserved

second place and six Championship points, which put him third in the title standings.

Walker had a solid drive to tenth. Having started badly, he benefited from the retirements of others as well as passing several other drivers to work his way up through the order. He even managed to pass the Tyrrell of Francois Cevert for ninth position with eight laps remaining but was re-taken two laps later. Nonetheless he was pleased to have completed a Grand Prix for the first time. The difference in physical stamina required to finish a 200-mile Formula 1 race in hot dry conditions at altitude in South Africa compared to a 20-lap Formula 3 race in Britain was clear for all to see, as mechanic Rex Hart recalls. 'We had to lift him out of the car after the race. He never got himself fighting fit, he was overweight - he didn't help himself at all. I remember in Argentina the guys said, "You've got to go down to this restaurant, the steaks are fantastic". So we went down, the things were bigger than a table-mat and they were brilliant. Walker had two of them! We all struggled to get half-way through ours but he ordered another!'

Charlton's race in the privateer Lucky Strike 72 was over virtually before it had begun, the belt on the mechanical fuel pump breaking on the opening lap. He pitted for repairs to be effected and then did one more slow lap before retiring, a bitter disappointment in his home race.

There was a fortnight before the next event on the calendar, the non-Championship Race of Champions at Brands Hatch. Before then, there was much work to do, because the cars had to be flown back to the UK and there was also the small matter of building up Emerson's new car, 72/7, with the target of running it at Brands. As was so often the case in a busy racing team, the build programme on 72/7 slipped behind schedule and it was the regular pairing of cars – 72/5 and 72/6 for Fittipaldi and Walker respectively - which were taken to the rolling Kent circuit. Fittipaldi had been testing his car at Jarama in the week leading up to Brands when a telephone call came through from Hethel, recalling the car. The car was on a plane

within the hour, just in time to make it back to Brands. At least there were no new-car sorting troubles to deal with, and Fittipaldi put his car on pole, emphasising that his form in South Africa had been no fluke. Walker was still struggling, qualifying on the fourth row, nearly two seconds slower than his team-mate.

In the race, Fittipaldi jumped straight into the lead, a position he held until the chequered flag. In the opening laps he pulled out quite a lead on his pursuers. By half-distance he had an advantage of 12 seconds and was able to cruise home to take a comfortable victory, the second of his Formula 1 career. Walker had a lonely race to eighth, the difference in pace of the two drivers illustrated by the fact

that he only just avoided being lapped by his team-mate after 40 laps of racing.

Although Fittipaldi had not beaten the likes of Stewart, who was absent from the race due to a dispute over starting money, the win at Brands Hatch was an excellent morale booster for a team which was used to winning but hadn't done so for a long time.

Nine days later, the teams reconvened at the Interlagos circuit in Brazil for what was, in effect, Fittipaldi's home 'Grand Prix', even though it was a non-Championship

Above Left: The 72 started off the 1972 season with the oil tank literally hanging off the back of the cars, helping give a pronounced rearward weight bias. These shots give a good view of the arrangements, as well as the ducting for the oil coolers and faired-in rear light (obligatory for that year), plus inboard rear brakes and surprisingly thin rear drive-shafts. **Above Right:** Texaco joined John Player as a sponsor of Team Lotus in 1972. The adaptation of the Texaco logo to conform with the black-and-gold livery of the tobacco brand was not well-received at the oil company's head office… Note ventilated discs and extinguisher mounted far forward in nose. Walker's office: The cockpit was best suited to those of a slight build and the Australian never felt truly comfortable in his car. Note warning to driver! **Left:** Peter Warr and Eddie Dennis wheel Fittipaldi's 72/5 – shorn of its nose-cone and rear wing so that it fits in the transporter – through the Brands Hatch paddock at the Race of Champions meeting.

'rehearsal' race in preparation for a fully-blown Championship round in 1973. Unusually, the race was to be held on a Thursday, with practice sessions taking place on the Tuesday and Wednesday. Again, there was a relatively small field, consisting of the two John Player Team Lotus entries, the works Brabhams, BRMs and Marches, plus several privately-entered and 'rent-a-drive' Marches.

Of most interest was the first appearance of Emerson's new car, 72/7. This was visually similar to the other two cars, with the exception of the new wing with deep side-plates and an aerodynamically shaped conical oil tank. This new set-up was tried in practice but in fact for the race, Emerson reverted to the standard arrangement. Meanwhile, Walker was in his regular car, 72/6.

After a slow start which saw Ronnie Peterson setting the pace in his March 721, Fittipaldi put his car on pole by more than two seconds from Carlos Reutemann with only five minutes of practice left. Walker qualified fifth, ahead of all the BRMs, albeit nearly five and a half seconds off the pace of his team-mate – not surprising really, given that Emerson knew the track like the back of his hand!

At the start, the field roared off towards the first bend in a cloud of dust and sand, which actually caused the retirement of three cars on the first lap with sticking throttle slides. Despite starting from pole, Fittipaldi was outdragged by brother Wilson in the Brabham BT34 and, unbeknown to his pit or legions of enthusiastic fans, he too was afflicted by sand in the throttle slides. Not wanting to stop so early in the race, the Brazilian gambled that the dust

and sand would gradually clear from the track and that the problem would eventually right itself if he kept going.

During the third lap, going into the slightly banked first left-hand corner, Emerson's throttle stuck open and he shot up the inside of his brother, forcing him virtually off the track in what was described in reports at the time – obviously oblivious to the cause – as 'a most unbrotherly manoeuvre'. Once in clear air, the Lotus's throttle slides

Above: Start of something: Fittipaldi's victory in the Race of Champions was the beginning of a rich vein of form. *Top Right:* Stevie May fits the distinctive slats to the rear wing of Walker's car. *Right:* Dave Walker, seen here at the Race of Champions, moved up to the Formula 1 team on a full-time basis in 1972.

began to clear and Emerson seemed set for a very popular victory when, with five of the 37 laps remaining, he spun wildly coming round the very fast-left hand bend leading on to the start/finish straight. Fortunately, he managed to skilfully avoid contact with the barriers and was able to engage second gear and drive slowly on into the pits and retirement.

It transpired that a lug in the bottom of the rear upright had come adrift, causing instantaneous and uncontrollable toe-in. It was of little consolation to the team that Walker came home in fifth, his best placing of the year so far. Fittipaldi's problem had cost the team £2,800 in prize money and was a major disappointment to both the driver and spectators, who had been confidently expecting a home win. Instead, victory went to an Argentinian, Carlos Reutemann!

A third successive non-Championship race took place just over three weeks after the Brazilian event, this being the GKN/Daily Express International Trophy meeting at Silverstone. Fittipaldi was in his new car, suitably repaired after its Interlagos mishap, while Walker was again in 72/6. On the first day of practice, the Brazilian set a blistering pace, equalling Stewart and Reggazoni's British Grand Prix pole times from the previous year. He was fastest in the Saturday session too, garnering the £100 prize for the day's quickest lap and underlining his superiority.

The pleasure gained from this pole was somewhat spoilt

for John Player Team Lotus when Walker crashed his car heavily. "I had a cracked front disc and they set off back to Hethel and brought one disc back, so I had one brand new disc and one well bedded-in disc. When I complained about it I was told, "No, no, it'll be alright, just do a dozen laps bedding it in gently and it'll be the same as the other one." So I did precisely that. It was getting towards the end of practice so I thought I'd better crank it up a little. Going into Club Corner, I went onto the brakes and, needless to

say, one of the front wheels locked up and I ended up putting my outside wheel in the rubble and the dust and it just understeered me into the bank. They weren't prepared to rebuild the broken car overnight. So I sat on the sidelines. It was disappointing because I probably could have finished in the first two or three, maybe even won that one, because I knew Silverstone pretty well and I'd had a lot of success there." Although Walker felt the car could have been repaired, the impact had in fact crumpled and

split the monocoque, putting it beyond repair at the track. It was a bitter blow for the Australian because he had already set a time good enough to put him on the third row and this was a track he was very familiar with from his Formula 3 days.

At the start, the BRMs of Gethin and Beltoise outdragged Fittipaldi, but he was past and into the lead after seven laps. However, the handling of his car was deteriorating and he was not getting away from his pursuers. A bolt in the rear suspension had come loose, allowing the top link to slip out from the radius arm and causing the car to slide around much more than normal. Mike Hailwood, who was having a storming drive in the Surtees, caught the Brazilian and passed him, only to retire soon after, with the result that Emerson slipped and slid to a lucky victory, finishing only 1.8 seconds ahead of Beltoise.

Opposite Page Top: At the International Trophy meeting, Silverstone, Peter Warr, Eddie Dennis and Chapman tend to Fittipaldi in the pit lane.
Opposite Page Bottom: Fittipaldi started from pole, the second successive race he had done so. **Left**: After his practice accident Walker was disappointed that his car could not be repaired in time to start the International Trophy, as he felt confident of a good result on a track he knew so well. **Above**: Fittipaldi's victory at Silverstone owed a lot to luck, as loose suspension forced him to slow and let Mike Hailwood (Surtees) past before the Englishman also faltered.

1st
Spanish
Grand Prix
John Player Special

Left: Fittipaldi's faultless drive in the Spanish Grand Prix was smooth, controlled and calculated and bore all the hallmarks of a potential World Champion. **Above:** In the early stages of the Spanish Grand Prix at Jarama, Fittipaldi leads Ickx, Hulme and Regazzoni.

Team morale was now at a high point after this run of good form, so it was the perfect time to return to the World Championship trail for Round 3, the Spanish Grand Prix at the tight and twisty Jarama circuit near Madrid. For this race, there were further small revisions to Fittipaldi's car, with the rear wing now mounted five inches further back on a sub-frame attached to the gearbox, while the front top wishbones had been revised to a simpler design. Walker's car for the weekend was Emerson's old mount, 72/5, since 72/6 could not be repaired in time following its Silverstone practice shunt. This car retained the old oil tank and wing positioning.

Practice took place over two days, with a two hour session on both Saturday and Sunday. The race was scheduled for the Monday, which was a bank holiday in Spain. On Saturday, Emerson topped the timesheets, while Walker languished down in 21st position on his first visit to the circuit. On the Sunday, Emerson managed to improve on his previous day's time but had an engine blow and slipped to third on the grid, on the outside of the front row. When his engine let go, Walker was summoned into the pits and made to give up his car for the Brazilian, which can't

have made the Australian feel particularly good as this was only the second Grand Prix of the year and it was already obvious where the team's loyalties lay.

In fairness, 72/5 was supposed to be Fittipaldi's spare car and was only being used by Walker because he had shunted his regular chassis, so it is easy to see why he was treated in this way. However, it did allow an interesting comparison of the driver's lap times in an identical car, with Fittipaldi setting a time in 11 laps that was 2.1 seconds faster than Walker had managed in 21...although it should be remembered that the Brazilian was also considerably more familiar with the circuit than his team-mate as a result of having raced at Jarama in Formula 2 and from having carried out Firestone tyre testing with the 72 earlier in the year. Walker's time was only good enough for the final row of the gird, so John Player Team Lotus had achieved the dubious distinction of qualifying one car on the front row and the other on the back row. Although the race was only 190 miles in length, the tight, twisty nature of the Jarama circuit meant that fuel consumption was heavier than normal and Lotus were concerned that the existing tank capacity would not be enough.

Before the race started, a fuel leak had been found in

Fittipaldi's car, as Eddie Dennis describes. 'One of the front fuel bag tanks leaked. He came into the pits and was sitting in a bath of petrol. This was in the warm up for the race. So we drained the front bag tanks and drilled holes in the bottom of the undertray to let the fuel out! He changed his overalls and we filled it as brim-full as we could get it.' Even before the off the Brazilian knew he was going to be marginal on fuel. The starter dropped the flag somewhat casually, which caught a lot of drivers off-guard, Fittipaldi included, so he came round in fifth place on the first lap.

His second lap was more dramatic, for his on-board fire extinguisher went off, fortunately doing nothing worse than making him feel a bit colder for a few seconds! On the third lap he slipped past Reggazoni's Ferrari and then, three laps later, he jumped two places in one fell swoop with a magnificent manoeuvre to pass Ickx and Hulme into the right-hander at the end of the start/finish straight. Reigning World Champion Jackie Stewart was in the lead by this stage but instead of the Scot's customary pattern of pulling away to win comfortably, he was actually being caught by the flying Lotus. On lap nine, Fittipaldi executed a clean pass on the Tyrrell at the end of the straight and immediately began to pull out a lead.

After 20 laps he led the Ferrari of Ickx, who had also managed to pass Stewart, by 6.3 seconds. Shortly after this, a brief rain shower saw the Belgian 'rainmeister' close right up on the 72, cutting the gap to one and a half seconds, but the rain passed, the track dried quickly in the wind and Emerson began to build his advantage once more. With 60 of the 90 laps gone, his advantage was up to nine seconds. However, by this stage he was already saving fuel by changing up early and cornering in a higher gear than normal, worried that he would run dry before the finish. His shrewd approach paid dividends, and he eventually took the flag 20 seconds clear of Ickx, who had been troubled by tyre problems.

Team-mate Walker made steady progress up the order, mainly as a result of other people's retirements but also through making up places by passing Pescarolo's March, Schenken's Surtees and Wilson Fittipaldi's Brabham, all the time following in the wheel-tracks of Carlos Pace's March. Eventually, Pace and Walker latched on to the battle for fourth between Andrea de Adamich's Surtees and Revson's McLaren. Just as it looked as if Walker might be able to make use of his experience of starting the last lap among a tight bunch of cars and emerging in front when it mattered, his car (which had been carrying the extra four gallons) coughed and spluttered and ran out of fuel. This was a cruel blow, because he had been seventh at the time and a points finish was a definite possibility. What this demonstrated was just how carefully Fittipaldi must have driven to have been

able to cover 90 laps on four gallons less than Walker, who ran out on his 88th lap. Or that Walker's engine was consuming more fuel...

In the Championship race, Emerson was now tied on 15 points with Denny Hulme at the head of the table, five ahead of Ickx and six clear of title-holder Stewart. It was early days, but at least he was at the sharp end of things. With two weeks before the Monaco Grand Prix, the mechanics had plenty of time to strip down and prepare the cars before making their way across the South Coast of France to the Principality. Unfortunately, this apparently simple task became somewhat more complicated when the John Player Team Lotus transporter was involved in an accident while driving through Spain and approaching Barcelona, when the driver of an oncoming car fell asleep and veered into its path. The impact severely damaged the cab and side panels but fortunately none of the mechanics were injured. Eddie Dennis had to stay behind to appear in court because the driver of the car was killed, while a local transport firm was hired to take the other mechanics, cars, spares and tools on to Monaco. As a result, they arrived considerably later than they had wanted.

Since they had come straight from Jarama without going back to Hethel, the cars were to the same specification that had been used in Spain. In practice, while Emerson stuck with his regular four-speed gearbox, Walker opted for a five-speed set-up with closer ratios. Having won the Formula 3 race at Monaco the previous year, he was

obviously looking forward to getting stuck in to a circuit he obviously felt very comfortable on. The first session on Thursday afternoon was shortened to only 50 minutes after a dispute between the teams and organisers concerning how many cars would be allowed to start the race. Fittipaldi was only sixth fastest, hampered by trying a new compound of Firestones which didn't work too well, while Walker, encouragingly, was eighth quickest, only half a second slower than the Brazilian.

The session held early on Friday morning turned out to be the decisive one, for the Saturday afternoon one was blighted by rain. Fittipaldi quickly showed that he was back on the pace and ended up setting the fastest time, and ultimately taking pole position. Although Walker knocked nearly a second off his Thursday time, he slipped down the order but still ended up 14th on the day, good enough for the seventh row, his best grid position of the year. The three fastest car/driver combinations on Friday had been Fittipaldi (Lotus), Ickx (Ferrari) and Reggazoni (Ferrari). Even the rain made no difference, with these three still out front, albeit Ickx pipping Reggazoni and Fittipaldi.

Race day dawned wet, and the rain wasn't just coming down steadily, it was torrential. At the start, the two cars on the second row (Reggazoni and Beltoise in the BRM) 'anticipated' the drop of the flag and burst through to pass Fittipaldi and Ickx before the first corner. However, on the fifth lap, Reggazoni overshot the new chicane on the approach to Tabac and Fittipaldi, using the Ferrari's red

Emerson. Just after the 50 lap mark, Reggazoni crashed too and the Lotus was up to fourth. This looked to be the best possible result, as Stewart was some way ahead but Lady Luck decided to smile on Emerson when the Tyrrell began to slow with water in the electrics and, on the 76th lap, the Lotus 72 snatched third place and four valuable points. Meanwhile Walker soldiered on, unhappy with the handling of his car, to finish a lowly 14th, five laps down on Beltoise, who had driven a magnificent race to score a well-earned victory. The result put Emerson on his own in the lead of the Championship, for Hulme had endured a miserable race to finish one place behind Walker. The Lotus driver's nearest challenger was now Ickx, who had driven a steady race to second behind Beltoise and was now three points behind Fittipaldi in the title standings.

Between Monaco and the next Grand Prix in Belgium, there was yet another non-Championship race, this one being the Rothmans Gold Cup at Oulton Park, now held on the end of May bank holiday. Two JPS Lotus 72s were entered for this race, these being 72/5 for Fittipaldi and the freshly rebuilt 72/6 for Walker. Fittipaldi's new car, 72/7 was back at Hethel being prepared for Belgium.

In practice, Emerson put his car on the outside of the front row, alongside pole-man Peter Gethin (BRM) and Denny Hulme (McLaren), while Walker was very competitive, only six-tenths behind his team-mate on the inside of the second row. Race day was overcast and spots of rain began to fall on the warm-up lap, prompting Fittipaldi to go out on intermediates. On the grid, he changed to slicks as all the other teams had opted for them but, with four minutes to go the JPTL mechanics put the intermediates back on, Emerson gambling on a bit of rain to liven things up. Unfortunately for him, the rain did not materialise and, as the only Formula 1 car not on slicks, he was at an immediate disadvantage. Consequently, Gethin and Hulme disappeared off into the distance, the Lotus inheriting second place when Gethin retired. Walker had another frustrating race, being forced to pit after only six of the scheduled 40 laps with a softening rear tyre and rejoining having lost a lap. Later on, just after half distance, he lost fourth gear and so coasted into the pits to retire.

light as a reference point in the spray, followed him, letting Ickx by. The Brazilian then ran a steady fourth until, troubled by oil on his visor, he overshot the chicane once again, this time letting Gethin and Stewart through. Fittipaldi's 1971 team-mate Reine Wisell, now driving for BRM had been laying a trail of oil down on the track from his engine, which finally blew on lap 17. The result of this was that the average lap time of the leading cars increased from around 1m 40s to nearly 2 minutes. Walker was the first to come across the oil, which made the track so bad that he thought something had broken on his car and came into the pits on lap 15 but was sent on his way again as nothing could be found. This was a shame as he had worked his way up to ninth place by this stage and a good result looked to be on the cards.

Fittipaldi ran in sixth place for around 10 laps until Gethin crashed, promoting the Lotus to fifth. On lap 36 out of 80, Beltoise, who was flying in the BRM, lapped

Opposite Page: Wet weather conditions in the Monaco Grand Prix saw Fittipaldi unable to capitalise on his pole position, the Brazilian coming home third. Above: Is it a boat, is it a plane? Walker splashes his way through the torrent at Monaco. Grip was so non-existent that he pitted, thinking there was something wrong with his car! Left: Fittipaldi gambled on intermediate tyres for the Rothmans Gold Cup at Oulton Park and finished a distant second.

For the Belgian Grand Prix, held at the featureless circuit of Nivelles, John Player Team Lotus was back to full strength, with 72/7 as Fittipaldi's race car and 72/5 as his spare, and 72/6 for Walker. The main change in specification was that 72/7 had a different rear wing with a shorter chord length. A Team Lotus drawing dated May 25th 1972 titled "Drawing for installation of F2 rear wing on 72/7" suggests that the wing had been cannibalised off a Formula Two Lotus and was adapted to be fitted to the 72. The revised wing was mounted on a new conical oil tank with the oil coolers slung on each side, as Geoff Aldridge, at that time a 22 year-old junior draughtsman on the design team, explains. 'In those days, you never knew what to do with the oil tank. They used to sit on top of the gearbox and they were pretty awful things. Martin drew an oil tank that actually provided the mounting for the trailing edge of the wing and it had stays on the front, so it was a three-point mounting'. The only change to the driver line-up was that a new, slim-line Dave Walker emerged, having lost 10lbs after a fitness course!

Emerson dominated practice, setting the fastest time in every session to secure pole position. He even had time to show Walker the way round the circuit after the Australian had got stuck at a particular lap-time, this enabled his team-mate to improve by more than half a second, which put him on the fifth row of the grid.

In the days before pole-men were able to select which side of the track they started from, Fittipaldi was forced to

Left: Crowded house. This pit shot taken in practice for the Belgian Grand Prix at Nivelles shows the team's three cars – from top to bottom 72/7, 72/5 and 72/6 – the first time that year the team managed to have a spare on hand. This is one of those shots where the more you look, the more you see: a relaxed looking Chapman in red shirt (top left) oversees operations. Dave Walker looks on rather impatiently as Rex Hart tightens a wheel nut on his car, while Stevie May wheels away the old tyres. Eddie Dennis and Steve Gooda are trying to get 72/5 out of the way while Trevor Seaman straps Fittipaldi into 72/7 and Jim Pickles inspects the rear of the car.
Bottom Left: Walker's 72/6 returned to the track for the Belgian Grand Prix after its Silverstone accident. Eddie Dennis leans into the cockpit while Steve Gooda changes a rear wheel and Stevie May checks the oil level.
Below: Those ain't no cowboys, they're Team Lotus! Even Chapman, always one with an eye for a good publicity opportunity, doesn't seem quite able to bring himself to wear a Texaco cowboy hat for this shot taken at the Belgian Grand Prix.

start from the right-hand side of the track, which happened to be the dirtiest as the cars ran on the left past the pits. Although his mechanics actually swept the track clean in front of his car, the Brazilian was still unable to match the start of fellow front-row man Reggazoni in the Ferrari. However, on the ninth lap, he found a way past and was never headed again, coming home 26.6 seconds clear of his nearest challenger, Francois Cevert in the only Tyrrell in the race. Jackie Stewart was a non-starter due to having

Italiana attracted something of a sparse entry of only eight Formula 1 cars, it being a long haul for the teams just for a minor event. This was particularly the case for John Player Team Lotus, who were still without their transporter following its accident in May. They had been forced to resort to a Will-Hire truck, which had engine trouble on the journey and would only do a maximum speed of 55mph downhill with the wind behind it!

The team entered one car and used it as an opportunity to try out one or two new ideas in competition without compromising their Championship challenge. The main changes concerned the wing, which was now positioned even further back than before, with just a single mounting point attaching to the top of the oil tank. This was effectively the beginning of the team's flexible or 'bungee' wing, as Geoff Aldridge explains. 'The derivation [of the previous three-point mounting arrangement] was to put a flexible mounting on top of the oil tank, which became the sole wing mounting. They were enormous rubber bushes and by enormous I would say two inches in diameter. I remember going up to Metallastic in Leicester to pick them up. The whole assembly was about 10 inches long, two inches diameter and with dog drives on the end. We had, effectively, a large diameter cross-tube which disappeared into the centre of the wing, so you couldn't see the cross-tube because that was inside the wing and it was simply a rubber bush and torsion.'

The effect of this modification was to enable the wing to reduce its angle of incidence (and therefore drag) at high speeds on the straights but revert to its normal position in the corners to provide downforce and drag when needed, according to Eddie Dennis. 'The rubber bush was pre-loaded and it would deflect down the straight and then come back up again for the slower corners' he recalls. The whole arrangement was a variation on the theme adopted

developed a stomach ulcer. Walker endured another eventful race, working his way up to 10th by lap 19 before he tangled with Andrea de Adamich's Surtees, which he was lapping. He lost several places but was up to 11th again when he was forced to pit for a new front tyre on lap 31. Seven laps later, he was in the pits again, asking if he should continue because he was worried about the oil pressure but he was sent on his way once more, eventually finishing 14th and last. Vic McCarthy remembers that there was an amusing explanation for the Australian being sent back into the fray. 'He came into the pits, saying he'd got no oil pressure. Rex [Hart] put his head in the cockpit and it turned out that the needle had fallen off the gauge!' The symmetry of Jarama practice (front row/back row) had been repeated in Belgium, with John Player Team Lotus topping and tailing the results, in first and last position.

Fittipaldi's dominant win further extended his

Championship lead over Hulme, who finished third, to nine points. Local hero Ickx, who had been lying second in the points standings, failed to finish.

Between races, works Formula 3 driver Tony Trimmer was brought in to do some aerodynamic and testing work that was deemed unnecessary for the regular drivers to attend. 'Most of the time I spent in the car was doing some test work at Hethel. I remember going round many, many times, doing aerodynamics and things like that, sticking bits of wool on the bodywork to see which way they blew in the wind. They don't do any of that these days, they have £2 million wind tunnels, don't they?'

The Dutch Grand Prix of 1972 was cancelled due to the Zandvoort circuit being pronounced unsafe for Formula 1 cars, so the gap in the calendar was filled by another non-Championship race, this time held at the Vallelunga circuit near Rome in Italy. The Gran Premio della Republica

Above: Vic McCarthy (left), Steve Gooda (right) and Eddie Dennis (squatting) work on Fittipaldi's 72/7 prior to the Belgian Grand Prix.
Right: These two shots show the subtle differences between the cars of Fittipaldi (72/7, right) and Walker (72/6, left). Fittipaldi's has the new conical oil tank and shorter chord rear wing, with the oil tank providing the rearward mounting point for the wing. Fittipaldi's rear wing is positioned considerably further back than the one on Walker's car, which still has the old style oil tank and wing arrangement.

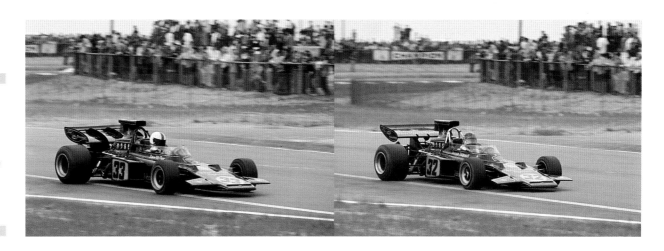

mountains just to the west of the city. Once again, Fittipaldi had the choice of his regular race car, 72/7 or the spare 72/5, while Walker was in his usual car, 72/6. The Brazilian's spare car was again fitted with the flexible wing arrangement as tried at Vallelunga, while the race car was to the same basic specification as it was at Nivelles. The only change was that the oil cooler arrangements had been tidied up with a single large cooler positioned behind the conical tank under the rear wing and two narrow scoops either side of the tank to help channel air to it.

Neither driver had competed at Clermont-Ferrand, so they were at something of a disadvantage compared to the likes of Stewart (back behind the wheel after his enforced break), Ickx, Hulme and Amon who knew their way around the circuit very well. Another problem for the Brazilian was that he had a bout of 'flu, which made him feel decidedly second-hand for much of the weekend. A third 72 was entered under the Lucky Strike Racing banner for the South African Champion Dave Charlton, who had secured additional sponsorship from Sasol, the fuel company, South African Airways, Firestone, Champion and Wynn's to fund a three-race trip to Europe. This chassis 72/3, had been updated at Hethel to the same specification as the works cars, prior to travelling to France.

In practice, the drivers spent the first session becoming accustomed to the circuit, with Walker overcooking it a bit and smashing the left rear wheel, shredding the tyre and knocking off an oil cooler. Emerson ended up way down in 11th, while Walker was even further back. In the first of the two one-hour Saturday sessions, the Brazilian moved up to

by Chapman in 1968 and 1969 with the high-winged Lotus 49Bs, where the wing would be feathered by a foot pedal and then would return to a high-downforce setting for corners. Dennis recalls that it was almost impossible to move but that the wing still provided useful download, even in its feathered position. 'You could bounce on it all you liked with a man's weight, you wouldn't budge it but down the straight the Old Man reckoned it had about 400lbs download'.

Since the abolition of high wings mid-way through the 1969 season, moveable aerodynamic devices had been prohibited by the rules. This was just another example of Chapman challenging the boundaries, by adopting a creative interpretation of the rules. Ironically, a furore blew up in the late 1990s when several Formula 1 teams began experimenting with the same idea of flexible wing mountings in pre-season testing and they were eventually ruled to be illegal. The difference was that Chapman came up with the idea 30 years before Ferrari and McLaren, illustrating how far ahead of his time the Lotus boss was.

Using the new wing set-up in the Saturday practice session at Vallelunga, Fittipaldi found an improvement of nearly a second over his previous day's time and ended up comfortably quickest, nearly a second faster than his

nearest challenger, Howden Ganley in the BRM. In the race, Fittipaldi jumped straight into the lead and, despite losing an end-plate and part of the Gurney-flap off his rear wing on only the fifth of the 80 laps, he continued to extend his advantage. He lost the other end plate and the rest of the Gurney flap at around half distance but this didn't seem to slow him noticeably. Towards the end of the race he eased off slightly, having already set the fastest lap, as there was a possibility that he might again be marginal on fuel, but he was fine and coasted home 32.8 seconds clear of second man, Andrea de Adamich in the Surtees.

A fortnight later, after some tyre-testing at the Österreichring on the way home from Vallelunga, the teams re-assembled for Round 6 of the World Championship, the French Grand Prix. After a hiatus of two years, the race returned to the picturesque and rolling Circuit de Charade near Clermont-Ferrand, the track being based entirely on public roads around the

1st
**French
Grand Prix**
John Player Special

First Person

Dave Walker on Colin Chapman

"I had very little to do with Colin. He was not that much involved, he handed the reins over to Peter Warr. Colin was very heavily involved with Moonraker Yachts and that was taking up a lot of his time and whatever other pressures he had on him. So he wasn't really around a lot. He turned up at the race meetings and that was about all you saw of him. I never talked to him in between races, never had any meetings or discussions with him, he was almost a non-identity to some extent."

Opposite Page Top: The Gran Premio Republica Italiana saw the first appearance of the flexible 'bungee wing' mounting. Unfortunately, the wing began to disintegrate during the race, although this didn't stop Fittipaldi from taking victory, albeit from rather weak opposition.
Opposite Page Bottom: The French Grand Prix at Clermont-Ferrand saw the return of 72/3 as Dave Charlton embarked on a three-race tour of Europe. **Left:** Fittipaldi struggled to get the 72 to work at Clermont-Ferrand and not even the 'bungee wing' could help him beat Stewart in the Tyrrell, even though the team had printed the victory stickers!

a more competitive fifth-fastest, while Walker's run of bad luck continued with an engine failure. For final practice, the flexible wing was fitted to Emerson's race car but he was forced to switch back to the spare after only doing one lap, due to low oil pressure. This also put paid to Walker's chances of improving, since there was no time to change the engine in his car and he had been hoping to have a run in Emerson's spare. A marginal improvement of only 0.1 seconds meant that Emerson slipped down the starting order, ending the day in an unaccustomed seventh. This left him eighth on the grid, since his position was determined by his best time – done in the first Saturday session - in his race car.

Charlton's practice was interrupted by a constant run of niggling minor problems and he was never able to get on the pace, managing a best time nearly six seconds slower than the final qualifier. It later transpired that the plucky South African had been suffering from a middle ear infection, which could only have added to the disorientating nature of the French circuit.

An untimed practice session on race-day resulted in Fittipaldi feeling much more confident about his car and his prospects, with a fresh engine and his 'secret weapon', the flexible wing, fitted to his car. When the flag dropped, Fittipaldi got the better of his fellow fourth-row man, Cevert in the Tyrrell, but was passed by Mike Hailwood's Surtees. Clermont-Ferrand is not the easiest circuit in the world on which to pass, and it was not until the third lap that Emerson found a way through. On the next tour, he was past his eternal nemesis from 1971, Tim Schenken, in another Surtees and a lap later he overtook the BRM of Helmut Marko to capture fifth place. He maintained this position, behind the Ferrari of Jacky Ickx, for many laps until, at just over half distance, leader Chris Amon was forced to pit with a puncture to the left-front tyre of his Matra. Three laps later, the retirement of second-placed man Denny Hulme promoted the Lotus to third and then another retirement, this time of Ickx, lifted Emerson into second with less than 10 laps to go, a position he held until the chequered flag.

Team-mate Walker had another frustrating race, reflecting the fact that he was short of practice and experience of the challenging circuit, as well as suffering from a down-on-power engine. 'There was a very fast section and that was one of the races I had one of the older engines in and people were just passing me left, right and centre as I went along the straight and then I'd clamber all over them through the twisty parts of the circuit.' A crown wheel and pinion failure while running in a lowly fourteenth, one lap down and with three laps to go just about summed up his weekend. 'I lost fourth gear originally, then third gear went and eventually I retired. I got accused of being heavy on gearboxes when I never broke a gearbox in Formula 3 in my life!'

It hadn't been an inspired drive by Fittipaldi and he had finished almost half a minute behind the winning Tyrrell of Jackie Stewart, but it gave the Brazilian a further six valuable World Championship points. He now led his closest rival, Stewart, by 13 points, a decisive advantage after six races.

CHAPTER 11 HOLDING IT TOGETHER

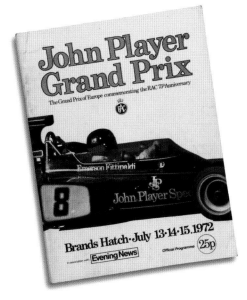

The next race was the 'home' event for both Team Lotus and sponsor John Player, the British Grand Prix at Brands Hatch. The race was even renamed the John Player Grand Prix in deference to its sponsor. Originally, the intention had been to field three JPS Lotus 72s, with Tony Trimmer being the driver of the extra entry as a reward for his testing duties. However, like many of the best laid plans, it did not come to fruition. The reason given was a shortage of engines, but there may also have been an element of the team deciding that at such a crucial stage of the Championship all their efforts should be focused on their existing cars and drivers, particularly Fittipaldi.

The team were at full-strength, with three cars once again. Emerson had his regular 72/7, with 72/5 as a spare. The latter had been updated to the new specification with the conical oil tank, single oil cooler and smaller aerofoil layout of 72/7. However, as Geoff Aldridge recalls, both cars had gained additional support for the wings, in an effort to prevent rival teams becoming suspicious about the mounting arrangements. 'We grew some struts from the trailing edge back down to the gearbox. That was yet another cheat because they were telescopic struts!' The Team Lotus drawing for this modification, simply titled "Drawing for adjustable link, rubber mounted wing" is dated 12th July, the Wednesday prior to the Grand Prix (which took place on a Saturday) suggesting it was something of a last-minute decision to bolster up the mounting! The effect of their addition was to give the

impression that the wing was fixed in one position but because they were telescopic they still allowed the wing to feather.

Dave Walker was at the wheel of his regular car, 72/6. It is perhaps illustrative of the effort being put into Fittipaldi's Championship push that his car still retained the old oil tank and wing mounting arrangements last used by Fittipaldi at the Gold Cup in May. As at Clermont-Ferrand, Dave Charlton had entered his privately owned, Lucky Strike-sponsored 72/3 and was hoping that this time he might qualify.

Using 72/5, Emerson immediately set the pace, recording the fastest lap in the first of the two practice sessions on Thursday to secure 100 bottles of Champagne, courtesy of the Evening News. He had started the session in his race car but had been forced to switch when cracks

were found in his rear suspension. It transpired that some distance pieces had been added above the shock absorber bump rubbers to try and help with the problem of bottoming on the bumpy Kent circuit and this had placed too much strain on the frames, which the dampers were fixed to, causing them to crack. The same problem was found on Walker's car, meaning that some frantic stripping and re-welding had to be done in the paddock before the cars could practice again. In addition, Fittipaldi's car had developed a leak in the internal piping of the oil tank and this was causing the breather catch-tank to pressurise.

For the second session, Emerson was back in his race car and managed to match the time he had set earlier with the spare, although he was half a second slower than pace-setter Jackie Stewart, in the new Tyrrell. During the first session on Friday, the Brazilian concentrated on full-tank

Above & Right: Fittipaldi tightened his grip on the Championship with victory in the British Grand Prix. It was a good day for Team Lotus – a win on home ground and in an event sponsored by John Player.

LOTUS 72

runs to achieve a perfect race set-up. However, for final practice, he was sent out in qualifying trim, with only five gallons of fuel on board. The initial set of tyres didn't feel right, so Fittipaldi pitted and a set was taken off Walker's car. The times he recorded were, according to the Team Lotus stopwatches, well inside Ickx's pole but eventually Emerson was given a time some four-tenths slower that would put him on the outside of the grid. As this was considered to be a better starting position than pole on the sloping start/finish straight at Brands, the team were very satisfied and did not contest the times they had been allocated. Walker found it very difficult to make any headway and it was only in the final session that he made a notable improvement. This gave him a time 1.8 seconds slower than his team-mate, only good enough for the eighth row. Charlton managed to up his game sufficiently to qualify on the penultimate row of the grid, his first Grand Prix start of the year.

When the flag dropped, Fittipaldi didn't get away as cleanly as he had hoped, and he slotted in behind the sleek red Ferrari of Ickx in the run up to Druids hairpin. However, almost immediately, he could see that the Ferrari was trailing a small amount of oil. Figuring that this could not last, he settled in to bide his time. Meanwhile, Stewart, who had been held up in the early laps, was relentlessly closing in on the leading duo. At around one-third distance he passed Fittipaldi when the Brazilian had a bit of a moment at Druids and ran wide. However, only 11 laps later he returned the favour when Stewart did the same thing and was back up to second place. At the two-thirds mark the inevitable eventually happened and Ickx dived into the pits to retire with no oil pressure.

Despite relentless pressure from Stewart, Fittipaldi reeled off the remaining laps in calm, confident fashion to take his third Grand Prix win of the season. That luck was once again on his side was revealed by the fact that his car had a puncture on the slowing down lap!

In contrast to the steadfast reliability of Fittipaldi's 72, the two other Lotus runners had poor races. Walker was in the pits after only four laps with fuel pressure problems, losing four minutes in the process. 'I had a fuel line crack behind me, spraying me in fuel and stuff and I pulled into the pits and spent some time there.' Eventually he rejoined and actually ran in close company with the leaders when they lapped him before dropping back. 'They repaired it and I went back out again and put up a fairly competitive lap time. I seem to remember somebody saying that I did the fourth- or fifth-fastest lap of the race.' He later retired

with a broken radius rod, caused by a failure in a shock absorber mounting. After making a reasonable start, Charlton slipped back down the order and was running last of the unlapped runners for a long time. Eventually, he pulled off the bottom straight and took the short-cut into the pits to retire, apparently unable to find any gears but it later transpired that he had again been suffering from sickness from the undulations of the circuit.

Emerson's World Championship points tally now stood at 43, giving him a 16-point lead over Stewart. Although it was still a little early to think about these things, the Championship title was looking very much a possibility if the team could maintain its fantastic reliability record – for the lead car at least!

The Grand Prix circus moved on to Germany and the daunting Nürburgring which, despite its reprofiling in

Top Left: Charlton qualified for the British Grand Prix in 72/3 but retired with gear selection problems. **Top Middle & Right:** These shots again illustrate the difference in the specification of the cars of Fittipaldi and Walker. The rear wing is visibly further back on Fittipaldi's car, which sports the new conical oil tank and flexible rear wing mounting. **Right:** Fittipaldi waits patiently as Eddie Dennis and Jim Pickles work on his car during practice for the John Player Grand Prix.

caused by a short, sharp rain shower made him spin off on the approach to Aremberg, resulting in damage to the left rear corner. 'Merzario in the Ferrari lost it coming out under the bridge there and rolled and smashed it to pieces. I guess he was probably the first to hit the few sprinkles of rain and the flags weren't out. Then I came around and there were still no flags and I lost it on the left-hander [Schwedenkreuz], did a few 360s and eventually parked it against the barrier with not a significant amount of damage.' Charlton also had a huge slide at the same spot but was fortunate enough to escape unscathed.

Walker sat out the second Friday afternoon session while his car was being repaired. Meanwhile, Emerson lopped a full seven seconds off his best time to go third-quickest, although his time in the T-car was 25 seconds slower. Charlton was battling against sickness induced by the G-forces and constant undulations of the circuit and was barely able to break through the 8 minute barrier, compared to Ickx's best time of 7m 10s.

On Saturday, Emerson signalled his intent by going almost as fast as the day before in the T-car when he was

Left: Thumbs up! A delighted Fittipaldi salutes the crowd having won the British Grand Prix, flanked by his wife Maria-Helena (left, in green jacket and hat) and Colin Chapman (right). Also visible are Peter Warr (far left) and mechanic Stevie May (far right). *Below:* The crew: the John Player Team Lotus mechanics take a rare break to pose for a photo. Back row from left – Jim Pickles, Rex Hart. Front row from left – Vic McCarthy, Stevie May, Steve Gooda. *Bottom:* Charlton again suffered from sickness induced by the undulations of the Nürburgring and was forced to retire from the German Grand Prix.

1971, still represented a considerable challenge to any driver. Fittipaldi's main problem was that he was not as familiar with the track as his closest rivals in the Championship chase, Stewart, Hulme and Hill. With that in mind, it was decided to take Emerson, the spare car 72/5, and a couple of mechanics to the Eifel mountains a week before the race, in order to enable him to fully familiarise himself with the terrain prior to the start of official practice on Friday. However, this plan did not work out because he only managed two laps in the dry on the Monday before it started raining and then on the Tuesday the gearbox pinion bearing failed. Usually, this would be a relatively straightforward job but the bearing was new, one of a special batch a sixteenth of an inch wider than standard, so the box wouldn't go back together again. So, it was not until the first session on Friday that Emerson put in any more serious lappery.

Walker was even less prepared than his team-mate. 'I had never seen the place in my life. It's hairy enough at the best of times but to have to jump into a Formula 1 car and drive round there for the first time was something else!'

Fittipaldi had his usual car, 72/7, with 72/5 as the spare, while Walker was in his trusty 72/6. The only changes were the introduction of smaller adjustable tabs on the front spoilers and revised top shock absorber mountings following the failures experienced at Brands, while Emerson's spare car was fitted with cross-drilled brake discs as opposed to the regular ventilated ones. Once again, a third car was entered for the race, this being Charlton's 72/3.

In first practice, Emerson drove both his cars, setting a faster time in 72/7, but some four seconds slower than Jackie Stewart, while Walker was still playing himself in on his first visit to the circuit when a damp patch on the track

bedding in brakes. Reverting to his race car saw a further five seconds sliced off his lap-time, putting him in an elite group of only three drivers who had lapped in less than 7m 10s – Ickx, Stewart and Fittipaldi. Walker rejoined the fray for the final session but was never in the hunt and ended up almost 20 seconds slower than his team-mate. Charlton continued to suffer from sickness but at least managed to improve his time by more than 25 seconds and was only about five seconds slower than Walker. Initially, Charlton was one of two drivers deemed to have not qualified, but after pleading with the organisers, they were allowed to compete without receiving any start money.

At the start, Fittipaldi got away well but was forced to ease off to avoid an unnecessary coming-together at the first corner. The result was that both Peterson and Reggazoni slipped by, so that at the end of the first lap the order was Ickx, Peterson, Reggazoni, and Fittipaldi. At the other end of the field, Charlton had made a good start and came round one place ahead of Walker. On the second lap, Fittipaldi achieved the seemingly impossible and managed to pass the Ferrari of Reggazoni. Three laps later, he was past Peterson's flying March but by this time Ickx was already long gone, some 15 seconds ahead of the Lotus on the road. It looked as if second – and six very valuable points - was the best Emerson could hope for.

However, everything went wrong on the 11th lap. Before half-distance, the 72 had already begun to jump out of third and top gears. As Fittipaldi had left the start/finish area to start his 10th lap, a mechanic had noticed a tell-tale haze of blue smoke coming from the car. Sure enough, when it returned at the end of that tour, it had escalated into a billowing cloud of smoke and, shortly after crossing the finish line and rounding the South Curve, the gearbox failed and the car briefly caught fire. The Brazilian hopped out quickly and the blaze was soon extinguished. The problem had been a cracked gearbox casing, which had caused loss of oil, the gearbox to seize and the fire to break out. The other two Lotus fared no better, Charlton having to pull out sick after five laps and Walker retiring just before the halfway mark with a split oil tank. Emerson now had to sit in the pits and contemplate the prospect of Stewart, his closest title rival, clawing back some points on him.

It was not to be, for the Gods were again looking after Fittipaldi, courtesy of the swarthy Swiss, Clay Reggazoni. He and Stewart had been locked in a near race-long tussle for second place, which climaxed with the two cars having a coming-together at Hocheichen on the final lap. This left a seething Stewart up against the barriers and out of the race, unable to reduce the points deficit on his young Brazilian rival. So Fittipaldi retained his 16 point advantage over the Scot, while Ickx moved up to third place, two points adrift, with Hulme fourth, a further four points back.

A fortnight later, the Österreichring played host to the third Austrian Grand Prix. This purpose-built circuit, set in the hills above Zeltweg, was a high-speed blast, which had in previous years tended to favour the more powerful 12-cylinder Ferrari, BRM and Matra engines. Fittipaldi arrived in Austria early, well prepared and in a strong position. If Stewart or Ickx were going to have any chance of claiming the Championship title, then they were going to have to start winning and pushing the young Brazilian back down the order.

Fittipaldi's spare car, 72/5, was the first to arrive with several mechanics and was testing on the Thursday, the day before official practice began. A new engine cowling which was intended to deflect air down towards the rear oil cooler was being tried but the results proved inconclusive. Walker had his regular car, which had been updated to the single rear oil cooler/aerodynamic oil tank specification.

Emerson spent the first session swapping between his race car and the spare. He was already familiar with the circuit, having been there in June for Firestone tyre testing. Therefore it was no surprise that he was immediately on the pace, setting a time in the spare car that was ultimately good enough for pole position. Somehow, his race car, complete with new gearbox after its Nürburgring conflagration, didn't quite seem right, and he was unable to get closer than 1.6s to the time he set in the spare. Poor Walker, using an early 9 series engine due to a shortage of DFVs, was well back, his best time being some three and a half seconds off Emerson's pace.

First Person

Emerson Fittipaldi on Peter Warr

"He was one of the best team managers I ever worked with. He was a great guy, extremely efficient and - when Colin allowed him to - he would run the team in a very professional way. But Colin was the Maestro, sometimes he'd come in and take over everything, and that was typical of his personality. Peter was a very strong personality as well. To succeed in racing you have to be. I did a lot of testing with Peter and he was very methodical. I liked to test with him because he did his homework the way I like to, phase to phase not jumping around. Sometimes it is so easy to get lost in racing, when you start jumping from different set-ups. Colin could solve an emergency, quickly but Peter was more the day-to-day development guy."

Saturday's session took place in the height of the afternoon heat, and many of the top runners found it difficult to improve on their times from the day before. Emerson was quick in both his cars, being slightly faster in 72/7 (for second-best time of the session) but still not as fast as he had gone in 72/5 on Friday. Meanwhile, Walker - still struggling with his old engine – managed a small improvement but this was good enough only for the tenth row.

After much deliberation, the decision was taken to race the spare car. The night before the race, 72/5 was stripped down to its bare tub and then thoroughly rebuilt by its four mechanics, Eddie Dennis, Steve Gooda, Jim Pickles and Trevor Seaman. The team were so confident of their prospects that they didn't bother participating in the race-morning untimed session. The only other change was the

decision of Colin Chapman, after much pleading on the part of the Australian, to put a 12 series DFV in Walker's car. However, as this had been the unit used by Fittipaldi at the German Grand Prix, it had plenty of miles on it already, so no one in the team was overly optimistic that it would last to the finish of a 200-mile flat-out blast.

Race day, just like both practice days, dawned hot and dry and the crowds flocked into the circuit, with well over 100,000 people basking in the sunshine. The flag was dropped so quickly that it caught the front-row men off guard and it was the fast-starting Stewart – no doubt desperate not to get stuck behind Reggazoni again – who burst through from the second row to grab the lead. At the end of the first lap, he came through ahead of the Ferrari and Fittipaldi's Lotus, while Walker had made a tremendous start with his 12-series DFV and had passed Pace, Stommelen and Gethin already.

On the fifth lap, Fittipaldi found a way around Reggazoni and set off in pursuit of Stewart. Walker lost a place to Gethin for a couple of laps but managed to re-pass him on lap seven and was running in 16th place, when a cloud of smoke from his engine signalled the end of his race. Unfortunately this occurred on the far side of the circuit, leaving him a long walk back to the pits. His mechanic Stevie May remembers the occasion well. 'He came back and said, "I had an engine problem, I think I just caught it". Rex [Hart] and I went out to sit with the car so that bits didn't get pinched from it. And as we walked there, we could see this oil slick about a quarter of a mile long, bits of piston and engine, all over the track! And I thought,

yeah, right, you just caught it, didn't you?' For the next twenty or so laps, Fittipaldi closed in on Stewart and then waited for the right moment to pounce. It was a tremendous battle of wits and skill: two drivers obviously right at the top of their game, with nothing less than the Championship at stake. If Fittipaldi were to pass Stewart and win, it would virtually spell the end of the Tyrrell driver's title aspirations.

On lap 24 of 54, the black-and-gold Lotus dived up the inside of the blue Tyrrell at the Bosch Curve around half-way round the circuit and was through. It soon became clear that the slowing pace of Stewart was not down to any canny tactics at all – his car was handling very oddly, as if something was not quite right with the suspension and three laps later Denny Hulme in his McLaren M19C passed the Tyrrell to move up into second.

The Yardley-liveried car closed in steadily on the Lotus but was unable to find a way past. The McLaren was quicker round the corners but the Lotus had the edge on

Opposite Page Top Left: Up in smoke: Fittipaldi's hopes of a good finish in the German Grand Prix disappeared when his car caught fire behind the pits. Fortunately, the blaze was extinguished quickly and neither driver nor car were harmed. **Opposite Page Top Right:** Walker, seen here rounding the Karussell, retired from the German Grand Prix with a split oil tank. **Above:** Fittipaldi ran in second prior to his retirement. Luckily, his closest rival Jackie Stewart did not finish either, leaving the Brazilian's lead in the title race unchanged.

straight-line speed. Although Hulme got almost alongside Fittipaldi at one stage, the Brazilian remained calm and reeled off the remaining laps to take victory, punching the air with delight as he crossed the line.

An indication of the extent of the team's confidence in car and driver was given by Peter Warr after the race, as Rex Hart explains. 'He actually had the sticker printed for coming 1st in Austria and as soon as the car came in, he stuck it on to the back of the wing!' As Jim Pickles explains, this confidence came from the fact that Fittipaldi, the Lotus 72 and the mechanics were all gelling. 'Emerson was growing more comfortable with the car and we could interpret what he wanted, understand what he was asking for. I think we felt confident with the car as well, and conversant with it. You could put your finger on it instantly if there was something amiss and go straight to it. Also, while the 72 may have been a little bit on the difficult side to work on, we knew it so well that we could do everything almost blindfolded.'

Fittipaldi's drive had more or less assured him of the World Championship title, for Stewart's challenge had faded away and he eventually finished a disconsolate seventh. With Ickx retiring, Fittipaldi now led Stewart and Hulme by a clear 25 points with three races remaining. This meant that one of these two had to win each of those races, with Fittipaldi finishing no higher than fourth in any of them – an unlikely scenario given the form and reliability of the Lotus so far in the season.

It was at this meeting that a rival team finally rumbled the 'bungee wing'. Eddie Dennis remembers the moment well. 'Denny Hulme was following Emerson [in his pursuit of the Brazilian towards the end of the race] and he was noticing that, as he went down the straight, his head appeared above the wing. He could see his helmet coming into view and yet on the rest of the circuit he couldn't see it. Alistair Caldwell [McLaren Chief Mechanic] came round the back of the car and said "What the hell's going on here? There's something funny going on!" We had some little pip pins we used to put in the [telescopic] struts that supported the wing and at the start of the race, we'd pull the pins out, so the wing could then operate on its own. But what we didn't realise was that it gave you an inch or so of wear mark on the strut where we'd had them painted. He'd spotted the movement there and in the end we had to take it off. But that was just one of the Old Man's innovations. It took a long while before people realised.'

Before the serious business of trying to wrap up the World Championship, there was the slightly more frivolous, if no less financially rewarding, issue of the Rothmans 50,000 race. This event, which would take place over a distance of 312 miles (therefore about 50% longer than the average Grand Prix) had been devised by John Webb, boss of the Motor Circuit Developments group which owned Brands Hatch, Oulton Park and Snetterton. It was to be run as an allcomers

event to Formula Libre rules, with a huge £50,000+ prize fund (hence the name of the race) to be spread among the participants.

The week before the race, a story ran in the motorsports press claiming that Colin Chapman had signed an option to secure Ronnie Peterson's services for the 1973 season. On the day of the Rothmans 50,000, this was confirmed by John Player Team Lotus, who announced that the talented and rapid Swede had signed to drive for the team in 1973 and 1974 as an equal number one with Emerson Fittipaldi. The rationale for the move was quite simple, as Peter Warr explains. 'We'd got fed up with not producing any results with the second car. What we wanted were a few 1-2s and points in the Constructors' Championship. Also, we reasoned that, if one car didn't win, the other one would.' Fittipaldi was also pleased at the prospect of having a team-mate who he felt he would get along well with, and who would push him more. 'I was very pleased about Ronnie because he was my best friend since arriving in Europe in 1969. We had a great relationship, my wife and Barbro Peterson were very good friends and I knew we would make a very strong team.'

Only one car was entered by Lotus, for Fittipaldi to

John Player Team Lotus announced that the Swede Ronnie Peterson had signed

Right: Aided by the 'bungee wing' Fittipaldi was able to fend off Denny Hulme's McLaren in the final laps of the Austrian Grand Prix.
Opposite Page Top: Fittipaldi flashes a smile to his wife Maria-Helena after winning the Rothmans 50,000 race at Brands Hatch. The auxiliary fuel tank required for the 312-mile race is just visible behind the driver's head.
Opposite Page Bottom: John Player-sponsored Team Lotus took great pleasure in taking money off a rival tobacco company when Fittipaldi won the Rothmans 50,000.

drive. Because the race was sponsored by rival cigarette brand Rothmans, a decision had been taken to respray his spare car, 72/5, in the green and yellow colours of Café do Brasil. However, a late change of heart by John Player meant a quick respray was required and the car appeared for practice in its usual black and gold JPS livery. The only change to its specification was the addition of an extra three-gallon fuel tank fitted behind the roll-over bar, so that it could avoid the need for a refuelling stop during the race.

The rest of the entry was very disappointing. The organisers had hoped that the size of the prize fund would have tempted Can-Am, Interserie and USAC cars and certainly more Formula 1 cars than turned out, with second-string entries from McLaren and BRM

and no cars from the likes of Ferrari, Tyrrell, Brabham and Matra. Although the field was large, it consisted primarily of Formula 2 and Formula 5000 cars plus a sprinkling of 2-litre sports cars of varying capabilities.

Emerson was on top form right from the start, having already won two races at the Kent circuit that year. He was fastest in every practice session, securing pole position by a margin of nearly one second. The beginning of the race was unusual in that it was a rolling start rather than the more usual standing start but still Fittipaldi was able to outdrag his fellow front-row man, Brian Redman, into Paddock Bend. In fact, this was probably the most exciting part of what was otherwise a dull and dreary contest, which was too long considering the sparseness of the entry. The Brazilian led from start to finish, with Redman being the only other finisher on the same lap as the Lotus. Fittipaldi also set the race's fastest lap. What a great way to prepare himself for the biggest race of his life – the Italian Grand Prix – which was due to take place in less than two weeks.

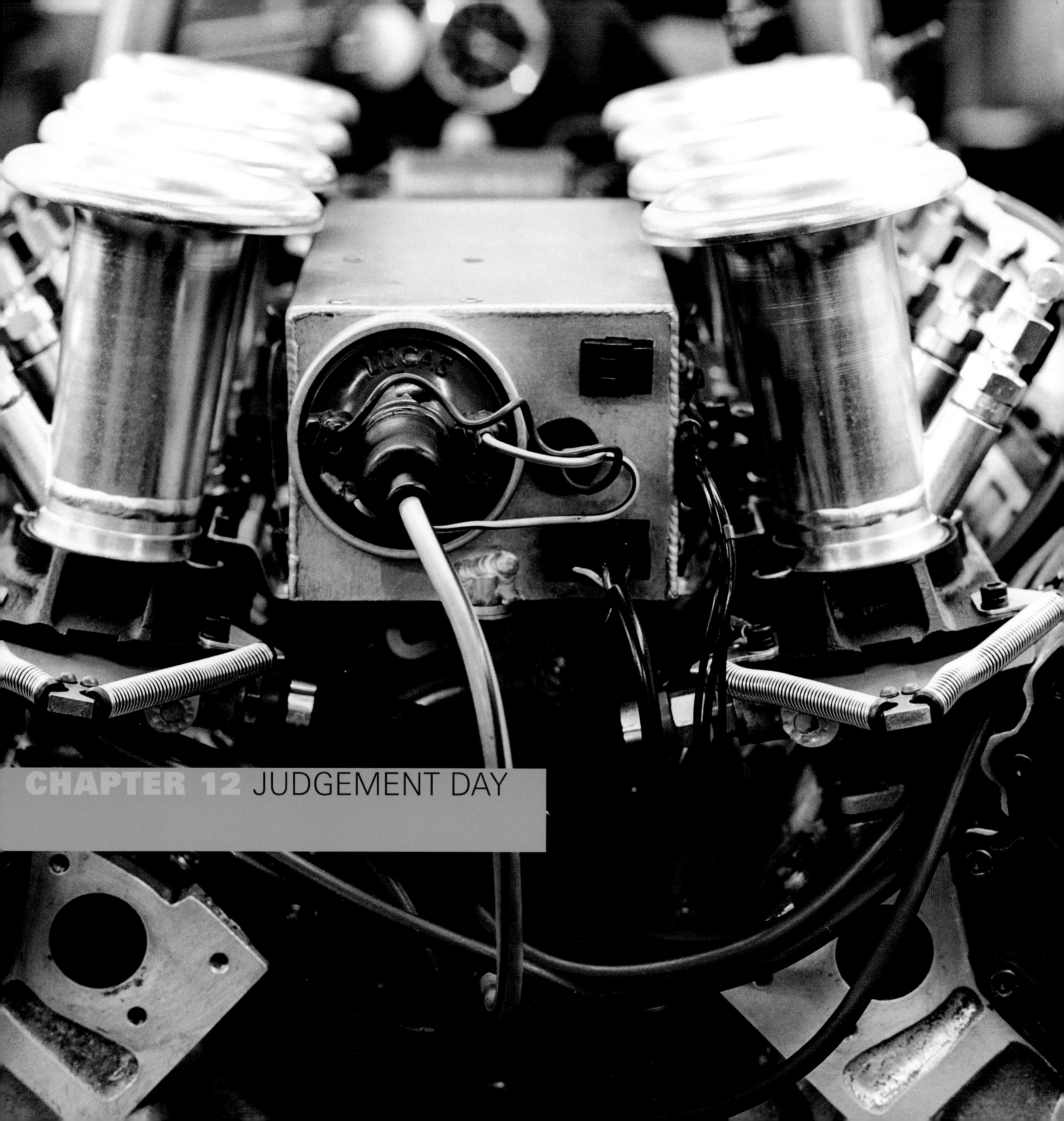

CHAPTER 12 JUDGEMENT DAY

Despite Fittipaldi's strong position in the World Championship standings, development work was obviously still continuing on the 72, illustrated by a drawing, dated August 20th 1972, for a full-width front nose rather than its distinctive chisel-shaped one. Geoff Aldridge recalls that this was just part of the normal process of exploring all avenues. 'It was purely about trying to find something on the aerodynamic front. I can't say that I'm aware of there being a particular problem. I know that there was much discussion as to whether you should go full-width or not in the same way as there was about airboxes and whether you should have tall ones or big ones or small ones.' That the car never ran with such a nose indicates that the team concluded there was no major benefit to be had over their existing arrangements – something which fans of the clean lines of the 72 will probably be thankful for.

There had been much discussion and speculation within the motorsport press as to whether Team Lotus would field any entries in the Italian race, for Chapman feared that his cars might be confiscated and he might even be arrested in connection with the ongoing investigations surrounding Jochen Rindt's death at Monza in 1970. However, the Italian Grand Prix organisers obtained a categorical assurance from the relevant authorities that nothing like this would happen and that he was more than welcome to enter the event.

Nevertheless, Chapman was not prepared to take unnecessary risks, so he entered just a single car, 72/7, for Fittipaldi, under the World Wide Racing banner he had used 12 months before when he ran the Brazilian in the turbine. Dave Walker was rested for this meeting, while Emerson's spare car, 72/5, was taken down in the team's Formula 2 transporter and left just across the Italian/French border, at Chamonix, in case of emergency. This turned out to be an astute move on the part of the Lotus boss.

Since the accident on the way to Monaco from the Spanish Grand Prix, which had destroyed the team's regular transporter, Team Lotus had been using an old Bedford borrowed from Tim Parnell. On the Tuesday before the Monza race, the team had their second big transporter crash of the season, an incident which might have seen Fittipaldi's Championship hopes destroyed had it not been for the forward thinking of Colin Chapman. Eddie Dennis remembers it well. 'We'd all travelled in convoy to Mont Blanc and then Stevie [May] and I picked up a hire car and we'd just caught up with them coming up to Milan when Vic [McCarthy] had a tyre blow. That sent him off onto the soft shoulder and, as the truck went along it hit a big gully, virtually took the front axle off, and then turned over on its

Driver Vic McCarthy took these snapshots of the wrecked Team Lotus truck on the day after it crashed off the autostrada near Milan.

side. Steve Gooda went out through the windscreen and fractured his ankle and cut his hand badly and Vic was still in the truck, unhurt apart from his glasses being busted. The car went out through the roof - it had like a translucent top - and finished upside down in a green pepper patch, which was someone's garden, with all the tools scattered around it!

'Steve was rushed to hospital. We got in touch with Novamotor and they came up with a truck and a crane and lifted the car out of the pepper patch. We just gathered everything up and they transported it to Monza'.

Fittipaldi had set out the same day to drive down to Monza. When he arrived at the Hotel de Ville, the receptionist told him that his transporter had been involved in an accident but no further details were available as Peter Warr had already departed to go and inspect the damage. 'A bit later he called me and said, "Emerson I need your help, I'll come and pick you up at the hotel and we'll go to the motorway because the transporter is turned upside down and we have pieces everywhere. I don't speak Italian, I need your help." I thought "Shit!" I couldn't believe it. It was a big shock. That's how we started the weekend.'

Close inspection of the damaged car revealed that it would have taken quite a lot of work to get it raceworthy again, as Dennis explains: 'It had a fair amount of damage, mainly wings and the screen and I think the bottom of the undertray might have had a hole punched in it. It was nothing serious but we went with the spare.' A decision was made to go and collect the spare car from across the border in Chamonix. Fittipaldi drove Trevor Seaman up to the transporter and then had to go to a prize giving at Bra, south of Turin to receive some trophies on behalf of Eddie Dennis and Peter Warr, who were unable to attend because of the accident.

The next day, the mechanics were working hard to get the spare car prepared and Emerson got out for some unofficial practice late in the afternoon. This was the first

Left: Shaky start: The transporter crash on the way to the Italian Grand Prix damaged Fittipaldi's race car and put a mechanic in hospital. It also meant a lot of rushing about for Fittipaldi but this didn't stop him from attending the Amici del Volante prize-giving (below) to receive an award for being the 'worthiest pilot of the year' and accept awards on behalf of Chapman and Eddie Dennis. **Bottom:** A Telex from Peter Warr set out the pre-conditions for the participation of Team Lotus in the Italian GP. Although an entry for Walker was mooted, it did not materialise.

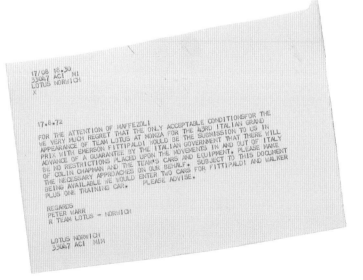

time that the new circuit layout had been used, so there was a lot for the drivers to become accustomed to. Designed to prevent the slipstreaming which had been a characteristic of past races at Monza, it featured a tight chicane just after the start/finish area and a swooping 'S' bend at the Curva Vialone before the long run down to the Parabolica.

On the first day of official practice, Fittipaldi was fourth quickest, behind Stewart, Hulme and Ickx, his three-closest Championship rivals. He spent much of the session exploring the limits, finding out how hard and how late he could brake for the tricky first chicane. On several occasions he overcooked things and was forced to take to the escape road, rejoining the track through a gate controlled by a marshal. The race would be all about balance: between the front and rear brakes; between the rear end weaving and locking the fronts up; and with the wing and spoiler angles of incidence to provide the right mix of straightline and corner speed.

For the Saturday session, a brand new Series 12 Cosworth DFV was installed in Fittipaldi's car. After a good start when he was running on full tanks, the engine seemed to go off the boil a bit and it actually seemed to be slower than the tired old unit it had replaced. There was some concern among Team Lotus because the engine had been in the transporter when it crashed. Although Gianni Pedrazanni had looked it over and pronounced it OK, there were fears that it could have been damaged internally. However, these were assuaged when Eddie Dennis found that the throttle slides were not opening fully, going some way to explaining why the Brazilian had not been able to do better than eighth-quickest in the session. The decision was

taken to leave the engine in the car for the race but to revert to Friday's suspension settings, with which Fittipaldi had been more comfortable. A lowly grid position was just what he didn't need at this crucial stage of the season but it was exactly what he ended up with: sixth, on the outside of the third row, was his worst position since his 'flu-bound performance at Clermont-Ferrand.

The morning warm-up was wet, which scuppered the team's plans to try and perfect the handling of the car following their decision to revert to the Friday settings. It also revealed a worrying brake vibration, so the team decided to change the front discs before the race. In addition, Fittipaldi elected to go one turn to the rear on the brake balance, as he felt that the car would lock up too much with full tanks. As the pre-race tension began to build, there was more drama. With only 35 minutes to go a leak was discovered in one of the fuel tanks, necessitating the draining of all the car's tanks, disconnection and removal of the offending item and then putting a new one in, reconnecting and refuelling – hardly the work of a moment. Eddie Dennis, Trevor Seaman, Stevie May and team manager Peter Warr worked like demons and, with only 10 minutes to go, the car was fired up and ready to go and Fittipaldi took his place on the grid.

The Brazilian was not renowned for his lightning starts but, if ever one was required, it was in this race. He duly obliged, surging through into third place behind the two Ferraris of Ickx and Reggazoni on the blast down to the Curva Grande. Almost before the race was started the Championship hopes of Jackie Stewart were over, for his clutch had failed when the flag dropped and he fed the

power in. This left only Hulme, who needed to win this race, as a potential challenger for the title. At the end of the first lap, he came round in seventh, so things were already looking good for Fittipaldi.

The Brazilian played a waiting game, which first produced results on lap 17 of 55, when Reggazoni collided with Carlos Pace's March at the Vialone chicane and was eliminated in the ensuing accident. This left Ickx and Fittipaldi running nose-to-tail. A second place would be enough to secure the Championship title but the urge was there to win the Championship and the race. The Lotus driver spent a number of laps weighing up very carefully where he felt he could pass the Ferrari under braking. However, he need not have bothered for, with only 10 laps remaining, Ickx raised his arm as he exited the Parabolica to signal that he was heading for the pits, an electrical short-circuit ending his race.

This left the black-and-gold Lotus in the lead by 10 seconds from Mike Hailwood's Surtees. Not sure whether his car was still leaking fuel, Fittipaldi began to lift early for corners and change up before reaching maximum revs. Consequently, Hailwood began to close in, causing some consternation in the pits, although they were fairly sure that Fittipaldi had everything under control. The final lap was agonising for everyone concerned, both in and out of the car. Fittipaldi was watching the fuel pressure gauge like a hawk, being ready to weave to get every last drop of fuel out of the tank should the engine begin to falter. He also went through the Parabolica – the final corner – as fast as he could so that he could coast across the line if he ran out.

As it turned out, such worst-case scenario planning proved unnecessary, for the car never missed a beat. Emerson crossed the line nearly 15 seconds clear to clinch the 1972 World Championship title, aged 25 the youngest driver ever to do so. Chapman threw his hat high into the air in his now traditional victory celebration and the mechanics and everyone else connected with the team leapt around, elated and relieved in equal measure that the dramas of the previous six days had been overcome. Almost un-noticed, Fittipaldi's win had also secured the coveted Constructors' Championship title for Team Lotus.

The team's transporter driver Vic McCarthy recalls the

day vividly, explaining that Chapman was just as happy about beating an old rival as he was about taking the title. 'I can see Chapman now, walking along the pit road and the biggest thing he loved about it was the fact that "Hey, we beat Ferrari in their own backyard again!"' Another thing he remembers is the Lotus boss's apparent lack of concern for his welfare in the wake of the transporter crash. 'I don't think he ever even asked me how I was after that accident. He was a funny character really. A bit of a cold fish as Andretti would call him.'

The day after the race, the jubilation of victory was slightly dampened by the news that Firestone, a long-time technical partner of Team Lotus, was withdrawing from all European motorsport activities and that it would no longer be providing any Formula 1 team with its rubber. The most serious impact of this decision would be on the works teams supplied free of charge by the company – Lotus, Ferrari and BRM – for it meant that they had to quickly find an alternative source and there were concerns over whether rival company Goodyear had the capability to supply the entire Formula 1 grid.

With the business of sewing up the Championship now complete, the remaining races on the calendar seemed something of an irrelevance. Two weeks after Monza, the first of the two season-ending North American races took place, the Canadian Grand Prix at Mosport Park. Consequently, there was little opportunity to bask in the glow of being World Champions as the team had to pack up the three cars they were sending and ship them over to arrive in good time for practice.

The usual three cars were sent to Canada, with 72/7 having been repaired after the transporter accident on the way down to Monza. However, there was a notable absentee when it came to the driver line-up. Dave Walker had been omitted, the result of a bit of 'wrist-slapping' on the part of Peter Warr. Soon after the announcement was made that Ronnie Peterson would be joining the team for

the 1973 season, Walker tested a Formula 2 GRD. This was deemed by Team Lotus to be in breach of his contract. Initially, he was told that his services wouldn't be required for either Canada or the US but eventually they settled on a one race 'suspension'.

Walker's place in Canada was taken by the team's 1971 driver, Reine Wisell. The genial Swede had signed up for four Grand Prix starts with BRM but had achieved disappointing results in these races. Having fulfilled that commitment, he was looking for drives which would raise his stock and bring him to the attention of team managers for 1973. With John Player Team Lotus having just won the Championship, it was too good an opportunity to miss. He was signed up for the final two races, which meant that, for the first time since 1970, Lotus would run three cars, one each for Fittipaldi, Walker and Wisell, in the US Grand Prix at Watkins Glen. Wisell was lined up to drive 72/6, Walker's regular car and the very same chassis the Swede had driven for the team in the second half of 1971.

A small but important milestone (particularly to the mechanics!) was reached in the week prior to the Canadian Grand Prix when Team Lotus finally took delivery of a new transporter for the Formula 1 team, to replace the one written off in May. The vehicle was state-of-the-art, having been built to order by Marshalls of Cambridge.

An intriguing addition to the Lotus technical staff in Canada was former designer and team owner of Brabham,

Ron Tauranac. Since selling the Brabham team to Bernie Ecclestone at the end of 1971, he had undertaken various freelance work during 1972 (including helping out on the Frank Williams Marches and revising the suspension on the recalcitrant Tecno) and there was some speculation that he would become technical chief of Team Lotus for 1973.

The first practice session on Friday afternoon at the bumpy Mosport Park circuit, situated about one hour's drive north of Toronto, was headed by Jackie Stewart, finally getting to grips with the new Tyrrell 005. Fittipaldi was a comfortable fourth quickest, while Wisell played himself back into things with a midfield time. For the Swede it was an interesting opportunity to compare the car to when he had last driven it in 1970 and 71 and also with the BRM. 'It felt better, much more civilised and stronger. They had made a few improvements on the suspension, hubs etc. But unfortunately, we were on the wrong tyres…' On Saturday morning, proceedings were dominated by the two Goodyear-shod McLarens of Revson and Hulme, making the most of their detailed familiarity with the circuit as a result of the numerous Can-Am races they had done there. Fittipaldi was the 'best of the rest' in third, while Wisell was still marooned mid-grid.

In the final session on Saturday afternoon, Fittipaldi was second-quickest behind his soon-to-be team-mate Ronnie Peterson in the March. The Brazilian's time was good enough to give him fourth place on the grid overall, on the inside of the second row, behind the two McLarens and

Opposite Page Top: Fittipaldi rolls down the pitlane at Monza during practice for the Italian Grand Prix. **Opposite Page Bottom:** Fittipaldi's car is wheeled into the Team Lotus garage at Monza during the Italian Grand Prix meeting. Note DFV dumped on floor – a contrast to today's sterile Formula 1 environment! This shot also shows the neat oil cooler arrangement at the back of the conical oil tank under the rear wing, which had first appeared at the British Grand Prix. **Right:** Despite starting from a lowly grid position, Fittipaldi came through to take victory and clinch the World title in the Italian Grand Prix.

LOTUS 72

First Person
Vic McCarthy on life as Team Lotus transporter driver

"I started working for Lotus Cars in 1968, in their transportation division. I managed to get some work with Team Lotus, going out with Jim Pickles and Ian Campbell, driving the Formula 3 transporter. Then at the end of 1970, early 1971, there was a mass exodus: Herbie [Blash], Joe 90 [Derek Mower] and a couple of other guys just vanished. Then there was this void, I guess. They brought in some new people and Peter Warr came up to me one day and asked me if I'd like to work full-time for the team. That year was terrible, we never won a race. What was wonderful was that the same group with the same car won the Championship the next season. You can't beat that. We came from the valley to the peak in one year."

Above Right: After a torrid year which had seen the team suffer two transporter crashes, Colin Chapman took delivery of a new 'state-of-the-art' vehicle from Marshalls of Cambridge in September. **Opposite Page:** Back in the fold: Reine Wisell returned to the team for the Canadian (shown here) and US rounds of the 1972 World Championship. In Canada he was a replacement for Dave Walker, who was forced to sit out the race as 'punishment' for testing a GRD, while at the lucrative Watkins Glen race the team ran a third car for the Swede.

the March and fastest overall of the Firestone runners. This race was notable for Goodyear's introduction of super-sticky 'qualifying' tyres, which undoubtedly contributed to the company's monopoly of the front row. Wisell improved his previous time by only a tenth of a second and so would start from the seventh row of the grid.

Race day dawned with a dense fog. At one stage it seemed as if it would have to be cancelled and the start was terribly delayed, the flag eventually being dropped at 3.47pm. Peterson shot into the lead, while Fittipaldi settled into fifth, a position he held until lap 18 of 80, when he passed the Ferrari of Ickx, which was losing revs. Wisell made a good start and managed to pass Pace, Hill and Beltoise in the first quarter of the race. Fittipaldi was struggling to get past the McLaren of Revson. His engine had been misfiring on the grid and was down on power so these positions were maintained until the demise of Peterson's March on lap 56 promoted them to second and third respectively.

Two laps later, Fittipaldi suddenly began to lose ground and was passed by Reggazoni. The reason was a damaged nose fin, which was rotating and upsetting the handling. A change of nose-cone pushed him right down the order and he emerged from the pits in 12th. While the Brazilian's Lotus was being worked on, Wisell, who had worked his way up to 11th position, also came in, with a broken fuel line. As a result, all the lubrication on the throttle slides had been washed away, causing them to stick. This was fixed

and he was sent on his way but five laps later his race was over with a dropped valve in his DFV.

Fittipaldi plugged on to the end of the race but the motivation to drive hard was simply not there. In addition to his down on power engine, he lost second and third gears, eventually coming home two laps behind winner Stewart, in 11th place.

The twelfth and final round of the Championship took place a fortnight later at the Watkins Glen circuit, scene two years ago of the triumphant first and third positions of Fittipaldi and Wisell. This was the most lucrative event on the Formula 1 calendar, another reason why many teams such as Lotus had chosen to run extra cars. Twenty three drivers were automatically qualified to run and receive a minimum US$6,000 prize, while the same amount was also available to the next two fastest drivers in practice. The remaining six cars were welcome to start the race but would only be eligible to compete for a share of the not-inconsiderable overall prize fund of US$116,500, some US$50,000 of which would go to the winner. With US$3,000 on offer for pole position and the same amount for fastest lap, there was no question of the level of competition being blighted by 'end of term blues'.

The first practice session turned out to be crucial, since although it was overcast, it was dry and warm. Fittipaldi spent much of the time swapping between 72/7 and 72/5, while Walker sat and twiddled his thumbs in the pits, his regular 72/6 being used by Wisell. Eventually, Team Lotus management took the decision for the Brazilian, assigning him 72/5 and giving Walker Emerson's regular race car. Unfortunately, this meant that he didn't have much time to dial himself in, and ended the session propping up the timesheets with the slowest lap. Meanwhile, Fittipaldi's time was only good enough for a disappointing ninth-quickest, while Wisell was again in mid-field, albeit only around a second slower than his old team-mate. The Swede claims that he would have been faster but that he was prevented from going out by the team management! 'They brought me into the pits and took my wheels off because I was quicker than Fittipaldi at that time – very frustrating!'

Tyres were once again an issue, with Goodyear-shod cars occupying the first five positions. In the week before the race, Firestone had announced a change of heart, reversing its decision to quit but the damage appeared to have been done in terms of staff morale and development of new compounds. Consequently, the Firestones supplied for this event did not perform well, with Reggazoni the best of their runners in sixth place and Fittipaldi the next-best. When rain, wind and low temperatures afflicted Saturday's sessions, it became clear that the grid for the race was already settled. Although the conditions for the afternoon session were markedly better, times were still some 15 seconds off those achieved on Friday, with Fittipaldi ending up second-quickest behind Carlos Pace. Wisell was higher than he had been and Walker was well up but frustrated at being unable to get a crack at qualifying in the dry again.

Thankfully, race day dawned dry but it was still very cold, which was bad news for the Firestone runners. Fittipaldi gambled on an experimental tyre compound in the hope that it would give him an edge. When the flag dropped, it did indeed give him superb traction, and he ended the first lap in third position, behind Stewart and Hulme. However, the tyres were already beginning to overheat and, on the fifth lap, he suffered a puncture. When he came into the pits, it could be seen that both edges of the tread were blistered and had peeled off. A tyre change saw him rejoin in last position but only nine laps later he was back in the pits with the same problem. He set off again but after another three laps it was decided to retire him because the team was running out of suitable tyres and rims and all hope of a good result was gone.

Wisell had a poor start but recovered to pass Pescarolo and de Adamich on the second lap and later got the better of Beltoise and Ganley to move up to 13th on lap 13. A measure of the speed of race leader Jackie Stewart was that he lapped the Swedish Lotus driver on the 25th lap of 59.

Wisell then ran consistently to the finish, being lapped a second time towards the end, to come home a rather uninspired 10th. Walker had engine problems, with oil spraying from the breather onto the back of his neck for some time before the engine eventually lost all its oil and failed. All in all, a rather deflating end to the season for Team Lotus but nothing could take away the fact that they had achieved their goal of winning the World Championship, the second title for the Lotus 72 in its third year of competition.

This wasn't quite the end of the racing season for Team Lotus, for a special non-Championship race, the John Player Formula 1 Challenge Trophy, was being run at the Brands Hatch circuit two weeks after Watkins Glen. A single car was entered for the new World Champion, this being his normal race car, 72/7.

Before then, there was some good news for the team when it was announced that Emerson Fittipaldi had re-signed for the 1973 season, to drive alongside Peterson. There had been some speculation that he was considering offers from other teams, rumoured to include Porsche (apparently contemplating a Formula 1 effort) and Ferrari. An illustration of the improvements in tyre performance in the latter half of 1972 was that, despite the cold weather, Fittipaldi managed to set a pole position time for the Brands race some 1.4 seconds quicker than the best practice time for the British Grand Prix at the Kent track in July.

Race day was cold and a fine drizzle was falling. This put the teams and drivers in a predicament regarding tyre choice. Many leading drivers, including Fittipaldi, opted to start on wets. The BRMs went for intermediates, while Carlos Pace – having his first drive for Surtees - started on slicks. These choices turned out to be crucial to the outcome of the race. At the start, Fittipaldi was out-dragged into Paddock by Peterson and Hailwood but quickly disposed of the Surtees to move into second. However, after 13 of the scheduled 40 laps, he pitted to change to slicks, dropping him right off the leader board and losing nearly a lap in the process. After setting fastest lap of the race, the Brazilian came back into the pits after 30 laps to retire, reporting that the engine's oil pressure had dropped and oil temperature had risen. The race was eventually won by Beltoise's BRM, from Pace, both of whom benefited from their tyre choices. The race was a disappointing finale to the season for John Player Team Lotus but one which proved the new Champion had lost none of his raw speed.

The next day, he returned to his native Brazil to a tumultuous welcome, with crowds lining the streets in their thousands to greet their hero. However, it wasn't just a pleasure trip, for Fittipaldi also competed in the Torneio Formula 2 series, which he once again won at the wheel of his trusty Lotus 69.

Looking back, Fittipaldi believes it was the year he came of age. 'I had much more confidence in myself, the car and the team. Everything came together tremendously in 1972.' He singles out his drive at Monza to clinch the Championship as the best of the season. 'We had the accident [with the transporter], it was likely to be decisive for the Championship and then we had the fuel leak just before the race. I was running very strongly behind Ickx and I would have secured the Championship [even if he hadn't retired]. I was extremely happy with the way I was driving under such tremendous pressure.'

For Dave Walker, it is hard not to look back on his season with John Player Team Lotus in Formula 1 without a tinge of bitterness. 'Part of my problem in 1972 was that they were only prepared to go so far in making it comfortable for me knowing that, as number two driver to Emerson, if he had a problem, he had to step into my car. So I never, ever felt comfortable sitting in the car, I was always crunched up or gear changes were awkward. That's the lot of the number two driver, basically. To be competitive at that level of motor racing, you certainly have to be comfortable.' Lack of testing is another sore point which he believes contributed to his poor performances. 'I had expected a lot more testing, particularly as I was coming up from Formula 3 and it was a pretty big jump in those days. During that the winter I did some laps at Brands Hatch and that was about the end of it. After that, I never

went testing. In contrast, they were taking Emerson off to every Grand Prix one to two weeks beforehand, spending two or three days getting everything sorted out at the circuits while I stayed at home.'

Walker also felt he was given the leftovers when it came

to engines. 'I was getting the bottom end of the scale of motors that they had. I don't know whether they had eight or nine engines but they only had two series 12s or whatever they were in those days and they were kept for Emerson. I always remember racing in Austria, getting towards the end of the season and I qualified 19th. I went to Colin, over Peter's head and I said, "Look, can I please have a decent engine?" Emerson had 3-400 hours on his engine, so Colin agreed to let me have it. I will honestly never forget it. What I recall was coming out of corners, literally getting a run and being able to pull out and go past all sorts of cars in front of me that had previously passed me down the straight, whether it was a BRM, or whatever. I was just storming along but it had too many hours on it and it lasted about 10 or 12 laps and then it let go. Not that I'd over-revved it but it was just at the end of its life-expectancy I suppose. But the difference between that particular motor which Emerson had all year and what I'd been using - it was just chalk and cheese. You could get yourself up behind somebody, get a slight drag out of them and pull out and go past. With the previous engines, I didn't have a hope in hell of doing that.'

Eddie Dennis, Chief Mechanic in 1972, vehemently denies that any favouritism was shown to Fittipaldi or that this was a factor in Walker's performances. 'He could have been using engines out of Jim Clark's car because all the blocks were updated. We didn't know how much horsepower they pushed out, Cosworth just didn't release that information. He had pretty equal machinery really. Obviously, Emerson would get preference of the Old Man's attention and Walker had to make his way as he went along, so he didn't get the coaching perhaps from the Old Man as Fittipaldi had done, the inspiration that the Old Man could push into drivers. He was a great motivator really, he could put his arm round their shoulder and get another second out of them, just by talking to them and pumping them up! But I really just don't think he [Walker] had it in him.'

Walker, unsurprisingly, disagrees, saying that he was never allowed to go his own way on set-up. 'That was another minor problem I had with the 72. Every time I wanted to change something I wasn't allowed to do it because it had to be left for Emerson in case he needed to jump into it. So that was another battle. It was frustrating because I wanted to set up roll bars and change torsion bar tensions and get the car more suited to my style of driving. But I was never permitted to do any of that stuff. So I had to try and learn to drive like Emerson drives. And that is not always easy after several years of developing your own technique and style of driving.

Opposite Page Top: Fittipaldi's season tailed off with car problems in both North American races.
Opposite Page Bottom: Walker finds it hard not to be bitter but the team maintain that he was fairly treated. **Left:** Fittipaldi took pole for the John Player Challenge Trophy but retired.

WORLD CHAMPIONSHIP TABLE 1972

Pos	Driver	Race	Argentina	S.Africa	Spain	Monaco	Belgium	France	Great Britain	Germany	Austria	Italy	Canada	USA	Total	(dropped)
1	Emerson Fittipaldi			6	9	4	9	6	9		9	9			61	
2	Jackie Stewart		9			3		9	6				9	9	45	
3	Denny Hulme		6	9			4		2		6	4	4	4	39	
4	Jacky Ickx		4		6	6				9				2	27	
5	Peter Revson			4	2				4		4	3	6		23	
6	Francois Cevert						6	3						6	15	
6	Clay Reggazoni		3	4						6			2		15	
8	Mike Hailwood						3	1			3	6			13	
9	Ronnie Peterson		1	2				2		4			3		12	
9	Chris Amon					1	1	4	3		2	1			12	
11	Jean-Pierre Beltoise					9									9	
12	Mario Andretti			3										1	4	
12	Howden Ganley									3	1				4	
12	Brian Redman					2				2					4	
12	Graham Hill			1						1		2			4	
16	Andrea de Adamich				3										3	
16	Carlos Reutemann												3		3	
16	Carlos Pace				1		2								3	
19	Tim Schenken		2												2	
20	Arturo Merzario							1							1	
20	Peter Gethin											1			1	

Pos	Constructor	Race	Argentina	S.Africa	Spain	Monaco	Belgium	France	Great Britain	Germany	Austria	Italy	Canada	USA	Total	(dropped)
1	Lotus-Cosworth			6	9	4	9	6	9		9	9			61	
2	Tyrrell-Cosworth		9			3	6	9	6				9	9	51	
3	McLaren-Cosworth		6	9	2	2	4		4	2	6	4	6	4	47	2
4	Ferrari		4	3	6	6			1	9			2	2	33	
5	Surtees-Cosworth		2	3			3	1			3	6			18	
6	March-Cosworth		1	2	1		2	2		4			3		15	
7	B.R.M.					9				3	1	1			14	
8	Matra-Simca					1	1	4	3		2		1		12	
9	Brabham-Cosworth			1						1		2	3		7	

Barely three months elapsed between the John Player Trophy race at Brands Hatch and the first round of the 1973 World Championship, at Buenos Aires in Argentina. During this time John Player Team Lotus had been busy re-organising, seeking to consolidate their position and ensure that they would be able to supply their joint number one drivers with equal equipment.

The first such move was to bolster the technical staff, including the appointment of a new chief designer and several more experienced mechanics. At the end of October the surprise announcement came that Ralph Bellamy had been appointed chief Formula 1 designer as from November 13th. Australian Bellamy had worked at Brabham between 1966 and 1969, and then had a spell at McLaren during which he penned the very neat and effective M19 Formula 1 car, and had returned to Brabham at the beginning of 1972, where he oversaw the running of the BT37 design. He saw his appointment at Lotus as being pretty much the ultimate for a Formula 1 designer. 'At that time, you'd aspire to work either for Colin or for Ferrari, I suppose, they were the 'gun' teams of the time. You have got to understand that also Bernie [Ecclestone] had taken over Brabham and had staggered through 1972 with literally no money. So to be asked to go and design Formula 1 cars for Colin, who had a reasonable budget and it was a famous time – you'd really arrived. So I was more than happy to accept his offer. He apparently, it turned out, was brassed off that he'd missed out on catching me when I was at McLaren because he'd admired the McLaren M19 and when I moved from there to Brabham that all happened too quickly for him. He'd not managed to intercept me on the way, if you like.'

Bellamy's appointment was not universally popular among the mechanics, as Eddie Dennis recalls. 'Ralph was a rather staid designer really, nothing outlandish or original. We used to call him Rigor at one time, as in rigor mortis. You'd go past his drawing board and he'd be standing there and you'd go past an hour later and he was still in the same position, as though rigor mortis had set in!'

At the same time, stories began to circulate that both Lotus and Ferrari had signed up with Goodyear for the 1973 season, despite Firestone's recent reversal of its decision to quit the Formula 1 tyre arena.

The suggestion was that both teams had signed with Goodyear in rather unseemly haste and that, by the time Firestone changed its mind, it was already too late for the two teams to continue with them. This was disputed by Goodyear at the end of November, when it confirmed that John Player Team Lotus and Ferrari had indeed joined its ranks, the company claiming that discussions had taken place over 'a considerable period', certainly long before Firestone announced their plans to withdraw. A programme of intensive testing for the forthcoming season was revealed, taking in the Buenos Aires track in Argentina and Interlagos in Brazil in December before moving on to Kyalami in January.

In early December, more details emerged as to how exactly Lotus intended to maintain dual number one status for each of its drivers. The team announced that Emerson Fittipaldi would be allocated chassis 72/7 and 72/5, while Ronnie Peterson would be given a new car yet to be built, 72/8 and Dave Walker's regular race car from 1972, 72/6. The mechanics were also shuffled around. Eddie Dennis was retained as Chief Mechanic, while Ian Campbell and Steve Gooda would look after the revived works Formula 2 team. Keith Leighton and Yoshuatsu Itoh both joined Lotus from Rondel, with Leighton being assigned to look after Peterson's Formula 1 car and Itoh given responsibility for the chassis programme.

Preparations were already well under way for the forthcoming season. The same week as the announcement about who would be driving what chassis, Fittipaldi and Peterson were both in Brazil, conducting tyre testing with Goodyear and, by all accounts, setting very competitive times. Emerson was reported as having lapped Interlagos in 2m 32.4s, while Peterson recorded 2m 33.0s. Rival Stewart couldn't better 2m 34 in his Tyrrell and his team-mate Cevert could not break 2m 36.0s. For designer Ralph

Bellamy, the trip provided an embarrassing start to his new job, due to an inadvertent run-in with the Brazilian authorities. 'The Team Lotus secretary had obviously never sent an Australian to Brazil before and she was under the misapprehension that an Australian didn't need a visa to enter Brazil, so I got myself locked up for a few days. That I remember! I found out the requirement when I arrived there. Emerson got me sprung to do the test but I had to be escorted onto an aeroplane to leave the country, which impressed the other passengers no end!'

Switching to Goodyear was not without its disadvantages. Peter Warr recalls that its rubber was probably not best suited to a car with such a pronounced rearward weight bias and low unsprung weight as the 72. 'The engineers working for Goodyear had been more used to working with cars with weight bias further forward. Therefore their knowledge and understanding of what made tyres work had been garnered from working with those cars, so there was always the suggestion that the tyres would work better on cars that weren't quite the same as ours.

Above Right: Texaco continued their involvement with the team for 1973 (with a red and white logo on the rear wing this time, although the logo remained in black-and-gold on the cockpit surround), while Goodyear came on board, replacing Firestone as tyre supplier. Here, Stevie May adds some of Texaco's finest to Fittipaldi's car.

'The biggest hurdle was the front tyre and we managed to get over that with some honking front downforce and some geometry changes and, in a way, sort of masked it. The other thing was that we'd got Ronnie behind the wheel and he overcame quite a lot of what was not handling quite right by the car because he wouldn't ever stop and adjust it, he'd just drive round it. It would take him a couple of laps to sort out the way it was behaving and then he'd just drive it that way. And that was a tremendous advantage.' Fittipaldi concurs with Warr's assessment of the switch to

Switching to Goodyear tyres in '73 was not without its disadvantages

Goodyear. 'At that time, I think the front tyres from Firestone were more efficient. We lost a little bit of grip at the front and then I had to go for more front wing. But we adapted the car well to the Goodyears and they adapted well to our cars and, as you recall, we were very fast from the beginning of the season.'

Initially, Goodyear's policy of testing with the top team of the time worked in favour of Lotus, as Ralph Bellamy explains. 'Goodyear had a pretty simple policy in so far as they tested and developed tyres with whoever was quickest and Lotus was quickest so they developed tyres for our car. And those tyres were supplied to everybody. Now that stuffed everybody else royally!'

Emerson was a busy man: the week following testing in Brazil he was back in England to receive the BRDC Gold Star in a presentation held at the new John Player factory in Nottingham. Despite thick fog, Emerson did a lap of the factory grounds in a 72 and even managed to spin the car! Also, in the first week of January, one of the 72s (it isn't clear which) was whisked off to the Racing Car Show at Olympia in London, where it was the centrepiece of the exhibition.

Only a couple of weeks later, the Formula 1 circus arrived in Buenos Aires for Round 1 of the World Championship, the Argentinian Grand Prix. Due to space restrictions on the CL-44 air freighter used to carry all the cars en masse, John Player Team Lotus took only two cars with them, these being Emerson's regular race car, 72/7 and the new chassis 72/8. In fact, it was so new that it hadn't actually turned a wheel before first practice in Argentina, nor did it have a proper chassis plate!

Small modifications to the specifications of the two cars were evident. Revisions to the gearbox sideplates meant that the track of both cars had been widened slightly at the rear, while the method of attachment of the rear brake disc centre-sections to the discs themselves had been changed.

In addition, the fire extinguisher on the new car had been relocated and was now between Peterson's legs rather than in the front sub-frame as was the case with Fittipaldi's car.

Four official periods of practice had been laid on, two on Friday and another two on Saturday, each in the afternoon, separated by an hour's break. During the first Friday session, Clay Reggazoni proved to be the surprise package in the BRM, setting the fastest time, ahead of Stewart and Fittipaldi. Meanwhile, Peterson had some new car niggles and then a gearbox bearing failure towards the end, which meant that he had to miss the second session later that afternoon, in which Fittipaldi improved his time to emerge fastest, with Stewart and Reggazoni again his closest rivals.

Stewart was quickest in the first Saturday session, from Reggazoni, with the two Lotus drivers setting exactly the same time only slightly further back. In final practice, the new found form of Reggazoni and the BRM was underlined by his taking pole position, while Fittipaldi was the only other driver to get below 1m 11.0s to join the swarthy Swiss on the front row. Peterson, suffering from his lack of track time in the new car, could only manage a time good enough for fifth on the grid, on the inside of the third row but this was a pretty good effort all things considered.

Race day was dry, hot and breezy. At the start, Cevert jumped into the lead after Stewart overdid things at the first corner and got on the 'marbles'. But before the lap was out, Reggazoni had passed him to put the BRM in the lead, a position he maintained for the first 28 laps, hotly pursued

Player Special-sponsored cars.

They continued in this vein until two-thirds distance when Peterson, who had been keeping an eye on his oil pressure because it had been dropping in corners, pulled into the pits with a seized engine. Fittipaldi was pushing Stewart harder and harder, trying to find a way past and, on lap 76, he did so and set off in pursuit of Cevert, setting a new lap record in the process. The Frenchman held him at bay for 10 laps but, on lap 86 with 10 tours remaining, the World Champion came round in the lead, having forced his way up

by Cevert and the two black and gold Lotus 72s of Fittipaldi and Peterson. Stewart recovered from this poor first lap to catch up the leading quartet, making a train of five cars, all covered by around a second. Around quarter-distance, the Scot found a way past Peterson and then, seven laps later, he passed Fittipaldi as a result of a mix-up while the leaders were lapping a back-marker. At around this time, the tyres on Reggazoni's BRM started to go off, and he was passed for the lead by Cevert and then quickly deposed to fifth by the other Tyrrell and the two John

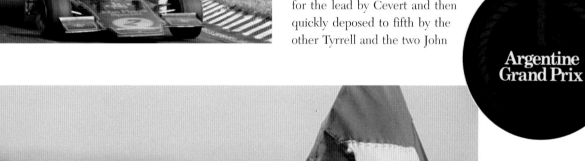

Argentine Grand Prix

the inside of the Tyrrell into the final hairpin. Fittipaldi reeled off the remaining laps with ease to finish the race four and a half seconds clear of Cevert, with Stewart third. Chapman having already left for the airport, it was left to Peter Warr to provide the traditional Team Lotus celebration by throwing his cap in the air. It was the perfect start to his title defence, a signal to his rivals that the reigning Champion meant business.

Today, Fittipaldi ranks that race as his best in a Lotus 72. 'Francois was leading, Jackie was second, I was running third. I took a long time to pass Jackie, because he made his Tyrrell very wide! Then I passed

Opposite Page: The 1973 season began with a car being displayed at the Racing Car Show at Olympia. Chapman makes a point, while Fittipaldi and mechanic Stevie May look on. The car displayed at the Racing Car Show got a young Gordon Murray into trouble when, at the behest of Ron Tauranac, he tried to get close enough to it to measure the rear wing and found himself being frog-marched off the stand by security! **Above:** Ronnie Peterson made his Team Lotus debut in the Argentinian Grand Prix but retired after running in the leading group. The race also marked the first appearance of 72/8. **Left:** Start as you mean to go on: Fittipaldi began the 1973 season in a determined mood, passing both Tyrrells on the way to victory in the Argentinian Grand Prix. Fittipaldi, flying the flag, described winning in front of his home crowd as emotionally the best victory he had with the 72.

Brazilian
Grand Prix
1973

Francois with not many laps to go. I overtook both of them in the same place, at the hairpin before the pit straight, with two wheels on the grass! I was driving very aggressively, I wanted to win the race, I wanted to win the Championship again. I think that was my best-ever performance with the car.'

Two weeks later, the second South American race took place, at Fittipaldi's home track, Interlagos. With no time for the cars to return to the factory, only small detail changes were made to their specification, the most notable being a slightly larger airbox aperture. In addition, some modifications had been carried out to the oil tank on Peterson's car as this was thought to have caused his engine problems in Buenos Aires.

After the bitter disappointment of having to retire with a handful of laps to go whilst leading the non-Championship Brazil Grand Prix in 1972, Emerson was determined to make amends. He knew the 7.96km (about 5 miles) track intimately, having raced there countless times as a youngster. Therefore it was no surprise that a black and

gold Lotus 72 topped the timesheets for each of the four official practice sessions. What was a surprise was that, for the first three of these, it was Ronnie Peterson who pipped his team-mate and set the pace, with Fittipaldi only recording the fastest time in the final session and this was still slower than Peterson's best. The gauntlet had been well and truly thrown down by the Swede for the season to come.

The Lotus 72s were head and shoulders above the competition. They seemed perfectly balanced, cornering quicker, braking later and putting the power down earlier than their rivals. In the first session, Peterson was a tenth quicker than Fittipaldi but a whopping 2.3 seconds faster than the nearest non-Lotus driver. In the second the Swede was again 1.5 seconds quicker than Ickx's Ferrari, with his Brazilian team-mate this time 1.1 seconds adrift. The two John Player-sponsored cars were again fastest in the first Saturday practice, although times were generally slower than at any other part of the weekend. For the final session, Fittipaldi turned the tables on Peterson, setting a time two seconds faster than his team-mate, while only another Brazilian, Carlos Pace, was able to match the Swede's time. In fact, the general consensus of opinion was that Saturday was much slower than the previous day because of the

intense heat. This was unfortunate for Emerson, since he had practiced on Friday with a rather tired engine, whereas Peterson had a fresh one. On Saturday, the Brazilian had a fresh unit installed but was unable to make the most of it.

The day of the race was also exceptionally hot, perhaps favouring local drivers used to the stifling conditions. Fittipaldi made a superb getaway, leading into the first corner and he was never to be headed, the first ever time that he had led a Grand Prix from start to finish. Peterson made a poor start and dropped to fourth, but quickly moved up to third. He was just shaping up to try and pass Stewart's

Above: Fittipaldi's winning start to the season continued in the Brazilian Grand Prix, with a dominant lights-to-flag victory. Early in the year it looked as if the partnership between Chapman and Fittipaldi was as strong as ever with the Brazilian winning the opening two races. **Left:** Peterson waits patiently in his car for the start of the Brazilian Grand Prix, umbrella shielding him from the heat of the afternoon sun, while Eddie Dennis oversees last-minute checks. **Far Left:** Close-up of the rear brake and disc arrangement on the 72.

Tyrrell when he spun on lap six and brushed the barrier. The Swede had felt the back end go loose when he was putting the power down and closer inspection when the car was returned to the paddock found that the centre had pulled out of the pressed and bonded Melmag right rear wheel, causing the car to spin out of control. Unbeknown to the team, this would be the first of many problems with these wheels, which would probably cost Team Lotus the World Championship title and led to it taking the producers of the wheels, Magnesium Electron, to court. Emerson crossed the line 13.5 seconds clear of Stewart. This time, Colin Chapman stayed on to celebrate his driver's victory and a popular one it was too, with the home crowd, who mobbed their hero when he finished his slowing down lap, as he recalls. 'Emotionally, that was the best win I had with that car because Sao Paolo was my home town, I was the World Champion and it was the first official World Championship race in Brazil.'

It was a storybook start to the season for the Brazilian. The South American campaign had yielded a maximum 18 points, with his closest rival Stewart already some way back on 10 points. In contrast, the Brazilian's team-mate Peterson had yet to score any points. Just as significant for the team was the fact that this was their 49th Grand Prix victory, equalling the record of the mighty Ferrari despite the fact that Lotus had been racing for a much shorter period of time. A team once dismissed by Enzo Ferrari as mere 'garagistas' had matched the feats of the mighty men from Maranello.

The teams now had less than three weeks to pack up their cars and transport them to another 'fly-away' race, the South African Grand Prix. At one stage there was some doubt whether the event would take place at all, since the fuel crisis had led to the banning of all motor sport in South Africa. However, after considerable pressure, the ban was lifted and the race was allowed to go ahead.

Once again, Fittipaldi had on hand his regular chassis 72/7, while Peterson was driving 72/8. The reason for the continued absence of spare cars was explained by the fact that the other two chassis, 72/5 and 72/6, were back at Hethel being converted to conform with new regulations which were to be introduced for the first European round of the World Championship, the Spanish Grand Prix, at the end of April. A third 72 was entered for this race, the Lucky Strike 72/3 of Dave Charlton, which was actually the lap record holder at the Kyalami circuit.

As usual in South Africa, the race was scheduled to take place on a Saturday, so practice was held over three days, with three hour sessions on both Wednesday and Thursday and one and a half hours on Friday. A number of teams had been unofficially testing in the run-up to the race and from this it was apparent that McLaren's new M23, driven by the vastly experienced Denny Hulme, was going to be the car to beat.

This proved to be the case, with the absolute domination by Lotus of practice at Interlagos now nothing more than a memory. Hulme was fastest on the first day, with the M19s of Revson and Scheckter filling the next two places to make it a McLaren 1-2-3. The Lotus 72s of Fittipaldi and Peterson were next up. On Thursday, Peterson set the pace, closely followed by his Brazilian team-mate, Lotus turning the tables on McLaren this time. However, in the crucial Friday session, it was Hulme who was back on top, while Fittipaldi's practice was prematurely curtailed by a broken rear subframe after he had set the second-fastest time. Peterson was unable to match, let

Top: Formation flying: a slightly ragged-looking Fittipaldi fights to hold Peterson at bay as they round Clubhouse Bend during the South African Grand Prix. **Left:** Fittipaldi drifts 72/7 through Kyalami's Leeukop Bend.

Charlton attempted a rather ambitious passing move on the Argentinian going into the fast right-hander Crowthorne, at the end of the main straight. He partially spun and came to a halt on the outside of the corner and was then hit by the Surtees of Mike Hailwood, who drove over the Lotus 72's nosecone. Although Charlton limped off to the pits to retire, this incident set in motion a chain of events that caused Clay Reggazoni to crash into Hailwood's car and his BRM to catch fire. It was only the bravery of Hailwood, who pulled him from the burning wreckage, which saved Reggazoni's life. It also resulted in race leader Hulme sustaining a puncture, forcing him to pit.

In amongst all the smoke and chaos, Jackie Stewart had been moving up through the field and, on lap 6, he passed Peterson for third. On the next lap, he had passed both Fittipaldi and Scheckter to take the lead and, from this point on, he was never headed. Four laps later, Fittipaldi lost third to Revson and for over 30 laps, the Lotuses ran together in fourth and fifth positions. However, Scheckter's tyres were gradually going off, and Fittipaldi passed him for third on lap 44 of 79. Only five laps later, Peterson's race was all but over, a ball joint in the throttle linkage having broken he was forced to sit in the pit for six laps while it was repaired, re-joining to finish a lowly 11th. Fittipaldi and Revson continued to run in close company, while Stewart stretched his lead. Try as he might, Emerson could not squeeze past the McLaren. This was partially due to a mistake in set-up which saw too great an angle of incidence on his car's rear wing, hindering speed on the crucially important main straight, which was the principal

alone beat, his previous day's time, with the result that the black-and-gold cars ended up in second and fourth places on the grid, Emerson in the middle of the front row and Ronnie on the outside of the second row. Meanwhile, Charlton was putting his local knowledge to good use and lined up on the outside of the fifth row in amongst several of the works drivers such as Ickx, Lauda and Hailwood.

At the start, Fittipaldi was out-dragged by both Hulme and Scheckter and settled into third place at the first corner, while Peterson slotted into fifth place behind the other McLaren of Revson. On the third lap the Swede passed the American to move up to fourth. Behind this gaggle, carnage was about to unfold. Dave Charlton had made a fantastic start from his mid-grid position and came round in seventh place at the end of the first lap, right behind the Brabham of Carlos Reutemann. On lap three,

overtaking place. However, this did not stop the Brazilian from setting the fastest lap of the race in his pursuit, with only three tours remaining.

Fittipaldi had to be content with four points for third place, giving him a total after three rounds of 22, while Stewart closed the gap to his Championship rival to three points by winning the race comprehensively. Things were thus very evenly matched as the Grand Prix teams returned to Europe for two non-Championship races prior to resuming the title battle in Spain.

The first of these events was the Race of Champions at Brands Hatch. This marked the re-appearance of the two cars which had been converted to conform with the new regulations requiring cars to have deformable structures surrounding their fuel tanks in an effort to try and reduce the risk of fire from exposed tanks splitting. The solution

Top Left: Fittipaldi finished a disappointing third in South Africa, although he did set the fastest lap. **Top Right:** Peterson and Fittipaldi gave the deformable structure cars their debut at the 1973 Race of Champions. Here Peterson in 72/6 is pushed through the paddock by Eddie Dennis. **Left:** These two shots show how the radiator ducts were incorporated into the deformable structures to make a one-piece 'jacket' that went over the tub. The meeting point of the two side skins is just visible below the Texaco logo on the cockpit surround.

adopted by Lotus was to clad the sides of the tub with a flexible foam around 1cm thick, covered in fibreglass. As Ralph Bellamy recalls, some typical Lotus creative thinking enabled the 72 to conform to the letter, if not the spirit of the new regulations. 'We had to convert the Formula 1 cars to the new regulations, which gave the opposition some hope. The Lotus 72 was seen as being pretty formidable and they thought that the change in regulations might detract significantly from its performance and others would be able to match it. But we managed to comply with the rules and really we didn't change the car all that significantly. You had to have 100mm of deformable structure in some areas and 10mm in others, so we literally just made a 'jacket' to go over the car. It was just fibreglass and then some bloody diddy foam, goodness knows what it was, nothing structural, I assure you of that, just the lightest rubbish we could get our hands on. The 100mm section was the radiator inlet ducts, top and bottom, because they were alongside the fuel tanks. We could just fill the inlet ducts with foam and job done! You would have to be an astute observer to pick the difference between a 1972 car and a 1973 car.' The cowling for the side radiators and the deformable side jacket were now all one piece, with the leading edges of the ducts now blended neatly and smoothly into the side of the bodywork. All this work came at some cost in terms of the overall weight of each car, which was reported as being some 30lbs heavier.

Other changes to the cars included a wider front track, as well as new cast rear uprights. In typical Lotus fashion, the work to the cars was still being finished on Friday, so both Fittipaldi (allocated chassis 72/5) and Peterson (72/6) missed practice that day and were able only to take part in

the Saturday session. With all the changes to the cars, it was no surprise to see that they were slightly off the pace and unable to get near the times set by Fittipaldi in practice for the non-Championship race at the end of 1972. Peterson ended the day in sixth and Fittipaldi in an unaccustomed seventh. For the Sunday morning warm-up, the wider front

track was abandoned and both drivers reported that the cars felt better.

In the race, Peterson got a good start from the third row and moved through to second place, while Fittipaldi jumped into fourth. So much so, in fact, that the stewards penalised him one minute for a jump-start. However, at the end of the second lap, the Brazilian was into the pits to retire, with a broken metering unit. On the fifth lap, Peterson took the lead, a position he held until the 18th lap, when he peeled off into the pits with a broken differential. Such was the rate of attrition in this race, that it went down in the record books as the only International Formula 1 race to be won by a Formula 5000 machine, Peter Gethin taking the spoils in his Chevron B24.

After the disappointments of Brands Hatch, the mechanics' attention turned towards converting the team's two other cars, 72/7 and 72/8, to the deformable structure specification in time for the next Grand Prix in Spain.

Above: Mechanics Rex Hart and Keith Leighton working on Fittipaldi's car at the International Trophy meeting. **Right:** Fittipaldi prepares to go out in the rain in practice for the International Trophy meeting at Silverstone.

LOTUS 72

However, before this, there was the second non-Championship race, the GKN/Daily Express International Trophy Meeting, which took place three weeks after the Race of Champions. The fertile brain of Colin Chapman had been at work once again, with drawings dated 30th March 1973, laying out a design for a 'Power Clutch'. It was not long before this was fitted and tested by Peterson in 72/6 at Silverstone on the Wednesday before the International Trophy in unofficial practice. The system incorporated an electrically-actuated clutch activated by a knob on the gear lever.

Before much impression could be formed as to its worth, Peterson had a coming together with a Formula 3 car at Maggotts, resulting in him spinning wildly towards Becketts and smacking the bank hard enough to cause considerable damage to the front end of the car. It was so bad, that the car could not be repaired in time for the race on Sunday, so the order was given to speed up the work on 72/8 and ready that instead. This was easier said than done, since it was about as stripped down as a tub could get, even

lacking an undertray, but by dint of a posse of mechanics working shifts round the clock the work was finished on Friday morning and the car arrived just in time for the first practice session in the afternoon.

When practice started, neither 72 had the power clutch fitted, so clearly more work needed to be done. While Peterson struggled to set up his hastily rebuilt car, Fittipaldi set to work and was soon inside his pole time from this race in 1972 of 1m 18.1s, ending up joint fastest with Peter Revson's McLaren M23 on 1m 17.5s. On Saturday, he improved even further to sew up the pole with an astonishing lap of 1m 16.4s, an average of 137.56mph on this fast, flat, former airfield circuit. Meanwhile, Peterson got his car dialled in and responded superbly by recording 1m 16.6 to line up in the middle of the front row alongside his team-mate, while Jackie Stewart was the only other driver inside 1m 17s and thus occupied the final front row slot.

The race was a disaster for Fittipaldi. He had decided to use a higher first gear than before and had overheated his clutch on the warm-up lap doing practice starts to try to get

used to it. When the starter held the cars on the grid for an unusually long time, this appeared to spell the end for the clutch on the Brazilian's 72, and when the flag dropped, the rest of the field charged round him, leaving Emerson to limp part way round the circuit before pulling off just before Club with no drive to the rear wheels. It was later reported that the flywheel had sheared.

Peterson made a lightning start and jumped into the lead, a position he would hold for only a lap before Stewart forced his way past. However, the Scot uncharacteristically spun on lap six, allowing the black-and-gold Lotus back into what was now a comfortable lead. Although Stewart quickly made up the ground he had lost, he was unable to find a way past Peterson and it looked as if the popular Swede would at last win his first Formula 1 race. It was not to be, for just after three-quarters distance, a freak snow storm dampened the track at Becketts and caught out Peterson, who spun off, fortunately without hitting anything. By the

time he had gathered everything together and rejoined the track, Stewart had slipped by. Peterson gave chase but it was a hopeless task and he eventually eased off, coming home in second place, 10.4 seconds behind the winning Tyrrell.

What a difference a year made! In 1972, Fittipaldi had won both the Race of Champions and the International Trophy, setting him up for a run of victories which formed the basis of his World Championship title. In 1973, his sum total for the two races was a paltry two laps and two DNFs.

Opposite Page: Super Swede as we all remember him, doing it in style. But for a spin during a snow flurry (shown) he would have won the non-championship race at Silverstone. **Above:** The conversion of Peterson's 72/8 to deformable structure specification was hastily completed after he crashed 72/6 in practice for the 1973 International Trophy meeting while testing Chapman's 'Power Clutch' concept.

The two cars were converted to conform with the new regulations requiring cars to have deformable structures surrounding their fuel tanks

Despite the fact that there was a three-week gap to the Spanish Grand Prix, it was not possible to repair 72/6 in time for the transporter to leave on the long journey down to Barcelona, so Peterson was restricted to 72/8 while Fittipaldi had 72/7. The Brazilian's spare car, 72/5, was still on its way down from Zolder, where he had taken the opportunity to test at the circuit which was to be the venue for the upcoming Belgian Grand Prix. The worth of this exercise was slightly negated by the fact that, shortly after their visit, the entire circuit was resurfaced in preparation for the race. The only changes to the specification of the two cars was the addition of an enlarged rear wing incorporating a shallow slot, in an attempt to gain more downforce with less drag.

The Montjuich Park circuit was in the heart of Barcelona, held on public roads. The lap started off near the Olympic stadium rising up and then falling away dramatically over a hump, which was the scene of the huge accidents that befell Jochen Rindt and Graham Hill in 1969 when the high wings on their Lotus 49Bs collapsed. It then plunged downhill into the city itself, via several hairpins before making its way back up the hillside and looping round to finish the lap. It was a tough street circuit, not as narrow as Monaco but just as formidable a test for the drivers because it was lined by unforgiving Armco barriers. The combination of the humps and bumps, high speeds and heavy braking meant that it was exceptionally hard on cars as well.

This was the first race to take place under new FIA regulations which required crushable 'deformable' structures to surround all fuel tanks and to be of specified materials and dimensions. Fuel tank capacity was also limited to 250 litres (55 1/2 gallons), which had to be divided so that no more than 80 litres could be carried in a single tank. Finally, the minimum weight of the cars was increased, from 550kg to 575kg, reflecting the fact that the

addition of deformable structures alone added considerably to the weight of each car.

As a result of being rebuilt to conform to these regulations, in addition to having modified suspension with cast rear uprights added, Fittipaldi's chassis 72/7 had not turned a wheel in its new form before first practice at Barcelona on Friday afternoon. When he ventured out onto the circuit, he found the car almost undriveable, with what he described as 'diabolical' handling, and problems with the brakes. As a result of this, he spent much of the session in the pits, while the left front hub assembly was taken to pieces and examined. Meanwhile, Peterson was really flying and set the fastest time, a feat he went on to repeat in the

second Friday session, leaving his time at 1m 21.8s, considerably faster than the lap record from the 1971 race of 1m 25.1s. Midway through Friday practice, the transporter with 72/5 rolled in after its long cross-country trek from Zolder, giving Fittipaldi an alternative car to try, which was a relief after the troubles he had experienced that day.

On Saturday, Emerson again tried 72/7 but it seemed no better, so he decided to revert to his trusty 72/5, the very same car he had driven at the circuit in 1971, albeit now in a rather different specification. Conditions were hotter than the previous day, so times started off slower but as the heat went out of the sun, they started to come down. Peterson was on fine form again and topped the timesheets with a lap exactly the same as he had done on Friday. No one else could get close to him, so his second pole of the year was secure. Fittipaldi finally started putting together some reasonable laps in the spare car, eventually ending up seventh-quickest, good enough for a starting position on the

Above: Let's hope it's a John Player Special! Trevor Seaman doing his best to keep the team sponsor in business while working on Fittipaldi's 72. **Left:** For 1973 the oil cooler and rear wing mounting arrangements were tidied up into a very neat, compact package.

The status quo was maintained for another 20 laps, until Stewart suffered a broken brake disc mounting and pulled off into the pits, leaving the black-and-gold cars in a commanding 1-2 position. Just as it looked as if Peterson would finally break his duck, he began signalling to his pit that he was in trouble. It transpired that he had lost top gear. Shortly afterwards he lost third gear and soon he had lost all drive. It was a bitterly disappointing end to a dominant performance. This left Emerson, complete with a now almost flat rear tyre, at the head of the field, although Carlos Reutemann was cutting huge chunks from his lead and with ten laps remaining was just over three seconds behind. But it wasn't to be: with nine laps remaining, he pulled into the pits with a broken driveshaft and Fittipaldi was free to complete his remaining laps at a considerably reduced speed and take the chequered flag, to his huge relief. 'That last lap, I couldn't believe it. I was looking in the mirror, and it was like running with three legs, I had lost one of my legs! I remember the Esses just before the finish line, and the car was very, very tricky, it was moving everywhere. I was just trying to balance it, to be able to cross the finish line and I did it, I was extremely happy that I won.'

Emerson's victory was as a result of his considerable skill in bringing home a car with such a major handicap

inside of the fourth row. As a result of his problems with his race car, he elected to start in the spare.

Race day was again hot, sunny and dry. Peterson made a great start and led the field round at the end of the opening lap, with Fittipaldi maintaining his position, a poor getaway fortunately being matched by even worse starts by Ickx and Revson in front of him, which compensated for being passed by the BRMs of Lauda and Beltoise. The young Austrian was duly despatched on lap 2, with the Frenchman being deposed a lap later. At the front, Peterson was obeying Colin Chapman's pre-race orders and maintaining a lead of around four seconds over Stewart's Tyrrell. Denny Hulme was a little further back, just ahead of a developing scrap between Cevert in the second Tyrrell and Fittipaldi. When Hulme pitted with tyre troubles on lap 20 of 75, Fittipaldi was promoted to fourth but still couldn't find a way past the determined Frenchman. However, on lap 27 the Tyrrell ran wide at the first hairpin, allowing the Lotus through.

Nine laps before this, Andrea de Adamich had crashed his Brabham heavily and deposited debris across the track. It seems that Cevert had picked up a couple of punctures

as a result and he pitted, while shortly afterwards Fittipaldi also began to experience handling problems and realised he had a slow puncture. At this stage, he was some 17 seconds behind second-place man Stewart, who was 10 seconds adrift of Peterson. The Brazilian evaluated the situation and determined to keep going rather than pit, for a stop for a new tyre would surely lose him too much time.

While there is no doubt that luck played a part in Emerson's victory, it was scored primarily as a result of the Brazilian's considerable skill in bringing home a car with such a major handicap. After the race the Goodyear technicians inflated the tyre and it went flat again within five minutes. Meanwhile, Peterson was left once more to reflect on what might have been. The fact that he emerged

as the moral victor of the race was scant reward. However, all this was forgotten in the celebrations of a record-breaking 50 Grand Prix wins for Lotus, taking them to the top of the all-time lists, one ahead of the mighty Ferrari. Just as important in the short term was the fact that Fittipaldi had stretched his lead over Stewart to more than the equivalent of one race win, his tally of 31 points being 11 ahead of the Scot's. Already at this early stage it was starting to look like shades of 1972 for this was a commanding lead by any standards.

Back at Hethel, there was further investigation into the cause of the mysterious handling affliction of Fittipaldi's car at Barcelona. Closer, more considered assessment revealed that the steering rack had been too long, causing the front wheels to bump-steer. As soon as this was fixed, the problem was immediately solved. Attentions also turned to John Player Team Lotus's stated aim of being able to provide both its lead drivers with a race car and a spare. There had been no time to rebuild Peterson's 72/6 after its Silverstone shunt but this was done in the period between the Spanish race and the next Grand Prix in Belgium. Consequently, for the first time ever, the team took four 72s to a race meeting, an event considered so historic that Peter Warr lined up the four cars and all the team personnel in front of the pits and asked photographer David Phipps to record it for posterity! On a technical level,

the basic specification of the four cars was unchanged from Barcelona.

By contrast with Montjuich Park, Zolder – venue for the Belgian Grand Prix - was pretty featureless, although it did incorporate at least some undulations. Up until the last minute, there was some doubt as to whether the race would

be on at all, since negotiations between the organisers and Formula 1 teams were not concluded until a very late stage. The result was that the circuit was rather hastily resurfaced on the weekend of the Spanish race and was not really given the chance to 'cure', playing host to a saloon car race only two days later.

Opposite Page Top: 72 laid bare: Fittipaldi's car sits in the paddock at Montjuich Park prior to the start of practice for the Spanish Grand Prix.
Opposite Page Bottom Right: A jubilant Chapman celebrates Fittipaldi's victory, on the rostrum with Emerson and his wife Marie-Helena.
Above: Peterson dominated the race but once again retired when leading.
Right & Opposite Page Bottom Left: Fittipaldi inherited the lead and then drove a finely-judged race to take victory with a deflating rear tyre.

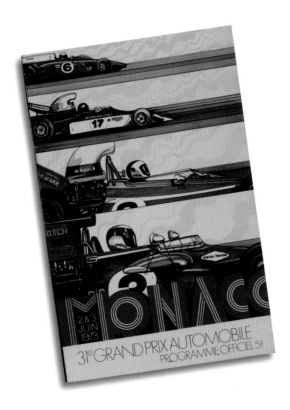

In the first practice session on the Friday, the track began to break up under strain from the very grippy slick tyres of the Formula 1 cars. Just after halfway through the scheduled duration, practice was abandoned for the rest of the day, with Fittipaldi having set the fastest lap and Peterson in fifth, although the times were not particularly representative due to the state of the track. Overnight, the organisers arranged for the sections of track which had

broken up to be resurfaced and, true to their word, the work was completed in time for the final two sessions on Saturday afternoon. Fittipaldi spent much of both sessions switching between his two cars, due to the fact that one had brake trouble and the other had problems with its fuel system. He was able only to set fifth-best time in the first Saturday session and slumped to ninth in the final session. Meanwhile, Peterson began to string together some quick laps, setting the third best time in the first session and then moving up into pole position with a stunning lap more than half a second quicker than the next fastest driver, Denny Hulme in the McLaren M23.

Overnight, 72/6 was thoroughly race prepared, while Fittipaldi still couldn't decide between his two cars and would not do so until just before the race. In the Sunday morning warm-up, Peterson crashed his race car, wiping off the oil tank and rear wing against the guardrail. The accident had been caused by brake failure, with the pedal going straight to the floor, possibly connected with the fact that he was supposed to be bedding in new pads. He then went out in his spare and, after a few laps, was given the 'In' sign. However, on his slowing down lap, he lost concentration and spun off at the same corner, this time making a mess of the front end of the car, it returned on the tow truck with its front wheels hanging off and pointing in different directions.

The mechanics toiled away to make a serviceable car out of the two crashed ones, transplanting the undamaged oil tank, oil cooler and rear wing off the spare and putting them on Peterson's race car. Fortunately, this was achieved in good time but the Swede was still undecided about which

tyres to run and only just made it in time to his rightful position on the grid after the team made the decision for him. Finally, on the grid, he made a last-minute decision to increase the angle of his front nose fins. By contrast, Fittipaldi's preparations were much more relaxed, although he was still switching between 72/5 and 72/7 on the Sunday morning and, even as the cars were going out on their warming up lap, 72/5 was brought out to the pits 'just in case'.

At the start, Peterson shot into the lead but it was quickly clear that his untried car's handling left a lot to be desired and on the second lap he was demoted by Cevert in the Tyrrell. On lap 19 of 70, both Fittipaldi and Stewart – who had steadily been working their way up through the order after the reigning Champion passed the former Champion on lap 5 – slipped by the struggling Swede. Peterson was suffering from chronic oversteer and fading brakes and his seemed a lost cause even at such an early stage of the race.

A lap later, Cevert spun away all his hard work and Fittipaldi was into the lead. However, Stewart was determined to make up for the disappointment of Barcelona and on lap 25 forced his way past the Lotus, which was already suffering from fuel pressure problems. Fittipaldi's engine was losing power in fourth and fifth gears as a result of the pressure going down and so was slow on the straights. Frustratingly, it was fine in the lower gears. The astute Brazilian quickly determined to try and nurse his car to the finish – the second successive race he had been required to do this. Meanwhile, Peterson had slid further down the order, being passed firstly by the

Opposite Page & Right: Fittipaldi was unable to match the pace of Stewart in the Monaco Grand Prix and had to settle for second. **Below Left:** Stewart's tongue-in-cheek reply to a fake invoice sent to him by Lotus in the wake of the Monaco slowing down lap collision was typical of the friendly atmosphere prevailing in Formula 1 during the 1970s. **Below Right:** Peterson finally scored his first points of the season at Monaco, coming home third.

McLaren of Peter Revson and then the Surtees of Pace as well as Cevert's Tyrrell.

Although he regained one place to fifth when Revson crashed out, the Swede fell victim to the increasingly treacherous track surface on lap 43, spinning off into the catch fencing and putting an end to a thoroughly ignominious weekend, during which he had crashed three times. In fairness to him, Peterson was feeling distinctly below par, having suffered a high fever for the whole weekend. Five laps later, the fast recovering Cevert passed the sick Lotus of Fittipaldi to make it a Tyrrell 1-2, a position that he maintained to the flag. Emerson kept the car going to the end, finishing one and a half minutes behind Cevert, the only other car on the same lap as the leaders. Stewart's win reduced the gap in the title race between him and Fittipaldi to only seven points, the Brazilian's third position taking his tally up to 35 points. Already, the Championship was developing into a two-horse race between these two, with Peterson still unable to finish a race, let alone score points.

The Saturday after Zolder, the Italian judicial authorities dropped an unexpected bombshell with the announcement that, after nearly three years of on/off investigations, Colin Chapman would be charged with manslaughter in connection with the death of Jochen Rindt, in practice for the Italian Grand Prix in 1970. This was despite the fact that he had since been allowed back into the country and given an assurance that he would not be charged.

Eleven days after the Belgian race, the teams had reassembled in the far more glamorous surroundings of Monte Carlo. The famous circuit had been reprofiled since 1972, with a new section skirting round the swimming pool and rejoining the old track at the Gasometer hairpin, freeing up the old approach to the Gasometer for use as the pits. Despite several parts of the track having been resurfaced, it was still just about the toughest test of man and machine that the Grand Prix circus would face that year.

The damage to Peterson's spare 72/8 had been found to be worse than initially thought, with the result that there was not enough time to repair it on its return from Zolder and get it back on the transporter, before it left on the long journey down through France to Monaco. Consequently, Peterson was left with just one car, 72/6, while Fittipaldi had his usual pair, 72/5 and 72/7, available to switch between. Once again, there were no major changes to the specification of both cars, the

reasoning being along the lines of 'If it ain't broke, don't try to fix it'.

Practice took place over three days, each session being held in warm, dry conditions, making a pleasant change from the cold, torrential rain which afflicted the 1972 meeting. While Peterson was quickly into the groove, setting the second-quickest time of the Thursday afternoon session behind Stewart, Fittipaldi was switching between his two cars hampered by a troublesome gear-linkage on 72/7 and clutch problems on 72/5. As a result, he ended up half-way down the timesheets. On Friday morning, Stewart was again quickest, with Peterson just two-tenths slower. Fittipaldi finally got going in 72/7 and set the fourth fastest time. He also drove 72/5 but could not match his pace in the other car.

Saturday's practice followed two Formula Three heats, with the result that the track was deemed to be slightly slower for the leading runners. Of the top five from Friday, only Francois Cevert managed to improve, pushing Fittipaldi down to fifth place on the grid, while the Stewart-

After Peterson crashed twice, the mechanics toiled away to make a serviceable car out of the two crashed ones

Peterson front row remained unchanged. At the start, Cevert made a tremendous getaway to lead the field up the hill from St. Devote, hotly pursued by Peterson, an order that was the same at the end of the opening lap. However, after two tours, it was Peterson who came round in the lead

LOTUS 72

after the Frenchman had got carried away and thumped a kerb, causing a tyre to puncture.

The Swede pulled out a huge gap in these early laps, aided by the fact that there was a furious queue building up behind Reggazoni's BRM. When he shot off up the chicane escape road with brake failure, the pursuing pack were released like a Champagne cork out of a bottle, but by now Peterson was in trouble yet again. This time it was his turn to suffer fuel pressure problems and his Cosworth DFV would not pull more than 9,500rpm and was not picking up properly out of the hairpins. Within two laps of Reggazoni's demise, Stewart had caught the black-and-gold Lotus and, on lap eight, the Tyrrell and the other Lotus of Fittipaldi swept past the frustrated Swede. The next time round Lauda (BRM), Ickx (Ferrari) and Wilson Fittipaldi (Brabham) had got past but after this he seemed to get to grips with the problem and only lost one more place, on lap 34 of 78, to Denny Hulme's McLaren.

For much of the race, the gap between Fittipaldi and Stewart stayed at around three seconds but this concealed the truth about the difference in performance of the two cars. While the Brazilian was hurling his Lotus around in an effort to keep up with the leader (and in fact hit the guard rail on at least one occasion) the Tyrrell was handling far better and the Scot was simply controlling the race from the front. At one stage, his lead grew to 12 seconds but then he let it dwindle in the closing laps. Although the crowd and Lotus pit fervently hoped that it meant there would be a do-or-die battle for victory over the final few tours, it was just Stewart's canny way of preserving the car and he crossed the line 1.3 seconds ahead, but in complete

command. To cap off a slightly underwhelming weekend, Fittipaldi drove up alongside Stewart to congratulate him on his win and the cars promptly touched, spinning Emerson round through 360° and breaking two wheels!

Peterson plugged away, making the best of a difficult situation, and was rewarded with elevation up the order as a result of the retirements of Ickx and Hulme ahead of him. When third-placed man Wilson Fittipaldi retired with only six laps to go, it promoted the Swede to third place, albeit a

full lap behind the leading duo.

One sensed that the balance of power in the Championship race was subtly shifting from the Lotus to the Tyrrell camp. Stewart's victory enabled him to close up even further on Fittipaldi, although the Brazilian's second position meant that he was still the leader with 41 points against the Scot's 37, while Peterson was at last off the mark with four points to his name.

If the FIA had tried, they could not have thought of a much longer trip for the teams than travelling from Monaco on the coast of the Mediterranean right up to the Anderstorp circuit in Sweden, except perhaps from Barcelona or Monza! So it was, that everybody gathered for the first Swedish Grand Prix, a home race for Peterson on a circuit he knew well. He also had his full complement of cars, for 72/8 had at last been repaired following its encounter with the Zolder barriers, while 72/6 was also at his disposal. Fittipaldi had his regular pairing of 72/5 and 72/7. Reflecting the fact that it was getting difficult to improve an already finely honed design, there were no changes to the cars' specification from Monaco.

In the first session on Friday morning, Peterson was second fastest in 72/6 behind Cevert's Tyrrell, while Fittipaldi in 72/7 was playing himself in gently, ending up seventh-quickest. In the Friday afternoon session, Peterson really turned up the wick, recording the fastest time with 72/6 and the second fastest time with 72/8 just to underline his superiority. Fittipaldi continued to focus on 72/7 and set the sixth-best time. By Saturday, the track was becoming more polished and slippery and many drivers found it

difficult to improve on their times from the previous day. Peterson was one of these, but he need not have worried, for he retained his pole position, despite the fact that Cevert, Stewart and Fittipaldi all improved. Although the Brazilian tried his spare, he had two separate incidences of suspension upright failure, something which appeared to be linked to his slowing-down lap coming together with Stewart at Monaco, since the parts in question had been transferred to his spare car for Anderstorp.

Once again, it looked like being a Lotus vs Tyrrell battle, with Cevert lining up on the front row alongside Peterson and Stewart and Fittipaldi sharing row two. On the morning of the race there was a minor panic when it was found that the rear crankcase oil seal on Fittipaldi's car was leaking, so

this had to be changed, while both Lotus drivers felt that the different wind direction compared to practice warranted a ratio change after the warm-up.

When the Swedish flag was dropped, Peterson made a great start, with Fittipaldi slicing his way up the middle to slot in behind his team-mate at the first corner. Incredibly, this was the way it stayed until lap 70 of the scheduled 80, with the Lotus drivers circulating virtually nose to tail. However, Fittipaldi's brakes were playing up, due to oil from the gearbox leaking onto the rear discs. This forced him to use

the gearbox more to slow the car and, since it was now running low on oil the box was beginning to break up. Eventually, both Stewart and Hulme passed the stricken Lotus on the same lap and, although the Brazilian clung on to fourth place tenaciously for the next three laps, he was then passed by Cevert and Reutemann on successive laps. He managed another two laps before parking his car near the finishing line, with only four laps remaining.

Meanwhile, at the front of the race, Peterson had appeared to be cruising to an easy victory but his left rear tyre was softening as a result of a slow puncture. Stewart had been harrying the Swede for several laps in an effort to get by, but Ronnie had been making his car extra-wide, determined to hold on and win his home race. At about the time that Fittipaldi stopped, Stewart ran into brake troubles similar to the ones he had experienced at Barcelona, except this time at the rear and it looked as if Peterson might hold on after all. However, Denny Hulme took up where Stewart had left off, badgering the sliding Lotus all the way round the lap. With cruel precision, he passed Peterson on the last lap, robbing the local boy of what would have been a long-overdue and very welcome victory.

Stewart had struggled on despite the problems with his car, and was able to nurse it home in fifth place, to earn two valuable points. This took his tally to 39 compared to the 41 of Fittipaldi. Other title contenders at this stage were Cevert (25 points), Hulme (19), his McLaren team-mate Revson (11) and Peterson, now into double figures at least (10).

Opposite Page Top Left: Peterson confers with Peter Warr, while Ralph Bellamy checks over the rear of the car during practice for the Swedish Grand Prix. **Opposite Page Top Right & Bottom:** Denied again: Peterson led the Swedish Grand Prix with Fittipaldi acting as tail gunner until first the Brazilian retired and then the Swede was forced to relinquish the lead just miles from home due to a puncture. **Above:** Peterson and Fittipaldi get ready for practice at Anderstorp. Peter Warr (standing, left) is overseeing operations, while Colin Chapman is keeping a watchful eye on proceedings just to the left of Peterson. **Left:** On Peterson's home soil, Fittipaldi played the role of dutiful team-mate before his retirement. His car shows evidence of contact during the race, since the left-front nose fin is drooping.

CHAPTER 15 MIDSUMMER MADNESS

The problems experienced by Fittipaldi with his gearbox were symptomatic of the greater loads being placed on this part of the car by the combination of tyre technology and aerodynamics during the 1973 season, as Ralph Bellamy describes. 'We used a pretty straightforward Hewland gearbox. The problems were predominantly crown wheel and pinion and gears as well. The 72 had a significant rearward weight bias and bloody huge rear tyres, so the amount of tractive effort was enormous and that's what kills gearboxes. So, the load on the gearbox was, at that time, greater than probably at any other time in Formula 1. I can remember spending a lot of time talking to oil companies about better lubricants, for keeping crown wheels and pinions alive and stuff.'

The other area of concern for the team, according to Bellamy, was the 72's braking performance. 'While they had an inboard brake system, the calipers were made by Girling and they were pretty agricultural. Being inboard, there wasn't a lot of cooling around and they got hot and weren't particularly good. The front brakes were OK when the design was new, but through the life of the 72, the amount of aerodynamic downforce went through the roof because we were just stuffing bigger and bigger wings on and therefore the amount of braking capacity the car needed, or could use, went up dramatically. In those days what was available off the shelf from the brake manufacturers, which were only Girling and Lockheed, was not super-brilliant, and I can remember having shouting matches with them about it all.'

After the long trek up to Sweden, the Formula 1 teams returned to the south of France two weeks later for the French Grand Prix at the Circuit Paul Ricard. This was a venue where the 72s had gone particularly well in 1971 when the race was last held at the venue, so John Player Team Lotus were extremely optimistic about their prospects.

Drag was particularly important on this circuit with its seemingly endless back straight, which dominated the circuit: if a car was not quick on this part of the track it could not compensate by clawing back any deficit on the twisty bits. As a result, for this event, all four John Player Team Lotus cars sported subframes attached to the gearbox casing which placed the rear wings a whole 10 inches further back than before. The reasoning behind this was that they would be more effective because they were positioned in less turbulent air and also that they would exert more leverage for less drag, as Ralph Bellamy

explains. 'The further back you went, the more clear air you got. You could run the wing at a shallower angle and produce the same amount of downforce because it was running in clearer air. The thing you have to understand is that there was no drag penalty for having more and more front wing.

'When eventually we went into the windtunnel [for the Lotus 78] we found that you could put more and more front wing on and get more and more downforce and the drag didn't go up. It seemed to me that this was because the front wing was immediately followed by the front tyre and suspension, which created all the drag anyway. The front wing, in effect, was free. So, if you could move the rear wing back and improve its efficiency, and then add front wing - which was free - to balance the car and keep the centre of pressure in the right place, then you'd made a net gain.' In true Lotus fashion, there had been no opportunity to try this new tweak before setting off for Paul Ricard, so the first time that the drivers would have a chance to find out whether it worked or not would be when practice began.

Both drivers had their regular chassis but Fittipaldi had reverted to 72/5 as his race car, with 72/7 as the spare. The reason for this was that the team had apparently had a close look at the car he drove in Sweden and found that it had become warped during the process of conversion to deformable structure specification, which upset the handling. Due to the tight schedule involved in travelling back from Sweden and then down to Paul Ricard, it had not

been possible to address the problem back at the works, so it was consigned to the role of spare for the meeting. Similarly, Peterson chose to continue with the older 72/6, since 72/8 was fitted with the wrong torsion-bar rate and changing torsion bars was a complicated task requiring several hours work, since it necessitated the removal of the deformable structure 'jacket' around the tub.

Once more, it was the Tyrrell and Lotus teams who were the dominant force in practice at Paul Ricard, except for the fact that there was an interloper in the form of the McLaren team, which had really got its M23s working well. The two Lotus drivers were well matched and in the first session on Friday afternoon, Peterson was around half a second quicker than Fittipaldi, while on Saturday morning the Brazilian returned the favour. In the final session, Fittipaldi again edged out the Swede, who had been troubled for much of practice by fuel system woes which caused the engine to cut out on the long sequence of right-handers as well as by a misfire at peak revs on the straight. Notwithstanding these problems, the two JPS cars still lined up in third and fifth places on the grid, Fittipaldi squeezing onto the outside of the front row in the 3-2-3 formation and Peterson on the outside of row 2.

The scene was set for a superb race and what followed didn't disappoint, from the crowd's point of view at least. 'New boy' Jody Scheckter, having his first race in the McLaren M23, made the best start, while Peterson burst through from the second row to come round in second at

Left: They're off! Fittipaldi and Stewart set off from the second row in pursuit of new young hotshot Jody Scheckter's McLaren. Peterson is already aiming for the gap between them, having started from the third row. Note the rear wing and oil tank/cooler assembly, now mounted some 10 inches further back on a sub-frame.

the end of the opening lap, ahead of Stewart, Hulme and Fittipaldi, who had rather squandered his good grid position. This gaggle of five pulled clear of the rest of the field and proceeded to run nose-to-tail until Hulme was the first to break, swinging off into the pits at the end of lap 17 with a puncture and two laps later Fittipaldi was past Stewart. After a further two tours had elapsed, the Scot was in the pits, also with a softening tyre, leaving the lone McLaren to fend off the two Lotus 72s. On the same lap that Stewart pitted, Fittipaldi decided that he had given Peterson enough of an opportunity to get past the flying Scheckter and pushed his way into second.

For nearly 20 laps, the Brazilian pondered where he might pass. He saw his opportunity as they came up to lap the BRM of Jean-Pierre Beltoise and pounced into the slow right-hander leading onto the start/finish straight. He takes up the story. 'I started attacking Jody, very aggressively. I worked out a few laps before that it was the only place I could pass him. He was very slow on the infield, on the corner before the pits. I'd never tried to pass him because I didn't want to show that I could pass him there but I knew that I could overtake him on the right side, on the inside, because the Lotus was very good under braking there. I said to myself "Now is the time, now or never" and I went to the inside of Jody. As he saw me, he was shocked, and he closed the door before the corner! I hit the side of the

McLaren with my front wheel and bent my front suspension.'

The resulting collision damaged the suspension on both cars, Emerson just managing to coax his car out of harm's way off the track and the McLaren driver limping round to the pits to retire. All this left Peterson, no doubt smiling to himself inside his helmet, as the comfortable leader, by some considerable margin from the Tyrrell of Cevert and with only 12 laps remaining. With everything crossed for good luck and listening for any slight change in engine note or tyre profile which might spell trouble, the Swede reeled off those laps to take the chequered flag, his debut Grand Prix win and the first for his new team.

The delight among the team members at finally achieving this landmark victory was tempered by the fact that Fittipaldi had failed to score for the second successive race, while Stewart had recovered from his puncture to come home fourth and pick up three points, enough to topple Emerson from the lead of the World Championship by one point. Cevert's second place had brought him closer to Fittipaldi with 31 points, while Hulme and Peterson were now tied for fourth in the standings with 19 points apiece.

For the British Grand Prix at Silverstone, the two John Player Team Lotus drivers stuck with the cars they had used at Paul Ricard, the damage to Fittipaldi's car being confined to suspension components rather than the tub itself. The only specification changes were on the two race cars, which had been fitted with extra transmission oil coolers in an

First Person
Ralph Bellamy on developing the 72 in 1973

"It was an extremely efficient motor car, simple as that. The inboard brakes and stuff like that gave it an advantage. In those days, one was just putting more and more downforce on the cars and going faster. So, literally all the development was aerodynamic, we barely touched the rest of the car. We just put bigger wings on the back and moved them further and further back and bigger wings on the front to counteract that, and that was the development. It was almost entirely aerodynamic, anything just to get more and more grip."

effort to try and prevent the gearbox problems which had afflicted the cars at several of the races so far.

Practice got off to an ignominious start for the team, when the fuel pump on Peterson's 72/6 seized and then the pump drive belt on the front of the engine broke, forcing him to use the spare. Despite a down-on-power engine and a gearbox that was leaking oil, he managed to put up second-quickest time, two-tenths slower than Denny Hulme, while Fittipaldi in his race car was another two-tenths slower to place fourth in the session.

In the second session on Friday afternoon, Emerson

equalled Peterson's time of the day before but the Swede, back in his race car, really turned up the wick and took pole with a superb lap, which had the crowd at Woodcote on the edge of their seats. His time of 1m 16.3s was two-tenths quicker than the two McLaren M23s of Hulme (unable to improve on his Thursday time) and Peter Revson, while Stewart and Fittipaldi achieved the same time, taking up fourth and fifth spots on the grid, Stewart ahead of the two by virtue of having posted the time first. The first seven cars were fielded by Lotus, McLaren and Tyrrell (the odd number being due to McLaren running Scheckter in a third car), so once again it seemed as if a close battle between these three teams was in prospect.

This race became famous for the huge accident at the end of the opening lap caused by Jody Scheckter, when he ran wide at the ultra-fast Woodcote corner and then spun across the track into the pit wall and rolled back into the path of the rest of the field. For Lotus, this turned out to be a fortuitous incident, because both cars emerged unscathed from the melee. Peterson had been ahead of it all in second place, having been caught by surprise by the fast-starting Tyrrell of Stewart, which had slipped past him into Becketts. Meanwhile, Fittipaldi had been in among it all in a lowly 11th place, having been chopped by Reutemann at the start, causing him to lift off, losing momentum and several places. Somehow he had managed to steer his way through without hitting anything. Both drivers complained that on the opening lap their cars had been oversteering badly on full tanks, so some adjustments were made while awaiting the restart to try and counter this. There was also a minor drama when fuel was found in the cockpit of Peterson's car but it was decided this was just a spillage and a plastic sheet was inserted before the Swede got back into the cockpit in order to protect him 'just in case'.

The two Lotus drivers made a better job of the start second time around, Peterson leading through Lauda's BRM and Stewart, with Fittipaldi in fourth this time. On lap seven, Stewart spun just as he was attempting to overtake Peterson into Stowe and Emerson got past the BRM, so all of a sudden the two John Player Special Lotus 72s came round in first and second positions, leading the John Player Grand Prix – a sponsor's dream. This order was maintained for the next thirty laps, although Fittipaldi was increasingly having to fight a rearguard action to hold off the McLaren of Peter Revson, with the result that he was getting closer and closer to his team-mate.

On lap 37, there was a light sprinkling of rain and then all of a sudden Fittipaldi was pulling off at Abbey Curve, his race over due to a broken CV joint. This left Peterson exposed to the McLaren and two laps later the American driver was through into the lead, a position he held until the end to score his maiden Formula 1 victory. Peterson held on to come home in second place but once again a good points-scoring opportunity had slipped out of the grasp of Fittipaldi. The only saving grace was that Stewart's spin had cost him a lap in the pits while the debris was cleared out of his radiators and air scoops and the Scot came home in 10th position, also out of the points. Thus, there was no change in the standings, with Stewart still leading Fittipaldi by one point, Cevert (who finished fifth at Silverstone) maintaining third eight points further back and Peterson now up into fourth place, another eight points adrift.

After the race, the first rumours began to circulate about Marlboro making a big offer to Emerson Fittipaldi and that he would be joining a new, as yet unspecified, team for 1974. With Jackie Stewart almost certain to announce his retirement at the end of the season, many 'insiders' felt that Tyrrell was the logical place for him to go but at this stage it was no more than idle speculation.

For the next race, the Dutch Grand Prix at Zandvoort, new airboxes were introduced with a larger aperture which

Opposite Page: At last: Peterson's long-awaited first Grand Prix victory was a long-time coming, even prompting Team Lotus to produce a special sticker to celebrate! **Above:** Peterson keeps a close eye on Stewart in his mirrors in the early stages of the British Grand Prix at Silverstone. **Left:** Fittipaldi's car is pushed onto the grid prior to an eventful John Player British Grand Prix.

significantly increased engine revs, by as much as 1,000rpm according to Rex Hart. However, as Ralph Bellamy explains, no-one was certain whether this gain was due to the airbox itself, or other related factors. 'One was never sure when you put a bigger airbox on whether the increase in revs was because you had disturbed the airflow to the rear wing and therefore reduced its drag or whether you'd actually made an improvement in the engine performance. So there was this question mark hanging over where the extra revs had come from.'

Due to the close proximity of the German Grand Prix, set to take place a week after Zandvoort, it was decided that the two drivers would concentrate on their regular cars, 72/5 for Fittipaldi and 72/6 for Peterson, while the spare cars would be prepared for the Nürburgring and left in the garage back in the town rather than brought to the circuit. The only concession was that they were fitted with Zandvoort ratios, just in case they were needed.

The first practice session on the Friday afternoon was largely spoilt by heavy rain which, when combined with the wind blowing off the North Sea, made for particularly cold and unpleasant conditions. Peterson still went out, setting the fourth-best time, while Fittipaldi was eighth after missing the best conditions as a result of a puncture. On Saturday, the weather was still very overcast but at least dry. Disaster struck in the first of the two sessions. Fittipaldi had already set the third-fastest time and he and Peterson were

circulating in close company when the glued centre of his left front parted company with the rest of the wheel, sending him spearing off into the barriers at one of the fastest points on the circuit, just where the cars are coming onto the long start/finish straight. The impact pushed the whole of the left front corner, including the brake disc, back into the footwell, trapping the Brazilian's feet. 'What a disaster. That was the worst accident I've ever had. My fuel was leaking but I couldn't get out of the car.' Fortunately, although it was a big impact, there was no fire and eventually Emerson was released by the combined might of Mike Hailwood, a Tyrrell mechanic and Graham Hill, using a length of pipe as a lever.

The car was badly damaged. There was no question of it being rebuilt, either for the race or in the foreseeable future. This was particularly sad because it had really been 'Emerson's car'. He was the first to drive 72/5 at Monza in 1970 and the two of them had since been through good and bad times. After an examination at the Grand Prix Medical Unit, the World Champion took some pain-killers and hobbled off to get into 72/7, which had been brought down from the town in the interval between sessions. In considerable pain, he drove this very gingerly round, doing just enough to qualify, his time good enough for the inside of the seventh row.

Peterson pulled a 'fast one' in the final session. In first practice, Goodyear had provided Stewart, Hulme and

Fittipaldi with a new compound tyre, which proved to be about 0.7s per lap quicker than any other, but which had grained badly and therefore the company withdrew them. Peter Warr went along to Goodyear, invoked a clause in the team's contract which stipulated that all drivers would be provided with equal equipment and came away with a set of these tyres for Peterson, who had not tried them in the earlier session. He promptly used these to excellent effect, putting his car on pole, half a second clear of Stewart, with the other Tyrrell of Cevert completing the front row. This was despite the Swede's engine refusing to rev to its maximum, being some 400 revs down by the end of practice.

The race was totally overshadowed by a terrible accident involving British driver Roger Williamson, who died trapped upside down in his burning car due to the scandalous ineptitude of the marshals and lack of suitable fire-fighting equipment. Fittipaldi, barely able to walk, managed but two laps in his spare car before pulling into the pits to retire, while Peterson led for 63 of the 72 laps before his engine blew up. It had been under some considerable strain for the previous 20 laps or so because the Swede had gear selection problems, which eventually saw him lose second and fourth and so he was revving it particularly hard at certain points of the circuit in order to maintain speed. Two laps after he lost the lead to Stewart, he coasted into the pits to retire, leaving the Tyrrell team to

Opposite Page: Hammer blow: Fittipaldi's accident at Zandvoort when practising for the Dutch Grand Prix severely damaged his favourite chassis and caused the Brazilian injuries that blunted his ability to challenge for the Championship. **Left:** The German Grand Prix was not a successful meeting for John Player Team Lotus, Peterson (shown here rounding the Karussell) retiring on the first lap and Fittipaldi battling on despite his injuries to a brave sixth.

score an emphatic 1-2. Stewart now led Fittipaldi by a clear 10 points, while Cevert was only two points behind the Brazilian in the standings and Peterson still fourth.

The one-week gap between races now proved to be a considerable disadvantage to the cause of Fittipaldi's World Championship challenge, for it did not permit sufficient time for the Brazilian to recover from the injuries sustained in his Zandvoort accident. The three remaining Lotus cars which appeared at the Nürburgring were virtually unchanged in specification: for first practice the ten-inch subframes on which the rear wing and oil tank were mounted were replaced by shorter, three-inch versions but the team actually reverted to the familiar set-up for second practice and the race.

In the first session on Friday, Peterson set a time good enough for second on the grid, while Fittipaldi was some eleven and a half seconds slower. As it turned out, this was the crucial session, since Saturday practice was blighted by intermittent rain showers. In this session, Fittipaldi was fractionally

faster than Peterson but it was all to no avail as he was unable to improve on his Friday time. As a result, he was again down in a lowly grid position, on the outside of the seventh row, alongside his brother Wilson's Brabham. Peterson's session came to a premature end when a ball joint on the left front suspension broke at the Pflanzgarten jump and he was lucky not to have a big accident.

At the start, the Tyrrells of Stewart and Cevert chopped across the bows of Peterson into the South Curve and were never to be headed, scoring their second successive 1-2 finish. Mid-way round the first lap, the Swede pulled off at the Breidscheid bridge with distributor failure, while Fittipaldi had an unspectacular race to sixth just behind his brother, having been passed by Wilson on the second lap. Clearly, he had done well to finish considering the pain he was in and one point was just reward for his efforts.

It was about this time that Ralph Bellamy began design work on the new Formula One Lotus for 1974

First Person

Eddie Dennis on Peterson and Fittipaldi

"I think Ronnie was possibly the quicker driver in equal machinery. It's often spoken about him not being quite as good a car sorter as Emerson and Ronnie probably profited from some of Emerson's settings. There was no secrecy between them – the Old Man would share the same information between both of them. But once you gave Ronnie a quick car, he would go blindingly fast, come what may. That was the only thing he knew. He just drove as fast as he could. We never had any moaning from Ronnie at all. Emerson's wife started to say that they thought Ronnie was getting the better equipment and I got quite short with her

because that was not the case. What they got was what they'd always had, nothing had changed. It was just that Emerson had the luck in the early part of the season and Ronnie had it in the second part."

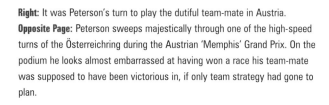

Right: It was Peterson's turn to play the dutiful team-mate in Austria.
Opposite Page: Peterson sweeps majestically through one of the high-speed turns of the Österreichring during the Austrian 'Memphis' Grand Prix. On the podium he looks almost embarrassed at having won a race his team-mate was supposed to have been victorious in, if only team strategy had gone to plan.

However, another nine points for Jackie Stewart meant that he had now built up a virtually unassailable lead in the World Championship standings. To rub salt into the wounds, Cevert's six points elevated him into second place in the title race behind his team-mate, three points ahead of Fittipaldi.

It was about this time, according to Ralph Bellamy, that design work began on the 1974 Formula 1 Lotus. 'Colin came up to me and he said, "I want you to go back, go to Ketteringham Hall, set yourself up in a separate office there and design this car. It just wants to be an upgraded, tidied up version of the 72 because it's getting a bit long in the tooth, it's got some structural problems and all that sort of stuff, just tidy it all up". And that's what I did. So it really had no inherent performance advantages built in. What it had built in was a tidier engineering package. '

With four Championship rounds remaining, the situation was becoming critical for Fittipaldi if he was to have any chance of mounting a challenge for the title. He just had to score points at the next round in Austria and, realistically, anything less than a maximum haul of nine points would be a disaster. The three cars that appeared at the Österreichring were as they had appeared in Germany, except that 72/8 was fitted with a longer, lower oil tank which also acted as the rear wing mounting. This removed

the need for the temporary space-frame which had been used to mount the wing 10 inches further back since Paul Ricard.

Fortunately, the high speed sweeps of the Österreichring were known to suit the Lotus 72s and Tyrrell had always struggled at the circuit, so the team were optimistic that a good result could be achieved. This optimism seemed to be well grounded, for Peterson set the fastest time in the first session and actually ran out of fuel on what he felt was going to be a faster lap. Fittipaldi was down in ninth, suffering from understeer, which was definitely not where he wanted to be, even if that was one place ahead of Stewart. Everything came right in the final session, when Emerson really got everything wound up and put his car on pole, to make an all black-and-gold front row. More encouragingly in terms of the Championship, Stewart could only qualify on the fourth row, with Cevert on the fifth row.

When the flag dropped, it was Peterson who made the best start, while Denny Hulme pushed his McLaren through into second as the field streamed up the hill and disappeared out of sight. Hulme was the meat in a Team Lotus sandwich for the first 11 laps but then a plug lead came loose and on lap 12 it was the two John Player cars that came through some way clear of the rest of the field.

1st
Memphis
Grand Prix
1973
John Player Special

Before the race, Colin Chapman had sat down with his two drivers and discussed tactics if just such a situation arose. Between them, they agreed that it would be better for Fittipaldi's Championship chances if he could win and so, on lap 17, Peterson allowed the Brazilian through into the lead and then faithfully followed his team-mate at a respectful distance.

Everything seemed to be going to plan, although they would have been even happier if Stewart had not been running in third behind them. However, with just six laps remaining, Fittipaldi pulled off the circuit. A pipe running to the fuel metering unit had come off, something which had never happened before but it was enough to end his

TEXACO

race and, with it, almost extinguish the Brazilian's Championship hopes. Peterson continued, almost embarrassedly, to take his second Grand Prix victory of the year ahead of Stewart, whose six points virtually assured him of the title. Although Peterson's win took his tally to 34 points, he could not now win the Championship, even if he won the next three races, since Stewart already had 66 points. With Cevert failing to score, Fittipaldi remained in third place in the title race but he was now the only non-Tyrrell driver who could win the Championship. To do this, he had to win the remaining three rounds, with Stewart scoring no more than three points, an almost hopeless situation given the Scot's results to that point.

CHAPTER 16 THE FIRST SIGNS OF DISCORD

After the Austrian race there was further speculation about Fittipaldi's plans for the 1974 season and there were repeated stories of Marlboro trying to sign him up, taking their sponsorship to either Brabham or McLaren for the coming year. Even Colin Chapman openly acknowledged that the Brazilian had received approaches from other teams but said that he felt there was no reason for him to go anywhere else and that he was confident Emerson would be driving for him the following year.

The next race was the Italian Grand Prix, held in the picturesque setting of the park at Monza. What used to be a high-speed slipstreaming blast had been emasculated in the name of safety to incorporate a chicane just after the start and finish area and a left/right/left sweep on the return leg. Nonetheless, the same teams which had monopolised the front row at the high speed Österreichring circuit – Lotus and McLaren – were once more the dominant forces at Monza. Once again, only three black-and-gold cars were rolled out of the transporter – 72/7 for Fittipaldi and 72/6 and 72/8 for Peterson. Although a ninth chassis (effectively a new car built out of the remains of 72/5) had been finished and was on its wheels back at the Hethel works, it was decided to leave it in England and concentrate the team's efforts on thoroughly preparing for Italy. The only changes made to the cars for the Italian race were that the low-line oil tank/wing mounting arrangement which had first appeared on Peterson's spare in Austria was now fitted to the two race cars, while 72/8 had reverted to the previous arrangement.

After the two Friday practice sessions, Revson was at the top of the timesheets in his McLaren but Peterson was only five-hundredths of a second slower. Fittipaldi was well

Below: Peterson and Fittipaldi ran in formation throughout the Italian Grand Prix at Monza, except that the team did not order Peterson to move over and let Fittipaldi through, as the Brazilian had thought they would… Note larger aperture of airbox, first used at Zandvoort.

down the list as the heavy braking required for the chicane was making his ankles hurt as well as the fact that his engine would not rev properly. In an effort to help his ankles he had them strapped up in the Grand Prix Medical Unit. On Saturday, he was clearly much happier, moving up to fifth fastest in the first afternoon session, while Peterson was again second quickest, this time behind the other McLaren of Hulme. The final session took place in the cooler air of the late afternoon, so that most of the leading runners improved their times. Peterson bolted on a set of sticky Goodyears and put pole out of reach, the only driver to lap inside 1m 35s, while the two McLaren's continued their good form to occupy the next two grid slots on the two-by-two grid. Fittipaldi was next, for a position on the outside of the second row, with Championship rival Stewart content with sixth, right behind the Brazilian on the grid.

Race day was hot, sunny and dry and a huge crowd filtered into Monza to see the Championship showdown. At the start, both Peterson and Fittipaldi made superb getaways, the Brazilian forging through to snatch second as the field hurtled towards the Curve Grande. They came round at the end of the first lap in team formation and, for the next 55 laps ran like clockwork. Although no team orders had been issued prior to the start, Fittipaldi quite naturally assumed that Peterson would at some stage allow

him to pass as he was the only one of the two with a mathematical chance of still winning the Championship, albeit a slim one.

In the pits, the situation was discussed by Chapman and Warr. It was further complicated by the position of Stewart. The Tyrrell driver had punctured on lap eight and dropped right down the order from the resultant pit stop. If he was going to finish outside the points then there might be some justification for waving Fittipaldi through. However, the Scot made a fantastic recovery moving through the field and back into the points by lap 37. He was into fifth place on lap 42 and then up to fourth, the position he needed to secure the title if Fittipaldi remained where he was, on lap 49. To take the title, Fittipaldi had to win at Monza, then in Canada and the US, with Stewart not scoring at all. If this happened, the Brazilian and the Scot would be tied on points but Fittipaldi would be Champion by virtue of a greater number of wins.

Chapman and Warr realised that this was an unlikely scenario and decided to do nothing. As the latter explains, they were also aware of the chance that the Brazilian would be moving on at the end of the year and so they didn't want to upset Peterson, who would be staying with them for 1974. 'We both knew that Emerson had had conversations about driving for McLaren, as we expected he would. Ronnie was absolutely at the top of his form, having done very little else but win since Paul Ricard and Emerson was definitely not the fastest driver. His mathematical chance of winning the Championship relied, not only on Ronnie giving him the last two races, which is a hell of a lot to give away, but it also relied on Stewart not scoring any more points. I think that was just so remote, and when Colin and I discussed it we didn't talk for more than a few seconds on

these was the Canadian Grand Prix, at the Mosport Park circuit. With first practice being only 12 days after Monza, there was no time to make any changes to the specifications of the cars, so they were unchanged.

Peterson dominated all three practice sessions, setting the fastest time in each and by a considerable margin over all the other competitors. On Friday, Fittipaldi was troubled by his car pulling to one side but this was resolved for Saturday and the Brazilian promptly ended the day second on the timesheets. However, because Saturday was the slower of the two days, his time was only good enough for the inside of the third row.

Once again conditions on race day were wet, although they weren't quite as bad as they had been the previous year. At the start, Peterson splashed into the lead but it was the Firestone tyres which appeared to have the upper hand in the rain and Niki Lauda passed the Swede on the third lap, opening up a huge advantage over his pursuers, the nearest of which became Scheckter when he passed Peterson on lap eight. Meanwhile, Fittipaldi had briefly lost out to Stewart and was down in fifth but got past the Tyrrell seven laps later. Around this time, Peterson supplanted Scheckter to regain second and three laps further on Fittipaldi also passed the young South African to make it Lotus second and third. However, it wasn't long before the incident-packed race turned up another drama, when Peterson suffered a puncture on lap 16, causing him to spin, breaking a torsion bar link as he went up over the kerbing and then hitting the guardrail hard enough to end his afternoon's racing.

the pit wall before both of us just said "No, we can't do it". So we let the race run out as it was.' Of course there was some risk involved in this strategy since there was still the possibility that Stewart might encounter further problems in the final few laps and score no points at Monza.

It wasn't simply that Fittipaldi was looking likely to join McLaren that had upset Chapman and Warr either, for it transpired that his departure would have financial implications for the team as well. 'We had very good information that he was planning to decamp. I think he had suffered a considerable wound to his pride because Ronnie had come along and proved to be quicker than him everywhere. The thing which didn't predispose us particularly kindly towards Emerson at that moment in time, was we learnt that– everybody knew what a struggle it was to fund race teams, it was then and it is now – as part of the package he was going to do with the Marlboro/Teddy Mayer/McLaren set-up, he was going to take our sponsor, Texaco, with him.'

Despite a big effort on the part of Fittipaldi to pass Peterson in the dying laps when

1st Italian Grand Prix 1973 *John Player Special*

Nice One Jackie World Champion 1973

he realised he was not going to be waved through, the Swede crossed the line 0.8s ahead, triumphantly punching the air. Fittipaldi recalls the frustration he felt in the closing laps when it became apparent that his team-mate was not going to be ordered to let him through. 'With ten laps to go, Colin didn't give any sign and then I started attacking Ronnie. Then Ronnie realised what I was doing and we raced to the end. I couldn't pass him and I finished right on his gearbox. That's when I decided to go to another team'

The normally placid Fittipaldi was privately seething at this perceived lack of support from his team, and made the decision there and then to leave. He was not even certain of second place in the title race, either, for Cevert had finished fifth in Italy and lay only one point behind him, while Peterson was now only five points behind.

The two remaining races in North America, as was so often the case, therefore became inconsequential in terms of the outcome of the World Championship but there was still second place in the standings, as well as personal pride, to play for. The first of

First Person

Peter Warr on the arrival of Ronnie Peterson

"It didn't put Emerson's nose out of joint to start with but it did very soon after! Ronnie was just so fast, he'd come through the Curva del Sol at Interlagos with smoke coming off both rear tyres! Eventually, Emerson had a word and we did a deal with Ronnie – if he let Emerson win in Brazil, Ronnie could win in Sweden. In the first half of the season Ronnie overdrove the car. Then he put together a series of pole positions that showed he was the quickest driver in Formula 1, which got up Emerson's nose. Ronnie didn't have the slightest idea on setting his car up and what happened a lot was that he'd be all at sea while Emerson was quietly working away getting his car just right and then we'd bolt Emerson's settings on at the last minute and Ronnie would go out and take pole!"

Another three laps further on and Fittipaldi found himself in the lead as Lauda pitted for new tyres. The Brazilian enjoyed a dozen laps in the lead before he decided that the track was dry enough to warrant a change to slicks and he also lost some additional time having some wing taken off to better suit the conditions. Around this

time, there was a collision between Cevert and Scheckter, which brought out the recently-introduced pace car. Unfortunately, it positioned itself in front of the wrong car, allowing the first three runners – Beltoise (BRM), Oliver (Shadow) and Revson (McLaren) – to run round and join the back of the field, now almost a lap ahead of everyone else.

What followed was a tremendous drive by Fittipaldi. Once the pace car unleashed the field, he forced his way past Howden Ganley's Iso (the 'leader' the pace car had picked up) and then drove on the limit to make up an entire lap on the BRM and Shadow – Revson had already slipped past these two and had a comfortable lead of half a minute or so – in 40 laps. With just two tours remaining, Emerson passed both cars to snatch second place, although because of the huge number of pit stops the Lotus lap-scorers had lost track of who was where and thought Fittipaldi had won! Chapman therefore did his customary 'hat in the air' victory celebration but it was a lap too early and was promptly flattened into the tarmac by the rest of the field as they completed their final lap…

After the race, Chapman and Fittipaldi left the circuit together to discuss contracts. The Lotus boss had apparently made Emerson a much more attractive financial offer than before and was keen to secure his services to drive alongside Peterson for 1974. Rumours continued to abound of some kind of a tie-up between Fittipaldi and McLaren or possibly Brabham but no official announcements had been made.

The fifteenth and final round of the World Championship, the United States Grand Prix, took place as usual at the Watkins Glen track in New York State. John Player Team Lotus fielded the same three cars as in Canada. The damage to Peterson's car following its race accident at Mosport Park was worse than initially thought,

Opposite Page Top: Peterson punches the air in delight, having resisted the attacks of Fittipaldi in the closing laps of the Italian Grand Prix. Opposite Page Bottom: For the second successive race, Peterson climbs up onto the rostrum to receive his victor's garland. Below Left: Fittipaldi probably would have won the Canadian Grand Prix had it not been for a pace-car blunder on the part of the officials, which forced him to make up nearly a lap on the cars in front of him. Below Right: Peterson ran strongly in both North American races at the end of the season. In Canada he took pole and led the race until a puncture caused him to crash.

with the result that the tub had to be flown back to Hethel to be straightened in the jig and then returned to America to be rebuilt. In order to give Peterson a chance to dial in his repaired chassis, a special test session was laid on for the Swede, as Rex Hart recalls. 'On the Tuesday before the race, the Old Man wrote a programme out to give Ronnie a bit of a chance and we ran no wings, dampers backed right off and we then went through, gradually introducing bump and rebound, then front wings, then back wings. We finished up with the rear wing almost flat and he was flying, inside the lap record! But the Old Man wouldn't run it because it didn't look right. He just said, "No, we're not running that".'

Official practice was scheduled over two days – Friday and Saturday. On the Friday, there was a four-hour session, while the next day there were two sessions, one in the morning and a second in the afternoon. Practice started badly for Peterson when, after only two laps, his left rear wheel came off due to a hub unscrewing itself and he made light contact with the barriers. As a result, he spent the rest of the session in the spare car, 72/8, but this didn't seem to slow him down much, since he emerged at the top of the timesheets, with Fittipaldi languishing down in ninth, still troubled by his painful ankles.

The Saturday morning session was the fastest of the three, with all the leading runners setting their best times. Back in his favourite 72/6, Peterson was again quickest, the first time a Formula 1 car had lapped under the magical 100 second barrier and the only driver to do so. This secured his ninth pole position of the season – a truly remarkable achievement and testament, if any were

needed, to his blistering turn of speed. Meanwhile, Fittipaldi moved up the order and put in a lap which was good enough for third on the grid. However, the whole session was overshadowed by the tragic death of Francois Cevert, who crashed his Tyrrell in the high-speed Esses section of the track and was killed instantly.

Cevert's accident guaranteed that Fittipaldi would

finish second in the World Championship, although the Brazilian would not have wanted it this way. Similarly, when Elf-Team Tyrrell announced the withdrawal of their remaining entries, for World Champion Jackie Stewart and Chris Amon, it also assured John Player Team Lotus of the prized Constructors World Championship, although again they would much rather have fought it out on the track to

win it in the final round. The afternoon session, quite understandably, took place in a rather subdued atmosphere, with everyone affected by the morning's events. The circuit also seemed to be slower and none of the front-runners improved their times.

The race took place over 59 laps of the 3.377 mile circuit and was held in cool, cloudy but dry conditions. Peterson made a superb getaway and was never headed. James Hunt in a privately-run March owned by Lord Hesketh moved into second place on lap four and closed up to the back of the black-and-gold Lotus but was unable to pass, even though he moved alongside at one stage when Peterson was lapping some backmarkers. It was a game of cat and mouse. The Swede was driving just fast enough to stay ahead (he was troubled by locking rear brakes due to a bit too much bias to the back) and the Englishman was

applying just enough pressure to try and force the Lotus driver into an error. It was all in vain, for Peterson drove a finely judged race to come home 0.7s ahead of his rival, taking his fourth victory of the year, equalling the tally of Champion Stewart and one more than his team-mate Fittipaldi.

Emerson had endured a frustrating race, slowing due to a vibration in the front wheels (no doubt bringing back memories of the moment just before his wheel broke up at Zandvoort) and also being troubled by vicious oversteer. In the early laps he ran fourth but slipped back to seventh after being passed by Hulme, Hailwood and Scheckter when the vibration began. After a few more laps he managed to repass Hailwood and had a relatively uneventful race until lap 37 of 59, when due to the rear wing coming off, Merzario spun his Ferrari right in front of

the Lotus. Fittipaldi was forced to brake heavily to avoid the errant red car and in doing so, flat-spotted both his front tyres. A couple of laps later, he pitted, losing a place to Peter Revson in the process and continued in sixth position to the finish.

Peterson's win elevated him to third position in the final Championship standings, just three points shy of Fittipaldi. While Emerson had ridden his luck sometimes (or made his own) in the first half of the season, without doubt Peterson had enjoyed the better luck in the second half and had also driven exceptionally well, too.

It quickly became apparent that the Brazilian had driven his last race for John Player Team Lotus. Although Marlboro and McLaren were tight-lipped at the race itself, in the aftermath of the event it emerged that Fittipaldi had said he was '99% certain' to join the team as number one driver for 1974. Clearly, the idea of continuing his joint number one status with Peterson was not one that appealed to him. This was not surprising, as there had been times during the year when it was obvious that the team were struggling to field four competitive, properly prepared cars and the already overworked mechanics had been swamped with work. In addition, the team wasn't that desperate to hold on to his services, as Peter Warr relates. 'The fact of the matter is that in Ronnie, we had got the driver that we really wanted. Emerson had been fantastic, had done a brilliant job, but the edge was going off him in the sense that he was no longer hanging it out on the line to get the pole position, he was thinking about his financial security, he was thinking about things that real racers don't think about. Although he went on and did a very, very good job to win the Championship in 74 with McLaren, he never figured from the point of view of going out and blitzing

Opposite Page Top : After Fittipaldi's Dutch accident, Peterson was the only driver with a spare car. From left to right are Peterson's spare 72/8, Fittipaldi's 72/7 and Peterson's race car, 72/6. Opposite Page Bottom: Goodbye: Fittipaldi bowed out of Team Lotus with a sixth place in the US Grand Prix. Above: Man of the moment: Peterson's win at Watkins Glen was his fourth of the year and his third in four races. Left: Victory from pole was the achievement of Peterson in the US Grand Prix at Watkins Glen, despite the race-long attentions of the Hesketh of James Hunt.

them from the front. That was the sort of race-driver that Colin wanted, the sort of driver who was out front.'

Of more concern on a financial note, Texaco, the team's second largest backer after John Player, would be taking its sponsorship with Fittipaldi to McLaren. In some ways this was not really a big surprise: it was well-known that the company had been disappointed at the way it had been forced to take a back seat to John Player, including having to change the company's distinctive red and white logo on the cars to a gold one in order to fit in with the JPS livery. Nonetheless, it was frustrating for the team, having nurtured the relationship, to lose the Texaco money to a

rival, as Warr explains. 'It wasn't a fantastically significant proportion of the budget but what was good about the Texaco thing was that they were involved in the team and they were so keen to establish their own identity. It was all the groundwork that we had done to get this huge company interested, they had never previously been involved in Formula 1, and were so big at the time compared to other fuel sponsors that there was the potential to unlock the door to further and greater riches in the future. Just at the moment when we'd done all the hard work and got them really keen and enthusiastic, they jumped ship with Emerson and went off to McLaren.'

Colin Chapman resigned himself to the fact that he was going to lose Fittipaldi and began casting around for a suitable replacement. He asked Jody Scheckter if he would consider joining Lotus but the South African had already agreed to join Tyrrell for the coming season. Ken Tyrrell had already begun scouting round after the Canadian Grand Prix when Jackie Stewart had confirmed that he intended to retire after Watkins Glen but the death of Francois Cevert meant that he had now lost both his drivers. The choices available to Chapman were therefore relatively limited: Chris Amon had endured a disastrous year with Tecno which had damaged his credibility, while Jacky Ickx had fared little better with the recalcitrant Ferrari. Revson appeared to be on his way to UOP-Shadow, while Reutemann was committed to staying at Brabham.

Perhaps more surprising is that Chapman didn't attempt to sign up James Hunt, who had put in some amazing performances in the Hesketh March. Having said that, it is hard to imagine two characters more different in outlook and the tall Englishman would probably not have fitted in very well at Hethel. This assessment of Hunt is confirmed by Peter Warr. 'Hunt was not Colin's sort of driver. It was the same as Ron Dennis and Nigel Mansell – they were just

First Person
Emerson Fittipaldi on Colin Chapman

"Colin was a genius. What I learned in four years of driving for Lotus I think would take 10-12 years driving for another team. Sometimes during Friday practice the car wasn't so good. Then Colin and I had dinner together and I explained to him, I tried to go through the track from corner to corner from place to place, exactly what the car was doing. He'd call the mechanics and they'd all go very early the next morning, to change the whole set-up and bingo, the car was fast! On the suspension side, on the set-up he had fantastic intuition, he could feel what the car was doing and just change it and 99.9% of the time it would work."

Top: Peterson enjoys the spoils of victory at the US Grand Prix. **Right:** The loss of Fittipali was a 'double blow' for Team Lotus, as he took sponsor Texaco with him.

never, ever going to hit it off. I have to say that, although James did a pretty decent job, there was never any great admiration of him at Team Lotus, no-one ever thought he was really the "Dog's Whatsits"!'

With a new car on the way, Chapman was keen to 'clear the decks' and, only a week after the US Grand Prix, it was announced that Team Lotus had sold a pair of 72s to Team Gunston in South Africa, for Ian Scheckter and Paddy Driver to drive in the South African Drivers Championship. The new car was being penned, in conjunction with Chapman, by the team's Chief Designer Ralph Bellamy. So busy had the Australian been on its design, that he had not attended any of the last five rounds of the 1973 World Championship.

In mid-October, Lotus said that it would announce the identity of its second driver at the end of the month. Peter Warr also said that Fittipaldi had been given a release to conduct a tyre test with McLaren at Paul Ricard but there were tight conditions placed on him – the car had to be painted a neutral colour (white) and he was to wear his usual insignia on his overalls as he still had two and a half months to run on his contract. Warr pointed out that the Brazilian was not at liberty to associate himself with any other tobacco product except John Player until his contract expired on December 31st.

True to their word, at the end of October, John Player Team Lotus announced that it had signed the Belgian Jacky Ickx to drive alongside Peterson for 1974. A new sponsor also joined the ranks, with Duckhams picking up where Texaco left off as the team's official supplier of lubricants.

Peter Warr recalls that there was a sound theory behind the signing of Ickx. 'We wanted a driver who had class and a good reputation, one who wasn't going to throw it into the scenery, because we knew Ronnie was going to do that from time to time! And Ickx was absolutely the perfect mix because he was blindingly fast on his day.'

Ickx's motivation was one of a fresh start in a new team, with the added bonus that he knew his future team-mate very well. 'I didn't want to go back to Ferrari. We had a good relationship and everything but I was fed up at the time and I felt it was a good idea to take some fresh air somewhere else. Especially because I didn't feel the 1974 season with Ferrari was going to be good, but I was wrong. That's the way things are in life – sometimes you make the right choice, sometimes not! So I signed a deal with Colin Chapman to join Ronnie Peterson at Lotus for two seasons, 1974 and 1975. I knew him already because we were in the same Ferrari prototype sports car championship team in 1972 and 1973.'

After the seemingly endless toil of the 1973 season, it was not surprising that there were some changes to the line-up of mechanics. Chief Mechanic Eddie Dennis, who had held that position for the previous three seasons, decided that he wanted a quieter life and took a job back at the Lotus factory. His place was taken by Ronnie Peterson's mechanic, Keith Leighton

WORLD CHAMPIONSHIP TABLE 1973

Pos	Driver	Argentina	Brazil	S.Africa	Spain	Belgium	Monaco	Sweden	France	Great Britain	Netherlands	Germany	Austria	Italy	Canada	USA	Total	(dropped)
1	Jackie Stewart	4	6	9		9	9	2	3		9	9	6	3	2		71	
2	Emerson Fittipaldi	9	9	4	9	4	6					1	6		6	1	55	
3	Ronnie Peterson							4	6	9	6		9	9		9	52	
4	Francois Cevert	6			6	6	3	4	6	2	6	6		2			47	
5	Peter Revson		6	3			2			9	3			4	9	2	38	
6	Denny Hulme	2	4	2	1		1	9		4						3	26	
7	Carlos Reutemann							3	4	1				3	1	4	16	
8	James Hunt								1	3	4					6	14	
9	Jacky Ickx	3	2					1	2				4				12	
10	Jean-Pierre Beltoise				2						2		2		3		9	
11	Carlos Pace											3	4				7	
12	Arturo Merzario		3	3													6	
13	George Follmer			1	4												5	
14	Jackie Oliver														4		4	
15	Andrea de Adamich					3											3	
15	Wilson Fittipaldi	1											2				3	
17	Niki Lauda					2											2	
17	Clay Reggazoni		1											1			2	
19	Chris Amon					1											1	
19	Gijs van Lennep										1						1	
19	Howden Ganley														1		1	

Pos	Constructor	Argentina	Brazil	S.Africa	Spain	Belgium	Monaco	Sweden	France	Great Britain	Netherlands	Germany	Austria	Italy	Canada	USA	Total	(dropped)
1	Lotus-Cosworth	9	9	4	9	4	6	6	9	6		1	9	9	6	9	92	4
2	Tyrrell-Cosworth	6	6	9	6	9	9	4	6	2	9	9	6	3	2		82	4
3	McLaren-Cosworth	2	4	6	3		2	9		9	3	4		4	9	3	58	
4	Brabham-Cosworth	1				3		3	4	1		2	3	1		4	22	
5	March-Cosworth								1	3	4					6	14	
6	Ferrari	3	3	3			1		2								12	
6	B.R.M.		1		2	2					2		2		3		12	
8	Shadow-Cosworth			1	4										4		9	
9	Surtees-Cosworth											3	4				7	
10	ISO-Cosworth										1				1		2	
11	Tecno					1												

The 1974 season started earlier than ever, the first World Championship round being held on January 13th. No sooner had the employees of John Player Team Lotus arrived back from the Christmas/New Year break than it was time to set off globe-trotting again!

New regulations introduced by the FIA for 1974 limited the positioning of the rear wing in an effort to prevent the wings from being hung so far back in the way that Lotus had been doing from mid-way through the 1973 season. As Ralph Bellamy concedes, this was probably the right thing to do. 'Yes, that stifled that area of development. Probably not a bad thing actually, it was all getting a bit bizarre!' The new regulations required that the trailing edge of rear wings be a maximum of one metre behind the centre line of the rear wheels, so the team was forced to abandon the lower, longer oil tank/wing mounting they had perfected and revert to a more conventional position of wing mounting. In addition, the regulations demanded that all oil storage tanks situated outside the main structure of the car had to be surrounded by 10mm thick crushable structure and that no oil tank could be situated behind the gearbox or

final drive casing. Consequently, Lotus was forced to revert to mounting the oil tank over the gearbox rather than as an integral part of the wing support. Finally, although this did not affect the 72, all fire extinguishing systems had to be located within the main structure of the car.

The cars taken to Argentina were 72/8 for Peterson and 72/5 for Ickx. The latter had been rebuilt, salvaging as much as possible from Fittipaldi's Zandvoort wreck. Following the sale of the two cars to South Africa, neither driver had access to a spare, so a serious accident was likely to mean withdrawal from the race for the driver involved. The relocating of the oil tank and wing was found to have upset the handling balance of the car, giving less grip at the rear, with the result that after first practice both drivers reported excessive oversteer. Peter Warr confirms that, on top of the difficulties posed by running Goodyears, which the team had just about managed to counter in 1973, these changes had contributed to a further deterioration in the balance of the overall package. 'The furthest back we ever got the wing was when it was mounted on the top of the conical-shaped oil tank, so in one fell swoop, a lot of changes had to be made. One of the problems, of course, was that everything else that we were doing around the engine and the engine cover interfered with the flow of air to the rear wing, so if you brought the rear wing further forward you were just putting yourself in deeper shit'.

Despite the problems, Ickx was raving about his new car, saying to Autosport's Pete Lyons: "It's so difficult to find the limit. You put that tail out so far that you think you must spin but then the car begins to grip even better. It's fabulous really". The Belgian was having a baptism of fire, having only driven the car briefly at Paul Ricard just before Christmas. There had been no time in the New Year to test because the cars had to be packed up and air-freighted to South America in good time for the race.

In the second afternoon session, when the track was a little less green and conditions were much cooler, some new contenders for victory revealed themselves, the two Ferrari 312Bs, first and fourth with Reggazoni and Lauda respectively, the brand new Shadow DN3 of Peter Revson,

which was second-fastest and the Brabham BT44 of Carlos Reutemann. Also showing a good turn of speed was Mike Hailwood, now driving a McLaren M23 in Yardley livery. The two Lotus 72s were slightly off the pace and when the session times for the day were combined, they were 8th and 12th fastest – a rather unaccustomed position for the team.

Some hard work overnight on settings produced better-handling cars on Saturday. In the slower first session Peterson was only three-tenths off the fastest time set by James Hunt in the Hesketh March 731, although Ickx was still adjusting to his new surroundings and was more than a second slower than his team-mate. In the final session, everything came right for Peterson and he bolted on some sticky Goodyears and snatched pole from Reggazoni. Ickx also improved his best time by nearly two seconds, good enough for a slot on the inside of the fourth row. Meanwhile, the team's former driver, Fittipaldi, slid easily into the cockpit of his McLaren M23 and showed that he would be a title contender with his third-fastest time.

John Player Team Lotus were so happy with their cars that they didn't even bother coming out for the morning warm-up on race day. However, this proved to be a mistake

Left & Right: New regulations for 1974 aimed at eliminating extreme outrigged rear wings set a maximum distance that the trailing edge of a rear wing could extend back from the centre line of the rear wheels and also stipulated the oil tanks had to be in front of the rear face of the gearbox or final drive casing.

LOTUS 72

First Person

Ralph Bellamy on Jacky Ickx

"Ickx was a huge talent, he really was. Different to Ronnie but still a huge talent. In some ways, the handling and structural shortcomings of the car just disillusioned him and he didn't get the hearing that he should have got from Chapman, that was the problem. I had a better rapport with Ickx than Colin did. He wanted us to fit outboard brakes and I wanted to do that because I could see that that was the way to go but politically with Chapman that wasn't on. On occasions we thought that maybe we would get the OK to do it but it never happened.

Jacky was just massively demotivated. He and Colin didn't have a lot in common, either. Jacky was a European gentleman of the old school, a lovely bloke and a gentleman. Colin definitely wasn't!"

since, at the end of the warming-up lap immediately before the start, Peterson came rushing into the pits reporting a top end misfire. In the time available, nothing could be done to sort the problem, so the Swede was sent round to take his pole position on the grid.

When the flag dropped, Peterson led the charge down to the first corner but halfway round the opening lap Hunt got past him, only to go off the track a few corners later. The Swede maintained his lead for two laps but it was already clear that he was in trouble, as Reutemann was catching him quickly. At the end of the third lap the Brabham came round in the lead. In addition to his misfire, Peterson was struggling with chronic oversteer and fading front brakes, which were causing the rears to lock. On lap 10, Denny Hulme passed him and on the next lap team-mate Ickx was through, followed shortly by Lauda, Hailwood and Pace as well.

Ickx ran in third for 15 laps or so, comfortably holding off the challenge from Lauda's Ferrari but at half-distance he pulled into the pits with a punctured rear tyre. For some time he had been changing gear without a clutch and the effort of engaging first gear as he left the pits meant that he

lost bottom gear. In addition, the new tyre put on was mis-matched and this upset the handling. Eventually the transmission failed completely but by this time he was already out of contention.

Peterson continued to coax his car round and, by the halfway point, he was up into fifth, largely by dint of other people's retirements. However, his battery, mounted at the back of the gearbox, had come loose and was hanging off by its wires. Eventually it fell off and he was forced to pit for a new one to be wired up. While he was in the pits, he had a new left rear tyre fitted as this was heavily worn, and also had more rear wing added. The combined effect of this lengthy stop was to drop him right out of the running, so the rest of the race was little more than an extended test session for the team. He rejoined in last place and remained there, caming home in 13th position, five laps behind the winner Hulme.

Some valuable lessons had been learnt by the team in Argentina. Firstly, the changes required by the regulations had upset the balance and handling of their car. Secondly, there were a number of new contenders who were obviously going to be challenging strongly for race wins in 1974. In addition to the established big teams of Lotus, McLaren and Tyrrell, Ferrari were back on form and the Brabham of Reutemann had run strongly, leading until two laps to go when a loose plug wire slowed him and allowed Hulme through to win.

After the race, John Player Team Lotus stayed on at the Buenos Aires circuit to test, with each driver finding a set-up which was more to their liking, particularly in terms of curing the oversteer which had afflicted both cars throughout the weekend. Meanwhile, Colin Chapman returned to Hethel to collect some fabricated uprights that had originally been run on the cars in 1973. These provided alternative pick-up points which would be better suited to the larger diameter (28 inch) rear tyres Goodyear were now supplying to their teams. He also returned with a strengthened battery carrier to avoid any repeat of the problem with Peterson's car in Argentina.

The venue for the Brazilian Grand Prix, the Interlagos circuit in Sao Paulo, had been the scene in 1973 of one of the most dominant performances of the year by John Player Team Lotus, with the 72s being very stable over the bumpy surface and literally seconds faster round the lap than anybody else. However, it became obvious after the first practice session that this was not going to be the case in 1974, for they were in only second and eighth places.

During this session, the Swede had achieved the dubious distinction of running over his former boss, Max Mosley, in the pits, fortunately without serious injury! More worryingly from the team's point of view was that he was experiencing trouble with the hot conditions and was becoming very dehydrated, eventually having to be given a glucose injection in the pits.

It wasn't just Lotus though, everybody was struggling to come close to the time set by Peterson the previous year and Fittipaldi's eventual pole position lap was nearly two and a half seconds slower than the 1973 mark. There were several possible explanations for this: the cars were heavier, as they had been in non-deformable structure specification when they last raced in Brazil and they were also running to the new regulations which restricted rear wing and oil tank positioning. The impact on weight distribution and aerodynamic download, had certainly affected handling and grip levels.

In the Saturday sessions, Peterson was unable to improve on his Friday time but Ickx did go faster, with the result that they lined up on the outside of the second row and the inside of the third row respectively. In an effort to try and provide his neck with some support on the long, fast corners, Peterson had rigged up a head restraint system, whereby his helmet was attached by hooks and string on both sides to the cockpit windshield. However, he found that this transmitted too many forces from the car through to his head, so for race day he appeared with the string tied to the shoulders of his race suit instead.

From virtually first light, race day saw the grandstands full of rabidly enthusiastic, chanting Brazilians, anticipating a 'home' victory for Fittipaldi. Blissfully ignorant of the consequences, all sorts of debris, including bottles and nails, was being thrown onto the track by spectators and this delayed the start of the morning warm-up while it was removed.

Peterson made another of his trademark quick getaways at the start and slotted into second place behind front-row man Reutemann in the Brabham. As early as the fourth lap, the tyres on the Argentinian's car were going off and Peterson was into the lead, followed almost immediately by Fittipaldi. For just over ten laps, the former team-mates played out a tense battle for supremacy, with Peterson's car looking more and more ragged on the long left-hand corners. On lap 16 of the scheduled 40, the Swede could hold out no longer and the red and white McLaren was through into the lead, to a roar of approval from his fans. Three laps later, Peterson was into the pits, realising that the poor handling of his car was not, as he had originally thought, down to tyre wear or blistering, but a puncture, perhaps as a consequence of the earlier over-enthusiasm of the crowd. He blasted back into the race in 10th place, once again out of contention for victory but determined to drive flat out to the finish.

Peterson's stop elevated Ickx to third. The Belgian had driven a steady race but his car was ill-handling and he had moved up only as a result of the slip down the order of Reutemann and his team-mate's misfortune. However, he maintained his pace and was able to keep ahead of his nearest challengers, Pace in the Surtees and the McLaren of Hailwood, to claim his first points for the team. With Peterson dropping down the order, Fittipaldi had a comparatively easy time for the rest of the race, although things did become tricky when it began to rain, which eventually forced the curtailment of the race eight laps earlier than had been scheduled. Peterson's determined drive resulted in him overhauling Reutemann three laps from the eventual end of the race, for sixth place. He actually finished the race in the pit lane, having come in to change to wets, unaware that the officials had chosen to stop the race. After the race, the Swede was taken off to hospital, suffering from slight heat exhaustion.

The first two Championship rounds in South America had yielded just four points for the black-and-gold cars from Hethel, a stark contrast to the two wins scored by Fittipaldi in these races in 1973. In fact, Peterson had led both races and had been denied a good finishing position by technical problems rather than a lack of outright pace. Another positive aspect was the forthcoming debut of the new car, which the team felt sure, would revive their fortunes and place them firmly back at the sharp end of the grid again. Peter Warr summed it up succinctly: 'The real problem was that everybody was panicking to build the new car and trying to run the old cars as well. There wasn't a lot of development done on the old cars but we had to make some regulation changes to them anyway, so they went out in a relatively undeveloped situation, just made to comply with the regulations, while we were waiting for Nirvana, which was Bellamy's 76.'

A White Elephant

Although some teams stayed on in Brazil for a non-Championship race at the new Brasilia circuit, John Player Team Lotus hurried back to the UK to concentrate on getting the new car out on track. Just eight days after the Brazilian Grand Prix, it was seen for the first time in public, testing at Silverstone.

The car was officially revealed to the press in early February. As it followed on after JPS/8 (72/8) the first chassis was designated JPS/9, although the official Lotus Type number was 76. Chapman's brief to Ralph Bellamy had been to design a car which retained the characteristics of a Lotus 72 but that was 100lbs lighter and it was claimed at the launch that not only had he succeeded in doing so but had made the car stronger as well.

The most interesting innovation on the car was the use of a hydraulically operated clutch actuated by a button on the gear lever and powered by a pump driven from the

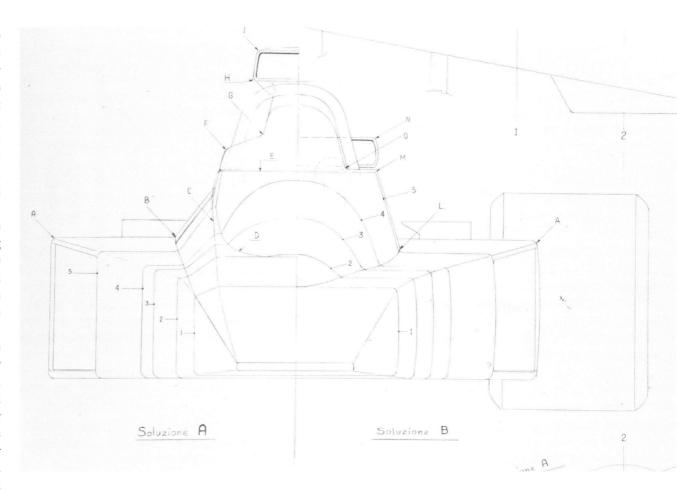

Soluzione A   Soluzione B

Opposite Page Top: Peter Warr was never convinced of the merits of the 76.
Opposite Page Bottom: R Drops was a red dye sprayed on to components to help with identifying cracks. **Above:** Giugiaro sketch done for Chapman of how a Formula 1 car could look, bears striking resemblance to final shape of 76.

LOTUS 72

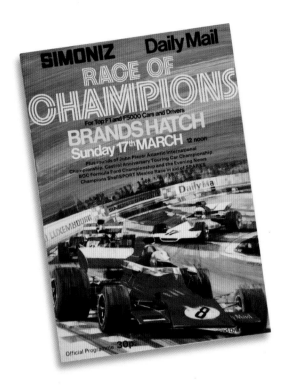

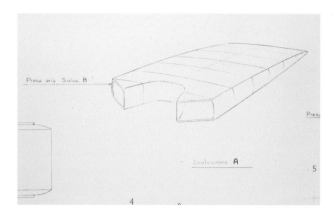

starter motor. There were four pedals in the footwell consisting of, from right to left, a throttle pedal, two brake pedals and a clutch pedal. The brake pedals were joined together in a 'V' shape, so that the driver could choose to brake with either his right foot in the traditional manner or with his left foot. The clutch pedal offered a normal foot release for getaways from the grid.

The tub was fabricated in 16 gauge L72 aluminium sheet, extending forward of the front wheel centre-line rather than using the complicated front sub-frame of the Type 72. Fuel was carried within the tub in glassfibre-lined cavities, with a total capacity of 40 gallons. Suspension was, as with the 72, through compound torsion bars with Koni dampers all round. Front suspension was by fabricated steel wishbones with cast magnesium uprights, featuring variable rate geometry and 3° of anti-dive. At the rear there were twin parallel top links and a single bottom link, paired with twin radius rods and fabricated steel uprights.

The body shape was very sleek, with side water radiators angled back sharply at the side of the tub in the same way as had been seen on the Formula 2 Type 74 (also the work of Bellamy), a narrow nose section with wide fins and a long tapered engine cover covering the oil tank and blending into a distinctive bi-plane rear wing. In fact, the whole car bore a striking resemblance to a drawing produced for Colin Chapman by Giugiaro (who was working with Lotus on the Esprit at the time) of a Formula 1 concept and there seems little doubt that this acted as a heavy influence on the final shape. The

engine air box was angled forward, bearing a slight similarity to the Brabham BT42, while motive power was, as always, provided by the ubiquitous Cosworth DFV V8, coupled to a Hewland FG400 5-speed gearbox.

At the launch, Peterson and Ickx posed happily with the car that many believed would enable them to dominate Formula 1 in the same way that the 72 had done at its height. Its first race appearance was scheduled for the Race of Champions, more than a month away, by which time it was expected that most of the normal new car niggles and glitches would be sorted.

The week after the launch, John Player Team Lotus were down at Goodwood testing the new car. In addition to his normal driving duties, Peterson was enlisted to help clear the ice off the track prior to running. In early March, they switched to testing in the warmer climes of Spain at Jarama, choosing to focus on testing instead of going to the Race of Champions, where a lone 72 was entered for Ickx. A lack of spares also influenced this decision, since Britain was in the grip of the three-day week where, due to the energy crisis, companies were allowed only to operate for three days out of five. This meant that insufficient spares could be built to guarantee being able to supply one car at the Race of Champions as well as two at the South African Grand Prix, scheduled to take place only 13 days after the Brands Hatch race.

Ickx therefore was entered for the non-Championship race in his regular car, 72/5. The main modification it

sported was a revised oil tank, which was of the 'saddle' variety, hung over the gearbox rather than sitting atop it, in an effort to improve airflow to the rear wing. In the wet first practice, the 'Rainmaster' was anything but, suffering from an off-colour engine. The same was true in the second session on Saturday, which was held in the dry, for his engine just would not pull and he ended up well down the grid on the sixth row. Engines were in short supply at John Player Team Lotus and the team did not want to use one of the engines assigned for South Africa, so they left things as they were. However, the matter was brought to a head when the engine blew up in the warm-up on race morning and a new DFV had to be installed.

The race was held in appallingly wet and cold

with typical modesty. 'Practice was not too good and then we changed a lot of things for the race and it worked well. Brands Hatch was a circuit that always suited me and I loved the rain'.

It was intended that the Race of Champions was to have marked the last ever appearance of a works Lotus 72 in competition. A second new car, designated JPS/10 (i.e. 76/2) had been built up for Ickx, and testing had gone well and been trouble-free enough for there to be some optimism in the Lotus camp. However, this was quickly extinguished in the first practice session at Kyalami, a circuit with peculiar characteristics which seemed to change from day to day, let alone year to year.

Several changes had been made to the cars as a result of the testing programme. Visually, the main one was that the nosecone had been mounted further forward but less obvious was a shuffle around of the pedal layout. This saw the brake and clutch pedals swopped over so that, from right to left, the order was throttle, brake, clutch, brake, although the two brake pedals were still linked together as before using a cross

shaft. This modification had been made only to Peterson's car, while Ickx's had reverted to a conventional layout without the hydraulically-actuated clutch. Although his road-going Elan plus 2 was fitted with the system he didn't feel that it was sufficiently well developed to use it on a racing car being driven flat out in the hustle and bustle of a Grand Prix.

As well as the two works 76s, the pair of orange and brown Team Gunston 72s were entered for their home race, with 72/6 for Jody Scheckter's older brother Ian and 72/7 being driven by Paddy Driver. These cars had also been revised to conform with the new regulations concerning oil tanks and rear wings but were making their first appearance of any kind as a result of the ban on motor racing in South Africa having been lifted just prior to the race. For Driver, this was an 'in at the deep end' introduction to Grand Prix racing, as he explains. 'I had an unfortunate operation [to have a rib removed] the same time as I was given the drive in the Lotus. Then the Grand Prix came along and that was the first time I sat in the car. I certainly wasn't fit!'

Problems with the new 76 began to manifest themselves almost straight away. In the first practice session, the starter motor which provides drive to the hydraulic pump failed. A knock-on effect of this failure was that it created a short-circuit so that whenever Peterson depressed the button on the gear lever, the whole engine cut out – definitely not a desirable thing! In the second Thursday session, a rear suspension mounting broke, forcing the Swede to take out the spare, which was 72/8, his car from the first two races of the season. Although the cockpit fire extinguisher system

conditions, which anyone who was there that day probably still remembers! However, it was livened up by a tremendous battle for the lead. Niki Lauda in the Ferrari had overhauled initial leader Reutemann (Brabham) and was pursued by Emerson Fittipaldi and Ickx, who had made his way up through the field from his lowly starting position. On lap 15 of 40, Ickx got past the McLaren and set about closing the gap to the Ferrari. With 10 laps remaining, the Belgian was on the tail of the Austrian and, on the 35th lap he pounced, driving around the outside of his rival at Paddock, the plunging downhill right-hander at the end of the start/finish straight. It was a tremendously popular victory and one which showed that Ickx had not lost his touch (in the wet at least) after a couple of fairly mediocre seasons by his standards. Ickx recalls the weekend

Opposite Page Top: Giugiaro sketch for airbox on the Type 76. This style would later be seen on the 77. **Opposite Page Bottom**: Peterson carried out early testing of the 76 at a cold Goodwood. **Above**: In what should have been the last-ever appearance of a works Lotus 72 in a Formula 1 race, Ickx scored a superb win in the rain-lashed Race of Champions at Brands Hatch. **Right**: Ickx's JPS/10 (76/2) made its debut in the South African Grand Prix, minus its hydraulically-actuated clutch. It was a disastrous start, the sister 76 of Peterson colliding with the Belgian's car at the first corner, effectively eliminating them both.

promptly decided to set itself off, he still managed to record a reasonably competitive time in the car. Then, when he went back out in the 76 the engine lost its oil pressure and Peterson was forced to pull off and watch the rest of the session as a spectator. Meanwhile, Ickx in his conventionally-clutched version showed the new car's potential by setting the sixth-fastest time.

On Friday, with a new engine installed, Peterson managed only to reach the grand total of four flying laps because the new unit had developed a mysterious misfire. Both cars were afflicted by severe understeer, which could be changed to oversteer only by the most extreme methods,

such as the drivers searching out dusty patches of track on which they could 'lose' the tail. With the Friday session not proving generally to be as fast as the day before, Ickx was unable to improve on his time, while Peterson knocked four-tenths off, leaving the Belgian on the outside of row five and the Swede back on the eighth row – not quite the places they had envisaged starting the race from in the new car! In total, Ronnie managed more laps in his 72 (27) than he did in the 76 (19), while Ickx at least notched up 73 laps in his car. Meanwhile, the two Gunston drivers played themselves in gently, ending up on the 11th and 13th rows.

After final practice had ended, Lotus persuaded the organisers to lay on an extra half-hour unofficial session and also used the full time of the unofficial practice session on the morning of the race to work through the full gamut of set-up options such as wings, torsion bars, roll bars, wheel sizes and tyres and by the end of the process felt they had improved both cars considerably, although they ended up running on different diameters of tyre!

The race was short and not at all sweet for the two John Player Team Lotus drivers. As the field streaked down the straight to Crowthorne Corner in a cloud of dust, the throttle slides on Peterson's car jammed open and it careered, brakes locked up, into the side of Ickx's car, sending them both spinning. Although both cars restarted and made it back to the pits, Peterson's steering had been damaged in the collision and he retired after two more slow laps. Ickx had a new nosecone put on his car and continued, treating the rest of the race as an extended test-session, making adjustments and going out, then coming in again to report on their effect, making more adjustments and so the

process continued. Eventually, due to brake balance problems that couldn't be solved quickly, he retired having notched up 31 laps.

Six days later, practice began for the 26th Daily Express International Trophy meeting, the second of the big UK non-Championship Formula 1 races. The freighter flight from South Africa delivered the cars back into the UK on Wednesday night, so there was precious little time to prepare for the first practice on Friday. However, there was still time for the mechanics to make some revisions to the 76 entered for Peterson. This involved the removal of the complex hydraulically actuated clutch system and its replacement with a standard three-pedal layout. The other change was the repositioning of the low rear wing to a position some eight inches further back to try and place it

Left: Same car, new livery: Paddy Driver (top) and Ian Scheckter (bottom) gave Team Gunston's newly-acquired 72s their first outing in the South African Grand Prix, Driver in 72/7 and Scheckter in 72/6. **Above:** A 72 was taken along to the 1974 International Trophy at Silverstone as a spare car for Peterson in case of problems with the new 76. **Opposite Page:** The 76 continued to be troublesome at the International Trophy meeting at Silverstone, switching from understeer to oversteer and proving very unpredictable. Peterson qualified nearly two seconds slower than pole-man James Hunt in the new Hesketh. These shots show the streamlined engine cowling which ran back to the rear wing and the 'bi-plane' wing format. The lower wing had been moved back for this event to try and get out of turbulent air.

experiments with different wings and mounting positions providing no discernible increase in performance and then to cap it all that evening another cracked engine mounting plate was found. Nonetheless, Peterson's performance was good enough for second on the grid in the middle of the front row, albeit some 1.7 seconds slower than poleman James Hunt in the new Hesketh.

In the race, Peterson led from laps 2 to 28, until the slow-starting Hesketh finally overhauled him. By this time, the left rear tyre on the wildly-oversteering Lotus was chunking badly and the Swede was just about to swing off into the pits for a replacement when the engine seized and his afternoon's work was over.

Chapman, Bellamy and Warr were so appalled at the problems they had experienced at Silverstone that they decided to stay on at the circuit and conduct further tests the day after the race. By tuning the chassis to the tyres through changes to springs and roll bars and ride heights they reportedly managed to improve lap times by around 1.5 seconds, so were considerably more optimistic about their prospects for the next race, the Spanish Grand Prix.

The Spanish race took place at Jarama, a tight, twisty circuit which required maximum downforce. Consequently, the same two JPS cars that appeared in South Africa, ran with a new larger rear wing in place of the smaller bi-plane wing arrangement. The oil tank was also modified to the saddle format as re-introduced on the Type 72 at Brands Hatch, to move it out of the airflow. A spare car, 72/8, was taken along and this had been brought up to the same specification as 72/5 had been in at the Race of Champions.

In first practice, Peterson demonstrated the worth of the chassis fine-tuning by posting the fastest time, while Ickx was also competitive, in fifth. In the second session, the Swede was just pipped by Niki Lauda, whose time was quicker than Peterson's Friday best and therefore snatched

in less turbulent airflow.

On Friday the car was reasonably fast but still displayed an alarming tendency to snap from understeer to oversteer. When a wheel nut stripped its thread it meant the end of the car's participation since a repair required the replacement of the entire upright. In addition, overnight inspection revealed cracks in an engine mounting plate. Saturday's session was little better, a succession of

pole. Ickx was again fifth-fastest, so the JPS cars lined up on the outside of the front row and in the inside of the third. In a welcome contrast to previous races, the only problem they had in practice was a split exhaust pipe on Peterson's car.

It was during this 1974 season that, anxious to avoid the problems experienced by Fittipaldi the previous season, Ickx resorted to some strange antics to try and send his team-mate astray on set-up, as Rex Hart describes. 'He would make changes without the management knowing, because he'd sussed out that he would do good times and Ronnie was getting the information, so he would lead him up the garden path a little bit. At the right time he'd put settings on, which maybe management are still not even aware happened. Just before the race it would be "Let's have a couple more notches on that rear bar and the front bar this, and some more wing" and all the bits and pieces!' Of course the Swede had the last laugh, for Ickx never once outqualified him…

The race started in wet conditions and when the flag

LOTUS 72

dropped, Peterson jumped into the lead and held this position for 20 laps before the drying circuit persuaded him to pit for slicks. However, he was already in trouble with his engine overheating, this due to the fact that the radiators had been masked with tape in the anticipation of the cold, wet conditions that the race started in, continuing for the duration of the event. Two laps after he rejoined on slicks in 8th place he had moved up to 6th but was forced to pull out with a blown engine totally devoid of water. Ickx's pit stop had been a disaster of almost farcical proportions: a rear wheel hadn't been fastened properly and the Belgian had to stop at the end of the pit lane with his loose wheel and wait for the mechanics to run down and tighten it up. When they went to restart the engine, the wrong button was pushed and, instead of firing up the DFV, it activated the on-board fire extinguisher, enveloping the car and the far end of the pit lane in white mist! After that, all hope of a decent finish was gone and so the team were again left to treat the rest of it as a big test session. However, after only two more laps the brakes began to leak fluid and the car was retired.

Another frustrating race followed in the Belgian Grand Prix at the featureless Nivelles circuit. After qualifying on the third and eighth rows respectively, Peterson and Ickx both retired. Early in the race, Ickx (in JPS/10-76/2) had been hit from behind, eventually causing an oil pipe to break when he had worked his way up to 8th position. This was replaced and the Belgian set out again, only to return with spongy brakes. These were bled and he returned, only to have to retire with overheating. Meanwhile Peterson (in JPS/9-76/1) ran in a steady fifth place for a long time before also pitting with spongy brakes needing to be bled. After continuing for another dozen or so laps, he too retired, due to fuel leaking into the cockpit and burning him.

Above Left: Peterson was right on the pace in the Spanish Grand Prix at Jarama, qualifying on the front row of the grid and running strongly in the race before retiring with overheating problems. **Left, Above & Opposite Page Top:** Ickx was even less enthusiastic about the 76 than Peterson and, apart from an encouraging qualifying performance at the Spanish Grand Prix, generally languished well down the grid. In these shots, it can already be seen that the cowling running back from the airbox has been discarded in order to achieve a higher rear wing height. **Opposite Page Bottom:** The sleek, Giugiaro-inspired lines of the 76 are displayed in this shot of Peterson taken at the wet/dry Spanish race.

Les
John Player Specials
arrivent
Nivelles
12 MAI 1974

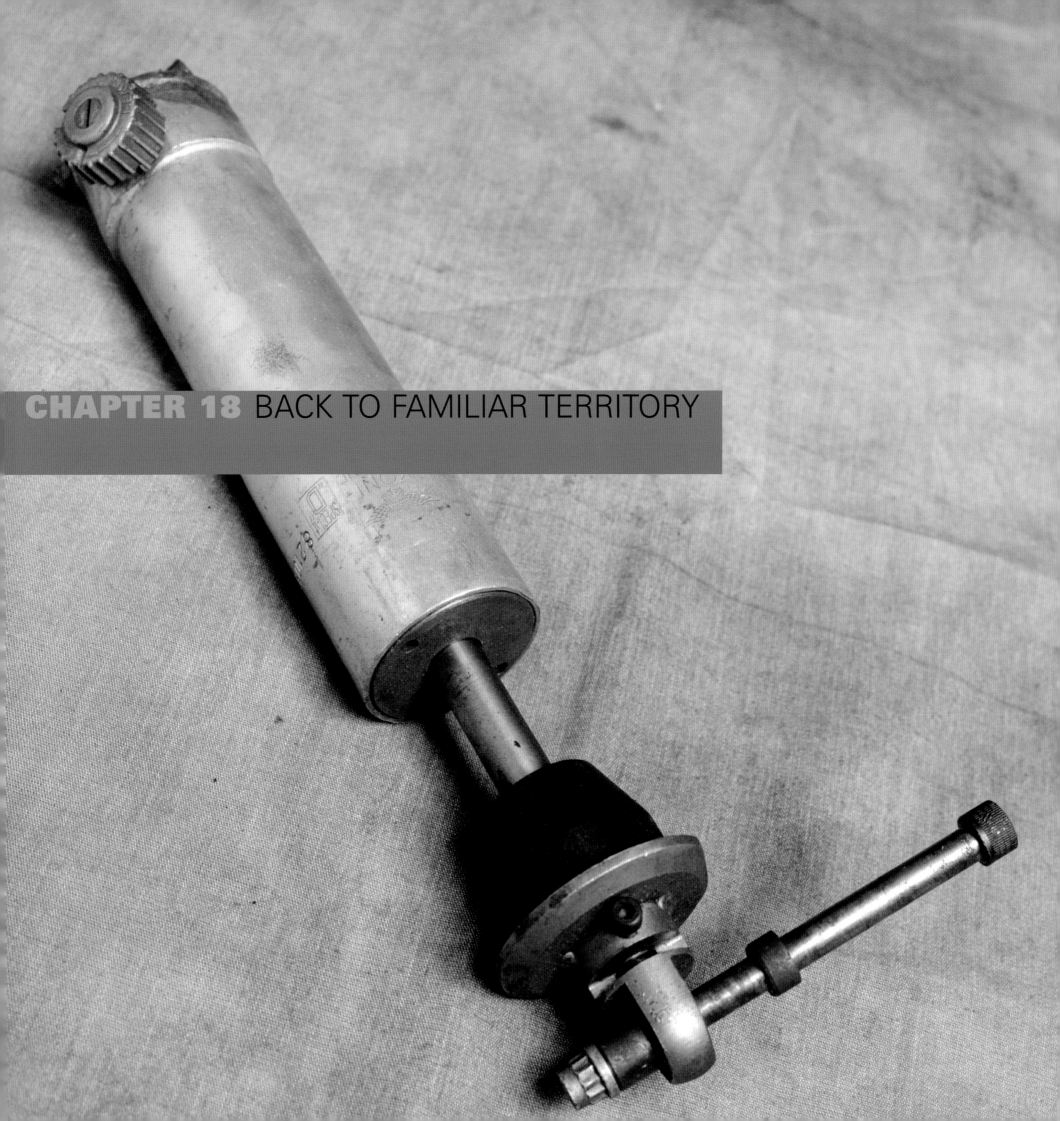

The four races it had contested had revealed that the 76 was lacking in competitiveness and reliability. So many problems had required attention that it had been impossible to spend any concerted amounts of time on track getting to know the car and finding out how it responded to set-up changes. If John Player Team Lotus and its drivers were going to start challenging for the Constructors and Drivers World Championships in 1974 it was clear that something had to be done and fast. The problem was that with the short intervals between races, it was not possible to conduct much testing, so all the development of the 76 was being done at the Grand Prix meetings themselves, hardly a sensible approach.

Peterson, desperate to notch up some wins or even get a few more points under his belt, was all in favour of bringing out the 72 again. He had driven the spare 72/8 at Grand Prix meetings whenever JPS/9 ran into problems and had still been able to set competitive times. The Swede felt that the venue for the next race, the Monaco Grand Prix, was hardly the place to put a new, yet to be proven, car to the test. Chapman and Warr relented, with the result that 72/8 was entered for Peterson, with 72/5 reclaimed from Chapman's personal museum(!) for Ickx and JPS/10 brought along purely as a spare.

As Peter Warr recalls, this was a painful decision for the Lotus team management, particularly after the high-profile launch of the 76. 'Colin was so upset that this car was turning out to be a disaster. He had done - for the first time ever - the Big Barbican launch in London and it had been built up so much. We didn't really want to throw any more money at building more of them or trying to make a lightweight version. In the end it was a 76 running in a 72 configuration so we thought we might as well stick to the original, why have a bad copy? It was Colin's forcefulness that said "No, right, that's what we are going to do" because I think the last thing he wanted to do was eat any more humble pie.'

Ralph Bellamy concedes that he could understand the operational logic from the point of view of someone like Warr in going back to the 72, even if in engineering terms it might have been a retrograde step. 'People like Peter just said, "All we need is a 72 and we can win races. Why are we

pissing around with this thing?" He didn't care, I mean he had no engineering axe to grind one way or the other, he just had this simple manager's approach of what'll work and what he knows, and what he's been successful with in the past.' Looking back today, Bellamy also feels that the team's decision was a bit of a knee-jerk reaction in the wake of defeat from a rival car/driver combination they believed to be inferior. 'It was a panic reaction. Who won the race in Spain? Lauda in a Ferrari. I mean, Niki Lauda: he was a nobody in a BRM, Ferrari: clowns! What had they ever done over the last couple of years? McLaren and Lotus had been flogging their arse for years! Suddenly, Lauda won the race in a Ferrari. Well, shit, to be beaten by Lauda and a Ferrari meant that you'd really stuffed up big-time! Analysing what had gone wrong two days later, it looked like a disaster. But looking at it at the end of the year, when Lauda and Ferrari were absolutely formidable, that was the start of it. So it was inability to read a situation I suppose.'

Looking back today, Warr describes John Player Team Lotus as having been in a state of total disarray at this time. 'What I mean is that you come back to the factory and the

buyer comes out and says "Oh, I've got those new bits for you" having just bust his balls, had vans running around England, people working through the night and so on and you say to him "We don't need those now, we're running the other car next week". That's a team in total disarray. Colin was rampaging because he wasn't a happy bunny, the drivers weren't happy and the people in the factory were working longer hours for less result than they'd ever done before.'

The 72s were as they had last appeared, with the exception that some components had been moved forward in an effort to shift the weight distribution further towards the front. The only other change was that Ickx's car was fitted with a special DFV with modified inlets, exhaust pipes and camshafts, which was supposed to give a faster torque curve at the expense of top-end power.

Ickx tried both cars in the first session after problems with his 72 forced him into the spare 76, which promptly blew its engine. After achieving a time on the Friday with his 72 that would eventually be good enough to put him on the tenth row, the Belgian stripped second gear in the final session on Saturday and was able only to get out again right

Right: The decision to revert to 72s for the Monaco Grand Prix reaped rewards, Peterson racing to a popular victory.

LOTUS 72

at the end. While his 72 was being repaired, he tried the 76 again but it was afflicted with fuel pressure problems and so was abandoned for the rest of the meeting. In stark contrast, Peterson had a relatively untroubled practice, apart from the fact that he also stripped a gear in the first session on Thursday. He was fifth in that session but improved to second on Friday and equalled his time again on Saturday, when he was third-quickest. This meant he would line up on the second row, behind the all-Ferrari front row of Lauda and Reggazoni.

Ickx decided that he would race the special engine, on the basis that it would place less strain on the transmission,

a key consideration on a circuit so hard on this part of a racing car. At the start, Peterson got away reasonably well but was pipped for third on the run down to Saint Devote by Jarier's Shadow. Meanwhile, behind the leaders, all hell broke loose as Hulme and Beltoise collided on the run up the hill from Saint Devote, the resulting pile-up eliminating seven cars. Ickx managed to pick his way through but did damage one of his nose fins in the process.

On lap three, Peterson found a way past Jarier and began to harry the two leading Ferraris. Then on lap six he overcooked it coming into the twisty Rascasse complex and spun the car. In his haste to get back into the race, he

reversed smartly back onto the racing line and hit Reutemann's Brabham, eliminating the Argentinian on the spot with a broken rear upright but with no discernible damage to the Lotus. He rejoined in sixth place and what followed was a tremendous tigerish fightback drive. The Swede moved up to fifth as a result of Mike Hailwood's retirement, then passed Scheckter, gained another place with the demise of Reggazoni's leading Ferrari and then disposed of Jarier on lap 25 of the scheduled 78. When Lauda's Prancing Horse went lame on lap 32, it was Peterson who came round in the lead, a position he held until the finish to score a first Grand Prix win of the year,

and a much overdue one at that, for himself and Lotus. The result also lifted him up to sixth in the Championship race with 10 points, 14 behind leader Fittipaldi but still not out of touch.

Ickx struggled with his broken nose fin, which eventually fell off. The effect of having only one nose fin skewed the nose cone over to one side and then it was found that his wheel rim was damaged so he was called in to have a new wheel and nosecone fitted. A lap later, the Belgian's gearbox failed and he coasted off up the chicane escape road to retire. The four points he had scored in Brazil remained the only ones to his name, and he was languishing in 10th in the title race.

Prior to this race, team morale had been at rock bottom with all the problems and it was only Peterson's never-say-die attitude which had made it all bearable. By contrast, Ickx was becoming increasingly disenchanted with the lack of progress as well as his inability to keep pace with his rapid team-mate. He recalls: 'It was clear that Ronnie was the number one of the team because he was the established driver. I was the newcomer and I had to make an impression. But I was very well treated. Colin was absolutely charming and totally dedicated to having a good season, although the team had difficulties. It was difficult for me because the car was not the type of car I was used to driving. Ronnie was basically not doing too bad and I was just average.'

Opposite Page: Once again Peterson tried the 76 in practice for the 1974 Swedish Grand Prix but still felt happier with his 72 and raced that. He seemed destined never to win his home Grand Prix, retiring with a broken drive-shaft. The team, though, had already printed the victory stickers! **Left:** Never-say-die: Seen at the Anderstorp test session, Peterson kept the spirits of Team Lotus up during a torrid 1974 season. **Above:** Ickx also preferred the 72 for Sweden but retired due to a lack of oil pressure.

An indication of the stresses and strains that the team personnel were under was the case of Chief Mechanic, Keith Leighton. He disappeared on the Saturday night of the Monaco meeting and never returned, reportedly going on a 'bender' and unable to face getting up the next day. The result was that Peter Warr, much to his disappointment, was forced to dismiss Leighton. 'It was very sad because Keith was, without a shadow of a doubt, one of the most intelligent people doing the job of a race mechanic that I've ever come across. He had this sort of ability to do his work, organise the crew and still have enough left to be able to read what was going on. I would turn round off the pit wall and say "Right, we need to do such and such…" and he'd already done it.'

Fortunately (or maybe unfortunately, from his wife's point of view!), former Chief Mechanic Eddie Dennis was on holiday with his wife and was spectating at Monaco. His trip quickly became a 'busman's holiday' as he was co-opted into the team to take over Leighton's job for the rest of the weekend. To underline how obvious the extent of the chaos within the team was to the outside world, after the Belgian Grand Prix John Player Team Lotus had been awarded the title of 'Team Shambles' by Motor Sport's European Editor, Denis Jenkinson, a moniker that it last garnered during the lowest point of the difficult 1971 season. However, after Monaco, this dubious accolade was passed on to Team Surtees, who were having an equally chaotic period.

On the way home from Monaco, Lotus, along with a number of other teams, stopped at the Dijon circuit, which was due to play host to the French Grand Prix for the first time later that year. Ickx did the driving and, struggling with

LOTUS 72

persistent fuel pressure problems, was just outside the 60 second barrier, compared to Lauda's fastest time in the Ferrari of 59.4s on super-sticky tyres. Later that week, Peterson tested JPS/9 at the Anderstorp circuit in Sweden, venue for the forthcoming Swedish Grand Prix. The day got off to a bad start when, after just 20 laps, the steering reportedly broke, sending the car spinning off into the guard rail. The car was repaired and, later in the day Peterson set a time only 0.2s slower than Lauda's Ferrari.

The main problem with the new car was not its speed but a lack of reliability. There were also still issues with the cooling, since the engine was still overheating. Consequently, it was decided to race the 72s again in Sweden, taking along JPS/9 as a spare car. The 72s were as they had been at Monaco, while the new car had sprouted air scoops on each side to try and funnel more air to the side radiators and a 72 style nose-cone. On Friday, Peterson concentrated on the 72, setting the second fastest time behind Lauda in both sessions. By contrast, the fire appeared to have gone out of Ickx's belly, for he was nearly two and half seconds slower than his team-mate. Saturday practice was dominated by the two new Tyrrell 007s of Scheckter and Depailler, while the two Ferraris filled the second row. Peterson was next up with a stirring performance on home soil in the 72 while Ickx picked up his pace and was only a couple of tenths slower, to put him on the inside of the fourth row. Peterson also tried JPS/9 in both Saturday sessions but was still more than a second slower in the new car than he was in the old one – hardly what could be called progress!

In the race, Peterson made one of his trademark dragster starts to get to the first corner in second place behind Scheckter and was maintaining this position when, on lap 9, a broken rear drive-shaft put him out. Ickx pitted with electrical problems and then retired with low oil pressure after only 31 of the 80 laps. Another disastrous race.

Two days after the Swedish event, the team went Goodyear tyre testing at Zandvoort with JPS/9. However, the test came to a premature end because Peterson left the track when his rear brakes failed on the approach to the Panorama Bocht chicane. He ploughed through several layers of catch fencing and hit the guardrail head-on. The front of the car was quite badly bent and the unlucky Swede was knocked out by one of the catch-fence posts and stayed unconscious for some 35 minutes. He was kept in hospital under observation for a couple of days before he was flown home. Meanwhile, Jacky Ickx was carrying out a parallel testing programme with JPS/10, driving the car at Brands Hatch and Silverstone and also taking along the 72 for comparison.

Back at Zandvoort for the Dutch Grand Prix, which

took place a fortnight after the Swedish race, the team continued with the 72s, both of which were now resplendent in shiny new paintwork. In addition to the 72s, a heavily revised JPS/10 was brought along for Ickx to drive as a spare car. The water radiators had been moved forward to just behind the front wheels, shrouded in new pods, to improve cooling and weight distribution, which had been deemed to be too biased towards the rear. The Belgian concentrated on this car in the first session but was well off the pace and for the second session on Friday he reverted to his 72. He went back to the new car only after the 72's engine let go in a big way during the Saturday morning session, when he set a time that would have just got him in the race, on the penultimate row of the grid! His time in the 72 was little better, good enough only for the ninth row. In

fairness to the Belgian, he didn't go out in the final session as the mechanics were just strapping him in (having done a super-fast engine change) when the flag went out to signal the end of practice.

Just to add to the team's woes, Peterson's normally reliable car was not behaving itself either. Having set the fourth best time on Friday, the Swede had the rear wing collapse during the Saturday morning session at around the same point on the circuit as he had his big testing accident. Fortunately, this time he managed to stay on the track. His car was repaired for the afternoon session but most of the top drivers went anything between one-and-a-half to two-and-a-half seconds slower due to a combination of hotter track temperatures and oil and rubber laid down on the track by a saloon car race. In those circumstances, Peterson's time, which put him second in the session, was very impressive, but because the faster times were done on Saturday morning, he was back on the outside of the sixth row.

At the end of his warm-up lap before the race, Peterson came rushing into the pits and asked that the angle of incidence of the nose fins be reduced. A good start lifted him to eighth at the end of the first lap and this became seventh when he passed Reutemann's Brabham on lap 17. He held this position until lap 36 of the scheduled 75, when he pitted, to have both his front tyres changed and a rear wheel nut tightened. It transpired that the decision to lessen the angle of attack of the nose fins had been a mistake and he was locking the brakes up many times, eventually flat-spotting the tyres. While he was in the pits he asked for them to be put back to their original position! Ten laps after Peterson's stop Ickx, who had climbed to 11th from his lowly grid position but then dropped back behind

Rikki von Opel's Brabham and Francois Migault's BRM, also called into the pits, with a loose wheel nut. The entire wheel was changed and this turned out to be unbalanced, further upsetting the already dismal performance of his car, which was hampered by fading brakes and a down on power engine. The two cars continued to circulate, both well out of contention, to finish in ninth and tenth places, three laps behind the winner. John Player Team Lotus appeared to be coming apart at the seams: could things get any worse?

By the next race, the French Grand Prix at Dijon, all pretence of resting the 76s while they were developed was abandoned and the full weight of the team was behind the 72 once more, although JPS/10 was brought along once more as a spare. It was modified so that the taller Peterson could drive it (his JPS/9 was still out of action following its Zandvoort testing shunt) by repositioning the brake cylinder system ahead of the footwell. The principal alterations to the 72s were the substitution of longer front wishbones, which had the effect of widening the track by around three inches. This was a specification that the team had tested in 1973 but never raced. To cope with the greater leverage such an arrangement exerted, stronger torsion bars were adopted, while the mountings for the front anti-roll bar were moved outboard to increase roll stiffness. A measure of the extent to which the team

was backing its efforts with the 72s was the news that a completely new 72 was under construction back at Hethel.

By this stage in the season, as Ralph Bellamy explains, the fact that the team were not regularly winning races meant that they were no longer the focus of Goodyear's tyre development work and this was beginning to hurt the team as tyres were developed which were more suited to other teams' cars. 'We got ourselves into a technical nightmare [with the 76] and, suddenly, we were off the pace. As a result of that, McLaren were quicker, so Goodyear instantly shifted over to developing tyres with McLaren, who had outboard front brakes. We got well and truly stuffed, and the 72 never handled again because the front tyre construction became too stiff and you could never make them work. We didn't understand quite what was going on for two years after that and it wasn't until we threw the inboard front brakes away that Lotus Formula 1 cars began to work again.'

Peterson was on majestic form at Dijon, a circuit which seemed to suit his enthusiastic, spectacular, press-on driving style. By the end of the two Friday sessions, he had recorded the third-best time and then on Saturday afternoon he was quickest of all, faster even than the all-conquering Ferraris, which had dominated the Dutch

Opposite Page Top Left: Although the team had a 76 as a spare they again chose to race the 72s in the Dutch Grand Prix. Peterson finished tenth in 72/8. **Opposite Page Top Right:** Over the hill? Ickx rarely managed to match the sheer pace of his team-mate and did not share the Swede's blind faith in the reliability of the cars either. He is pictured in the French Grand Prix at Dijon-Prenois, where he finished 5th. **Opposite Page Bottom:** Over the moon! Peterson celebrates a hard-fought victory in the 1974 French Grand Prix. **Right:** Peterson's victory in the French Grand Prix owed more to his sheer determination and skill than the merits of the car, which by this stage was becoming quite outdated.

LOTUS 72

Grand Prix. As a result, he joined pole-man Lauda on the front row. His only problem had been trouble with one front wheel locking up under braking for certain corners but it was decided this was due to the peculiar off-camber nature of the approaches to some bends rather than any inherent problem with the car. The Swede also tried JPS/10 in the Saturday morning session but was unable to come within a second of his times in the 72.

By contrast, Ickx was using the same engine that had proved recalcitrant at Zandvoort, as there were no others available. He got a new engine in time for Saturday's practice but that one broke a valve spring, so the tired engine was re-installed in the absence of any alternative for the final session. In the circumstances, it was hardly surprising that he ended up back on the seventh row.

At the start, Lauda jumped into the lead and immediately began to pull away from Peterson and the rest of the field. However, after the first few laps, the tyres and the handling of the Lotus really chimed in and he began to close on the leading Ferrari. On lap 17, Lauda ran slightly wide on the fast corner leading onto the main straight, losing momentum and allowing Peterson to get a superb tow up under the gearbox of the wailing scarlet car. At the end of the straight, the Swede darted out under braking and was through. The Austrian and the rest of the field waited in vain for something to go wrong with the Lotus and/or its tyres but this was Peterson's race. He reeled off the remaining 63 laps with clinical precision to take the chequered flag and his second Grand Prix victory of the year. This win pushed him up to fifth in the World Championship standings, with 19 points to leader Lauda's 36.

Team-mate Ickx had started in a downbeat mood because he was still using the engine which had performed indifferently at Zandvoort and in first practice. However, a great first lap, aided by a start-line skirmish which eliminated three cars and held up a great deal more, allowed the Belgian to make up six places and come round in seventh. The retirement of Reutemann promoted him up a place and, although he was subsequently passed by Fittipaldi, he managed to scrabble past Hailwood's McLaren to move back into the points. When Fittipaldi's engine blew on lap 28, Ickx was up into fifth, a position he

then held with great determination - despite the close attentions of Denny Hulme - for the remaining 52 laps, finishing six tenths ahead of the gritty New Zealander at the finish. This took his tally for the year so far to six points, for 12th place in the standings.

Just before the next race, the John Player British Grand Prix at Brands Hatch, Team Lotus took the unusual step of announcing that Ronnie Peterson had signed a contract with them to drive for a further two years. It seemed that several teams had been 'sniffing around' with a view to signing up the rapid Swede, and early measures had to be taken to ensure that he stayed with the team.

The two regular 72s were taken to Brands, plus JPS/10 as a spare, although the latter was never used. A programme of weight-reduction using titanium components had been prescribed for the rather corpulent 72s but the only evidence of this at Brands Hatch was a titanium roll-over hoop on Ickx's car. For the first time the

cars were using Lockheed instead of Girling brakes and these were paired with drilled discs for improved stopping power in an effort to prevent some of the braking problems the team had been having.

The time for all the competitors to aim for was Emerson Fittipaldi's 1m 20.8s pole-position lap, which had been achieved in the John Player Challenge Trophy race at the end of 1972. By the end of the first session on Thursday morning, fastest man Tom Pryce in the Shadow had got down to 1m 21.4s, with Peterson on 1m 22.1s and Ickx exactly a second slower. Then in the afternoon, Lauda and Peterson both went round in 1m 20.6s, so it became clear that perhaps a lap under the magic 80 second barrier might be possible. On Friday, Peterson was slower than Ickx in the morning but in the afternoon he really got everything

First Person
Ralph Bellamy on Ronnie Peterson

First Person
Ralph Bellamy on Ronnie Peterson

"Ronnie wasn't a good test driver but was unbelievably talented. In terms of sheer car control and ability he was just incredible. But he did tend to drive around problems. I remember being at Zandvoort when I was running his car and he came in and said "It's oversteering, terrible oversteer". So I changed the car, trying to fix it and he came back in saying "Still oversteering". I said, "Ronnie, I've changed the car a lot, what the hell's going on?" He said "Well, because I can't get it into the corner, I have to hurl it in, it flicks to oversteer and it's really difficult to control". I said "Ronnie, for Christ's sake, you've got understeer, then!" and he said, "Well, yes, I suppose so". And that was Ronnie. He just loved to drive cars fast."

wound up to record a stunning 1m 19.7s lap. Unfortunately, he did this just after Lauda had done the same time, so he would again start from the outside of the front row alongside the Ferrari. However, an indication of just how hard he had to try to do this lap time was that he took 49 laps to do it, whereas Lauda's pole was achieved from a total of just 16 laps. Meanwhile, Ickx's Friday morning time was the fastest of his weekend but good enough only for a place on the outside of the sixth row.

In the race, Lauda jumped straight into the lead and pulled clear, seemingly on his way to a dominant flag-to-flag victory, followed at some distance by Scheckter. Clay Reggazoni in the second Ferrari made a superb getaway from the fourth row and pushed his way in front of Peterson, who had been uncharacteristically slow off the line, hampered by too much wheelspin. The Swede then ran in a steady fourth until he was forced to pit for a new tyre after picking up a puncture, probably a legacy of Hans Stuck's big accident a few laps earlier, which had thrown a

lot of debris onto the track. He rejoined in 12th and, after another pit stop, trailed home in 10th, two laps down on the winner. Lauda was another victim of the puncture epidemic, handing an easy victory to Scheckter in the final five laps.

Ickx got past Stuck in the early laps and ran eighth behind Tom Pryce's Shadow for much of the race. Eventually, the natural process of attrition meant that he moved up the order, with first Reutemann's spin and then Peterson and Reggazoni's punctures promoting the Belgian to fifth on lap 42 out of 75. Five laps later, the Lotus passed the ailing Shadow and, when Lauda was forced to pit at the end of the penultimate lap to change his punctured tyre and then not allowed out again, this elevated the delighted Belgian into third at the chequered flag, his four points pushing him up to joint 10th in the Championship. The title battle was still tight at the top, with Fittipaldi's second at Brands Hatch keeping him on course for another Championship. His tally of 37 points was one better than the unlucky Lauda and two more than Scheckter and Reggazoni. Although Peterson was fifth, his failure to score in Britain meant that he was losing ground on the other title contenders.

Clinging on to Hope

A fortnight after the British race came the German Grand Prix, at the fearsome 14-mile Nürburgring circuit. The John Player Team Lotus line-up was unchanged from Brands Hatch, with the two regular 72s plus JPS/10 as the training/development 'hack'. In the first session on Friday afternoon, Peterson and Ickx were the seventh and eighth-fastest drivers, albeit more than eight seconds slower than the fastest man, Lauda. However, during this session, Peterson suffered a failure of a 15-inch Melmag wheel on the left-rear corner, causing him to crash heavily, the third

Opposite Page: Terrific trio. Chapman and everybody at Team Lotus admired Peterson's 'win or bust' attitude to racing. His wife Barbro was a constant figure at his side providing valuable assistance with lap-timing in the days before computerised timing screens. **Right:** Heavy revisions to JPS/10 for the Dutch Grand Prix included moving the water radiators forward so that they were just behind the front wheels, in an effort to shift weight forward and try and get more heat into the front tyres. As a result of this, the cowling in front of the rear wheels was abandoned, while metres of extra water piping were necessary to cope with the re-positioned rads.

incident of this type that the team had suffered with these wheels in 18 months. The car was heavily damaged, beyond repair at the circuit. As soon as he returned to the pits, Peterson was sent out to do a 'banker' lap in JPS/10, in case the weather the next day precluded any dry running.

An immediate decision was taken to stop using the wheels and revert back to cast 13-inch wheels. As Ralph Bellamy recalls, this was a decision that perhaps should have been made a long time before. However, uncertainty about exactly what was happening to the wheels (and whether indeed they were the cause of the accidents) lay behind the long time it took to identify the problem. 'It was a little while before we fully understood what was going on but the answer was simply to throw them all away and start again and just get some proper wheels. It was an awkward period for us, I have to say. Wheels being a life and limb item, you don't want them to fail.'

The most significant impact of the team's decision to revert to their old wheels was that they were unable to use the latest compounds of Goodyear rubber because these were made exclusively for 15-inch wheels, an impediment that the drivers believed cost them at least a couple of seconds per lap. The other pressing problem was what

LOTUS 72

Peterson was going to drive for the rest of the meeting. A decision was taken to graft the whole rear end of the 72, including engine, gearbox, suspension and wheels, onto the rear end of the 76 tub. This was not a simple task, requiring some considerable improvisation on the part of the tireless mechanics in terms of mounting/attachment points for radius rods. Eddie Dennis recalls that their work was well-received by Lotus boss Chapman, if not by the 76's designer. 'The Old Man was quite pleased with that - we were showing a bit of ingenuity. Ralph Bellamy said "No, what you should have done was put the 76 back end on the 72." He was a bit peeved about that really!'

On Saturday, conditions were generally accepted as slower. Peterson was out in his new car, a true John Player 'Special' in every sense of the word, but failed to match his times of the previous day in the 72. Nor did Ickx, or for that matter the two Ferraris that would occupy the front row of the grid.

Race day was overcast, with the threat of an occasional shower just to add spice to the already daunting prospect of 14 laps plunging and climbing through the forests in the Eifel Mountains. New regulations introduced for the 1974 season allowed Peterson to start from the grid position he achieved with the 72, placing him on the outside of the fourth row, while Ickx, who had set a time only one-tenth slower than his team-mate, was on the inside of row five.

Both had a good opening lap, helped by the elimination of Hulme in a startline accident which also delayed Fittipaldi, and the demise of Lauda, who crashed out even before the cars had gone out of sight of the grandstands. Peterson came round in fifth place, while Ickx was seventh, the two black-and-gold cars separated by the Tyrrell of Patrick Depailler. They continued this way until, halfway round lap six, an ambitious outbraking attempt by Depailler on Peterson ended with the Frenchman hitting the guard-rail.

On the next lap, Ickx managed to pass Peterson and both Lotuses got past the fast-starting German Jochen Mass, having a strong drive on home territory in a Surtees. A four-car scrap then developed between the two JPS cars, Mass and Mike Hailwood in the Yardley-McLaren. On lap 11, the engine in the Surtees blew, releasing Hailwood to challenge the Lotuses and he slipped past Peterson. For the next two tours he was the 'perfumed meat' in a 'tobacco sandwich' until, on the penultimate lap, he landed badly after the Pflanzgarten jump and crashed heavily into the barriers. This left the two team-mates to battle it out to the finish, although Ickx had enough of an advantage to feel that he would be able to maintain position.

Three-quarters of the way round the final lap, the more cautious Ickx (some might say prudent and considerate) lifted off considerably as he approached and passed the scene of Hailwood's accident, while Peterson kept his foot down, oblivious. This dramatically reduced the gap to his team-mate and, on the final run down the long main straight, the Swede was able to pick up a tow and slipstream past Ickx to snatch fourth. In fact, this nearly became third, as the two Lotuses had been closing in on Reutemann's third-placed Brabham, which had lost a large chunk of its rear wing (and therefore downforce). Although they made up 26 seconds on the last lap, they were just unable to catch the Argentinian, who finished a tantalising 0.9s ahead.

Privately, Ickx was upset at what he saw as the Swede's

Opposite Page Top: Old and new: Ickx's 72/5 stands in the foreground, alongside Peterson's JPS/9 (76/1) in the pit lane at the Nürburgring during practice for the 1975 German Grand Prix. **Opposite Page Bottom:** Having seriously damaged JPS/9 in a testing shunt at Zandvoort, Peterson used JPS/10 as a spare at the German Grand Prix. After crashing his 72 in practice, he resorted to a true 'John Player Special' for the race, consisting of a 72 back-end grafted onto a 76 front. Note the cut-down 72-type nose cone, replacing the more extravagant original…
Right: Caught on the hop! Some last-lap skulduggery on the part of Peterson allowed him to close right up on Ickx (shown here) and snatch fourth place in the German Grand Prix.

exploitation of the confusion surrounding the Hailwood accident for his own gain, although Peter Warr does not recall any confrontation between the two drivers. 'I can imagine Jacky not being too happy about that because he wouldn't have thought that was the done thing at all but I don't remember there ever being any shouting and screaming or dragging each other off to a corner at the back of the garage and having words or anything like that.' Nonetheless, in the weeks following the German race, there were stories in the motorsport press to the effect that Ickx and Peterson were no longer speaking to each other and that the Belgian had said he thought it was necessary for him to find a better car. However, the fact that he had signed a two-year contract with Lotus was thought likely to preclude this happening, at least without the team's permission, anyway.

In the Championship standings, Peterson stayed in fifth place even though his tally had increased to 22, while German Grand Prix victor Reggazoni moved to the head of the title race with 44 points. With four races remaining, Peterson was by no means out of the frame. However, to overhaul his rivals now required all of them to experience consistent unreliability in the final few events. Meanwhile, Ickx's two-point haul moved him up to eighth. In the Constructor's Championship, Lotus lay fourth with 29

points, some way behind leader Ferrari's total of 57.

Two weeks later, the teams reassembled at the high-speed Österreichring circuit for the Austrian Grand Prix. With Peterson reporting that the handling of the 76 had been improved by grafting on the rear-end of the 72 at the Nürburgring, the time between races had been taken up with converting the other 76, finally repaired after its Zandvoort testing shunt, to the same specification. As a result, the Lotus team appeared at the Österreichring with a total of four cars. Peterson's wrecked 72 from Germany had been rebuilt by scavenging bits from the still-to-be-completed 72/9. In addition, all the cars featured new 15-inch diameter cast wheels, replacing the previous Melmag models.

In the first session on Friday, both drivers concentrated on their 72s, although Peterson did some slow laps in JPS/9 as well. He remarked that, while the car he had raced at the Nürburgring (JPS/10) had actually been quite nice to drive, his JPS/9 to this specification felt different and he spent the rest of the weekend concentrating his efforts on the 72. As well as various dramas with the fuel system, the gearbox and replacing anti-roll-bars on Ickx's car, both the 72s were afflicted with chronic understeer, stemming from an inability to generate sufficient heat in their front tyres.

Overnight changes seemed to reduce but not totally

eradicate the problem but Ickx felt that they had made his car dangerously unpredictable. So he went out in JPS/10 and found that it was actually handling very well and set a time faster than he had achieved in the 72. As a consequence of their diametrically opposed experiences in practice, Peterson opted to race his 72, while Ickx chose the new car. The Swede was still, by some considerable margin (2.09 seconds) the faster of the two, lining up on the outside of the third row, whereas Ickx was almost at the back of the grid, barely faster than the Token of Ian Ashley which, without wishing to be disrespectful to either its driver or designer, was hardly in the same league in terms of resources or technical sophistication as the Belgian's Lotus.

In common with the two practice sessions, the race was held in blazing hot sun. For once, Peterson made a poor start and came round at the end of the opening lap in ninth position. After overtaking the Iso-Marlboro of Merzario on lap two, he benefited from the demise of Scheckter and a pit stop for James Hunt and then on lap 13 he passed the Brabham of Carlos Pace. The retirement of Lauda's Ferrari with engine problems promoted the Swede to fourth place, a position he held close up behind the gearbox of Fittipaldi's McLaren and Reggazoni's Ferrari for another 15 laps until Pace re-passed him.

On the 38th of 54 laps Fittipaldi's engine blew and

Left: Ickx enters the Karussell at the Nürburgring.
Opposite Page: Jim Crawford was signed up by Team Lotus in the hope that he would blossom into a top-flight star..

shortly afterwards, Reggazoni began to slow with a softening tyre, allowing Peterson through on lap 42. On the same lap, Pace also pulled off and suddenly the Lotus had leapfrogged into second place. Just as a fine result looked on the cards, the Swede coasted off the circuit with no drive to the rear wheels – an inboard CV joint bearing cage had broken up. His team-mate Ickx had made rapid progress up through the field from his lowly starting position to reach eighth place by lap 17. On lap 41, he passed eventual third-placed man Denny Hulme and was hotly disputing fourth with the Tyrrell of Patrick Depailler when the Frenchman spun his car and the Lotus had nowhere to go, T-boning his rival and putting them both out of the race. Therefore, within two laps, the hopes of Team Lotus were dashed, two DNFs was all they had to show for their weekend's hard labour.

Peterson's failure to finish had certainly not helped his Championship chances, dropping him down to sixth. Fortunately, all the other title contenders had struggled in Austria, Reggazoni recovering from his puncture to finish fifth, his two points leaving him in the lead of the title race with a total of 46, while Scheckter, Fittipaldi and Lauda all retired with blown engines. The man who had demoted Peterson from fifth in the standings was Austrian victor Carlos Reutemann. It was clear that to have any realistic chance of the title, Ronnie would simply have to win the next race in Italy.

The week after the Austrian race, it was announced that the promising British Formula Atlantic driver, Jim Crawford, had signed a one-year 'practice' contract with John Player Team Lotus. Scottish-born Crawford had for some time been mechanic to his friend Stephen Choularton, his reward for doing this job being a once-yearly race outing in his friend's Formula Atlantic March. Eventually, the obvious speed and talent he displayed on these occasional appearances resulted in Crawford taking the plunge and joining Choularton in a two-car team and, at the time of the Lotus deal, he was leading the John Player Formula Atlantic Championship. The one-year contract provided for the opportunity to test a Formula 1 car with the possibility of several outings in non-Championship races, the objective being to be seen to promote the interests of young British drivers while at the same time securing the services of someone who could turn out to be the next great British prospect.

A little later it also transpired that the team had signed up-and-coming French Formula Renault star Rene Arnoux on a similar deal. This had come about because of Colin Chapman's long-standing friendship with the French journalist, Jabby Crombac, who had recommended his young compatriot. Arnoux's first tests were due to take place at the end of October at Paul Ricard. In fact, he never even so much as sat in a Lotus Formula 1 car, but the publicity involved in having been singled out by Colin Chapman as having talent was enough to secure him other drives which eventually took him into Formula 1. Both Arnoux and Crawford were given a token sum of money in exchange for their signatures. It's not recorded what Crawford did with his money but according to Crombac, Arnoux immediately rushed out and bought a Basset Hound, which he named Lotus!

Despite the team's continuing problems, they had time to take JPS/9 to Mallory Park for Peterson to demonstrate at a Fordsport meeting. Two days later, they gave Crawford his first taste of a Formula 1 car on the Snetterton circuit, where he was reported as having lapped only fractionally slower than Peterson.

The following week, the team set off for Monza and the Italian Grand Prix, which had been the scene of so much joy and sadness over the years for them. Heartened by the strong performance of the 76 in Ickx's hands in Austria, they resolved to try and focus on the new cars once more, bringing down both JPS/9 for Peterson and JPS/10 for Ickx, with 72/8 as the spare for Peterson.

However, after the first Friday session, Peterson was still not happy with his new car and for second practice he reverted to 72/8, eventually setting the sixth fastest time of the day. Unfortunately, with no spare 72 to turn to, this was not an option that was open to Ickx, who ended the session three and a half seconds off the pace. It was the Saturday morning practice that was the decisive one, Niki Lauda grabbing pole in the Ferrari from a trio of Brabhams led by Österreichring victor Reutemann. Peterson's lap from Friday afternoon was his quickest of the weekend, leaving him on the inside of the fourth row. Although he tried JPS/9 again in the Saturday afternoon session, the time he recorded would barely have got him on the grid and he decided to race the spare. Ickx seemed to reach a plateau on Saturday morning and he was once again well down the grid, on the outside of the eighth row.

Overnight, a decision was taken to convert 72/8 back to its pre-French Grand Prix narrow track configuration in an effort to eke out more top-end speed. On the opening lap, Peterson made up a place by squeezing past Fittipaldi to come round sixth, while Ickx jumped four places as well and came past the pits in 12th. On lap two, Peterson dispatched John Watson's Brabham and five laps later it was another Brabham, this time that of Carlos Pace, which got the 'treatment'. When the lead Brabham of Reutemann also faltered on lap 12, the Swede was up to third behind the two dominant Ferraris of Lauda and Reggazoni, who were running away with the race.

Peterson had plenty to keep him occupied for, in a re-run of their battle in the 1973 race, Emerson Fittipaldi was applying constant pressure and was ever-present in the wing mirrors of the black-and-gold Lotus. The first cue for optimism in the Lotus pit came on lap 30 when Lauda's smoking car now began to billow and on lap 32 he came into the pits to retire. Pretty soon, Reggazoni's car started emitting tell-tale puffs of smoke and these gradually worsened until on lap 40 of 52, he too pulled into the pits and out of the race.

This left the last ten or so laps as a tense race between the past and present number one drivers of Team Lotus. Try as he might, Fittipaldi could not get the better of his Swedish rival, for the overnight changes to the 72 had given it a slight advantage on top-end speed which just about compensated for Peterson's softening front brakes. On one lap, Fittipaldi did manage to outbrake his rival into the first

chicane but overcooked it on the exit and the Lotus was back in front in a flash. At the finish, the gap was 0.8s and Peterson punched his arm into the air with delight as he took his third Grand Prix victory of the year, in a design that, by rights, should have been consigned to a museum (and had been!) by this stage in its career. In so doing, he kept alive his slim World Championship hopes, his tally of 31 points still within striking distance of Reggazoni, who despite his failure to finish, retained his lead in the title race with 46 points, one clear of Scheckter (who finished third at Monza) and three more than Fittipaldi, with Lauda (having failed to finish the last three races) now only just ahead of Peterson on 36. Ickx, in

JPS/10, had worked his way up to ninth, until forced to pit by a faulty ball-joint in the throttle linkage. This was repaired and he was sent out but, after another two stops, he retired with another part of the linkage broken – another frustrating race for the Belgian.

On the team's return to Britain, it was announced that a third John Player Team Lotus entry would be made for the lucrative United States Grand Prix in the form of Tim Schenken. Schenken had performed admirably in the under-funded Trojan Formula 1 car in several races during 1974 and he and Peterson knew each other well from their days driving for the Ferrari sports car team. The deal was that Schenken would drive providing the team didn't damage any of its cars or blow up too many engines in the intervening race in Canada.

With the - albeit remote - chance that he could still win the Championship, Peterson didn't want to take any chances in the remaining two races and told Chapman that he wanted to race the 72. Ickx had been none too impressed with his 76 at Monza and he too wanted to revert back to a 72. So a decision was made to take the two 72s plus a singleton 76 (JPS/9) to North America. Both of the 72s were to the same specification as Peterson's Monza-winning car, e.g. the narrow track format used earlier in the year.

The Canadian race was once again held at the Mosport Park circuit north of Toronto. The meeting began badly when the new engine in Peterson's car refused to pull properly, being 600 revs down, meaning that he ended the day 14th on the timesheets. Ickx fared little better, crashing

at the third corner and dinging the car against the barrier. Most of the rest of the day was spent converting JPS/9 to fit Ickx and so he only managed a few slow laps in the car before the day's practice ended.

For Saturday, the engine used by Peterson to win the Italian Grand Prix was re-installed, there having been insufficient time to have it rebuilt between the two races. This did the trick in terms of performance but the Swede was thwarted by a series of frustrating niggles, including a gearbox seal leaking oil into the clutch (not a new problem to Lotus by any means). The result was that he only truly got into the groove towards the end of final practice and could have done with more time to move up the order. As it was, his best time was good enough only for 10th on the grid, on the outside of the fifth row – not really what he

Peterson took his third Grand Prix victory of the year, in a design that by rights should already have been consigned to a museum

wanted when he needed to win to keep alive his Championship chances.

Ickx encountered a fuel pressure problem in the morning session on Saturday, so used the spare JPS/9 again in the afternoon, although his times in the car were well off the pace required to qualify. After practice it was discovered that the fuel pressure problems were down to a

Left: Monza magic. Peterson scored win number three for the team in the Italian Grand Prix, aided by reversion to narrow-track specification.

cracked internal pipe and it was hoped that, once this was sorted, the car would run cleanly in the race itself. The result was that the Belgian was left on the inside of the 11th row, slower than the overweight Lola of Graham Hill and only fractionally faster than the Surtees of Grand Prix newcomer, Helmuth Koinigg.

The main hi-tech modification for race day was the addition of a ladies' stocking across the airbox opening on both cars, with the toe-end running down into the cockpit. This was to keep dust out of the throttle slides on the first laps when the problem seemed to be at its worst due to the starting pack being bunched together. The idea was for the drivers to pull off the stocking after the opening lap and continue with nice clean throttle slides. Well, that was the idea…

Both 72s made average but not particularly noteworthy starts. Peterson was forced off the track by a wayward Carlos Pace as they accelerated away towards the first corner and the two black-and-gold cars came round at the end of the opening lap with Peterson in 10th and Ickx in 20th. Both drivers had forgotten to pull away their stockings, which were now trailing from their airboxes! Peterson took some 15 laps to size up Patrick Depailler, perhaps experiencing the same problems as his team-mate in being unable to generate enough warmth in the tyres. Finally, he slipped past the Tyrrell and then a lap later demoted Reutemann in the Brabham. Another 15 tours on, Jarier's Shadow was his next victim and then came trouble. He had been following James Hunt's Hesketh closely and when they lapped the McLaren of Jochen Mass, the

German pulled over for Hunt and then chopped back in front of Peterson. Just as the Swede decided to pass the McLaren on the other side, the German suddenly realised there was another car there and swung out right, collecting the Lotus and bending back its left nose fin.

A few laps later a pitstop by Pace and the retirement of Scheckter elevated Peterson to fifth. For thirty laps he followed the Hesketh. The incident with Mass had left Peterson not only fuming but also his car was now understeering badly. To make matters worse, the turbulence from the Hesketh combined with the bent nose fin was causing the front end to lift up off the ground over the little hump on the main straight! Finally on lap 60, with 20 to go, he found a way through and set off in pursuit of third-placed man Reggazoni. When Lauda crashed out with only 12 laps remaining they were racing for second. The gap came down and down until, going out onto the final tour it was only 0.4 seconds and a last-gasp lunge from Peterson looked likely. However, the Penske of Mark Donohue got between the two cars on the run-in to the finish, scuppering any hope the Swede had of snatching second.

Ickx's race had been unspectacular and uneventful, the Belgian suffering from poor handling under braking and a lack of traction from his tyres. At first glance, it was a performance distinctly devoid of 'fire in the belly'. However, closer inspection after the race revealed that the steering rack had been damaged in his practice shunt, causing the unpredictable behaviour under braking.

Peterson's third place gave him another four points but

it was now impossible for him to overhaul either Emerson Fittipaldi, who won the Canadian race, or Reggazoni, for the Championship title. These two were tied on 52 points and would fight it out in the last round at Watkins Glen, while Peterson's total of 35 points reflected the fact that, despite three Grand Prix wins (only one less than Fittipaldi) his title aspirations had been damaged by a general lack of reliability and organisation, plus the failure of the new car to provide him with a mount worthy of his talents. In hindsight, it seemed that, had the team opted to further develop the 72 for the 1974 season, the Swede may very well have won the World Championship, as Warr freely admits. 'In retrospect, and it's very easy to be wise in retrospect, then the answer is probably yes. If you'd have said "No, the 72 has still got two seasons' life in it, let's start with a clean sheet of paper: the races are only 200 miles now, so we can do away with the front tank installation and all the bits and bobs that go with it, why don't we make a lightweight monocoque, let's try and make some of the other bits out of the materials we know are available" I think we could probably have come up with a 72 that may not have been 100lbs lighter but it might have been 60lbs or 70lbs lighter, just by doing that. And that would have done the job, would have kept the car competitive, but we didn't know that at the time.'

By this stage of the year, the 'silly season' about which driver was going where was well under way. There was considerable speculation about whether or not Ickx would see out the second year of his contract with the team, the smart money being that he would retire instead of drive for Lotus again. Hot tip to take his place was the Irishman John Watson, who had enjoyed a very impressive year with the privately run Hexagon/Goldie Brabham team.

A fortnight after the Canadian event, the most lucrative Formula 1 race of the year, the United States Grand Prix, took place. With little to play for in terms of the Championship, there was just the small matter of pride (not to mention money!) to motivate the team and drivers in this final race of the season. Peterson was still in his regular 72/8, while Ickx was in 72/5 and Schenken was assigned JPS/9 (76/1).

It quickly became apparent that the latest Goodyear rubber just wasn't working for the Lotus drivers. They were reporting problems with low-speed understeer due to the fact that they simply couldn't get any heat into the front tyres. Chapman told Autosport reporter Pete Lyons, that temperatures at the front were 160 vs 210 at the rear. He opined that the construction of the tyres at both ends were too soft and springy to suit his soft suspension design. As a result, they had tried to stiffen up both cars, with Ickx's nearly solid at the rear and, although it seemed to work better, both cars were way off the pace. Other problems reported by the drivers were spongy brakes after a few laps – which did not bode well for the race – and recurring electrical troubles. In addition, Peterson ran out of fuel in the final session, stranding him out on the circuit.

The outcome was that Ickx qualified on the outside of the eighth row, while Peterson was back on the inside of the tenth row, the first time he had been outqualified by the Belgian and easily his worst grid position of his time at Lotus. For a man who scored an almost unprecedented nine pole positions for Grand Prix in the 1973 season, this must have been very depressing. Perhaps slightly more disheartened was Schenken, who never came to terms with his JPS/9, being another victim of terminal understeer, and failing to qualify for the race by some 1.3 seconds.

By the simple expedient of ignoring official procedure, Schenken managed to start the race anyway. As second reserve, he was permitted to have his car fuelled up and do a warm-up lap with the rest of the field in case some misfortune should befall two of the qualifiers. When the field lined up for the start, he and Jose Dolhem, the other non-qualifier in a Surtees, positioned themselves at the back, ever hopeful of a last-minute reprieve. As the flag dropped, they both charged off with the rest of the field and for five laps the Australian had his own little private battle with Dolhem before he was black-flagged. Oddly, Dolhem was allowed to continue, due to the fact that Mario Andretti had stalled on the start-line and so had, theoretically, not been able to take the start.

Meanwhile, the two black-and-gold 72s came round in formation, the Belgian in 15th place leading Peterson. By lap six, they were up to 11th and 12th, at which point Ickx spun trying to pass the Shadow of Jean-Pierre Jarier and went nose-first into the barriers. Although he was able to limp round to the pits, the damage was sufficient to force

1st Italian Grand Prix 1974 John Player Special

his retirement – an appropriate end to a miserable season that had promised so much and yet delivered so little.

By lap 21 of 59, Peterson was up to eighth but his car was not sounding too good, courtesy of a cracked exhaust pipe and eventually he came into the pits to have this removed, dropping him right down the order. Even so, he had worked his way back up to ninth again when, with seven laps remaining, a fuel line pulled loose just as it had for Fittipaldi in Austria the previous year, and his race was over.

Despite not finishing, the Swede just retained his fifth place in the World Championship, his tally of 35 points being three more than Watkins Glen race winner Carlos Reutemann. The title went to Fittipaldi in his first year with his new team, McLaren, the Brazilian's fourth place being good enough to secure the points he needed. Ickx finished 10th with 12 points, while in the Constructors title Lotus slumped to fourth behind McLaren, Ferrari and Tyrrell. It had not been a good year.

WORLD CHAMPIONSHIP TABLE 1974

Pos	Driver	Argentina	Brazil	S.Africa	Spain	Belgium	Monaco	Sweden	Netherlands	France	Great Britain	Germany	Austria	Italy	Canada	USA	Total	(dropped)
1	Emerson Fittipaldi		9		4	9	2	3	4		6			6	9	3	55	
2	Clay Reggazoni	4	6		6	3	3		6	4	3	9	2		6		52	
3	Jody Scheckter				2	4	6	9		3	9	6		4	2		45	
4	Niki Lauda	6			9	6			9	6	2						38	
5	Ronnie Peterson		1				9			9		3		9	4		35	
6	Carlos Reutemann			9	1							4	9			9	32	
7	Denny Hulme	9						1		1	1		6	1	1		20	
8	James Hunt							4					4		3	4	15	
9	Patrick Depailler	1		3		1		6	2							1	14	
10	Jacky Ickx		4							2	4	2					12	
10	Mike Hailwood	3	2	4					3								12	
12	Carlos Pace		3											2		6	11	
13	Jean-Pierre Beltoise	2		6		2											10	
14	Jean-Pierre Jarrier						4	2									6	
14	John Watson						1						3			2	6	
16	Hans-Joachim Stuck			2	3												5	
17	Arturo Merzario			1										3			4	
18	Graham Hill								1								1	
18	Tom Pryce											1					1	
18	Vittorio Brambilla												1				1	

Pos	Constructor	Argentina	Brazil	S.Africa	Spain	Belgium	Monaco	Sweden	Netherlands	France	Great Britain	Germany	Austria	Italy	Canada	USA	Total	(dropped)
1	McLaren-Cosworth	9	9	4	4	9	2	3	4	1	6		6	6	9	3	73	2
2	Ferrari	6	6		9	6	3		9	6	3	9	2		6		65	
3	Tyrrell-Cosworth	1		3	2	4	6	9	2	3	9	6		4	2	1	52	
4	Lotus-Cosworth		4				9			9	4	3		9	4		42	
5	Brabham-Cosworth			9	1		1					4	9	2		9	35	
6	Hesketh-Cosworth							4					4		3	4	15	
7	B.R.M.	2		6		2											10	
8	Shadow-Cosworth						4	2				1					7	
9	March-Cosworth			2	3								1				6	
10	ISO-Cosworth			1										3			4	
11	Surtees-Cosworth		3														3	
12	Lola-Cosworth								1								1	

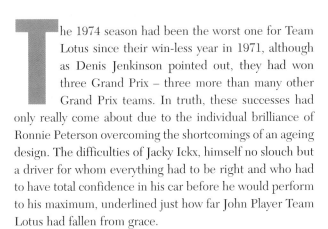

The 1974 season had been the worst one for Team Lotus since their win-less year in 1971, although as Denis Jenkinson pointed out, they had won three Grand Prix – three more than many other Grand Prix teams. In truth, these successes had only really come about due to the individual brilliance of Ronnie Peterson overcoming the shortcomings of an ageing design. The difficulties of Jacky Ickx, himself no slouch but a driver for whom everything had to be right and who had to have total confidence in his car before he would perform to his maximum, underlined just how far John Player Team Lotus had fallen from grace.

The reasons for such a slump in performance could be traced right back to 1973, when Chapman was engrossed in developing the Lotus Esprit and was also committing a lot of time to his boat manufacturing interests. As a result of this, he had been happy to brief his designer Ralph Bellamy to produce a car to the same basic concepts as the 72 but 100lbs lighter and stronger and leave him to get on with it. It seems that Chapman did not personally involve himself in the design of the 1974 contender as much as he had with the 72. His prolonged absences had also started to affect team morale, as Vic McCarthy explains. 'Chapman fell away

from the team a little bit. He was so busy trying to keep Lotus Cars alive. We actually asked Peter Warr to tell him to come over at least once a week because he was such a morale booster in a way, that when he came by the charisma of him, just bucked you up a bit.'

Peter Warr believes that the fundamental reason for the failure of the 76 was that it had failed to fulfil its design brief. 'I don't think, intrinsically, the chassis was actually that bad. I'm not saying it was that much better than the 72 but it finished up either no lighter or even a bit heavier than the 72, which was already being discarded because it was too heavy!

'I can't really ever believe or understand how it was that somebody persuaded Colin that the twin rear-wing it was

Below Left: Unjustly condemned? The 76 showed brief promise but lack of development time and management, left it to wither and die. **Below Right:** Alternative airbox detail from one of the Giugiaro drawings which inspired the Type 76 design.

launched with was a good idea. It was at that time that I started to suspect, from across the other side of the table from the engineers, that they didn't really understand aerodynamics. The twin rear wing thing just didn't work and the structure to carry it and the bodywork and all the rest of it was just outrageously over the top when you looked at what it had to compete against. Then of course, we got into the situation where we were having to change it to bring it back to a conventional set-up and in bringing it back to conventional set-up, we were in a panic. If you are in a panic you do the work, get the job done, get the car out to the next race and then all of a sudden you realise that what you have done is made it heavier. Then the radiator layout got changed, the oil tank radiators got changed and we finished up with a lump.'

Ralph Bellamy gets particularly aerated when the subject of the apparent ineffectiveness of the cooling system on the 76s is raised. 'We went to Jarama for the Spanish Grand Prix and it rained before the race. The rain had virtually stopped but the track was very wet. Colin, who was the tactician of the team, sent them out on wets and they came round on the parade lap and Colin rushed out to Peterson's car, stuck his head in the cockpit and saw that the oil temperature was low. In those days we had the oil coolers down the back end of the car, stuck out either side of the oil tank. Under those circumstances they copped a whole lot of water off the tyres. So, rather than being an air/oil cooler, it was almost like a water/oil cooler! Which of course kept the oil very cool. And Colin said "The oil's too cool, where's the tape, put the tape on". So he strapped tape around the oil coolers, as far as he was concerned to bring the oil temperature up. The race started and the first thing that happened was the track started to dry out, the racing

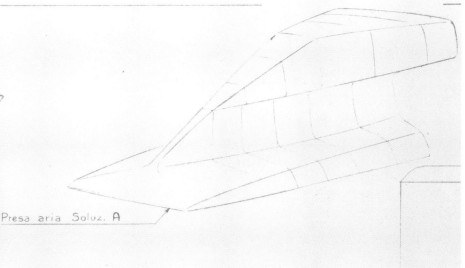

Presa aria Soluz. A

LOTUS 72

Left: Maurice Phillippe's Parnelli Formula 1 design was exactly what Team Lotus had wanted the 76 to be -a lighter, stronger version of the 72. However, it too was conspicuous for its lack of success.

line dried because it wasn't raining any more and the oil got 'stinko' because the coolers were all taped up!

'Then they came in for their tyres stops and there was that amazing stop that Jacky [Ickx] made where they just obliterated the whole pit road in fire extinguisher smoke. Anybody who was there that day will never forget it, it was the most extraordinary thing you've ever seen in your life, absolutely unbelievable. On the basis of that, and these long pit-stops and stuff-ups like that, Peter Warr decided that the thing overheated and the cooling system was no good. There was bugger-all wrong with the cooling system! Everybody subsequently copied it and ran it for years and years but it was the first one like that, and it worked fine. But it was internal Team Lotus politics, mate! I think Peter was more than ready to rip me down a peg or two if he could do it.'

Bellamy believes that, while the basic concept of the 76 was not particularly innovative, it was certain advanced aspects of its design which, in the end, let it down. 'It was crippled by the fact that Colin had this idea that he wanted a clutch-less gearshift because he wanted this left-foot braking thing. Then there was this bizarre bloody hydraulic system running off the starter motor that Lockheed did for

us. It didn't self-bleed, so every time you pulled the thing apart or did any work down the back of the car and broke into the system, you got air in it and it took half an hour's running before the air came out of it, by which time it was all over, whatever you were doing was over, because the thing wouldn't work. So you were forever stopping in the pits and buggering about and we never got to do any proper testing to make it work. All of these things compromised the design.'

It is perhaps surprising that more effort wasn't put in by the team to establish whether or not the power clutch concept was viable. Although there were stories that the power clutch had been tried on the Texaco Star Formula 2 car, Bellamy says this was not the case and, although it was tried extensively on Lotus road cars by the drivers, the conditions under which it was being tested were quite different. 'The Formula 2 car hardly ever ran. The engines grenaded all over the place - it was a dreadful fiasco the whole thing. We all gave up on it literally by mid-year, so we'd never have put it on that car. If you'd wanted to test something for five minutes before the engine exploded then that would have been a worthwhile exercise!

'It was fitted to their [Peterson and Ickx's] road cars. If

you fit it to a road car and get it bled and stuff like that and don't go pulling it apart all the time then it'll work. But obviously when it was fitted to a Formula 1 car and we were stripping it down and pulling the gearbox off and putting it back on and changing gear ratios and changing engines and all that sort of stuff on a fairly regular basis, it was forever getting air in it. So it really wasn't until we got it into the field that the true shortcomings were realised. Plus these guys, Ickx and Peterson, were driving for Team Lotus and this was a Chapman innovation and they weren't really going to go to him and say "Mate, this is a crock of shit and I don't want it on my Formula 1 car", even if they didn't like it!'

Peter Warr is not so sure that the power clutch was a mistake – more that it was just too far ahead of its time, as with many Chapman innovations. 'Not at all. It just showed that, again, Colin was 20 years ahead of his time. What wasn't available at the time was the technology, the electronics which can control hydraulic systems fast enough and with however many calculations per second, to do the job the way it is done now. To have an electric button on top of the gear lever to do a function which otherwise the driver would have had to have done with his left foot so that he could use it to brake instead was the right concept and it was brilliant and it was the right way to go.

'The trouble was, that as the car got into the mire of being uncompetitive and needing so many other things doing to it, and the fact that only Ronnie was really convinced of the advantage of left-foot braking, it was one of the easiest things to abandon. It was an added complication, it was extra bits on the car, we were looking to try and save weight which shouldn't have been there in the first place, and so it was easy to take it off.'

According to Bellamy, another problem with the 76 was that it was too softly sprung, due to the decision to retain torsion bars as in the 72. 'Having been designed for Lotus 72 torsion bars, it was sprung too softly for the current

which was a car that had all the good points of the 72, none of the bad points and was 100lbs lighter! The Parnelli was the car that we should have been racing. That car in a Team Lotus environment would have done the job.'

Also, there were signs that Chapman's approach of concentrating weight distribution towards the rear of the car – which had been successful with the 72 – was outdated. A new generation of cars like the McLaren M23 and Brabham BT42 had come through in 1973 which were better balanced through the use of a large central fuel tank between the driver and the engine and which generated sufficient grip at the front end to make the best use of their tyres.

Further problems with Lotus Cars in 1974 had

accident in practice for the 1974 German Grand Prix but had been forced to abandon them, as Warr explains. 'The joy of the MelMags was that what you basically had was two saucers and you had a central boss and the whole lot was bonded together. What you could do was ring up MelMag and say "Right we want a boss with an extra half inch in it or another inch in it or whatever" and this was the era when we were still experimenting with things like wheel widths, so you'd perhaps run different widths on wet tyres to dry tyres, on slow circuits to fast circuits and so forth.

'The concept of the wheel was not bad. It was light and it was rigid and it had everything that you basically wanted from a wheel. What it didn't have was the ability, as is the case with all composite structures, of being able to be tested without destruction. The only way you could test it to see if it was strong enough was to test it until it broke. The problem was that, in the early days, we didn't know whether the wheel failed in Brazil and at Zandvoort because it was incapable of accepting the load that the 72 was putting through it or whether it had been bashed up against something. It was after Ronnie's Nürburgring accident, that we actually had left the visible

The power clutch was not a mistake... as with many Chapman innovations, it was just 20 years ahead of its time

version of tyres, so the wheel rates were far too low to generate any heat in the tyres, which were designed to work with a McLaren, which they could just fling harder and harder coil springs into. Right from almost the time I got there, we were on the stiffest torsion bars in the box of bits, there was just not the space to put anything stiffer in.'

'In reality it probably did have some performance advantages if we had stuck with it and exploited it properly but again, it started off with the radiators down the back and, in a subsequent version because we couldn't make the front tyres work, I moved them up towards the front and things like that to try and solve the problem but really there wasn't a will within Team Lotus to make it happen.'

Jacky Ickx believes that lack of money was another factor that prevented the 76 being fully developed. 'It was good at Zeltweg, for the first time. Neither Ronnie nor I liked it but we kept trying. And maybe it could have worked well but it would have needed more development and they had no money for development.'

The impact of the departure of his co-designer of the 72, Maurice Phillippe, to the fledgling Vels-Parnelli Formula 1 team was not lost on Chapman either for, as Warr points out, he went on to do exactly what Chapman had wanted – build a lighter version of the 72! 'The car that we really, really should have had was the Parnelli because what Maurice Phillippe did was exactly Colin's design brief

continued to distract Chapman from his racing activities. A strike by miners had forced the Government to impose the three-day working week, putting back the planned March launch of the new Lotus Elite to May. The fuel crisis had also depressed demand for new cars, particularly sports cars, and there was real concern for the future of the company if it failed to sell enough of the new model. With only half an eye on Team Lotus, it was not surprising that Chapman was unable to develop the 76 into a competitive proposition, as Warr explains. 'During that period he was trying like crazy to learn how to run a big business and maintain his personal interest in the racing team. The car company threw crisis after crisis at him, which took up more of his time and he was never very good at delegating – he always wanted to get in and sort the problem out himself. He would have spent less time, having written the design brief for the 76, actually standing over the draughtsman's shoulders in the drawing office than he had done on previous cars. But then, equally, I think he thought that the various component parts that had made the 72 so good, like the torsion bar suspension system and so forth were being retained anyway, so he didn't have to spend so much time.'

Out of the public eye, John Player Team Lotus had quietly taken Magnesium Electron, manufacturers of MelMag wheels, to court and won. The team had used the MelMag wheels throughout 1973 and up until Peterson's

First Person

Geoff Aldridge on Colin Chapman's relationships with other designers

"Chapman always had this problem that he wanted things done his way but he liked to have people that he could feed off effectively, that he could pick up information from and it never really seemed to work. I think it probably worked best with Maurice Phillippe. You'd get somebody in who you think could do the job but Chapman would never let them do it and they'd get fed up and leave. And I think it was similar with Ralph Bellamy really. He thought that Ralph had a different approach to him and he could contribute but it didn't really work because Ralph wanted to do it his way and Chapman wanted to do it his way and they didn't hit it off."

What makes the John Player Special so special.

1. Inboard front disc brakes.
2. All independent rising rate torsion bar suspension.
3. Aerofoils and aerodynamically-shaped body to force the car downwards on to the track.
4. Aircraft-type fuselage. The rivetted, aluminium monocoque contains rubber puncture-proof fuel cells which hold forty gallons.
5. Twin, side-mounted radiators give low drag and increased driver comfort.
6. 480 h.p., V8 twin overhead camshaft 3-litre engine, turning at 11,000 r.p.m.
7. 16" wide tyres mounted on 18" wide wheels.
8. Airbox pressure-feeds air to engine.
9. Cooling ducts keep rear brakes temperature below 400°C.
10. Duckhams Q 20w/50 motor oil.

DUCKHAMS Q MOTOR OIL

Ask a man who knows about engines.

evidence that showed it hadn't been glued together properly, which was the basis then for the case against MelMag. 'It wasn't a malicious litigation, it was just a seeking of compensation for the money that we had spent on a product that had dropped us in it. We weren't looking to pay Emerson's hospital bills or the repair of the racing cars, we were just looking for our money back on what we'd spent with the whole bloody programme.'

Of more immediate concern from the point of view of the financial stability of the Formula 1 team, the three year contract with Players to race under the John Player Special brand came to an end in November 1974. Towards the end of the season, rumours of pull-outs by major motorsport sponsors began to circulate and Rothmans and Yardley were two high-profile examples of companies who decided to end their involvements. Persistent stories began circulating that John Player had also decided to quit.

Publicly, there was no comment from either party on the subject but privately John Player announced to Chapman and Warr that they intended to quit, setting in motion a remarkable behind the scenes drama. Peter Warr describes the sequence of events: 'The worst thing about it was that it was six weeks before the season started! There had been no warning at all, they just told us out of the blue. We only managed to salvage the season by saying to them, you do realise that what you have just done six weeks before the start of the season is basically put the company into administration? Because, we've got to lay off all the blokes, we've got commitments to drivers that are signed on contracts and we've got no money coming in.

'So what they actually agreed to do was to say, "Well,

perhaps we realise that this was a bit unpremeditated. All we can do is to say we will fund you to a level but not the same level that we were going to". So that determined what we had to do from then on.' In the end, John Player agreed to continue, but with a vastly reduced budget, something like 40% less than the team had been hoping for, raising doubts as to whether the team would be able to survive for the whole season, according to Warr. 'They cut it back to zero and we got it back up to about 60%. Well, given that you pay great chunks of money out when you are building cars and when you are paying drivers their contracts, it was obvious that we were going to run out of money halfway through the season.' Following their meeting with Players, Chapman and Warr flew off to the Lotus boss's holiday home 'Los Cuatro Horas' in Ibiza to consider their options.

One thing seemed certain at least – Peterson and Ickx would definitely be staying on for 1975, with the Swede having signed a contract for the 1975 and 1976 seasons as long ago as July 1974 and Ickx having signed for two seasons when he joined at the end of 1973. That the Swede would stay was no surprise but the Belgian had hardly excelled himself during his first season with the team and he was clearly disenchanted with the situation. Peter Warr believes that Ickx's poor performances were not necessarily down to the driver but more a symptom of the chaos in the team at the time. 'The problem was that the team was in a considerable state of disarray. In that state, it was then even clearer that, when you got a mod or an improvement, the chances are that there was only one of them. So he was driving the second-best car all year. Jacky was not happy. Anyone having the sort of season that he had with crises, decisions and changing cars, wouldn't have been happy because a driver needs to be able to settle down and get to know a car. He wasn't driving the same vehicle two weeks in a row.'

As a consequence, Warr says that there was no hesitation on the part of the team about continuing with Ickx for 1975. 'We felt he deserved another go because we hadn't given him a fair crack of the whip. There was never, as far as I'm aware, any suggestion that Ickx was not capable of delivering. It was one of the few occasions I remember, where no-one raised a question mark about whether he was up to it or whether he was capable of delivering because everybody realised he never had a chance [in 1974].'

With the cutbacks proposed by Players, it was by no means certain that they would be able to pay their drivers what they expected to be paid. Chapman and Warr agreed that their only hope was to ask Peterson, the better-paid of the two by some margin, if he would consider a pay-cut. By doing this, they could afford to build a new car but if they didn't then they would have to soldier on with the 72s. Peterson, who had gone through a similar process at March,

refused to countenance a pay cut, as Warr explains. 'We went to Ronnie and said "We love you dearly, we want you to stay, we don't want any other racing driver but we have had a kick in the goolies of a monumental size and what we are saying to you is that, if you want to continue with us, which we hope you do, we would like you to consider taking a cut in your contracted amount, because we've had to take a cut in our contracted amount. It's not because we don't love you or because we want to screw you, it's just that we haven't got the money any more". Ronnie said – and I have to say I was 100% with him on it – that the amount of money you earn as a Grand Prix racing driver is the measure of your status in the hierarchy and he was saying "If I do this, it is inevitable that the whole world will think that I am not where I should be in the pecking order". Ronnie wasn't interested terribly in money per se; he didn't have an exorbitant, flashy lifestyle. He was quite content with a pretty ordinary couple of cars in his garage at home but what he was concerned with was his position in the pecking order and I think that that is very important to a race driver. So he got his money, we didn't have the money so he didn't get a new car.' There was no choice but to carry on with the old cars for another year…

To the wider public at least, there was little indication of the turmoil within Team Lotus. In late November, it was announced that John Player would continue as a sponsor of Team Lotus, the Formula Atlantic Championship and the British Grand Prix. Meanwhile, two 72s were prepared for the first race of the 1975 season in Argentina, one of which was first taken to the Mount Fuji circuit in Japan for the World Winners Formula 1 demonstration being organised by Bernie Ecclestone as a precursor to a full Grand Prix at the circuit in 1976.

The week before the Argentinian race, Peterson was again the subject of great speculation, suggesting that he was going to sign for one of the American Formula 1 teams, either UOP-Shadow or Penske, after the first two South American races. It was well known that Penske had tried to tempt the Swede into driving his new Formula 1 car, while another rumour suggested that Peterson and Tom Pryce, Shadow's rising star, would swap places. Certainly, there seemed to be 'no smoke without fire'… Peter Warr takes up the story: 'What happened was that Colin said "Well, hang on a minute, if we've got to pay Ronnie his full whack, we're going to go bust anyway, so what we'd better do is look around and see if we can find anybody who is interested in taking his contract off our hands". We talked to Ronnie about it and he said, "Well, yeah, OK, because I want my contract, that is my ranking". Obviously he wasn't going to go to a team which was crap, so we came up with a couple of ideas and Shadow seemed to be one which was in a situation where he could have done some good and which

Above: Tug of love. Peterson was the subject of a bizarre swap proposal with Shadow – who had money aplenty but no top-line driver, whereas Team Lotus had the topline driver but no money… Eventually the deal was scuppered, along with any chance of a new car for the Swede in 1975.

possibly could have afforded him.' However, time was not on their side, and it proved impossible to set up a deal in time.

The story was still rumbling on when the teams assembled at the Buenos Aires circuit. Shadow boss Alan Rees admitted only that his team had come 'incredibly close' to signing Peterson. Negotiations had still been going on as late as the Tuesday before the race and the Shadow mechanics did not actually put Jean-Pierre Jarier's name on the side of their car until Friday morning!

The two 72s for Peterson and Ickx were visually unaltered from 1974, with Peterson retaining 72/8 and Ickx once again behind the wheel of 72/5. A host of minor modifications had been made over the winter, the most significant of which were the larger, stronger Girling calipers, which had been introduced at the front on Ickx's car. There was also a different design of 'straps' to mount the discs and stronger brake-shafts. All of this was aimed at overcoming the problem of spongy brakes, which had afflicted the 72 consistently the previous season. In addition, both cars were running in narrow track specification. In the Friday practice session, Peterson collided with the Copersucar Fittipaldi of Wilson Fittipaldi, tearing off a nose fin and puncturing a tyre, while he was also experiencing problems with locking front brakes. Ickx was also unhappy with the handling of his car on the high-speed sections of the track and, no doubt slightly envious of the options apparently available to his team-mate, joked that in fact all the reports were wrong and that it was really him that was joining Shadow!

On Saturday, Peterson's brakes were still playing up and eventually the problem was traced to a sticking caliper piston. By the time this had been sorted there wasn't enough time to balance the braking of the car and fine-tune the handling, so the Swede wound up mid-grid on the sixth row, more than two seconds off the pole time of…Jarier in the Shadow! As with many drivers, the prospect of being supplanted was clearly acting as an excellent source of motivation for the Frenchman. Ickx was on the outside of the ninth row, continuing the performance level he had perfected during the 1974 season. Overnight modifications were made to try and improve rear-end grip, which both drivers reported was a problem. This involved considerable improvisation: the suspension had been lowered by adapting front suspension damper units with two-inch spacers crafted out of sawn off jack handles, the latter having been borrowed from

McLaren!

In the race, Peterson profited from a rather blatant jump-start, which left him running fifth ahead of the Ferrari of Reggazoni. However, this did not last long because the brakes on the Lotus were fading badly and he was having to use the engine and gearbox more and more to slow the car down. Eventually, his engine gave up the unequal struggle with a dropped valve. Ickx continued to circulate in a small battle for ninth place, eventually getting past Brambilla's March and coming home eighth, albeit a lap behind the winner, reigning Champion Fittipaldi, in a McLaren M23.

The 'Peterson Saga' continued in the fortnight between the two South American races. Credence to the story was added by pictures of the Swede sitting in a Shadow, with Shadow boss Alan Rees alongside. Peter Warr takes up the story: 'The last meeting I had was with Alan in the hotel in Brazil and we got a deal as I recall'. However, as Warr explains, while Shadow were happy to take over Peterson's contract, the deal foundered because they were not prepared to countenance the payment of a football-style 'transfer fee' for doing so. 'Alan was completely clear and OK and signed up for paying Ronnie his contract. What they weren't clear about was paying us something in order to release him. We needed the money in order to top up our budget and this was, as it were, establishing the principle that drivers could be transferred like football players. That's where it all came unstitched and what actually happened was that we said we couldn't release him without a payment for that release.' On Thursday afternoon, the news broke that a straight swap would be performed between Peterson and Tom Pryce but by that evening, everything had changed again, with Peterson saying that, in Brazil at least, he would be driving for Lotus.

All this must have been very unsettling for the rest of the team but, in the gap between the two races, a lot of work had been done to the cars, aimed at finding a more permanent solution to the rear-end grip problem. Modifications to the pivot points of the cast rear uprights had changed the roll centre, through bolting an extra piece to the top of the uprights, there being no time to produce totally new uprights to the new dimensions. In addition to these modifications, Peterson's car had been adapted to take the larger Girling brakes.

The first day of practice was not very promising. Peterson was worried by a severe brake vibration in the first session, which turned out to be due to the fact that one of

First Person

Peter Warr on Ronnie Peterson and Jacky Ickx

"They got on very, very well. It is almost impossible to imagine a situation where you wouldn't get on well with Jacky because he is (a) a perfect gentleman and (b) a thoroughly nice guy. You can't imagine Ickx having cross words with anybody; he's not that sort of guy. And Ronnie was very laid back anyway and I think he had the supreme confidence from knowing he was quickest. I think Ronnie was basically quickest in every situation he found himself in throughout his Formula 1 career."

the front discs on his car was slightly distorted. There being no spares, he would have to suffer this for the duration of the weekend as no other car in the paddock used discs that would be suitable. As Alan Henry pointed out in his race report, it seemed as if the second Lotus had been prepared for a number two driver, reflecting the fact that almost up until the beginning of practice, it had looked as if Pryce would be joining the team…

In the second session, Peterson's engine refused to fire on all eight cylinders and he didn't even break the three minute barrier (the fastest time in the session was 2m 30.34s). Meanwhile, Ickx ended the day mid-way down the timesheets, for once faster than his team-mate. On Saturday, even though Peterson improved his time, he ended up seven tenths slower than the Belgian, who lined up on the outside of the sixth row. The Swede was on the outside of the eighth row while, sandwiched appropriately between them was the other player in the transfer saga, Tom Pryce in the Shadow which Peterson had been due at one stage to drive.

Not for the first time with Team Lotus, there was drama before the start when Peterson's car had a last-minute front tyre change on the grid after the Swede had decided, based on the handling on the warm-up lap that, in fact, he wanted

to run hard compound tyres all round, rather than hard rears and soft fronts. Then, when this had been done, the engine refused to fire up. By the time the mechanics got the car going, the rest of the field had already departed. At the end of the lap, Peterson came into the pits. In his haste to get away, he had not allowed the mechanics enough time to return the settings from full-rich (used to start the engine) to full lean. He rejoined just after the leaders had come by to complete their second lap, so already at this early juncture, he was effectively out of contention.

Ickx had come round at the end of the opening lap in 9th place but on lap six he lost a place to the McLaren of Jochen Mass and, on lap 11, John Watson passed him in the Surtees. James Hunt demoted the Belgian further down the order a lap later but then he gained a place with the retirement of Scheckter. After being passed by Andretti just before the half-way mark Ickx began to move up through the field by virtue of the retirements of others and was 8th with only three laps to go when Reutemann, recovering from a pit-stop, slipped past him. So the JPS cars ended up 9th and 15th, a dispiriting performance when what the team needed was some encouraging results to lift morale.

What was even clearer was that, despite the modifications to the suspension geometry of both cars, they were still woefully off the pace. An analysis of the fastest laps of the Brazilian Grand Prix found that Jarier had

recorded the best time in 2m 34.16s, with Ickx back on 2m 37.19 and Peterson on 2m 38.11s. Considering that the Swede was widely acknowledged to be among the fastest Grand Prix drivers at the time, the gap of nearly four seconds illustrated just how far off the performance 'tightrope' Lotus had fallen.

The team now returned to Hethel to lick its wounds. In mid-February, the Peterson saga was finally laid to rest with the news that he was now staying put, which must have come as a relief to Chapman, Warr and his faithful mechanics as his never-say-die attitude was what had helped them get through the difficulties of the 1974 season. It was reported that Imperial Tobacco, Players' parent company, had come forward with enough extra funding to enable the team to do a full season and that Chapman was working on a new car which was already at the wooden mock-up stage and could be seen 'in the metal' as early as the fourth round of the Championship in Spain.

The six week gap between the Brazilian Grand Prix and the next round of the Championship in South Africa enabled Lotus to finally finish off building chassis 72/9. This was to the same basic specification as the two cars raced in Brazil. The only difference was that the front uprights had been revised to give different geometry and this modification had been carried out on Ickx's car (72/5) as well. As well as the two works cars, the two Gunston 72s of

(something like twice as long as a typical South African Drivers' Championship round) and fell back. In the end, the four cars finished in 10th (Peterson), 11th (Tunmer), 12th (Ickx) and 13th (Keizan).

Gunston mechanic Andrew Thompson remembers that, after the race, Chapman visited their pits to congratulate them on their performance. 'He came over to us, shook our hands and said, "I have to say, that was a very good effort. It's not every day that somebody else beats us in our own cars! Don't do it again if you are thinking of buying any more cars from me!"' Although it was clearly meant as a joke at the time, one can imagine that the Lotus boss was probably not very amused that cars he had sold at the end of 1973 had managed to match the performance of the works entries…

A fortnight later, the first of the two major British non-Championship Formula 1 races took place, this being the Race of Champions at Brands Hatch. Peterson was entered in the new car, 72/9 and Ickx was in his trusty 72/5. Revisions to the rear suspension were evident, these being the substitution of steel cables instead of the regular steel torsion bar links, operating only under tension. The reason for this was that the steel links were causing the inside rear wheel to lift under hard cornering forces, causing wheelspin, whereas the flexible cable permitted much greater movement and enabled the wheel to stay firmly on the ground.

Practice revealed a problem with the cable actuation, with one of the new cables on Peterson's car snapping, causing the whole left rear suspension to collapse. Consequently, both cars were converted back to the original set-up for the rest of the meeting. Both sessions were run in damp or wet conditions, the two hours on Friday providing most people with their quickest times. Consequently, it was not surprising to find that Ickx had out-qualified his team-mate and would line up on the

Eddie Keizan (72/6) and Guy Tunmer (72/7) were entered for their home Grand Prix.

The new car suffered the usual teething bothers. Early in first practice, it stopped out on the circuit and when the mechanics reached the car it turned out that the fuel breakaway valve (which was only supposed to come apart in the event of a big accident) needed reassembling. Shortly after he got going, the Swede stopped again - this time a rubber fuel line in the vee of the engine had pulled off. Back on track once more, a scavenge pipe had been knocked off and oil smoke and spray was deposited all over the track by the black-and-gold car, nearly causing a following Eddie Keizan, in Peterson's old 72, to spin.

In the second session, a problem with a valve in the oil tank once again laid oil on the track, this time causing the other Gunston 72 of Tunmer to spin, fortunately without hitting anything. Peterson and Ickx were also both losing time through having to brake some 100 metres earlier than normal. It transpired that a new kind of fluid was being tried in the system and at the end of the session this was drained and the old type was put back in, while the master cylinder and rear calipers were changed on Peterson's car. Handling-wise, both cars were still afflicted by persistent understeer. During Thursday's practice, Peterson stopped out on the circuit again, this time with an electrical fault, which he managed to fix himself. Despite all these problems, the Swede was still comfortably faster than his Belgian team-mate in both sessions and lined up on the outside of the fourth row while Ickx languished on the 11th row, beside the quickest Gunston car of Keizan, while Tunmer was on the inside of the 13th and last row.

Race day was hot, sunny and dry. In the morning warm-up, on full tanks, Peterson had actually set the fastest time,

only fractionally slower than his practice lap, so the team were optimistic concerning his prospects for the race. When the flag dropped, he made one of his better starts and was third into the first corner, a position he held until lap 3. This heralded the beginning of a rapid descent down the order, his car understeering viciously, culminating in a pit stop on lap 11. A new front tyre was fitted, while the angle of attack of the front nose fins was increased but this did not seem to make any difference and the Swede continued to have to throw the car into a slide to kill the understeer.

Team-mate Ickx was similarly afflicted and was struggling to stay ahead of the two Gunston cars. For a long time, all four 72s circulated together, Tunmer causing great excitement in the Gunston pit when he actually got ahead of Ickx on lap 66 of 78. Team-mate Keizan had been in front of Tunmer but began to tire towards the end of the race

Opposite Page: Guy Tunmer took part in his one and only World Championship race when he drove Team Gunston's 72/7 in the South African Grand Prix, finishing a very creditable 11th sandwiched between the works cars of Peterson and Ickx.
Above: Peterson got his 'new' car for the South African Grand Prix but it was a new 72, chassis 72/9. **Left:** Eddie Keizan, shown here being followed by the McLaren M23 of Jochen Mass, ran well in Team Gunston's 72/6 in the early stages of the South African race but tired towards the end and fell back to finish 13th.

outside of row two, while Peterson was on the outside of the third row.

An electrifying start from the Belgian saw him lead the pack into the first corner in slightly damp conditions. However, before the end of the opening lap, Jody Scheckter was past him in the Tyrrell and, eventually first Pryce's Shadow, and then Watson's Surtees and team-mate Peterson also demoted him. After Scheckter's retirement, the battle between Watson and Peterson was for second place but the Surtees was the better car on the day and pulled clear, although the Swede closed in during the final few laps as the Irishman slowed with fuel surge. He finally finished 1.5s behind the Surtees, these two being the only other cars on the same lap as winner Pryce. Ickx soldiered on for fourth place, so at least both John Player cars had finished in the top six.

In the week after the Brands race, John Player Team Lotus suffered a double blow. Team Manager Peter Warr was involved in a serious road accident on the A11, which resulted in him being laid up in hospital with broken legs. Designer Ralph Bellamy was a passenger in the car but fortunately escaped unharmed. He recalls that nothing was allowed to stand in the way of the day's testing, even though he had just been in a bad car crash. 'Colin collected me from the hospital where I had gone with Peter, took me back home to show my wife that I was in one piece and then took me to Hethel and we flew to Silverstone to do the test that we'd intended to do. My chest hurt like buggery because of the whack that I'd got from the seatbelts but I was able to stand up and do my job, so off I went!'

That same day, Jim Crawford was testing Ickx's 72/5 at Silverstone as part of the team's continuing efforts to groom him for future stardom. However, it came to a premature end when a tyre (on an experimentally wide rim) deflated on the approach to the flat-out Abbey Curve (taken at

around 160mph). The car hit the Armco on the outside of the corner, flipped several times and came to rest the right way up. A shaken but unharmed Crawford climbed out and, an hour later, was reflectively sipping a pint in the Silverstone bar with Chapman and Peterson.

Despite the accident, it was decided that Crawford had shown enough promise to be given his chance in a race and Chapman contacted Jacky Ickx to ask if he would mind stepping down for the forthcoming International Trophy race at Silverstone. The Belgian was only too happy to oblige, and 72/5 was rebuilt in time for the young Scot. By virtue of the fact that John Player was once again sponsoring the British Grand Prix later that year, Team Lotus was the only squad permitted to enter more than one car, Peterson lining up in 72/9. Both cars were again fitted with the cable actuation on

the torsion bars, this time the fixing of the ends of the cables having been improved to prevent the chafing and fretting which led to the breakage on Peterson's car at Brands. For the second day, the Swede's car was also changed over to the wide track set-up that he had used with some success mid-way through 1974.

After the first of the two sessions on the Friday, Crawford had been 10th quickest, having done some 21 laps of practice. However, on his first lap in the second session, on cold tyres, he got out of shape at Club and smote the barriers, causing considerable damage to the car but hobbling away with nothing more than a sore left ankle. The tub was badly bent, beyond immediate repair, so the unlucky Crawford's entry was scratched. Meanwhile, Peterson was at last reasonably competitive, setting the third-fastest time to place him on the inside of the second row of the grid, two-tenths quicker than Fittipaldi's McLaren. However, the

Swede didn't get a chance to prove his form in the race for, in the morning warm-up, his engine blew. When the mechanics started up the replacement unit, it seized. With no time to replace that, there was no alternative but to scratch the second of its entries and head back to Hethel.

A week before the Spanish Grand Prix, it was announced that Team Lotus had employed Nigel Bennett, a former Firestone tyre technician and employee of the Hesketh team, as development engineer for the Formula 1 team. His brief was to take over Peter Warr's duties at Grand Prix meetings until the team manager was sufficiently well recovered, which he hoped would be in time for the British Grand Prix. At the same time as he announced Bennett's appointment, Warr emphasised that the team still retained faith in Crawford, despite his Silverstone accidents. He also said that the International Trophy practice crash could have been due to a seized engine, something that had been suggested by Cosworth when they inspected the engine afterwards.

The next race on the calendar, round four of the World Championship, took place on the road circuit in the grounds of Montjuich Park, Barcelona. Aside from Monaco, this was now the last Grand Prix run on closed public roads. After the Silverstone debacle, 72/5 had been rebuilt with a new front bulkhead and had also been brought up to the wide track specification of Peterson's 72/9. A spare car, 72/8, was also brought along in the transporter in narrow-track spec but was not used at all throughout the weekend.

The event got off to a bad start when the vast majority of drivers, who were members of the then quite militant Grand Prix Drivers' Association, refused to practice due to the fact that they considered the circuit to be unsafe. The reason for their concern was that many of the barriers had been incorrectly installed, or were missing nuts and bolts to hold them together. Given that there had been several gruesome incidents in recent history where drivers had

been killed due to poorly installed barriers that didn't do the job they were supposed to (e.g. Jochen Rindt, Roger Williamson, Francois Cevert, Peter Revson and Helmuth Koinigg), the reluctance on the part of the drivers was understandable, if a little ill-timed, coming when the event was already underway. Consequently, only two drivers, Ickx (who was not a GPDA member) and Vittorio Brambilla, practised on the Friday. Ickx's decision to practice pleased his mechanics immensely, as Eddie Dennis recalls. 'We were all quite proud of him. He came walking down the pit lane and he got into the car and went round. He didn't make a big song and dance about it but he went out and practised. He was quite solemn about it, he didn't treat it as something special. But he said, "Well, I'm here to drive and I'll drive."'

Overnight, the organisers promised to put a team of men to work to try and sort out the problem but the next day there was little significant improvement. Eventually, the teams themselves went out with their own tools, tightening up bolts which had previously been tightened only by hand. Although Colin Chapman, ever one for a photo opportunity went out and helped, his mechanics, led by Eddie Dennis, chose not to get involved and stayed back in the paddock. After this, most of the drivers, including Peterson, went out to practice but with just one session there wasn't much time to sort the cars out and it was a funny grid which formed up for the race.

Peterson was back on the outside of the sixth row, while Ickx was on the outside of the eighth row.

In the race, both Lotuses forged their way up through the field, Peterson running as high as second before colliding with a back-marker and crashing into the guard rail. Ickx actually led the race at one stage after previous race leader Rolf Stommelen had crashed over the barriers, killing a race marshal and four other people who had been standing in a prohibited area. At the end of the next lap the race was stopped, by which time the Belgian had been passed again by Jochen Mass. The race was declared a result, with Ickx officially second, 1.1s behind the winner, and half points were awarded because less than 60% of the official distance of 75 laps had been covered. It was Ickx and Team Lotus's best result of the year but not quite under the circumstances they would have liked.

Opposite Page Left: Tipping the scales. This unusual shot of the 72 shows Peterson's 72/9 in the paddock at the Brands Hatch Race of Champions meeting. Opposite Page Right: Peterson (shown here) and Ickx's 72s featured experimental steel cable links to the rear torsion bars in practice for the Race of Champions but after a breakage these were discarded for the race. Above: Jim Crawford's entry for the International Trophy had to be scratched after a practice accident, his second shunt in a 72 within a matter of weeks… Right: Peterson was unable to follow through on his practice form when his engine blew in the pre-race warm-up and then the replacement seized.

CHAPTER 20 THE UNEQUAL STRUGGLE

ased on their performance at Barcelona, John Player Team Lotus were reasonably optimistic that they would have a good race at round five of the World Championship, the Monaco Grand Prix. The same three cars were brought along as in Spain, with 72/9 for Peterson, 72/5 for Ickx and 72/8 kept in the transporter as a spare but never used.

For once, practice was reasonably uneventful for the team, Ickx only being bothered by a loose plug lead and a loose rubber fuel line on the Thursday and Peterson having a good two days. The Swede's best time on Friday was good enough to put him on the outside of the second row, although the grid was heavily staggered so he was well behind the third-fastest qualifier, Jarier in the Shadow. Ickx was back on the outside of the seventh row but less than a second slower than his team-mate.

With the race starting in wet conditions, both the Lotus cars began on wet tyres. Peterson made a great getaway and, aided by Jarier crashing on the opening lap, was able to move up to second, right behind Niki Lauda's Ferrari. On lap 24 of 75, Lauda pitted to switch over to slicks, so Peterson led for a lap before he too came in for dry tyres. Unfortunately, the Lotus mechanic's pit-work was not as fast as that of other teams and, after everyone else had made their stops, the Swede found himself in fifth place, Fittipaldi, Pace and Scheckter all having got past him. What followed was something of a procession, and it was only the retirement of Scheckter's Tyrrell which elevated the Lotus to fourth position, where he finished. Ickx was one of the last drivers to switch to dry tyres and had run as high as second before his stop. After rejoining well down the order, he managed to pass Donohue's Penske and, with the usual rate of attrition, managed to climb back up to eighth at the finish, one lap behind winner Lauda - not bad considering his lowly grid position.

At this stage in the season, Lotus drivers and cars were usually in a challenging position in the World Drivers' and Constructors' Championships but alas this was not the case in 1975. Peterson's Monaco result marked his first points of the year, putting him in joint tenth place in the standings along with team-mate Ickx, while John Player Team Lotus were in a lowly sixth place in the Constructors title race, one point behind Hesketh!

By this stage in the season, it was clear that the lack of testing caused by the budgetary cutbacks was really beginning to hurt the team. Other rivals were refining their car and tyre packages while Team Lotus were doing their testing and sorting at the races. In an effort to try and make some progress, the team spent two days testing with the narrow track spare car at Peterson's local track, Anderstorp, on the Thursday and Friday after Monaco.

Less than two weeks on from Monaco, the teams reassembled at the Zolder circuit for the Belgian Grand Prix. The John Player Team Lotus cars and drivers were unchanged, with Ickx eager for a good result to please his home fans. Practice at Zolder was relatively drama-free, it was just that the cars simply weren't able to go quick enough in the time available. Somewhat optimistically perhaps, Peterson reckoned that, with another two hours of dialling-in, he'd have been right at the front of the grid but there was little doubt that there was a degree of truth in what he was saying. The result was that the two black-and-gold cars lined up on the outside of the seventh and eighth rows, with Peterson just the faster of the two by 23 hundredths of a second.

In the early laps of the race, Peterson lost two places to Jarier and Depailler, after which he ran steadily behind the Tyrrell, gradually moving up through the order as others dropped out. By lap 26 he was seventh but 11 laps later his race was over when he suffered brake failure – ironically at the same place as he had crashed his three cars in 1973 – ploughing into the catch fencing and knocking off the left front suspension. On lap 52 of 70, team-mate Ickx, who was battling high speed oversteer, suddenly wiggled and ran very wide at the first corner. He drove round to the pits where it was found that a left front brake-shaft had broken at the outboard end. The team's race report made sombre reading, particularly the driver's comments. 'Very upset at his third brake-shaft breakage. Strong suggestion we should go to outboard brakes. Vibrating brakes

Right: Ronnie in the rain: Peterson splashing his way to fourth place in the Monaco Grand Prix, his best finish of the year.

LOTUS 72

throughout. Left front brake-shaft broke through outer spline (wide track large OD shaft had done Barcelona, Monaco, Zolder).'

Before the next race in Sweden, rumours intensified of the impending departure of Jacky Ickx from John Player Team Lotus. It was obvious to all outside the team that the Belgian had not been particularly happy with either his own or the car's performance during 1974 and the first part of the 1975 season. At the same time, it was revealed that Brian Henton was to be tested in a 72 at Silverstone in the week following the Swedish Grand Prix. This followed a recommendation from a long-time

First Person

Peter Warr on Jacky Ickx

"We never did get to know what it was that made Ickx just superb in a particular set of circumstances. I think he was a lazy driver, because it seemed to be that, when he was fast, it was when he was thrown a challenge that seemed so impossibly difficult or tricky that it suddenly awoke in him something that said 'Right this is an opportunity for me to try and prove something again'. If he didn't have anything to prove, you have to

say he was pretty steady. Every now and then something would happen and it would fire him up. There were just moments in Ickx's time with us when he was blindingly fast and you thought 'Wow!' and other times when he was just a regular race driver."

Right: The eyes have it: the despondent body language of Peterson and his mechanics reflect the fact that, in his home Grand Prix, he struggled even to qualify in the top ten and finished a lowly ninth. **Opposite Page:** Peterson's 72/9 is filled with fuel in the paddock at Anderstorp prior to the Swedish Grand Prix. Note 'saddle' oil tank, twin oil coolers and rear-mounted battery.

supporter of Henton, as Peter Warr recalls. 'We had a look at Brian Henton because Tom Wheatcroft suggested him as a likely lad. I actually signed him lying in bed in my front room in my house in Norwich with my legs still in plaster. I don't know what he thought he was letting himself in for when his appointment with the Team Lotus team manager was in the front room of a house!

'We didn't have any money to spend. We were looking for somebody who could be good and if he was British so much the better. We were in a position where we had to run a second car and, for relatively little cost, we could give someone an opportunity. In return they would then let us know whether they were any good or not. It was as simple as that. Any driver that came to us at that moment in time was in deep trouble, because they were on a hiding to nothing with an uncompetitive car and the number one driver was no good at sorting the car, so we'd had a year in which no-one knew where the hell they were on the whole set-up!'

Henton had developed a reputation as an excellent test-driver and car-sorter and had already tested a March Formula 1 car that year, so it came as no surprise to him when he received the offer from Lotus. 'Not to blow my own trumpet but at that time, everybody seemed to think that I was the 'boy on the block' the one to have. Having come back from the wilderness, I got three

offers. One was with Williams to drive for them, one with March and the other with Lotus. At that time Williams was probably the worst of the three, March were fine but they'd never got any money, Chapman was ruthless and the car was crap and five years old but they had the name and the potential and the track record. I did a test with numerous other English and foreign drivers at Silverstone. I was known as quite forthright in my comments, I did my stint of laps and everybody had been telling Chapman how good the 72 was, and I got out and said it was the biggest bag of shit I'd ever driven! And he said, "Well you're the man for me". Because he knew it was and that's how I got the job.'

Peterson dearly wanted to win his home race at Anderstorp but the omens didn't look particularly good. The only specification change was that, due to the failure of Ickx's brake-shaft at Zolder, the cars had reverted back to the narrow track layout. In the first practice session, with two cars at his disposal – his regular 72/9 as race car and 72/8 as T-car – he was unable to better eighth place after running out of road at the end of the main straight and damaging the front of 72/9. Ickx, in 72/5, was 1.3s slower than his team-mate, and well in the bottom half of the timesheets.

The main problem faced by the two Lotus drivers seemed to be that they were unable to find a balance for the cars – they either oversteered or understeered and

no amount of fine-tuning could even it up. Track conditions worsened as the weekend went on, with the result that the Friday afternoon session would prove to be the fastest of all. On Saturday, both Peterson and Ickx dropped further and further down the order, the Swede finding the spare car to be no better than his race mount. Final grid positions were depressing for both drivers, particularly the local hero, with Peterson on the inside of the fifth row and Ickx on the outside of row nine.

In the race, the highest that Peterson managed was a lowly seventh before he was demoted first by Mark Donohue's Penske and then by Scheckter's Tyrrell and he eventually trailed in a dispirited ninth. It probably came as scant consolation that this was only one place behind reigning World Champion Fittipaldi, who had an equally torrid weekend. Ickx struggled round with understeer, unable to stay ahead of Grand Prix new boys Torsten Palm and Alan Jones in their Heskeths and eventually, after a pit stop, finished 15th, behind even the Stanley-BRM of Bob Evans and the Williams FW03 of Damien Magee!

On the Wednesday and Thursday following the race in Sweden, Goodyear tyre testing took place at Silverstone. Peterson had gone round the flat Northamptonshire track in 1m 16.3s as long ago as 1973 but, with the regulation changes regarding where wings and oil tanks could be positioned, plus the demise of the tyre war following Firestone's pull-out, no-one had come close to that mark since. However, on this occasion Tom Pryce did actually beat that time by one-tenth of a second, whereas the two Lotus 72s present – for Peterson and Brian Henton – were able only to record 1m 18.52s and 1m 18.78s respectively. What the test demonstrated was that the supremely confident and opinionated Henton was also not uncompetitive when compared with Peterson, who was a good benchmark for anyone to aim for. Mechanic Ian Campbell remembers the occasion well because Henton also came out with a classic observation. 'He said, "We could do something with this car, Colin". Chapman turned away from him and rolled his eyes and I thought to myself "You silly bugger!" I mean it had only won two World Championships, hadn't it!"

The next race on the World Championship calendar

was the Dutch Grand Prix at Zandvoort, scene five years before of the 72's triumphant first win. The wider front track layout had been reintroduced as a result of new, stronger brake-shafts made of a maraging steel safe to 125 tons rather than the previous specification's 90. There had also been some attempt to get more heat into the front tyres by shifting the weight distribution forwards. On both cars, the battery had been moved from the rear to inside the nose, alongside the fire extinguisher (ironically where it started in 1970), while on Peterson's 72/9 the nosecone had also been made heavier through using a solid spar supporting the nose fins rather than a hollow one!

The changes didn't seem to result in significantly improved handling, the main problem still being chronic understeer or chronic oversteer, while Peterson was also suffering from a locking rear brake. The leading cars were all very evenly matched in practice. Consequently, even a small improvement catapulted people up the grid. From Clay Reggazoni on the outside of the front row to Peterson, way back on the outside of the eighth row, there was a gap of just 0.89s. Ickx once again

struggled to match the pace of his team-mate and was on the penultimate row among the tail-enders.

After two days of dry running in practice, the weather decided to add some spice to the proceedings, and with rain having lashed the circuit at around lunchtime, it was on wet tyres that the whole grid took the start. Peterson got away well and made up several places, although soon after the start, it was clear that the track was drying quickly and, as early as lap seven, the first cars were peeling off into the pit lane to switch to slicks. As a result of this, the Swede was up to sixth place by lap 10 before he too opted to swap. His stop was most notable for the fact that the Lotus hit the Ferrari team manager Luca Montezemelo, breaking his leg, as it left the pits.

By this stage of the race, Ickx was already out, his engine having blown after only six tours. Once everybody had pitted, the order settled down again and Peterson was in 10th. He gradually moved up, passing Mass in the McLaren on lap 30 of 75 and then Pryce's Shadow on lap 42. Reutemann's Brabham was the next victim on lap 49 and, when Jody Scheckter's engine

Right: By mid-1975, the team was experimenting with moving the weight distribution of the 72 forward, something it achieved by moving the oil tank to a position between the rear bulkhead and the engine. This necessitated longer engine mounting plates and lengthened the wheelbase, as well as 'helper springs' on the front suspension to cope with the weight that had been shifted forward. This is Ickx at the car's first appearance, the French Grand Prix at Paul Ricard. **Below:** Peterson soldiered on in '75, even when he had little chance of success. **Opposite Page:** Brian Henton made his Grand Prix debut in the British Grand Prix at Silverstone. This shot shows the rear coil suspension that replaced the torsion bars used since the car's inception in 1970.

blew with just eight laps to go, it finally looked as if Lotus might garner a decent haul of points. It was not to be for, on lap 69, the Lotus pulled off the track at the Tarzan hairpin, completely devoid of fuel. It appeared that the mechanics had fuelled it one churn short – a simple mistake but one which the team could have done without since it really needed the morale boost that a points-scoring finish would have brought.

A week after the Dutch race, it was confirmed that Brian Henton would drive a third John Player Team Lotus car at the upcoming British Grand Prix. He had taken part in a further test with the team, at Snetterton, to evaluate a new version of the 72, with a wheelbase lengthened by five inches. The team welcomed his input because he was widely regarded as an excellent car-sorter, one area where Ronnie Peterson was not felt to be particularly good, because like Jim Clark he would drive round faults by adapting his driving style rather than identifying them.

The long wheelbase car must have produced decent results at the test, for it was introduced on Ickx's car (72/5) and the spare (72/8) for the next World Championship round, the French Grand Prix at the ultra-fast Circuit Paul Ricard in the South of France. The lengthening of the wheelbase had been achieved by inserting an oil tank between the engine and rear bulkhead, shifting what Colin Chapman estimated to be an additional 25 pounds onto the front wheels, making a front-to-rear weight distribution of approximately 34:66%. Because the oil tank on these two cars had moved, a new wing mounting had also been designed. In addition, the spare car sported some 'helper springs' aimed at stiffening up the front suspension now that it was required to cope with the extra weight and also to try and generate some extra heat in the tyres, as Ralph Bellamy explains. 'I used little die-opening springs. They are very small springs about the same diameter as the shock absorber body made out of something like three-eighths square wire, and they are very short stroke and very high rate. I used to put these on the shock absorber as an extra spring to stiffen the wheel rate up, to try to solve the problems that we couldn't solve by changing the torsion bars. It was quite an exercise to work out how to mount them so that they came into action just at the right place and did the right thing and stuff like that because the whole thing wasn't adjustable of course. That was the last roll of the dice really.'

In the first practice on Friday morning, Peterson concentrated on his regular race car but in the afternoon

stopped.'

Ickx is more forthright, confirming that it was the run of breakages that finally convinced him to stop, although he also concedes that he probably wasn't driving with the commitment he had been – understandable in the circumstances. 'I had a succession of broken front half-shafts. Within a very short period of time, I had three failures, luckily always ending with only damaged front suspension, damaged steering arms and all these things. Honestly, I was lucky not to be involved in a bigger shunt. I lost my motivation and my interest because I didn't trust the car any more. Also, it was the end of my long descent 'into the inferno': when you start to go down it becomes so slippery you keep going and you go down, down, down and slowly it was the end of my Formula 1 career.' Eddie Dennis also feels that it was the mechanical failures that were the main reason why Ickx decided to stop. 'He was worried about the safety of the car. I remember him saying to the Old Man that, in all his time with Ferrari, he never had anything break.'

Despite all the problems, Ickx has fond memories of his time with the team, and particularly with the way he was handled by Peter Warr. 'He understood, probably as Ken Tyrrell used to, the psychological aspect of the relationship between a team manager and a driver. You have to feel happy, you have to feel loved and appreciated in a team. Although the success wasn't there and I was in difficulties, the team generally speaking – and especially Peter – was always there. I liked him very, very much and it made a difference to me, a big difference. I was very sensitive to that.'

he tried the long-wheelbase version, recording a time only fractionally slower, despite being able to manage only a few laps because of a loose water manifold bolt and problems with the oil tank. However, he cannot have been terribly impressed, because for the rest of the weekend, he concentrated on his race car. Ickx, unable to compare the two set-ups, found it difficult to comment, particularly as he stopped out on the circuit during Friday practice with low oil pressure.

Peterson steadily improved his times during the two Saturday sessions, but they were still only good enough for the inside of the ninth row again. Ickx was not far behind his team-mate, suggesting that the changes had made the car slightly better for him, at least, and he lined up on the inside of row 10. For the race, Peterson stuck with 72/9 but decided that he liked the stiffer ride provided by the helper springs on his spare car and so had them swapped over to his car for the race.

It was another uninspiring race for John Player Team Lotus. Ickx went out on lap 18 when a CV joint in one of the front brake-shafts broke, a repeat of what had happened to him in Belgium, while Peterson had a steady and unspectacular drive to 10th place, after fighting off the attentions of the Hill of Alan Jones and Jacques Laffite in the Williams FW04.

That second brake-shaft-related failure was a bridge too far for Ickx. After discussions with Peter Warr, a brief statement was issued, saying "John Player Team Lotus and Jacky Ickx have mutually agreed that Jacky will be free of the obligation of his contract to participate in Grands Prix with the John Player Special until the appearance of the new John Player Special Type 77

provided that the new car is competitive. Until then, Jacky will be free to drive for any other team in Formula 1 should he so wish." So ended a sorry and largely unsuccessful relationship between the Belgian and Team Lotus.

Warr had great sympathy for the situation Ickx found himself in. 'Jacky didn't want to kill himself in a race car. The Ronnies of this world never thought about it and, if they did, they thought, "It'll never happen to me". Ickx was a person who was intelligent and calm and reasoned and he wanted to live a full life. He couldn't see any reason why he should [die in a racing car], if he went about his work and the decision making that he had to do about cars and teams and so forth in a sensible way. We did have a couple of things which would have scared the pants off of him. But I

don't think they were per se, what motivated him to leave the team. I think what happened was that he got caught up in what should have been a fantastic era for Team Lotus but turned out to be one of its all time lows. In one and a half short seasons his extremely high reputation had been left in tatters through no fault of his own. I don't think it was an odd decision, what actually happened was that he said "My reputation is in tatters, if I stop it is not going to go any further" and so he

Good news came with the announcement that John Player had signed a new three year sponsorship deal

On the Tuesday before the British Grand Prix, it was confirmed by Team Lotus that Jim Crawford would get his second chance at qualifying for a Formula 1 race in 1975, joining Peterson and Henton in a three-car attack for the squad's home race. The team also said that it would continue to enter two cars in the remainder of the World Championship rounds and that it would be taking the opportunity to offer rides to a 'selected few British drivers'. Peter Warr says that the motivation to employ British drivers came from Colin Chapman. 'Colin was going through a period where he wanted British drivers for some reason. I think that he felt that if he could unlock the next great British driver, the great white hope, it would do enormous amounts for our prospects with John Player and also for sponsorship. What he didn't realise at that time was that a British driver brings you 'diddly squat' in the way of sponsorship. We had a look round at the available younger talent, mainly because it had to be virtually a freebie. I mean, we were going to pay them but they were going to cost us peanuts. And, of course, you sometimes come up trumps with one that's cost you peanuts but which pays you back in spades.'

Although on paper this seemed like a good way of bringing on new talent, Chapman was impatient for results, allied to which the car was not competitive enough to allow the drivers to fully display their skills. 'Instead of getting a youngster and nurturing him and trying to bring him along, Colin just wanted an instant result and of course that wasn't going to happen because you don't very often get instant results. Secondly, the car wasn't any good anyway, so there was no chance that Crawford could be competitive straight out of the box.'

One piece of good news for the team did come on

the eve of the British Grand Prix, with the surprise announcement that John Player had signed a new three year contract to sponsor Team Lotus. A dinner had been held the previous week at which this decision was announced to Chapman and the rest of the team, who were naturally delighted. The objective of the deal was to give Chapman sufficient funds to run the team at peak efficiency, while channelling funds into research and development. Players Chairman Geoffrey Kent said: "This long-term contract should enable Colin and his people to plan far enough ahead to put us back on top and keep us there." Given the performance level of the team at the time the announcement was made, such a transformation was hard to conceive. It was a bold, visionary move on the part of Kent and his company, who could not have been blamed if they had walked away from the team at the end of the year, given their

spectacular lack of results. In time, of course, it would turn out to be a very shrewd and perceptive investment that would prove rewarding to both parties.

A more pressing problem was lifting the performance of the three JPS cars in front of their home crowd, a tall order indeed. Contrasting approaches were adopted: the newest car, 72/9, to be driven by Peterson, was converted back as far as possible to 1973 specification, with narrow front track, battery at the rear, steel links rather than cables actuating the torsion bars, soft spring rates and so on. What could not be adopted was the incredibly far back mounting point of the rear wing, which incorporated the oil tank, since this had been outlawed since 1973.

The two cars for Henton (72/5) and Crawford (72/8) were left as they were at Paul Ricard, except for the fact that they now featured coil spring rear suspension. As Ralph Bellamy explains, it was easier to make major changes at the rear of the car than the front. 'In the front, there was no space, as you can imagine with the brakes and all that sort of stuff in there, whereas at the rear there was a lot more space to try different things. In the end, you could have thrown the whole rear end away and made a new one.' Finally, all three cars sported stronger CV joints on the front brake-shafts, taken from the rear suspension, in an effort to prevent a recurrence of the breakages experienced by Ickx in Belgium and France.

Left: "We could do something with this car, Colin." Brian Henton was never afraid to voice his opinion and came out with this gem after a test at Silverstone in 1975, causing Chapman to turn away and roll his eyes in disbelief. **Above:** Jim Crawford finally made his Formula 1 debut in the British Grand Prix at Silverstone. **Opposite Page:** These shots clearly show the oil tank on Crawford's car, positioned between the rear bulkhead behind the driver and the engine.

Practice revealed that the John Player Team Lotus cars were still woefully off the pace. The level of competition was tremendous, with only 3.5s covering the entire field. Peterson was the quickest of the three, benefiting from a fast time set on the Thursday. On Friday morning, Henton had been the fastest Lotus driver, setting his grid time in this session with a time nearly a second quicker than Peterson, while even Crawford went faster than the Swede. In the final session, Henton had a front torsion bar lever break, which ended his chances of improvement. Peterson was mid-way down the timesheets while Crawford went somewhat slower. The results left the Swede on the outside of the eighth row, with Henton on the inside of the 11th row and Crawford the penultimate qualifier on the inside of the 13th and last row. Still, at least both Grand Prix debutants had made the grid…

Race day was blighted by the weather. Although it was dry at the start, a rain shower before one third's distance resulted in many drivers pitting for wets and then again to switch back to slicks when the track dried out again. Peterson's race was mercifully short, his engine dropping a valve early on. Meanwhile, Henton and Crawford were driving steady, unspectacular races. Both cars pitted when the rain became too heavy to continue on slicks and then on lap 27, Crawford spun off into the catch fencing at the exit to Becketts and was out. At the end of lap 30, Henton pitted for slicks and ran as high as 14th before slipping back a couple of places.

The rains returned in the form of a steady drizzle with around 20 of the 67 laps remaining and then with just over 10 laps to go the rain became a torrent on the far side of the circuit and cars began sliding helplessly off the track at Stowe and Club corners as if pulled by some invisible gyrating force. Henton was one of these, ending up in a pile of cars which consisted of the Hill of Brise, Scheckter's Tyrrell, Pace's Brabham, Hunt's Hesketh, Morgan's Surtees, the Copersucar of Wilson Fittipaldi and the Lyncar of Nicholson. 'There was a big downpour at Stowe. I can remember vividly, I must have spun at least 20 times before I hit the bank at Club the other end. I looked round and there was Hunt spinning towards me and I just managed to jump out and get on top of the sleepers. I'd wiped the front of the car out and then Hunt went and wiped the back end out as well!' The race was stopped and eventually, when the officials had sat down and worked out where everyone was before they crashed, Henton was classified 16th.

When they got the cars back to the workshop, it was found that Henton's chassis was quite badly damaged, certainly beyond immediate repair, so only two cars would be available for the next Championship round in Germany.

Meanwhile, there was plenty of activity on the driver front. Following his statement about offering a place to a selected few British drivers, Peter Warr rang up leading Formula Atlantic driver Richard Morgan, who had been impressing at the wheel of Tom Wheatcroft's eponymous chassis, to offer him a drive in the Austrian Grand Prix. After discussing the matter with Wheatcroft, Morgan, who had only moved up from Formula Ford

for the 1975 season, declined the drive, feeling that he was not experienced enough.

Brian Henton continued to test the Type 72 at Snetterton but the news came that neither he nor Crawford would be driving for the team at the forthcoming German Grand Prix at the Nürburgring, although the team did extend their option on the latter's services for another three months from July 31st. Instead, Team Lotus had struck a one-off deal with the Irish driver John Watson, whose Surtees team had scratched their entry following a number of problems at the British Grand Prix. This made a lot of sense, since Watson was very familiar with the Nürburgring, whereas this was not the case with either Henton or Crawford. Additionally, he had proved himself to be the equal of most drivers on the grid, putting in some strong performances that year in a Surtees that was not regarded as being the most competitive car in the pitlane. 'I think one of the reasons why I got the drive was that, earlier in the year at the Race of Champions, in the Surtees, I'd overtaken Ronnie and finished second. Chapman was so pissed off that a Surtees had overtaken a Lotus that he thought he'd better give me a try-out! I was very flattered to be invited by Colin Chapman to drive one of his cars, despite the fact that it was an old war-horse.'

The two cars taken to Germany were to the same specification as they had raced at Silverstone, with Peterson sticking with his 'retro-spec' 72/9 and Watson driving the long wheelbase, rear coil suspension 72/8. The Irishman was no slouch round the 'Ring and settled

quickly into the car, ending the first session on Friday morning only eight-tenths slower than his team-mate. 'The first time I drove the car was the first practice on the Friday, so it was a real baptism of fire! I was cautious about it because of the circumstances and also because it is a hell of a circuit. There are several sequences of bends which are taken as one and you really need to have the confidence in a car to exploit it to the full and I didn't have that. The mechanics wanted to keep making changes and I said "No, no, no", because I wanted to get more familiar with the car as it was. The brake pedal feel was the thing I felt most strange about, due to the inboard brakes. From what I remember, it was a fairly insensitive brake pedal.'

Peterson didn't get out in the afternoon session, during which Watson improved to exactly equal the Swede's morning time. On Saturday morning, Watson lopped another four seconds off and, although Peterson also improved, he did not go as fast as his new team-mate. For the first time since Brazil in January, Peterson was the slowest Team Lotus driver on the grid. Both the 72s though were some ten seconds or so off the pace, with Watson back on the outside of the seventh row of the grid and Peterson two rows further back.

Race day was, thankfully, hot and dry. When the flag dropped, Peterson was last away due to a slipping clutch. He did one slow lap and then came into the pits to see if anything could be done. He set off again but didn't even bother going out onto the full circuit, turning off down the slip road at the North Curve and coming back round into the pits to retire. Meanwhile Watson had

made up a couple of places on the opening lap as a result of a crash by Mass and a slow getaway from Scheckter. Emerson Fittipaldi's pit-stop at the end of lap 2 elevated the Irishman a further place but before he had a chance to really get into the swing of things, a front torsion bar lever broke on the Schwedenkreuz section, one of the fastest parts of the circuit. 'I was under no illusions about the race – the people at the front of the grid were in cars they were confident and comfortable in. You go over the Flugplatz and then there's a double right-hander and then you get into some fast left-hand sweeps followed by an undulating straight and it was just on that straight where the right front suspension collapsed. It wasn't under any braking or cornering loads so I was just able to pull off at the side of the track but it was still pretty unnerving, as at that part of the track you'd be flat out!' So, yet again, it was an early and dispiriting end to the race for John Player Team Lotus.

The two cars used in Germany were also taken to the next round of the Championship a fortnight later, held at the Österreichring circuit in Austria. The only modifications evident were revised pickup points on the top of the rear uprights on returnee Henton's 72/8, while Peterson's 72/9 featured enlarged nose fins and a new pattern rear wing. The meeting started badly, with Peterson crashing his car at high speed in the first session when a slower car pulled over on him on the entry to the right-hand bend after the pit straight. The car was badly damaged but could be repaired. In the meantime, the Swede took over Henton's long wheelbase car for the Friday afternoon session, reporting it to be different

but not necessarily better than his own car, while the Briton had to sit out the session, which ultimately produced the fastest times of the weekend.

On Saturday morning, the two Lotus drivers were back in their regular cars. Henton improved his time to within 1.1s of Peterson and then one of the new brackets on the rear uprights broke, leaving him to crawl round to the pits with his left rear wheel leaning in drunkenly. Soon after that, he crashed heavily at the high speed Jochen Rindt Curve on oil laid down by the blown engine of Mario Andretti's Parnelli. 'The whole thing let go in a big way and I just skidded off on the oil. I had no chance. I was only 20 or 30 yards behind him when it blew. I think it must have been a rod through the side because the circuit was just lathered in it. I hit the oil, went skating straight on and whacked the barrier'. The impact pushed the front bulkhead back into the tub and, even if this could have been straightened out, the team had insufficient suspension parts to build the car up again after Peterson's Friday shunt, so Henton's weekend was over. With Saturday afternoon's practice spoiled by rain, there was no further chance for Peterson to improve and he lined up on the inside of the seventh row.

The race was held in atrocious conditions, with heavy rain falling throughout. At the start, Peterson made up several places and, on the second lap, passed Reggazoni in the Ferrari and the Brabham of Reutemann. On lap six he was past his old team-mate Emerson Fittipaldi, on lap nine it was Depailler's turn and on the next lap Hans Stuck fell into the clutches of the black-and-gold Lotus, the wet conditions masking its inferiority and placing a greater than usual emphasis on the skill of the driver. In passing Stuck, Peterson moved into a superb fourth place, a position he held for the next 11 laps, before he dived into the pits. The reason for his stop was that his visor had misted up so badly in the conditions that he could no longer see through it. A quick wipe from the mechanics and he was on his way again. The Swede's stop dropped him to seventh but within five laps he was past Reggazoni's

Left & Opposite Page Bottom: These two shots show the difference between the standard and long wheelbase versions of the 72. Taken in the Karussell at the Nürburgring, it shows Peterson (left) in 72/9 and Watson (right) in 72/8. **Opposite Page Top:** The up-and-coming Irish driver John Watson was given a drive in a works 72 for the 1975 German Grand Prix, something he attributes to Chapman being upset at a Lotus being beaten by Watson's Surtees earlier in the year.

Ferrari again and on lap 29 he slipped in front of the other scarlet car of Niki Lauda to take fifth. To his surprise, the chequered flag came out at the end of this lap. Although the race had been scheduled to run for 54 laps, the conditions were, if anything, worsening and the race officials decided to call a halt to proceedings. For the second time that season, half points were awarded, so Peterson gained a paltry point for his sterling efforts.

Just a week later, a curious non-Championship race entitled the Swiss Grand Prix was held at the French Dijon-Prenois circuit. An invited entry of 16 cars included a singleton Lotus entry for Peterson, in 72/9. Practice revealed an evil-handling car with the now familiar problem of snapping from chronic oversteer to understeer and vice versa and the Swede was 1.4s slower than he had been in practice for the previous year's French Grand Prix at the circuit. The only explanation proffered was that the tyres were different, which was undoubtedly true because there was no longer a tyre war. Instead of bringing along sticky qualifiers, Goodyear simply supplied one basic tyre to all the runners. From ninth on the grid, Peterson had an impressive race, hounding Carlos Pace into a mistake and then passing John Watson in the Surtees. By dint of several retirements, this translated into a satisfying fourth place at the finish.

The World Championship resumed a fortnight later with the penultimate round, the Italian Grand Prix at

Monza. Jim Crawford was recalled for his second Grand Prix appearance to drive alongside Peterson. In the week leading up to the Italian race the team's new car, designated the Type 77, finally turned a wheel for the first time at Hethel. It had been the team's intention to get the new car ready for Monza, but they simply ran out of time.

When the cars rolled out of the John Player Team Lotus transporter, Peterson's was unchanged from Austria, whereas 72/5 had now been rebuilt following Henton's Silverstone accident and took the place of 72/8, which had still to be repaired following Henton's Österreichring shunt! Crawford was generally unenthusiastic about the long wheelbase format, declaring a preference for the shorter car and throughout practice he was plagued by chronic understeer and brake problems. Peterson was, for a change, quite happy with the performance of his car and actually managed to set a time in practice two-hundredths of a second faster than he had done the year before, despite the lack of qualifying rubber this time around. However, this was only good enough for the inside of the sixth row, while team-mate Crawford scraped in once more on the inside of the last row.

At the start, Crawford's car was hit by Stommelen's Hill as the latter swerved to avoid the coasting BRM of Bob Evans. Although he was able to continue, his left

rear tyre was punctured and by the time he struggled round to complete the lap, it was a mangled mess. It was replaced and the Scot was sent on his way but by this stage he was already well down the order. By the time he had rejoined the race though, the number one Lotus was already out. At the start, the field had roared off down towards the Curva Grande without having to negotiate the tricky chicane just after the pits and at the end of the first lap Peterson came past in an excellent seventh place. However, there was a bit of a bottleneck at the first chicane and, out of the ensuing melee the Swede found himself out of the race with a wrecked car. Crawford continued to circulate in last place until, with ten laps to go, he passed Renzo Zorzi's Williams, coming home 13th, some six laps behind the winning Ferrari of Clay Reggazoni. The other Ferrari of Niki Lauda came home third to clinch the 1975 World Championship title.

Ten days after Monza, the new Lotus Formula 1 car, designated JPS/11 but known internally as the 77, was shown to the press. Designed by Geoff Aldridge and Martin Ogilvie, this was a relatively conventional car aimed at getting Team Lotus back towards the front of the field. Since there was little advantage now to introducing the car for the final race of the season, the intention of Team Lotus was to thoroughly test it during the winter, with the aim of having it fully sorted for the first race of the 1976 season. Testing of the new car commenced soon after the launch, with both Peterson and, later, Jim Crawford driving it. It was reported to be quickly on the pace, setting a new lap record around Hethel in the hands of the Scot.

The final Championship round of the year took place in the United States at the Watkins Glen circuit. Traditionally, the last two races of the season were held in Canada and the US. However, the Canadian organisers had been unable to agree terms with the Formula 1 Constructors' Association concerning the payment of a package fee for their members to attend. The result was that F1CA announced that none of its members would be going, effectively cancelling the event.

Brian Henton again returned to the John Player Team Lotus line-up at Watkins Glen, driving the car given to Crawford at Monza, 72/5, while Peterson was in his usual 72/9. Although the cars' specifications were unchanged, they differed in that the Swede opted for an entirely new tyre construction offered by Goodyear, which was much stiffer, with extra plies. He commented that it made his car feel like it used to. By contrast, Henton tried these tyres on his more stiffly sprung car and found them unsuitable. Practice saw both 72s well

off the pace, Peterson eventually qualifying one and a half seconds behind poleman Niki Lauda, while Henton was some 3.2s slower than the Ferrari.

Peterson made a good start, jumping three places on the opening lap, while Henton did even better, passing five cars. By lap three he had got up to 12th place, a position he held for three more tours before he spun at the first corner. Unfortunately Tony Brise, following in the Hill, was unable to avoid him and the ensuing contact broke the rear upright on the Lotus. Henton crawled back to the pits where it was repaired but he lost six laps in the process. Eddie Dennis remembers that the car was repaired because of the unusually lucrative prize fund, shared among all finishers – normally such damage would have resulted in the car's retirement. 'We rushed back and got another upright so he could continue to the finish because there was big prize money.'

Meanwhile Peterson moved steadily up the order, passing Depailler and Mass, as well as benefiting from the retirements of several others. By lap 19 of 59, he was up into fifth place and getting stuck into a fantastic scrap with the McLaren of Jochen Mass (who re-passed him), James Hunt in the new C-type Hesketh and Jody Scheckter in the Tyrrell. This lasted for the remaining forty laps and had the crowd on its feet. After pressurising Hunt for nearly 20 laps, the Swede finally forced the Lotus past and looked to be heading for a superb fourth place. But three laps from the end, he locked up his tyres and badly flat-spotted them. On the final lap in the new chicane at the Esses, he got out of shape and, while he was gathering it all together, Hunt slipped by again.

When they came round at the end of the final lap, just 2.7 seconds covered third to sixth place, with the old warhorse 72 coming home in fifth place to secure a points finish in its last ever Grand Prix. Henton also brought the second car home, but was 10 laps behind the winner having been forced to stop again to change a broken wheel after making contact with a guardrail at around half-distance. Peterson's two points lifted him to a total of six, for 13th in the standings, while Ickx finished in 16th with his tally of three. In the Constructors' Championship, Lotus was a lowly seventh, behind not just the big names like Ferrari, McLaren, Tyrrell and Brabham but also the tiny Hesketh equipe and the still-youthful Shadow team.

It was the final curtain for the Lotus 72. After a glorious Grand Prix career spanning six seasons, the grand old design was finally being put out to grass. There had been some tremendous highs and lows during its career but to score points in its last race just underlined what a fantastic concept Maurice Phillippe and Colin Chapman had penned back in 1969. The 1975 season had been particularly bad, one that Colin Chapman and Peter Warr would rather forget. However, thanks to the show of faith in their combined abilities on the part of sponsor John Player, the foundations had been laid for a dramatic revival of Team Lotus's fortunes in the years to come.

Opposite Page: Out of contention: a first lap puncture caused by a collision with another car meant that Jim Crawford had a lonely drive to 13th place in the Italian Grand Prix. **Left:** Final flourish: Peterson drove a typically determined race from 14th on the grid to bring his 72 home fifth in its last-ever World Championship start in the United States Grand Prix.

WORLD CHAMPIONSHIP TABLE 1975

Pos	Driver	Argentina	Brazil	S.Africa	Spain	Monaco	Belgium	Sweden	Netherlands	France	Great Britain	Germany	Austria	Italy	USA	Total	(dropped)
1	Niki Lauda	1	2	2		9	9	9	6	9		4	0.5	4	9	64.5	
2	Emerson Fittipaldi	9	6			6				3		9		6	6	45	
3	Carlos Reutemann	4		6	2		4	6	3			9		3		37	
4	James Hunt	6	1						9	6	3		3	2	3	33	
5	Clay Reggazoni	3	3				2	4	4					9		25	
6	Carlos Pace		9	3		4			2		6					24	
7	Jody Scheckter		9				6				4				1	20	
7	Jochen Mass		4	1	4.5	1				4			1.5		4	20	
9	Patrick Depailler	2		4		2	3			1						12	
10	Tom Pryce							1		1		3	2	1		8	
11	Vittorio Brambilla				1						1		4.5			6.5	
12	Jacques Laffite											6				6	
12	Ronnie Peterson					3								1	2	6	
14	Mario Andretti							3		2						5	
15	Mark Donohue							2			2					4	
16	Jacky Ickx				3											3	
17	Alan Jones											2				2	
18	Jean-Pierre Jarrier				1.5											1.5	
19	Tony Brise							1								1	
19	Gijs van Lennep												1			1	
21	Lella Lombardi				0.5											0.5	

Pos	Constructor	Argentina	Brazil	S.Africa	Spain	Monaco	Belgium	Sweden	Netherlands	France	Great Britain	Germany	Austria	Italy	USA	Total	(dropped)
1	Ferrari	3	3	2		9	9	9	6	9		4	0.5	9	9	72.5	
2	Brabham-Cosworth	4	9	6	2	4	4	6	3		6	9		3		54	2
3	McLaren-Cosworth	9	6	1	4.5	6				4	9		1.5	6	6	53	
4	Hesketh-Cosworth	6	1						9	6	3		3	2	3	33	
5	Tyrrell-Cosworth	2		9		2	6			1	4				1	25	
6	Shadow-Cosworth				1.5	1			1			3	2	1		9.5	
7	Lotus-Cosworth				3	3								1	2	9	
8	March-Cosworth				1						2		4.5			7.5	
9	Williams-Cosworth											6				6	
10	Parnelli-Cosworth							3		2						5	
11	Hill-Cosworth							1					2			3	
12	Penske-Cosworth							2								2	
13	Ensign-Cosworth												1			1	

Although the World Championship history of the Lotus 72 is a key part of the story of the car, it also played a major role in another significant single-seater Championship series – the South African Drivers' Championship (SADC). This series was open to a wide variety of machinery, ranging from Formula 1 to Formula 2/Atlantic and Formula 5000/A cars and provided a useful outlet for the leading manufacturers and teams wanting to sell on cars to make way for newer ones. The result was that some very exotic and exciting machinery found its way to the African continent, including amongst others the 72, which raced there in five different seasons covering the period 1971-75.

The first of the cars to make the long journey south was chassis 72/3. It was sold in July 1971 to United Tobacco Company (South) Ltd – owners of the Lucky Strike and Embassy brands in South Africa at the time. UTC purchased it for Dave Charlton to drive. Charlton had campaigned an ex-works Lotus 49C in the SADC in 1970 and the early part of 1971 but the design was becoming outdated and the writing was on the wall for the English-born driver. He came to England to look for a suitable replacement and in view of his previous dealings with the team, Lotus was the first place he looked. As he explains, 'I had known Colin Chapman for many, many years, so I just phoned him and said "Can we buy a car" and he said "Yeah, sure you can." He sold us the car, it was very simple, there was no problem about that sort of deal at all in those days.' The Lotus 72 also happened to have won the 1970 World Championship in the hands of Jochen Rindt and had clearly been one of the fastest cars on the grid. Charlton and his

sponsors wanted the best car money could buy. 'I knew that was the car for me and I was proved right. People said to me at the time "How can you buy that car, it breaks?" And I said "Balls, it does not break," and it never did. I believed in the designer and what his ways and thoughts were.'

In early June, United Tobacco wrote to Lotus confirming that Charlton was authorised on behalf of the company to negotiate for the purchase of a Formula 1 racing car and spares, with the car and spares 'to be the property of this company'. A maximum total expenditure was also set. In the week prior to the Dutch Grand Prix, where Charlton was scheduled to drive a 72 (although not the car it was intended he should purchase), Charlton wrote to Team Lotus, placing an order for chassis 72/3 to include DFV 052, modifications and spare parts for the sum of £16,500 (around £145,000 at 2003 prices). Wisell drove 72/3 for the final time in testing prior to the British Grand Prix in July, for which event the car was run for Charlton, although without much success, the engine blowing on the warm-up lap. Following this race, 72/3 was stripped down and thoroughly rebuilt to 'as-new' condition, complete with DFV 052 and a FG400 gearbox. It was then shipped out to South Africa, arriving just in time for the seventh round of the South African Drivers' Championship, the 25th Anniversary Trophy race at Kyalami. Despite his relative unfamiliarity with his new mount, Charlton posted the fastest time in practice to line up in pole position, with his arch-rival John Love, now driving a 1971 Surtees TS9, alongside him. Love got the better start to lead across the line first time round but Charlton was soon past and was unchallenged for the rest

of the race. Meanwhile Love had a huge crash, from which he was very lucky to emerge unscathed, when the throttle on his Surtees stuck open. To cap an excellent debut for the Lucky Strike 72, Charlton also set the fastest lap in a time quicker than the best lap set in the Grand Prix earlier in the year.

The next SADC round, the False Bay 100 at the Killarney circuit, saw Charlton underline his form with another pole position, with Love once again alongside, this time in his old March 701. However, the start did not go to plan when Charlton stalled. It took him 11 laps to recover and retake the lead but on the next lap, just as everything looked to be swinging his way, a valve broke in the DFV and that was the end of his race.

The Rhodesian Grand Prix at the Bulawayo circuit was hardly any more satisfying. In practice the track was slippery, causing Charlton to crash and damage one of his side radiators, leaving him in an unaccustomed fifth on the grid. A poor start saw him languishing in seventh, a situation not helped by having a slow puncture in his left rear tyre. Eventually the tyre burst, damaging the rear wing, which had to be hastily removed during the pit-stop to replace the tyre. Later in the race, Charlton had to stop yet again to have his front wings removed, as they were making the car virtually undriveable as a result of the lack of downforce at the rear. Although he finished two laps down on eventual winner Love, Charlton still came home fourth to secure further valuable Championship points.

The series returned to Kyalami for the tenth and penultimate round, the Rand Spring Trophy. Charlton was again on pole with Love and the other Lucky Strike team

Right: Starting as he meant to go on, Dave Charlton scored a comfortable victory in his first South African race in 72/3, the SCC 25th Anniversary Trophy at Kyalami in August 1971.

car – Peter de Klerk's Lotus 49 – alongside him on the front row. Although de Klerk took an early lead, he dropped back, leaving Charlton to lead Love. When Love dropped out, the Lotus 72 driver was left without a serious challenger and came home a comfortable winner. Since neither Love nor Pretorius, the only other people who could take the title, scored points, it also meant that Charlton had secured his second successive South African Drivers Championship. The final SADC race of 1971, the Welkom 100, took place at the Goldfields Raceway. Love and Charlton tied for pole position but Love took the place having set the time first. After running third in the early stages, the Lucky Strike driver was soon into the lead and was never headed, coming home a convincing 35 seconds clear of Love.

With no sign of any serious opposition likely to trouble the 72, Charlton and his sponsors elected to continue with the car for the 1972 season. The entry for the first race of the year, the Cape South Easter Trophy at Killarney in early January, was somewhat thin, with only three Formula 1 cars, both considerably less modern than Charlton's, these being Love's March 701 and the other Lucky Strike Racing entry Lotus 49 of Peter de Klerk. When Love broke a valve spring in practice, the result became almost a formality. Charlton did not disappoint, despite having to start from the rear of the grid in the first of the two 30 lap heats. He quickly caught and passed de Klerk and came home nearly half a minute clear. In the second heat, the two Lucky Strike cars again finished first and second from a field of only four starters.

A similar pattern was seen in the Highveld 100 at Kyalami three weeks later, with Charlton taking a comfortable pole, more than a second clear of Love, who was back in his newly-rebuilt Surtees, while de Klerk completed the front row. After Love crashed out early on, Charlton cruised to an easy victory, finishing more than a minute ahead of de Klerk. Already, it was looking ominous

for anyone wishing to challenge the Lucky Strike driver for the Championship.

After a disappointing South African Grand Prix, the Championship resumed at Pietermaritzburg with the Coronation 100. For the first two rounds, 72/3 had been in its 1971 specification with the 'periscope' airbox but for his home Grand Prix, Team Lotus had brought Charlton all the latest bits, including the anvil-shaped airbox as used by the works cars of Fittipaldi and Walker. This was a level of support which would continue throughout Charlton's ownership of the car, as he explains. 'Whenever we thought they [the works team] were going quicker than ever before, we used to talk. We were never short of the bits and pieces to update the car, that was what was good about Lotus.' The Lucky Strike car secured pole position by a whopping margin of nearly two seconds over John McNicol's McLaren M10B Formula 5000 car and Eddie Keizan in Alex Blignaut's Surtees TS5 F5000. A poor start saw Charlton swamped by the rest of the field, although he was up to seventh by the end of the first lap and second by the sixth. He then slowly narrowed the gap to leader John Love – who was driving a Brabham BT33 he had acquired after his rebuilt Surtees had been badly damaged in yet another crash at the South African Grand Prix. Love determinedly held off the Lotus for nearly 30 laps but eventually Charlton found a way past and once by pulled out a lead of almost three-quarters of a minute by the finish.

The series moved to Welkom for the Goldfields Autumn Trophy. A Lucky Strike car won again but this time is wasn't Charlton – Eddie Keizan emerging victorious after a race of attrition. Charlton had qualified on the outside of the front row behind McNicol's rapid McLaren M10 Formula 5000 car and Love's Brabham. When Love failed to start, it turned into a two-horse race between McNicol and Charlton. After 12 laps, Charlton finally found a way past at the end of the main straight but on the next lap McNicol retook the lead with an audacious manoeuvre in the same place but both drivers left their braking so late that they spun off. They both restarted and the battle resumed, but soon after both cars were eliminated when a wing stay broke on the McLaren, causing it to spin wildly and Charlton going off after taking avoiding action. Charlton admits that he was struggling to outwit his rival that day. 'I wasn't battling with him, I was just waiting for him to go slower! His car was very quick down the straight there, which was as fast as the old Kyalami – we used the same 5th gear. His wing collapsed and I was right up his chuff. All I could do was turn sharp right and I went into the grass – and that was the end of me.'

The next event was held at Bulawayo in Rhodesia but this did not count towards the South African Drivers' Championship. Charlton continued his dominant form in practice, taking pole by more than half a second. John McNicol again made the best start to lead the field through

Opposite Page Top: Charlton scored an easy victory in the Highveld 100 at Kyalami in January 1972. This was the last time the car ran with the old style 'periscope' airbox. **Opposite Page Bottom:** Peter de Klerk (right) shown here in the pits at Kyalami during the 25th Anniversary Trophy meeting, joined Charlton (left) in the Scribante/Lucky Strike team, driving Dave's old Lotus 49 in several races in 1971. **Left:** Charlton's car was kept as close to the works cars' specification as was possible. He is shown here at the 1972 South African Grand Prix. **Below:** The Republic Day Trophy at Kyalami in June 1972 resulted in another pole and victory for Charlton.

at the end of the opening lap but on the next tour Charlton was into the lead. He didn't have it all his own way though, because John Love was driving very well and the home star overtook the Lotus and had pulled out an advantage of four seconds by lap 11 when first a plug lead and then a wheel came loose. After this, Charlton was able to cruise home to victory, having set the joint fastest lap with Love.

Three weeks later the fifth round of the Championship, the Republic Trophy at Kyalami, took place. In his final appearance before leaving for Europe to take in three Grands Prix, Charlton blitzed the opposition in practice, his 1m 19.1s pole lap being nearly two seconds quicker than second man Love. At the start, Love jumped into the lead but his glory was short-lived for Charlton was ahead at the end of the opening lap and by the start of the third tour was already two and a half seconds to the good, never to be headed. By the finish, he was more than a minute clear of second man Paddy Driver, Love having retired.

After his frustrating foray into the world of European Grand Prix racing Charlton returned to the domestic scene in the Rand Winter Trophy at Kyalami. In the interim, Love had scored an easy win at Pietermaritzburg but Charlton still held a commanding Championship lead. His practice time of 1m 19.4 was again good enough for pole but by this time Love had got his Brabham BT33 handling much better and was only 0.1s adrift. In the race, Charlton hurtled off into the lead, never to be headed. No-one else could get close to his pace and eventually he broke the outright circuit record, his time of 1m 18.8s being 0.1s quicker than the previous record set by Mike Hailwood earlier in the year at the Grand Prix meeting.

For the next race, the Van Riebeck Trophy at the Killarney circuit in Cape Town, there were only two

Formula 1 starters – Charlton and his team-mate, Meyer Botha in a Lotus 49. The race started under grey skies and, at two-fifths distance, with Charlton leading easily, a steady drizzle began to fall. Most runners continued with their slicks but the conditions made the track very slippery. Charlton spun on lap 44 out of 50, removing his left front nose fin in the process, yet he still came home a lap clear of his nearest rival, Eddie Keizan, to score his sixth win of the year and clinch the 1972 South African Drivers' Championship title, with three rounds to go.

The teams then returned to the Bulawayo track for the second time that year to contest the Rhodesian Grand Prix. Charlton qualified on pole, 0.4s ahead of local hero Love, and these two proceeded to engage in a tooth and nail battle until, on lap 25 of 40, a left rear upright broke on the Lotus 72, spinning the Champion into retirement and leaving Love to score a popular home win. This was a rare mechanical failure for Charlton, in fact the only non-engine-related retirement he ever had with 72/3 during the time he raced it. 'It was a fabricated upright. I could see

something was wrong because down the straight the steering wheel was slightly offset. I took it easy and then it said "hello" on a pretty tight right-hander and I had to abandon the car there.'

The penultimate round of the 1972 Championship, the Rand Spring Trophy at Kyalami, saw Charlton take his third pole of the year at the circuit, this time with a blistering 1m 18.2s. He achieved this despite having to make clutchless gearchanges as his left ankle was in plaster after he had broken it two weeks earlier. He had been taking part in the 'Roof of Africa' rally and had been hit by a fellow competitor while trying to right his overturned Land Rover. In order that Charlton could get away at the start, the team came up with an innovative solution, as he explains. 'Ken Howes rigged up a hand clutch using a Honda 750 front brake lever, which he mounted on the left-hand side of the steering column between the steering wheel and the instrument panel.' The arrangement worked perfectly, the Lotus 72 driver coming round in second place at the end of the first lap. As the field started their third lap, the Champion blasted past his eternal nemesis Love and he led for the rest of the race, coming home nearly half a minute clear.

The final race of the 1972 Championship was the Welkom 100 at the Goldfields Raceway. Once again Love and Charlton set identical times in practice, this time Charlton taking pole by virtue of having set the time first. The Lucky Strike driver's leg was still in plaster, so once again he had to rely on the hand clutch to get him off the line. However, it failed on the dummy grid, with the result that the rest of the field was long gone before the Champion even departed. To make matters worse, in the wet conditions he spun on the opening tour and when he

lap but then proceeded to spin, rejoining in sixth. After the first few laps Charlton led Keizan and this was the way it stayed until three laps from the end, when the Tyrrell driver had a puncture and crashed, leaving the Lotus man to take victory, a lap clear of his nearest rival.

Three victories from three starts was Charlton's tally and already it was looking as if nobody would be able to prevent him from securing a fourth straight title. The Championship moved on to the Roy Hesketh circuit in Pietermaritzburg, where Charlton took another pole (although this time his margin over fellow front row man Keizan was only just over a second) and an easy victory, coming home 25 seconds clear of the Tyrrell driver. The fifth round of the series was held at Kyalami, a circuit where Charlton had proved virtually unbeatable in the past. This pattern was continued, with the Champion putting his car on pole by the substantial margin of 1.7s. Once again, his nearest challenger was Keizan in Alex Blignaut's Lucky Strike-sponsored Tyrrell 004 and at the start Keizan actually forced his way to the front, leading for the first seven laps before having to pit and have a loose front spoiler removed. Charlton led for the rest of the race, to take his fifth straight win. A pattern was beginning to emerge: Keizan could actually not only keep up with Charlton's 72 but also had the potential to get ahead of it in races. This was good for the race promoters and spectators but no so good for the Champion, whose thoughts began to turn towards getting a car which would keep him at the sharp end of races in 1974.

Meanwhile, the teams faced a long haul up to the Bulawayo circuit in Rhodesia for round six. Once again, Charlton put the Lucky Strike Racing Lotus 72 on pole, by 0.7s from Keizan and jumped into an early lead at the start. After nearly stalling when the flag dropped, Keizan caught Charlton within three laps and was pushing him hard for the first half of the 40 lap race, trying to find a way past. On lap 20 he finally managed to squeeze through and a lap later Charlton peeled off into the pits to have a front tyre changed. After a lengthy stop he rejoined in ninth place and proceeded to carve his way back up the order, inheriting fourth place on the final lap when the engine in John Love's Formula 2 Chevron blew up. Meanwhile, Keizan cruised to an easy victory, half a minute clear of Ian Scheckter in the

finally came through at the end of the lap, Charlton was almost one minute behind leader Love. Eventually though the rain stopped and when the track began to dry Charlton steadily closed the gap, which at half-distance was down to 20 seconds. Just as things were building up to a crescendo, Love threw it all away by spinning, letting Charlton through into the lead, a position he maintained until the finish.

Charlton had secured his third-successive SADC title and no-one had seemed capable of providing a real challenge to his domination. At the end of the season, his closest rival John Love conceded that his advancing years meant he could no longer compete effectively in the top division and announced that he would step down to Formula 2 (a new class introduced to complement the F5000s) for the 1973 season. On the positive side, Alex Blignaut was known to be negotiating to buy a Tyrrell from the works for his protégé, Eddie Keizan, which offered up the prospect of a more competitive season in 1973.

The addition of Formula 2 cars to the grid had the desired effect of boosting the number of entrants for the first Championship round of 1973, the Cape South Easter Trophy, held at the Killarney circuit in Cape Town. There were three cars in Lucky Strike livery – the two Scuderia Scribante entries, Charlton's 72 and Meyer Botha's March 721, plus Alex Blignaut's Tyrrell 004 for Keizan. In practice it was situation normal with Charlton clinching pole by the large margin of two seconds as his rivals struggled to accustom themselves to their new mounts. However, the race was much closer, with Keizan keeping in touch with the flying Lotus in the early laps before fading to finish 22 seconds behind. Charlton's race though was not without its

problems, for he suffered from a loose steering column and rear wing.

The series then moved on to Kyalami at the end of January for the Highveld 100. For this race, the Lucky Strike 72 had gained a bigger, deeper rear wing manufactured by the team. Once again, Charlton qualified more than two seconds clear of Keizan. After his engine blew in the morning warm-up it was a rush to get it changed in time for the race but such was his value to the event that the organisers delayed the start to allow the job to be completed. Paddy Driver made the best getaway from the front row in his F5000 McLaren but by the end of the opening lap Charlton was in the lead and was never headed. The result was made a formality when his nearest rival Keizan retired at three-quarters distance with a broken fuel pipe and worn tyres. The Lotus driver also had tyre trouble and was forced to slow his pace considerably in order to make it to the finish, something he achieved despite one of his rear tyres being in shreds.

After another disappointing appearance in his home Grand Prix, Charlton returned to domestic domination in the Goldfields Autumn Trophy at Welkom. He took a comfortable pole (this time by three seconds!) while Keizan did not even record a practice time due to problems with his differential. The work on the Tyrrell was still not completed by the time the race was due to start but Charlton – probably desperate for some decent competition – sportingly persuaded the officials to delay it until Blignaut's mechanics had finished. Despite starting from the back of the grid, Keizan had amazingly found his way to the front of the race by mid-way round the opening

Above: Charlton won the 1972 Rand Spring Trophy at Kyalami in 72/3 despite his leg being in plaster and having to make clutch-less gearchanges. **Opposite Page Top & Bottom:** His car now sporting a bigger, deeper rear wing, Charlton comfortably won the Highveld 100 at Kyalami in January 1973. At the start Charlton in 72/3 is on the left, flanked by Paddy Driver's McLaren M10B and Eddie Keizan's Tyrrell 004.

sister car to Love's.

The series returned to the Roy Hesketh circuit at Pietermaritzburg for the next race. Charlton struggled with differential problems in practice, eventually traced to a leaking oil seal. Just how well Keizan had got the Goodyear-shod Tyrrell working was illustrated by his near-one second improvement in practice time, which was good enough to net him his first pole position of the season. Meanwhile, Charlton was some 0.6s adrift but still alongside the Tyrrell

clearly felt that they would increase spectator appeal, rather than having one or two Formula 1 cars totally dominating proceedings as had been the case for the past five seasons or so. Back at Kyalami for the Rand Winter Trophy, Charlton was determined to re-assert his authority, under threat from the resurgent Blignaut-run Tyrrell. This he succeeded in doing, taking pole by a margin of 1.7s and then driving away from the rest of the field, having passed the fast-starting Keizan on lap 5 of 40. His eventual winning

margin was comprehensive – one minute and three seconds over the Tyrrell. Charlton was back in business! In late July, a surprise U-turn was revealed in terms of the proposal on the part of race promoters to make Formula 1 cars ineligible for the SADC from 1974. The National Competitions Committee met and decided that the present multi-formula format, combining Formula 1, Formula 2 and Formula 5000, should continue after all. It appeared that this change of heart was due to some fairly heavy behind-the-scenes lobbying on the part of the major owners and sponsors of Formula 1 cars, who faced being left with a lot of obsolete machinery at the end of the year.

Keizan took a surprise pole for the False Bay 100 at the Killarney circuit in Cape Town. Charlton had been unable to take part in official practice due to brake problems with the 72 and was forced to start from the back of the grid, so

With three victories from three starts, Charlton was looking as if nobody would prevent him from securing a fourth straight title

on the front row. At the start, Keizan jumped into the lead and was slowly eking out an advantage over Charlton when on lap 10 of 60, he was forced to pull off the track with a broken oil union. The Lotus 72 driver continued unchallenged to take the win, finishing with an oil-coated helmet as a testimony to the laps he spent following the Tyrrell with oil spraying out of its back.

Looking to the future, it was announced that a meeting of South African race promoters had decided to recommend to the National Competitions Committee that Formula 1 cars be dropped from the South African Drivers' Championship for 1974 and that it be run solely for Formula 5000 and Formula 2 cars. These two had proved to be very evenly matched during 1973 and the promoters

LOTUS 72

a good race looked to be in prospect. The first two rows of the grid rolled forward before the flag had been dropped, although they stopped again before it actually fell. Keizan led the opening laps, while Charlton scythed his way through the field in his customary fashion. By lap four he was second, about 10 seconds adrift of the leader, a gap which remained constant until they came upon backmarkers and then some oil was laid down on the track. The wily Charlton balanced his 72 on the edge and closed in for the kill. At half-distance he was through into the lead. As the oil was dispersed, Keizan again began to close on the Lotus but by this time it had been announced that the four drivers who had rolled forwards were to be penalised one minute for jumping the start. This effectively handed the race to Charlton on a plate, for it meant that he could afford to let Keizan past and only had to finish within a minute of the Tyrrell to win the race. This he did, coming home 23 seconds behind.

Above: Pole and a dominant victory saw Charlton back on form in 72/3 in the Rand Winter Trophy at Kyalami, August 1973. **Opposite Page:** Whatever the joke is, Paddy Driver doesn't appear to be in on it! His slightly bemused look sums up his 1974 season with Team Gunston, where he found himself unable to match the sheer pace of Ian Scheckter and manoeuvred out of the squad at the end of the year. **Both Pages:** Fans could keep up with developments in the South African Drivers' Championship through the publication Lucky Strike Racing, which contained comprehensive race reports.

Another long trek up to Bulawayo for the Rhodesian Grand Prix followed. Charlton took pole by 0.3s from Keizan and proceeded to win the race, although he finished only five seconds ahead of the Tyrrell driver. Around this time, stories began to circulate that Team Gunston – which had stepped down a class to run Formula 2 Chevrons in 1973 – was planning to buy a pair of ex-works Lotus 72s. Drivers were to be Ian Scheckter (Jody's older brother) and Paddy Driver, a former motorbike racer who had turned his hand, with some success, to racing cars, particularly 'big-banger' Formula 5000s. The cars in question were 72/6 – one of Ronnie Peterson's regular 1973 cars and 72/7, which had been driven in 1972 & 1973 by Emerson Fittipaldi. In early October, it was announced that a deal had been finalised with Team Lotus and that Scheckter would lead the team. Team Lotus records show that the cars were sold together with two DFVs, numbers 074 and 082.

The penultimate round of the 1973 SADC, the Rand Spring Trophy, took place at Kyalami. Charlton once again reigned supreme in practice, taking pole position by a clear one-second margin. At the start, Keizan made one of his trademark dragster starts, leading through Charlton's team-mate McNicol (March 721) and the Champion, in an unaccustomed third place. It was not until nearly quarter-distance that Charlton managed to find a way past the March, after which he set off in pursuit of Keizan, catching and passing the Tyrrell just after the half-way mark. From then on it was a cruise to the finish, the Lotus 72 driver coming home ten seconds clear.

The final race of the series, the Goldfields 100, was held at Welkom Raceway. The grid had a very familiar look to it, with Charlton on pole and Keizan alongside. However, the race followed anything but a familiar pattern, with the Champion going out on the opening lap due to a lack of fuel pressure and Keizan spinning out due to a stuck throttle, leaving John McNicol to win in the remaining Lucky Strike car.

On this 'against the form' note, the season ended. It was clear that Charlton was going to face stiffer opposition in 1974 than he had done for a long time. Keizan had started to be a regular thorn in his side with the Tyrrell and Alex Blignaut was making noises about getting a new car for the coming season, while Ian Scheckter had proved blindingly fast in the Chevron Formula 2 and seemed certain to challenge for overall honours now that he was moving up to a Formula 1 car. Charlton resolved to source a new car that would enable him to maintain his superiority, once again with the backing of United Tobacco Company, owner of the Lucky Strike brand. Lotus, from whom he had purchased his last two cars, were unable to offer him anything as they were still in the process of building their new car, the Lotus 76. Consequently, he was forced to look elsewhere and, towards the end of 1973, it was announced that he had purchased a McLaren M23 (chassis M23/2) from the factory.

Although this brought to an end the story of Charlton's racing career with the Lotus 72 in South Africa, a new chapter was just beginning in the form of the two cars being imported by Team Gunston. Ian Scheckter's place in the team was well deserved, as his pace in the Formula 2 Chevron run by Gunston in 1973 had been impressive. 'Not pushing myself but it helped because John Love was Charlton's big opposition at the time and John and I were

LUCKY STRIKE RACING

'First on the Championship Circuits'

- Clear win for Charlton
- Breathtaking opening battle
- McNicol has excellent debut
- Indy crashes—the aftermath

team-mates in the Chevrons and obviously, being much younger and that, I blew him away. I think they then thought they had a chance to beat Charlton, so they then took him head on and bought the Lotuses.' However, there was surprise in South African racing circles that one of the seats had gone to Paddy Driver and not Gunston stalwart Love, although the latter was nudging 50 years old by this time! No-one was more surprised than Driver (admittedly youthful by comparison!) as he explains: 'They phoned me up and said "We want you to drive one of these 72s" and I said to them "Where do you guys come from?" and they asked why. I replied that I wanted a Formula 1 car when I was 22 years old not 42!'

The cars arrived in November 1973, freshly repainted in the bright (almost McLaren-like) orange that was the base colour for the Team Gunston livery and were subsequently finished in a brown, almost maroon contrasting colour with gold trim lines and Gunston, Shell and Firestone decals adorning their sides. There was considerable doubt as to whether the Championship would start as planned in 1974, for the global oil crisis had led to a ban on all competitive motor sport in South Africa, while it was forbidden to sell petrol between Friday and Monday, to discourage non-essential driving. This was eventually lifted, just in time for the South African Grand Prix, which took place at the end of March. An abbreviated, nine-round SADC calendar was announced, with the first race taking place a fortnight after the Grand Prix.

During the winter of 1973/74, Charlton had ordered a large quantity of spares for 72/3, for the intention had been to enter the car in the South African Grand Prix, ostensibly as a spare car should he run into trouble with the McLaren, but for John McNicol to drive if all was well. These spares – the list ran to two pages – included a new lightweight nose, a pair of side skins (deformable structure ones to fit over the existing skin as these were now required by the Formula 1 regulations), and a super large airbox, among others. Reports at the time say that the car was not made ready in time for the race, and so did not appear at the Grand Prix meeting where Charlton drove his M23. McNicol though, was entered in 72/3 for the opening round of the South African Drivers' Championship, the Mercury 100 at Pietermaritzburg. However, the car did not arrive, because it was now in Alex Blignaut's hands, for Eddie Keizan to drive, although it could not be made ready in the time available and so the team ran their Tyrrell 004 for a final time.

Alex Blignaut Racing was a very different operation to the Gunston squad, as Keizan explains. 'I first drove for Alex in 1970. We raced saloon cars for a few years and then in 1972 we bought a Formula 5000. We were always backed by United Tobacco, plus we used to get some money from Ford. Alex was a hell of a busy guy as in between running Kyalami, he kept this racing team which comprised me! He ran it from his home, which was a farm on the outskirts of Johannesburg. I used to drive the car, the transporter and spanner the car with him. It was a very amateurish team but nevertheless we still managed to do OK with it.' However, for 1974, the team was expanded slightly, with the addition of two mechanics, the Englishman John McLoughlin plus a South African by the name of Pete Smith.

With the absence of the Blignaut car, the only 72s present at Pietermaritzburg were the two Team Gunston entries for Ian Scheckter (72/6) and Paddy Driver (72/7). It was a promising debut for the Gunston pair: Scheckter put his car on pole, while Driver was third, behind Keizan, for a position on the inside of the second row. Meanwhile, main rival Charlton was forced to start from the back of the grid, having missed official practice while his car underwent an

First Person
Dave Charlton on the Lotus 72

"Everyone said I had it easy because I had the best car. It is all very well to have the best car, but if you can't operate the bloody thing, you are going to get nowhere. The suspension was very 'trick' but I really understood it fully and that was what made the car. We hardly ever altered the mechanical set-up from one circuit to the next, only the aerodynamics and it worked beautifully for us. The only problem we ever had with the car was excessive temperature with the front inboard discs, which we cured by painting everything in the bay where the discs were matt black, that's all we did. It never broke, we didn't have any bulls**t from the suspension, the drive-shafts, the CV joints or anything. Look, our races were only 100 miles, not 200 miles like a Grand Prix but we stripped that car

after every race and checked all those parts in the normal manner then everything was put back in the same place it came off. In other words, we wouldn't have drive-shafts the other way round and opposite sides, everything was just the same. We never, ever had a failure, not even once. It never let us down."

engine change. The main excitement in the race centred around how long it would be before Charlton caught and passed Scheckter for the lead. In the end it took him 12 of the 40 laps, after which the results seemed a formality. However, problems with fuel starvation caused him to slow towards the end and his 20-second lead had fallen to only four seconds at the finish. Driver completed an excellent day for the Gunston team by finishing third. He was actually fourth on the road but Keizan – who finished ahead of him – was penalised one minute for receiving a push-start on the dummy grid and was therefore demoted to fourth once this penalty had been applied.

The Cape South Easter Trophy at the Killarney circuit in Cape Town was the second round of the Championship.

It also marked the first appearance of 72/3 for the Embassy Racing/Blignaut team. Now fully updated to 72E specification with the deformable structures and 1974-spec oil tank over the gearbox, the car was liveried in the striking blue-and-gold colours of Embassy, with other sponsors and suppliers including Goodyear, BP, Ferodo and Keizan's own Tiger Wheels concern. The only noticeable difference to the Gunston cars was that the team had adopted a Hesketh airbox in place of the normal Lotus design. Keizan explains how the deal to drive the 72 came about. 'With the fuel crisis and motor racing ban we didn't make any plans for the 1974 season. But then they lifted the ban so we just took the Tyrrell out of mothballs and dusted it off and raced the thing. But it was a terrible car. So Alex persuaded United Tobacco to take Charlie's car back from him and give it to us. Then we ran that for the rest of the season.'

Speaking in 2002, Charlton denies that 72/3 was ever loaned to Blignaut. However, the evidence suggests otherwise. The car and the spares had actually been paid for by United Tobacco, owners of the Lucky Strike brand,

Left: Paddy Driver, fresh from an operation to remove a rib and sporting a t-shirt from his good friend Dan Gurney, poses by the Lotus 72 that he would drive for Team Gunston in the 1974 South African Drivers' Championship. **Below:** Ian Scheckter loses the backend of the Gunston 72 on the last lap of th Republic Trophy at Kyalami, handing second place to Eddie Keizan in the Embassy 72/3. **Opposite Page Top:** In South Africa the team boss often got his hands dirty: Alex Blignaut works on Eddie Keizan's Embassy Lotus 72 (chassis 72/3) prior to its first race, with mechanics John McLoughlin (back) and Pete Smith (right). **Opposite Page Bottom Left:** In the early part of the 1974 season Alex Blignault's team experimented with a Hesketh airbox in place of the original 'anvil' model. **Opposite Page Bottom Right:** "Better than Jody" was Team Gunston Chief Mechanic Eddie Pinto's assessment of Ian Scheckter, who drove for the team in 1974 and probably would have run Charlton close for the title if tyre problems had been sorted out earlier in the year.

who sponsored Charlton's team and the purchase agreement specifically stated that they would remain the property of UTC, something Charlton freely acknowledges. Blignaut already had close ties with UTC, since the Tyrrell 004 he ran for Keizan in 1973 had been sponsored by Lucky Strike. For 1974, Blignaut's team switched to running in the livery of Embassy, another UTC brand. Therefore it appears that when UTC bought Charlton the McLaren M23, it decided that the 72 should still be raced, and handed it over to Blignaut.

Several references to this switch can be found in the contemporary motor sport press: Autosport (25/4/74 p3) reported that Keizan would be driving the 'ex-Charlton Lotus 72' while his problems with moving the pedals back 'having taken it over from Charlton just after the Grand Prix' were also reported in Lucky Strike Racing (Vol. 4 no 4, July 74 p2). In addition, if this wasn't the ex-Charlton car, it begs the question: 'Which chassis was it?' Since the whereabouts of all other 72s at the time can be established, they can be discounted. Extensive enquiries into the

They just phoned me up and said "We want you to drive one of these 72s" – Paddy Driver, 1974

in a race of attrition.

Keizan's sticking throttle at Killarney was attributed to the mechanics having moved the pedals back to tailor the car to fit their driver, which resulted in a sleeve on the throttle cable jamming intermittently against a small bracket. The problem was sorted in time for round three of the series, the Republic Trophy at Kyalami, and Keizan slotted into third spot on the grid, sandwiched between the two Gunston cars of Ian Scheckter (second) and Paddy Driver (fourth). Meanwhile, Charlton took pole in a time which would have put him third on the grid for the Grand Prix. Scheckter made the better start, leading away Keizan and Charlton. By Sunset bend, Charlton was through into second but it was not until the 9th lap that he caught up with Scheckter, whose tyres were beginning to go off again. The Gunston car stayed in front until lap 12, when Charlton finally got by into Crowthorne at the end of the main straight. As the race went on, Scheckter's handling problems intensified and he began to fall back into the clutches of Keizan. The gap came down from four seconds with three laps to go, to 1.5s with two tours remaining and on the final lap they were nose-to-tail. Coming through the Esses, the Gunston driver spun right in front of the Embassy car, as Scheckter recounts. 'By the time that corner came, I had nothing left at the back – it was just like riding on ice!' The two 72s just avoided a collision and Keizan went on to take a well-deserved second place. A disappointed Scheckter trailed in four seconds later, with his team-mate Driver the only other one on the same lap as the winner.

feasibility of a 'replica' 72 being constructed have suggested that this was not realistic, since the 72's tub was a very complex construction with double-curvature skins as well as the complex front sub-frame. Furthermore, following investigations among Team Lotus management at the time as well as fabricators and mechanics, no evidence can be found that a spare 72 tub had been built (which could perhaps have been brought out by the works team at the time of the Grand Prix), since the team was focusing all its energies on trying to develop the brand new 76 and make it into a reliable, race-winning proposition.

At Killarney, it was Ian Scheckter's turn to strike engine troubles during practice, requiring a change of DFV, while Charlton went on to take a comfortable pole, more than one and a half seconds clear of Keizan. Driver was fourth on the

grid in the second Gunston car, alongside John McNicol, making a return to the scene in the Lucky Strike March 721. Disaster struck on the warm-up lap when the throttle on Keizan's 72 stuck open and he spun into the sand and was unable to take the start. Charlton took the lead from the moment the flag dropped and was never headed. By lap four Scheckter had forced his way into second place but he and Driver suffered from problems with their Firestone tyres and both had to pit for new rubber. While Driver rejoined and finished third, Scheckter's transmission failed six laps from the end and he pushed the car across the line to take fifth

After three races, Charlton led the title race in his McLaren M23 with a maximum 30 points. However, the Lotus 72s were well placed, with Scheckter second, Driver third and Keizan joint fourth. A new circuit for the next round provided something of a level playing field for the teams and drivers. This was Brandkop, a bumpy, sweeping 2.1 mile circuit. Practice provided an upset, with Lotus 72s in first, second and fourth places on the grid, Keizan taking pole ahead of Driver, with Scheckter slightly off the pace. Charlton was unable to mount an effective challenge in practice as a result of engine problems. At the start, Driver took the lead but Charlton was soon ahead as the Gunston cars were once again in tyre trouble, both pitting for new left rears. This left Keizan in the Embassy 72 (running Goodyears) to finish second to the Lucky Strike McLaren, while Scheckter and Driver came home third and fourth.

This pattern was repeated at the Bulawayo 100 in Rhodesia, with Charlton taking pole from Scheckter and Keizan and leading home the Embassy car, with Scheckter the only Gunston car to finish, in third, after Driver's engine blew. There was little doubt that the Gunston drivers, particularly Ian Scheckter, had the speed to keep pace with Charlton but were being severely let down by their Firestone tyres, as Scheckter explains. 'The beautiful thing about the Lotus 72 was that it was the kind of car that needed to be driven sideways. Obviously it then gave the tyres a really hard time, so we did ruin them quicker than we should have. Maybe if I had backed off a bit and driven a bit straighter, things could have been slightly different but the car actually enjoyed being driven like a racing car should be, a bit of boot and throttle control and opposite lock, what Formula 1 is lacking today! The car was great while the tyres were good, I'd just pull away and lead and then, when the tyres went off, I was dead!' Consequently, the team took the decision to switch suppliers mid-season, moving to Goodyear rubber, which was as Scheckter recalls 'Night and day ahead'.

The switch to Goodyear proved to be a decisive turning point for the season and produced instant results at the next race, the Natal Winter Trophy at the Roy Hesketh circuit in Pietermaritzburg. A delighted Scheckter took pole by a tenth of a second from Charlton, with Keizan third. Sadly, Driver was unable to take part with the second Gunston car because he had another engine failure in practice and there were no spares left for him, as he explains. 'Ian got first dip of the engines. They were never rebuilt in South Africa, they were flown over to the UK, to Nicholsons. Every now and then we would get short of engines because one hadn't come back or two had gone over and none had come back and I'd have to use Scheckter's practice engine or something like that. I think that's possibly why I didn't finish a few races because they were engines that had done

too many miles. That's the only excuse I can give you! Having to take second place in the team. I don't think I was ever known, in any of my motor racing, whether it was cars or bikes, as being a machine breaker.' At the start, Scheckter once again shot into the lead but this time he did not experience tyre troubles and was able to hold Charlton at bay. Slowly, the Lotus 72 pulled clear and, by the finish, Scheckter's winning margin was five seconds. Such was the ferocity of the pace of the leading duo that they lapped third man Keizan in the Embassy Racing/Blignaut 72.

The series returned to Kyalami for the Rand Winter Trophy. Paddy Driver's run of miserable luck continued, when he lost control of his Team Gunston 72E and crashed, doing enough damage to the car to end his weekend there and then. However, team-mate Scheckter kept the Gunston spirits up by claiming pole position, two-tenths clear of arch-rival Charlton. With Keizan only nine-tenths slower than Scheckter, a close race looked in prospect. At the start, Scheckter led from Keizan and Charlton but after only seven laps the Embassy Racing 72 suffered a huge engine blow-up and was out. Six laps later, Charlton passed the Gunston car – which was

Above Left: Paddy Driver endured a frustrating season with Team Gunston in 1974 and was never quite able to match the pace of team-mate Scheckter. He is shown here in 72/7 at Quarry Corner at the Roy Hesketh circuit in Pietermaritzburg, during the Natal Winter Trophy meeting in July 1974.
Above Right: Turning point: When Team Gunston switched to Goodyear rubber for the Natal Winter Trophy, Scheckter immediately took pole and won the race. **Below:** Resplendent in its striking Embassy livery, Eddie Keizan's 72/3 sits in the pits at Kyalami, during the Rand Winter Trophy meeting in August 1974. The Hesketh airbox has been abandoned for a more conventional 72 version. Keizan is standing behind the rear wing, while mechanic John McLoughlin is standing by the right-front wheel.

Below Left: Ian Scheckter's exuberant style didn't suit the Firestone tyres Team Gunston started the 1974 season with but once they switched to Goodyear he was virtually unbeatable. He is shown here in 72/6 during the Rand Spring Trophy at Kyalami in September, which he won from pole position. **Below Middle:** Eddie Keizan's 1974 season in 72/3 petered out with a succession of engine problems and the Rand Spring Trophy meeting at Kyalama in September was no exception. After qualifying fourth, he went out with engine trouble, although he was still classified seventh. **Below Right:** Paddy Driver started and finished third in the 1974 Rand Spring Trophy at Kyalami in 72/7

LUCKY STRIKE RACING
'First on the Championship Circuits'

- Ian Scheckter beats Charlton !
- Five seconds at the flag
- Excellent race at Roy Hesketh
- Tunmer/Martin F2 struggle

obviously in some trouble – to take the lead. After another three laps, Scheckter pulled in to retire, due to a problem with the fuel pressure valve, leaving Charlton to cruise to another easy victory.

The False Bay 100 at Killarney proved that Scheckter's pace in the previous two races had been no fluke. Although Charlton took pole from Keizan, with Scheckter third, these three were covered by less than four tenths of a second! Driver was again waiting for a new engine and, as this did not arrive in time for official practice, he was forced to start from the back of the grid. At the start, Charlton jumped into the lead, with Scheckter passing Keizan on the opening lap. After only five laps, the Embassy car was out with a broken gearbox, leaving the Gunston car to fight it out with the McLaren. The two ran nose-to-tail until nearly half-distance, when Charlton finally succumbed to the pressure and spun. By the time he had gathered everything together, the Lotus was long gone and Scheckter came home to score his second victory of the year. To top a good day, Driver finished in third, while Scheckter also set the fastest lap of the race.

It seemed a cruel irony that finally, there was someone who could give Charlton a run for his money yet it was too late because the reigning title-holder clinched the Championship once more by finishing second at Killarney, with three rounds remaining. His supreme early season form, combined with the poor performance of the Gunston team's Firestone tyres, had effectively handed the Championship to Charlton on a plate.

A long trip back up to Rhodesia followed, this time to the Donnybrook circuit rather than Bulawayo, for the Rhodesian Grand Prix. Scheckter picked up where he left off, winning comfortably, while Charlton, Driver and Keizan all hit trouble. Keizan retired with broken

suspension, Driver's gearbox failed and Charlton lost four laps in the pits but still managed to finish third, due to the high rate of attrition in the race. Once again, and underlining his sheer speed, Scheckter took the fastest lap of the race.

Kyalami was the venue for the penultimate round of the Championship and Scheckter again pipped Charlton for pole position – a feat almost unimaginable in years gone by. Driver and Keizan lined up third and fourth to fill the second row. At the start, Charlton was jumped by the two 72s behind him and it was a Lotus 72 1-2-3 at the end of the first lap! The Champion soon disposed of the interlopers but could do nothing to reign in the flying Scheckter, who came home 3.3 seconds ahead. Driver finished a fine third, inheriting the position from Keizan three laps from the end when the latter's engine blew up again. Fastest lap of the race went – for the third successive time – to Ian Scheckter.

The Welkom Raceway played host to the final SADC round of 1974, the Goldfields 100. The Lotus 72 element in the field was depleted early on in practice when the engine in Keizan's Embassy Racing/Blignaut 72 blew up for the third time that year, forcing the team to non-start. Charlton

"The beautiful thing about the 72 was that it was the kind of car that needed to be driven sideways" Ian Scheckter

attempted to regain the initiative by taking pole by eight-tenths of a second from Scheckter, while Driver produced his best qualifying performance of the season, only six-tenths shy of his team-mate. The result of the race was settled on the first lap. Scheckter jumped into the lead and then Charlton spun in his haste to keep up. This resulted in sand getting in the throttle slides, causing the Champion to

spin again and he lost six laps in the pits having this put right. Meanwhile, the two Team Gunston 72s cruised to an easy 1-2, a fitting way to finish the season.

Scheckter had won five of the final six rounds of the Championship. Had it not been for the problems with the fuel pressure valve at Kyalami he would have scored a clean sweep of these races. If he had not spun away second at Kyalami early in the season the Gunston driver and Charlton would have been tied on points at the end of the year. However, the fact that the McLaren driver won the first five races of the series, then took Kyalami when the Gunston car wilted as well as his other two best finishes which were second places, meant that he ultimately emerged victorious. Looking back now, Scheckter says that it is easy to blame the decision to continue the team's relationship with Firestone into 1973 as the reason for him not securing the title but generously points out there were other factors at work. 'That [the tyre choice] maybe was a big reason but the whole team was new, we had no testing time so maybe it was just that we were all thrown in at the deep end. They went with the companies they knew. Goodyear would obviously have been a whole new ball game.'

For Paddy Driver, it had been a frustrating season but one which he now looks back on with some fondness. 'I had a good year. Ian Scheckter was always quicker than me: I could just never quite get on to the pace that Ian could do. I was always that second slower than him no matter how much I tried or what I did. I just put it down to age! I don't grumble about that but I enjoyed it very much, I'm just sorry that I never got into a Formula 1 car earlier than that – chances like that don't come very often.' Although he had performed reasonably, Driver's relative lack of pace compared to Scheckter's hadn't gone unnoticed. The Gunston bosses were keen to get a young hotshoe behind the wheel and Driver's contract was not renewed for 1975. Today, all Driver has to show for his year are his memories, some photos and a very special memento. 'They had

silhouettes of the cars on the side of the transporter – Scheckter on the one side and me on the other. The managing director was a good guy and I said to him "Seeing as you're booting me out, you might as well let me take that off the side of the transporter, because it doesn't match the next driver" and it's now hanging on my wall!'

For Alex Blignaut, running on very limited resources, it was clear that if his protégé was to progress, he needed more money behind him and/or better machinery. Consequently, Blignaut lobbied hard for Keizan to get a drive with Team Gunston and this was successful: he was signed to drive for the team in 1975. Meanwhile the Blignaut Racing Lotus 72 was returned to Charlton's workshops and hung in the rafters 'just in case'.

Above: Guy Tunmer scored his one and only race victory in the Gunston 72 in the False Bay 100 at Killarney when his team-mate Eddie Keizan spun on the last lap. **Below:** Keizan, who finished third, is pictured passing Nolly Limberis' McLaren M10B during the Rand Winter Trophy at Kyalami, July 1975. **Opposite Page Top:** Guy Tunmer qualified a promising second but crashed his newly built-up 72/3 during the 1975 Natal Winter Trophy at the Roy Hesketh circuit in Pietermaritzburg. **Opposite Page Middle:** Guy Tunmer crashed his Team Gunston 72/7 heavily in unofficial practice for the Rand Winter Trophy at Kyalami, forcing the tub to be sent back to the UK for repairs. **Opposite Page Bottom:** Once again, Keizan's luck deteriorated towards the end of the season but he still kept smiling. He is shown at the Rand Spring Trophy, where he failed to start after a drive-shaft broke on the warm-up lap.

Ian Scheckter had been persuaded to switch Rembrandt Tobacco Company brands and had moved to Lexington Racing to drive a 1974 Tyrrell 007 obtained from the works with a little assistance from his brother, Jody. 'We organised to buy the Tyrrell because Jody was driving for them. It's like anybody – you want the new car, don't you, whether it's better than the old one or not! And I gambled. They actually wanted me to stay in Gunston with the Lotus and they were going to give Keizan the Tyrrell. But I went the Lexington way. The Tyrrell was newer and we presumed it would be quicker. It wasn't more fun to drive by any means but I think it was maybe quicker by then.' The second vacant seat at Team Gunston was therefore filled by Guy Tunmer, a young, up-and-coming driver who had showed an impressive turn of speed in Lexington Racing's Formula 2 Chevron. The only significant modification made to the Gunston cars for the coming season was the replacement of the fabricated rear uprights with magnesium ones.

The series kicked off with the Cape South Easter Trophy at Killarney. The two Gunston cars were at opposite ends of the grid, Keizan sharing the front row alongside pole-sitter Scheckter's Tyrrell and Tunmer starting from the back due to blowing an engine in practice. After only five laps, Keizan's race was over due to fuel pump failure but Tunmer salvaged some pride for the team with a distant second place, more than a lap behind the winning McLaren

of Charlton. Tunmer found the transformation from Formula 2 to Formula 1 car quite a step up, and was eager to learn his craft from other drivers, particularly those who had experience of racing a 72. Gunston mechanic Andrew Thompson tells a story of how, on his first appearance in a 72 at Kyalami, (for the 1975 South African Grand Prix) Tunmer asked Dave Charlton for some advice on gearing for different parts of the circuit: He said to DC "The Barbecue Bend/Jukskei Sweep section – what do you do?" DC replied, "Oh, it's flat". So Guy went out to do a few laps and he came back into the pits looking very pale and with big eyes. He said to DC "There's no way you can go through there flat in top." And DC turned round and replied, "Oh, sorry, I should have told you I meant flat in fourth!'"

The two Gunston cars lined up alongside each other for round two of the South African Drivers Championship, the Goldfields 100 at Welkom and Keizan, with more experience of the 72, was over a second quicker than his young team-mate. In the race, the two orange-and-brown cars ran in second and third positions for a while, behind Charlton, before a recovering Ian Scheckter – who had spun on the opening lap – fought his way past them. Then, only seven laps from the end, Keizan was forced to retire due to dust having got in his throttle slides when he was lapping another car. With Charlton having to make a last-minute stop for fuel, Tunmer moved up to second and amid a chaotic finish, Tunmer was at one stage even

credited with victory but a protest by the real winner Scheckter saw common sense prevail.

Eddie Keizan's dismal start to the season continued when he had two engine failures in practice for the next race, the Mercury 100, at the Roy Hesketh circuit near Pietermaritzburg. As a result of his troubles, Keizan's team-mate was only two-tenths of a second slower than him and the two Gunston cars again lined up on the second row behind poleman Scheckter (Tyrrell 007) and Charlton (McLaren M23). Tunmer's race was run after only 12 laps due to a broken valve, while Keizan briefly ran as high as second when Charlton spun but the Champion was soon back ahead of him and he finished 15 seconds adrift of the leading duo, who fought tooth and nail all the way to the finish, Scheckter just coming out on top.

The series returned to the Brandkop circuit for the second time to contest the Brandkop Winter Trophy. After Keizan's two blow-ups at Pietermaritzburg, the Gunston team was woefully short of serviceable engines, so much so that Tunmer was forced to revert to driving a Chevron B25 Formula 2 car for this race. The new engine in Keizan's car did not sound right so they were forced to borrow one from Scheckter's Lexington Racing outfit. The lone 72 started from third on the grid and, just before quarter-distance was hit from behind by Charlton's McLaren, the latter having been forced to start from the back of the grid. It took Keizan three laps to restart his car and then after another three laps his fuel pressure disappeared and he was out.

Back at Kyalami for the Republic Trophy meeting, Team Gunston were still experiencing engine problems and both Keizan and Tunmer were off the pace of the leaders, ending up in third and seventh on the grid. Come race day, Keizan got bogged down at the start while Tunmer shot through to snatch third. Keizan recovered and had nearly caught his team-mate when he was forced to pit with a loose terminal. This dropped him to the back of the field

First Person

Ian Scheckter on driving the Team Gunston Lotus 72

"It was the most beautiful car I ever drove. It was the kind of car that, if you went off the road sideways, you could keep your boot in and it would come back on, it was really a great driving car. The next year we got a Tyrrell and, although it may have been slightly quicker, it was the kind you had to drive straight. If it got more than a metre out of line, it would want to go right round. Whereas with that Lotus you could hang the tail out and it would still come back! It was really great to drive. It was our first year in Formula 1, we were all quite new, so we didn't have much experience but certainly, once we got the tyres right, at every circuit that car was so driveable, it really was a pleasure."

but he continued circulating until around two-thirds distance when a puncture brought him into the pits for a second time, at which point he gave up the unequal struggle and retired. Tunmer was having his best race of the season and, aided by a wrong tyre choice on the part of the reigning Champion, started to catch second-placed man Charlton in the dying laps. As they came round The Kink for the final time Tunmer drew alongside the McLaren but just failed to take second by a matter of inches.

The False Bay 100 at Killarney provided a bittersweet result for the two Gunston drivers. Tunmer now really had the bit between his teeth and outqualified his team-mate for the first time. But for a timekeeping mistake, he should have been on the front row. Instead, the two 72s lined up in their by now customary second row formation. Initially, Charlton led the two Gunston cars but two spins by the Champion on a track surface littered with gravel allowed them through into the lead. Earlier in the race, Tunmer had also spun but without losing a position. The orange-and-brown cars then ran in team formation for the rest of the race until, on the final lap, Keizan managed to spin into the sand and stall, leaving a surprised and delighted Tunmer to claim the victory. Although he didn't finish, Keizan was still classified fourth but must have been kicking himself for throwing away the chance of an easy win.

Having really started to make an impact in the team, Tunmer blotted his copybook badly when he crashed heavily in unofficial practice for the next race, the Rand Winter Trophy at Kyalami. He lost control in the Barbecue Bend/Jukskei Sweep section (still trying to take it flat in top,

maybe!) and spun into the catch-fences. As he hit the fence, it pulled up one of the poles, which had been set in concrete, and this ripped off the undertray, very nearly doing the driver a nasty injury. With a front corner knocked off and the tub badly dented, the car was a terrible mess and there was no way that it could be repaired for the race. A decision was made to buy 72/3 from Charlton and try and ready this for the race on the Saturday.

The car acquired from Charlton was stripped down to the tub and rebuilt, using as many pieces from the Team Gunston store rooms as possible. It took three mechanics all of Thursday night and three-quarters of Friday to build the car up and it was finished for the last half-hour of practice that afternoon! Tunmer managed a few slow laps in an unfamiliar car, enough to qualify him on the back row at least, while Keizan was again third-fastest. In the race, Keizan ran in second behind Charlton before the slow-starting Ian Scheckter caught and passed him and he continued to finish in third. Meanwhile, not surprisingly Tunmer's car never ran properly and he retired early on, after just a few slow laps.

Below Left: Eddie Keizan waits on the grid before the Republic Day Trophy race at Kyalami, May 1975. **Below Right:** Guy Tunmer finished third in the Republic Day Trophy. **Opposite Page** Close-up! Tunmer fends off the advances of Charlton's M23 during the Rand Spring Trophy at Kyalami, October 1975.

The tub of the car crashed by Tunmer was too badly damaged to be repaired in South Africa, so it was packed up and shipped over to England, to the Hethel works of Team Lotus for repair, where records show that it had new side skins, undertray and a duct panel fitted. It would never race again as, by the time these repairs had been completed and the tub returned to Gunston, the 1975 season was finished and Formula 1 cars had become obsolete, as the SADC was switching to Formula Atlantic regulations for 1976.

The penultimate round of the series was the Natal

lap before he could fire the engine up again. Tunmer ran second to Scheckter in the early part of the race, and inherited the lead when the Tyrrell broke a drive-shaft. However, it only lasted for five laps before Charlton passed him and then Tunmer went and spoiled his day by crashing into the barriers with three laps remaining, fortunately without doing too much damage. Meanwhile, Keizan had recovered from his delayed start and came home second, albeit a minute shy of winner Charlton.

The final round of the Championship, the Rand Spring

frantic laps with Charlton climbing all over him trying to find a way by. After the Champion got through, the Gunston driver had a fairly uneventful run to the finish to claim third position. This finish also assured him of third overall in the SADC, overhauling the best of the Formula 2 drivers, Tony Martin, who failed to score. Keizan ended up fifth, a depressing outcome for a season that had promised so much.

There was one more race held for the South African competitors that year. This was the Donnybrook 100, a non-Championship event held at the circuit of that name near Harare in Rhodesia. The race was split into two heats. In the first one, Keizan led from Charlton and Tunmer before his engine blew in a big way. Tunmer finished second to Charlton and led the second heat before the McLaren driver pushed his way to the front and Ian Scheckter passed him in the Tyrrell. Tunmer's third was good enough for him to claim second on aggregate, a suitable high note to end the season on. It was a fitting result for chassis 72/3, which had first competed in 1970, the year the 72 design made its debut and was now the last of the chassis to compete in an international Formula 1 race, more than five years later. It was the end of a glittering racing career.

With the Type 72's final International Formula 1 race over, it was the end of a glittering racing career

Spring Trophy, marking the second visit of the series that year to the Roy Hesketh circuit. Tunmer was feeling more comfortable in his new car and promptly put it on the front row, alongside pole-man Scheckter. A good race seemed in prospect, for only 1.3s covered the leading four, with Keizan the slowest of the quartet, just behind Charlton, after his engine ran its bearings in practice. His dreadful season continued as he stalled at the start and lost nearly a

Trophy, was held at Kyalami. Once again, the 'Gunston twins' qualified third and fourth to take up their second row places. However, Keizan's appalling luck that year was underlined when he broke a drive-shaft as the field moved up from the dummy grid and was unable to take the start. Tunmer made up for this disappointment for the team with a great getaway to hold second place behind Scheckter in the early laps, a position he managed to maintain for six

Just how good was the Lotus 72? Was it a truly great Formula 1 design or merely a capable design flattered by great drivers? This chapter aims to answer these questions by considering the facts - in terms of bare statistics – as well as the opinions of those who ought to know: the people who drove the car and the people who competed against it.

A statistical analysis of the results of the Lotus 72 in Grand Prix racing shows that the car was almost as successful in terms of the percentage of races it won as the Lotus 49, but across a much greater number of races. It won 20 of the 74 Grand Prix it contested, a commendable win-rate of 27%. Its best years in terms of win-rate were 1970, when the car won half of the races it started, and 1973, when it proved victorious in almost half. Not even the Lotus 49 managed statistics as impressive as that. Similarly, Fittipaldi's 1972 World Championship-winning season yielded a win rate of 42%. Things started to slip slightly in 1974, while the nadirs were the win-less years of 1971, when the new drivers were struggling to come to terms with an ill-handling car and unfamiliar circuits, and 1975, when the design was becoming long in the tooth and tyre technology had gone in the wrong direction for the chassis.

Outright speed over a single lap is always a good measure of a car's abilities, and the 72 was no slouch in this department either. It achieved pole in a fifth of Grand Prix contested in 1970, a quarter in 1972 and an astounding two-thirds in 1973, as the blinding pace of Ronnie Peterson – who took all but one of these – lifted the performance of the car to a new level. Again, the dismal years of 1971 and 1975 are self-evident by the lack of pole positions, while 1974 was ruined by the failure of the 72's intended replacement, the 76.

Ronnie Peterson took the most starts in a 72, just two ahead of Fittipaldi. Between them, these two accounted for more than half of the total made by the car, with Ickx, Wisell and Walker the only others to get into double figures.

If Graham Hill was 'Mr 49', then Emerson Fittipaldi must be 'Mr 72': he was active in developing the car throughout 1971 into a competitive package and continuing to hone it through 1972 and 1973. By the time Ronnie Peterson had joined the team it was, without doubt, the quickest Formula 1 car on the grid, despite the fact that it was starting its fourth competitive season. The Brazilian is unequivocal in his opinions about the 72. 'That was definitely the best racing car I ever drove in my career, it was superb. It was outstanding on bumpy tracks. In 1972 and 1973 the car was unbelievable. To give you an example: Interlagos was bumpy, fast with long corners. The 72 was the best handling car, I mean it was fantastic. Then we really had two fantastic years.'

Fittipaldi is in the unusual position of having competed in a Grand Prix at the wheel of a Lotus 49, Lotus 72 and McLaren M23, three of the really great cars of the 3-litre Formula 1 era. How did he think the 72 compared with the 49? 'It was a different animal. The Lotus 49 was a very heavy car, softer riding, with slower, more conventional reactions than the Lotus 72. The 72 was a harsher car to

The Lotus 72's record in Grand Prix racing

Year	GPs contested	Wins	Win rate %	Poles	Pole rate %
1970	10	5	50	2	20
1971	10	0	–	0	0
1972	12	5	42	3	25
1973	15	7	47	10	67
1974	13	3	23	1	8
1975	14	0	–	0	0
Total	**74**	**20**	**27**	**16**	**22**

Driver	No. of wins	Win rate %
Emerson Fittipaldi	9	24
Ronnie Peterson	7	18
Jochen Rindt	4	67
Total	**20**	**27**

Only three drivers won a Grand Prix at the wheel of a Lotus 72 – Emerson Fittipaldi, Ronnie Peterson and Jochen Rindt. Fittipaldi scored the most wins, taking nearly half of the total, two ahead of Peterson. However, statistically, Jochen Rindt was the most successful because he won two-thirds of the races he started.

Grand Prix starts in a Lotus 72 by driver

Ronnie Peterson	40
Emerson Fittipaldi	38
Jacky Ickx	19
Reine Wisell	13
Dave Walker	10
Jochen Rindt	6
John Miles	6
Dave Charlton	5
Graham Hill	3
Brian Henton	2
Jim Crawford	2
Eddie Keizan	1
Guy Tunmer	1
Ian Scheckter	1
John Watson	1
Paddy Driver	1
Total	**149**

drive, quick on changing direction. The car felt lighter than the 49. It was a different concept and you could feel that in one lap.' And on the M23 vs. the 72? 'The M23 was a more conventional car, a simpler car but it was not as good as the Lotus 72, no way. The 72 was superior, much more consistent on different tracks. I think the whole package of the 72 was very good, the whole car, the concept was very good. It was right in terms of weight distribution, the shape, the downforce, suspension geometry – Maurice Phillippe was very good at that time, he was very much a detail guy.'

For an objective assessment of the significance and 'greatness' of the 72, who better to speak to than rival drivers and designers? One driver who can speak with authority about the performance of the Lotus 72 – in 1970 at least – was Jack Brabham, who spent most of that year's British Grand Prix in his BT33 tucked up under Rindt's rear wing before passing the Austrian and then running out of fuel on the final lap. 'There was very little in it between the

cars, whether it was handling or straight line or anything, they were very, very close. Well, I was having a lot easier time than he was! The Lotus 72 was a quick car but it wasn't all that easy to drive it that quick. Jochen had to be right on his toes to go that fast whereas our car was a lot easier to drive and I wasn't having such a hard time with it.' Like many rival designers and constructors at the time, Brabham still can't resist a little dig at the 72's perceived fragility. 'I felt a lot safer in my car than watching somebody else drive that one! At least I knew nothing was going to fall off it…'

It is probably true that the 72 was not really in its element on the bumpy surface of the Brands Hatch track and was more at home on high-speed, smoother circuits. Certainly, Chris Amon (a good friend of Rindt's) remembers several conversations with the Lotus driver where he alluded to how easy it was to drive. 'I remember having dinner with Jochen in London, during July or

August that year, when he was talking about retiring and he was actually saying how easy it all was at that moment, so I think that's probably a fair summary of where the car was at! 'Clermont-Ferrand in 1970 is the first time I can remember it being significant. For the first few laps I was in front of him and there were two or three others in front of us. Jochen said to me after the race "Oh, you weren't getting with it for the first two or three laps and the others got away". The Firestone tyres my team [March] were using – and Jochen would have been on the same ones – took a lap or two to actually get competitive. I remember thinking to myself "If Jochen thought I was hanging about for the first two or three laps, this car he's in must be pretty good!" He passed me going up the hill on the straight and eventually he won and I finished second.

'Also, at Hockenheim I was "best of the rest". There were the two Ferraris and Jochen plus I managed to hold on until the engine went but I was really just hanging on.

Jochen was able to swap places with the Ferraris so the 72 was obviously very quick in a straight line too. It was an unspectacular type of car to follow, it just seemed to go round corners and didn't do anything, whereas something like the March you had to drive the arse off it to get anywhere! If you think back to the 49, Jochen was pretty spectacular in that, as he could be, whereas he was very smooth in the 72, and I think that is a measure of how good the car was.

'Like so many of Chapman's cars, it was probably a year or two ahead of itself in that the basic concept remained competitive for a long time. It was perhaps not as significant as the 25 but Chapman had this huge ability to be one step ahead of everybody else in the concept department.' Amon's assessment is one with which Jabby Crombac, a long-time friend and ally of Colin Chapman, concurs. He cites the fact that it was the all-round package of wedge-shaped body, side radiators and the handling advantages bestowed by inboard brakes, which combined to make it a world-beater. 'It was trend-setting. The Indy car programme played a large part in the design of the 72 because it was the first time that Colin became aware of aerodynamic lift. At the time [of the Type 56 Indy wedge] he wasn't thinking of wings yet, so he made the car wedge-shaped and this was carried over to the 72. He had the side radiators which were very good for weight distribution and the inboard front brakes, which were OK as long as Firestone would do the right tyres for it.'

Many of the key features of the Lotus 72 can still be found on a modern-day Formula 1 car, such as side radiators and torsion bars, while the concept of an automated way of changing gear was also first tried out on a 72. Side radiators were not in themselves a new idea: they had been tried on Formula 1 cars before and the practice was already established in sports car racing. However, like so many concepts adopted by Chapman (such as the engine as a stressed member), this was the first truly successful example of their use in Grand Prix racing.

Although now considerably more compact, torsion bars are still utilised by the top Formula 1 teams today, such as Ferrari. Chapman was the first to use these in Formula 1 and the extent to which he was ahead of his time is illustrated by the fact that other teams such as Tyrrell tried to make them work and abandoned them in favour of a more conventional arrangement.

One innovation which did not make it onto the Lotus 72 (in the original designs, at least) was the power clutch. This eventually appeared four years later on the 76. Designer Ralph Bellamy explains ruefully that it appears Maurice Phillippe managed to talk Chapman out of that one. 'I was having a clear-up at one stage and I dug out a folder of paperwork relating to the early days of the 72. I looked

through it because I was always interested in who designed these things and who was the intellectual giant behind it. I found a spec sheet from Colin, with what he wanted and I'm reading through it and – bugger me – an electric clutch. I thought to myself "Maurice, you crafty bastard, you managed to avoid this and I got stuck with it!" So Maurice was better than me in that respect anyway, in that he managed to duck that one.'

Rival designers have mixed views about just how good the Lotus 72 was. Tony Southgate, who penned the successful BRM P153 and P160 designs of the early 1970s, is definitely of the opinion that it was a good package. 'When it came out it was a very advanced design compared to the opposition and it was oozing with trick bits and pieces which took quite a while to sort out. But, in true Lotus fashion, they'd muck around, change the suspension from one race to the next and so on, whereas the average team would take half a season to do that! It took them quite a while to get on top of it, because the thing had a huge amount of anti-dive and anti-squat in the suspension, which meant that it was very difficult for the drivers to know what the hell was going on, and so they dramatically reduced it. That was typical Chapman, he'd want to go to the limit all the time. And obviously they had a load of trouble with all

their drive-shafts for their inboard braking which presented them with a bit of a problem but of course they were in fairly new territory because most people had no experience of that sort of braking.

'It wasn't just one thing [that made the car good], it was lots of bits and pieces. It had centrally mounted radiators and fuel tank so obviously there was not much change in weight distribution and good low polar moment because it had nothing at the front – just pedals and brakes and a tubular frame so it could change direction quickly. It had things like torsion bar suspension that I don't think necessarily made the car any quicker, it just made for a nice package. The combination of torsion bars and rising rate geometry made it a very complex and sophisticated car but it meant that you needed to be careful with the setting up – you could easily get lost and I guess they did on a few occasions. But when it was all working, it worked a treat. The fact that it lasted such a long time shows that the basic concept was good. And it was constantly ahead of the opposition so they could just keep updating it to stay competitive.'

Given its complexity, Southgate was not surprised that the Lotus 72 did not spawn lots of imitators. 'Nobody actually made their version of a 72, I think because it was

LOTUS 72

too clever for them! Most of the designers wouldn't understand what the hell was going on, it would be too tricky, so they would take the mid-radiator and a pointed nose, thinking that was the secret but that would just be part of it. It is very rare that it is just one item on a car that makes it good. If there is, it is bad news because as soon as the opposition find out what it is, they copy it and they've beaten you or they're equal to you! Ideally, you have what you think are several new ideas to keep you ahead of the opposition.'

Gordon Murray, chief designer at Brabham from 1973

onwards, is less enthusiastic. 'If you start with the positives, it was refreshingly different, particularly in looks and layout and, on the surface, innovative. It was strikingly different from the normal square or coke-bottle Brabham or McLaren with the multi-layer rear wing and the wedge shape and inboard brakes and stuff. My first impression was "Wow - here's something a bit radical". But then as we got to race against it I looked at it in more detail, particularly as to whether we wanted to go inboard brakes and stuff. And then looking back on it now, as an ex-Formula 1 designer, I don't think it was one of the better Lotus Formula 1 cars. It

was a good car because it won a lot of races but I don't think it was one of the best designs to come out of Lotus to be honest. The first fundamental flaw was the whole layout of the wedge shape. It had no really good reason, apart from the fact that it looked a bit radical and modern. Plus it was too stylised, too complicated and cluttered and it was a total nightmare to work on, which was against all my principles.

'Having said that, purely as a place in history and because it was a Lotus – and I'm still a mad Lotus fan – it was a successful car, a radical car and it looked good. My funniest and overriding memory about that car was that I got "arrested" by a security man on a huge revolving stand at the Racing Car Show in London. It was the centre of attraction on this big raised turntable with spotlights on it and stuff. And Ron Tauranac, who was my boss in those days said "I want you to measure that rear wing" and I got right up to the car with a tape measure and got lifted bodily off the stand by several security men!'

But let us get back to the facts. Regardless of the 72's pros and cons, the truth is that it won more Grand Prix than any other single design of its era, the McLaren M23 (16 wins) being the only design to come close. It won Grand Prix in four of the six seasons in which it contested Grand Prix (1970, 1972, 1973 and 1974) and it showed that it was capable of winning even in the year in which its intended successor (the 76) was supposed to have taken over. Ironically, it seems that the decision to kill off the 72 may even have been a bit premature...

But what really sounded the death knell for the 72 was tyre company policy – specifically the decision of Firestone to pull out of Formula 1 at the end of the 1972 season. Even though they later reversed this decision, by that time Lotus had switched to Goodyear and the Akron firm's rubber never truly suited the 72 in the way that the Firestone's – specially tailored for the car – had, as Jabby Crombac explains. 'Goodyear refused to do special tyres for it and that was it, that was the end of the 72 really. I think Colin

was always hoping to convince the tyre people to work [more closely] with him. Also, having been a Firestone user for years, he wasn't the blue-eyed boy, they were Brabham and Tyrrell, who had been with Goodyear much longer.'

Brian Henton, who was brought in to the team in 1975 and did a lot of testing with the 72s, trying to make them work better, agrees with Crombac's assessment. 'The thing that absolutely destroyed the 72 was the tyre construction. Goodyear switched the carcasses on their tyres to a much stiffer construction. All of a sudden, it couldn't work the tyres, it was too light on tyres. And if you noticed, all the cars that started to go unbelievably well were the crude things like Marches! We did hours of testing to try and sort it out. We even went to conventional-type suspension and put springs on it and all this sort of thing. But we just couldn't get the tyres to work.'

Ralph Bellamy believes that, while the tyres were an issue, Chapman should have accepted that he was never going to get tyres from Goodyear tailored to suit the 72, and adapted his design to suit the tyres by switching to outboard brakes. However, as he explains, he believes there was a specific reason why this did not happen: 'What you have to remember is that Colin had a political thing going with this inboard brake issue. Jochen [Rindt] had been killed and he'd claimed that it wasn't the brakes that killed him and he'd had all sorts of difficulties in Italy as a result. So Colin

wanted to stick with inboard brakes for political reasons, whether or not they had a technical advantage, so that's what we did. The 76 had inboard brakes and the 77 had inboard brakes and the Formula 2 car [Type 74] had inboard brakes.

'It was only after a lot of distress with the 77 that Colin said to me "Look, can you fix it up, we've got to do something" and we got Len Terry involved. We talked to Len and we just put outboard brakes on the car. By this time, I was also designing the 78 [ground effects car] with outboard brakes and I said "Well, we may as well go to outboard brakes on the 77 as well" and when we did, suddenly, bingo, we were back on the pace, the understeer had gone and a whole new world had opened up!'

Ironically, in May 1976, only a matter of weeks after the 77 made its first appearance with outboard brakes, Chapman was finally acquitted of all charges relating to Rindt's death. The 77 got better and better and by June was starting Grand Prix from the front row and leading races. It was only a matter of time before Team Lotus were back on the top step of the rostrum and, sure enough, Mario Andretti won the season-ending Japanese Grand Prix. It was the dawn of a new era of ground effects, skirts and underbody aerodynamics and, once more, Team Lotus would be leading the way and others would be following...

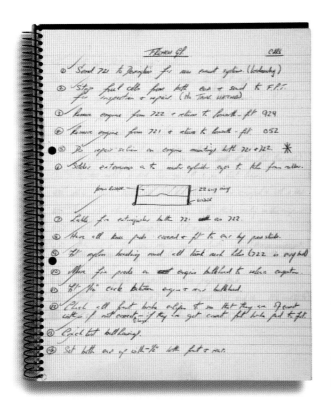

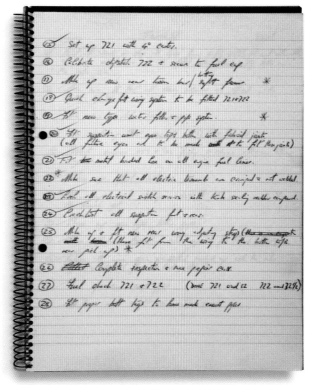

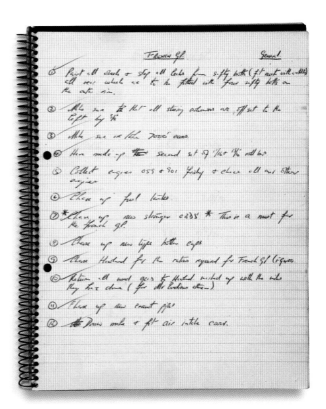

The complete competition record of the Lotus 72

This was the prototype car unveiled to the press on April Fools Day, 1970 **(see below)**. It enjoyed a brief and undistinguished career, failing to qualify on its first appearance at the Spanish Grand Prix, driven by John Miles, who was the only person to race this chassis. A retirement in the non-Championship International Trophy was followed by another non-qualification at the Monaco Grand Prix meeting, leaving the Englishman dejected about both his and the car's performance. The contrast was made all the more stark by the fact that team-mate Rindt won the race in the older 49C.

For the Belgian Grand Prix, 72/1 was substantially re-worked, with the removal of the majority of the anti-squat geometry from the rear suspension. However, it retained the DG300 gearbox, the anti-dive geometry at the front and also did not have the strengthening baffle added inside the tub to stiffen it up. These changes resulted in the car being given the designation 72B. Rindt drove it briefly in practice but his distrust of the new car was further reinforced when a rear hub seized and broke the suspension, so he switched back to his trusty 49C and Miles was put in the hot seat. After qualifying 13th, he lasted nine laps of the race before the car was withdrawn with deflating rear tyres, plus engine and gearbox maladies. At the Dutch Grand Prix Miles drove very well and was a tad unlucky not to score his first points, finally coming home seventh, while Rindt in the sister car demonstrated the 72's potential by scoring an emphatic victory. An eighth in the French Grand Prix at Clermont-Ferrand was followed by a retirement from the British Grand Prix due to a blown engine, after a strong qualifying performance.

After this race, Miles switched to 72/3, which was to the same 72C spec as Rindt's car. The decision was made to take 72/1 and totally rebuild it to 72C specification, before its sale to Rob Walker for Graham Hill to drive. The monocoque was literally taken to pieces and anything that could be carried over from the original was used in what resulted, chassis 72/4.

Debut:	Spanish GP, 1970 (DNQ)
Final race:	British GP, 1970
Race starts:	5
Grand Prix starts:	4
Race wins:	0
Grand Prix wins:	0
Other notes:	Re-built and re-numbered as chassis 72/4, sold to Rob Walker, August 1970

The Racing Record of Chassis 72/1

Year	Date	Event	Circuit	Spec	No.	Driver	Race	Notes	Practice
1970	19-Apr	Spanish Grand Prix	Jarama	72	19	J. Miles	n/a		DNQ
1970	26-Apr	International Trophy (NC)	Silverstone	72	9	J. Miles	Retired	11th Heat 1, Heat 2	23rd
1970	10-May	Monaco Grand Prix	Monte Carlo	72	2T	J. Miles	n/a	Sat practice only	DNQ
1970	07-Jun	Belgian Grand Prix	Spa-Francorchamps	72B	21	J. Miles	Retired	Puncture/engine/gearbox	13th
1970	21-Jun	Dutch Grand Prix	Zandvoort	72B	12	J. Miles	7th		8th
1970	05-Jul	French Grand Prix	Clermont-Ferrand	72B	7	J. Miles	8th		18th
1970	19-Jul	British Grand Prix	Brands Hatch	72B	6	J. Miles	Retired	Engine after 16 laps	7th

This car first appeared at Jarama for the 1970 Spanish Grand Prix, driven by Jochen Rindt and was inextricably linked with the Austrian thereafter. After an inauspicious debut, it again failed to impress at the International Trophy. Following these dismal showings, a decision was taken to go back to the drawing board, the car was totally redesigned and rebuilt, including the removal of most of the anti-dive and anti-squat geometry from the front and rear suspensions. There was also strengthening of the monocoque to help make it stiffer as well as the replacement of the DG300 gearbox with a smaller and lighter FG400 unit. Effectively, this resulted in an instant transition to 72C specification, leapfrogging the interim 72B spec applied to Miles' car. This transformed the car, although this was not apparent on its first outing, since Spanish driver Alex Soler-Roig had been entrusted with the task of driving it and he knew neither the car nor the Spa Francorchamps circuit.

It was in private testing during the week preceding the Dutch Grand Prix that the car truly came good and by the event itself, Rindt was unstoppable, easily securing pole position and running away with the race. This started a run of four straight victories, which effectively secured the 1970 World Championship for Rindt. Two of these were relatively lucky victories where the lead was inherited from a faltering rival – Beltoise in France and Brabham in Britain – but the Austrian won as he pleased in Germany, timing his passing move on Ickx's Ferrari to perfection. It was after this race that he made his often-quoted comment that a monkey could have won in his car, candid honesty from a driver obviously revelling in the

superiority of his machine and happy to tell anyone who'd listen.

An opportunity to consolidate his position at the head of the Championship table in Austria was lost with a blown engine and then came the fateful Italian Grand Prix. In practice, Rindt crashed very violently under braking for the Parabolica corner and was killed. The car was very badly damaged: the front sub-frame, suspension, wheels and pedal box were ripped off in the impact and the monocoque severely buckled. The chassis was impounded by the Italian

authorities for many years while they decided whether or not to proceed with legal action against Chapman relating to the accident. This they did and Chapman was not acquitted until May 1976. After this Team Lotus assumed that the wreckage would have been destroyed, in keeping with Chapman's wishes. In fact, the car continued to languish in a government-owned scrap yard where it remained until 1985.

The Italian collector Guido Romani discovered the car and acquired it from the authorities for a modest sum. It remained unrestored, in a garage at Romani's home, for a further eight years until 1993, when a friend of Romani, Pier-Luigi Mapelli, assumed ownership of the car in exchange for two historic Lola single-seaters. In 2000, the decision was taken to send the car back to England to be rebuilt to its former glory and in November 2001, respected restorer Simon Hadfield began the difficult task. Given that more than 30 years had elapsed, it was truly remarkable how much of the original car had survived. Romani had even found the cockpit surround with Jochen Rindt's name written on it next to the car. However, in a bizarre twist of fate, he at one stage arranged to meet someone to show them the surround and, while it was stored overnight in his car it was stolen and has never been found. At the time of writing the car was still under restoration.

Debut:	Spanish GP, 1970
Final race:	Austrian GP, 1970
Race starts:	8
Grand Prix starts:	6
Race wins:	4
Grand Prix wins:	4
Other notes:	Currently being rebuilt

The Racing Record of Chassis 72/2

Year	Date	Event	Circuit	Spec	No.	Driver	Race	Notes	Practice
1970	19-Apr	Spanish Grand Prix	Jarama	72	3	J. Rindt	Retired	Engine	8th
1970	26-Apr	International Trophy (NC)	Silverstone	72	8	J. Rindt	Retired	5th Heat 2	18th
1970	07-Jun	Belgian Grand Prix	Spa-Francorchamps	72C	22	A. Soler-Roig	Insufficient number laps	DNQ	-
1970	21-Jun	Dutch Grand Prix	Zandvoort	72C	10	J. Rindt	1st		1st
1970	05-Jul	French Grand Prix	Clermont-Ferrand	72C	6	J. Rindt	1st		6th
1970	19-Jul	British Grand Prix	Brands Hatch	72C	5	J. Rindt	1st		1st
1970	02-Aug	German Grand Prix	Hockenheim	72C	2	J. Rindt	1st		2nd
1970	16-Aug	Austrian Grand Prix	Österreichring	72C	6	J. Rindt	Retired	Engine after 22 laps	1st
1970	22-Aug	Gold Cup (NC)	Oulton Park	72C	2	J. Rindt	2nd		10th
1970	06-Sep	Italian Grand Prix	Monza	72C	22	J. Rindt	DNS	Fatal accident	-

This is probably the longest-serving and hardest-worked Lotus 72 of all, starting its competition life in 1970 and still being raced to great effect at the end of the 1975 season. This was the first to be built from new to 72C specification with reduced levels of anti-dive and anti-squat and a stronger monocoque. It was given to John Miles to drive and he raced it in Germany and Austria (where he had a front brake shaft fail but luckily managed to keep the car on the track). After the tragic weekend of the Italian Grand Prix, Miles was dropped and replaced by Reine Wisell, who took the wheel for the US and Mexican rounds. Wisell was then the regular driver of this chassis until mid-way through the 1971 season, when it was – unbeknown to the Swede – sold to the United Tobacco Company of South Africa for Dave Charlton to drive. The South African Champion had been looking for a replacement for his ageing Lotus 49C and the 72 fitted the bill perfectly. Just after the Monaco Grand Prix of that year, it had been converted to 72D specification, with twin parallel links at the rear.

After a very brief appearance in that year's British Grand Prix with Charlton at the wheel, 72/3 was thoroughly rebuilt, including the replacement of the 18swg side skins with 16swg ones in order to conform to the 1972 FIA regulations. It was then shipped back to South Africa, where it became the car to beat. He ran out an easy victor in the 1971 title race, scoring three wins, a fourth and one retirement from his five races with the car. This dominance became absolute in 1972, when Charlton either won races

or retired, scoring nine victories and two retirements from 11 race starts to become South African Drivers Champion for the third successive year. A venture to Europe to take in the French, British and German Grand Prix was less successful, with one DNQ, two lowly grid positions and two retirements to show for his efforts.

In 1973, as was the case in the World Championship, the 72 was still the car to beat, Charlton winning 10 out of 12 rounds. For 1974, the wily Charlton replaced his ageing steed with another state-of-the-art machine, a McLaren M23. Chassis 72/3 was then loaned to Alex Blignaut, who put his star driver Eddie Keizan in the cockpit, funded by sponsorship from another UTC cigarette brand, Embassy. He had a moderately successful year, ending up fifth in the Championship. The car was then returned to Charlton and moth-balled until, towards the end of the 1975 season, Guy Tunmer had a huge accident in the Gunston team's 72/7, badly damaging it, and needed a replacement car, quickly. Charlton offered 72/3 and a deal was done. The Team Gunston mechanics stripped the car down to the bare tub and then rebuilt it to 72E specification, using the spare parts they had and what was salvageable from the wreck of 72/7. This is why the car is found today with deformable structure panels. Tunmer contested the last three rounds of the Championship, without much in the way of results, although he did put the cat among the pigeons by placing it second on the grid at Roy Hesketh and finished second in the final non-Championship race at Donnybrook.

At the end of that season, the SADC switched to Formula Atlantic cars, making all the Formula 1 machinery in South Africa obsolete virtually overnight. Chassis 72/3 was retired to Rembrandt Tobacco's Heidelberg Motor Museum, where it remained until 1982, when it was mistakenly shipped to the English collector David McLaughlin instead of 72/6 (see page 225). It was then sent back to South Africa where it remained until 1989 when it was brought out of the country by John Brannigan and, via Rob Grant, found its way to the UK. After a rather perfunctory re-spray to put it back into Gold Leaf Team Lotus colours, the car failed to sell at auction and was later acquired by Michael Schryver, who had it fully restored by Simon Hadfield (see next page).

The car made its post-restoration debut in the HSCC Superprix in June 1993 and continued to compete regularly in historic races until the end of 1998, with Michael winning the TGP Championship in 1996. Appropriately, it returned to South Africa with the TGP group for a non-Championship race in October 1998, where Dave Charlton did a number of demonstration laps at Kyalami. In early 1999 Schryver sold the car to a Japanese collector by the name of Fakuda, in whose ownership the car remains today.

Debut:	German GP, 1970
Final race:	Rhodesian Grand Prix, 1975
Race starts:	59
Grand Prix starts:	14
Race wins:	22
Grand Prix wins:	0
Other notes:	

The Racing Record of Chassis 72/3

Year	Date	Event	Circuit	Spec	No.	Driver	Race	Notes	Practice
1970	02-Aug	German Grand Prix	Hockenheim	72C	16	J. Miles	Retired	Engine after 25 laps	10th
1970	16-Aug	Austrian Grand Prix	Österreichring	72C	7	J. Miles	Retired	Broken front brake-shaft	10th
1970	06-Sep	Italian Grand Prix	Monza	72C	24	J. Miles	DNS	Withdrawn	-
1970	04-Oct	United States Grand Prix	Watkins Glen	72C	23	R. Wisell	3rd		9th
1970	25-Oct	Mexican Grand Prix	Autodromo Ricardo Rodriguez	72C	23	R. Wisell	10th		12th
1971	24-Jan	Argentine Grand Prix (NC)	Buenos Aires Autodrome	72C	4	R. Wisell	7th	Not running at finish accident in Heat 2	3rd
1971	06-Mar	South African Grand Prix	Kyalami	72C	3	R. Wisell	4th		14th
1971	21-Mar	Race of Champions (NC)	Brands Hatch	72C	7	R. Wisell	Retired	Engine	8th
1971	28-Mar	Questor Grand Prix (NC)	Ontario Motor Speedway	72C	3	R. Wisell	Retired	Ignition	11th
1971	18-Apr	Spanish Grand Prix	Montjuich Park	72C	3	R. Wisell	12th		16th
1971	08-May	International Trophy (NC)	Silverstone	72C	3	R. Wisell	Retired	Engine	22nd
1971	23-May	Monaco Grand Prix	Monte Carlo	72C	2	R. Wisell	Retired	Collapsed hub bearing	12th
1971	13-Jun	Jochen Rindt Memorial Trophy (NC)	Hockenheim	72D	8	R. Wisell	10th		3rd
1971	20-Jun	Dutch Grand Prix	Zandvoort	72D	14	R. Wisell	Retired	Disqualified for reversing into pits	6th
1971	04-Jul	French Grand Prix	Paul Ricard	72D	2	R. Wisell	6th		15th
1971	17-Jul	British Grand Prix	Silverstone	72D	2	D. Charlton	Retired	Engine	13th
1971	07-Aug	25th Anniversary Trophy (SA)	Kyalami	72D	1	D. Charlton	1st		1st
1971	28-Aug	False Bay 100 (SA)	Killarney	72D	1	D. Charlton	Retired	Engine - broken valve	1st
1971	19-Sep	Rhodesian Grand Prix (SA)	Bulawayo	72D	1	D. Charlton	4th		4th
1971	09-Oct	Rand Spring Trophy (SA)	Kyalami	72D	1	D. Charlton	1st		1st

continued over page

Chassis 72/3

continued from previous page

Year	Date	Event	Circuit	Spec	No.	Driver	Race	Notes	Practice
1971	23-Oct	Welkom 100 (SA)	Goldfields	72D	1	D. Charlton	1st		2nd
1972	08-Jan	Cape South Easter Trophy (SA)	Killarney	72D	1	D. Charlton	1st		1st
1972	29-Jan	Highveld 100 (SA)	Kyalami	72D	1	D. Charlton	1st		1st
1972	04-Mar	South African Grand Prix	Kyalami	72D	26	D. Charlton	Retired	No fuel pressure	17th
1972	03-Apr	Coronation 100 (SA)	Pietermaritzburg	72D	1	D. Charlton	1st		1st
1972	22-Apr	Goldfields Autumn Trophy (SA)	Welkom	72D	1	D. Charlton	Retired	Spin, unable to restart	3rd
1972	14-May	Bulawayo 100 (SA - NC)	Bulawayo	72D	1	D. Charlton	1st		1st
1972	03-Jun	South Africa Republic Festival Trophy (SA)	Kyalami	72D	1	D. Charlton	1st		1st
1972	02-Jul	French Grand Prix	Clermont-Ferrand	72D	29	D. Charlton	-	Driver sick	DNQ
1972	15-Jul	British Grand Prix	Brands Hatch	72D	29	D. Charlton	Retired	Gearbox	24th
1972	30-Jul	German Grand Prix	Nürburgring	72D	29	D. Charlton	Retired	Driver sick	26th
1972	05-Aug	Rand Winter Trophy (SA)	Kyalami	72D	1	D. Charlton	1st		1st
1972	26-Aug	Van Riebeck Trophy (SA)	Killarney	72D	1	D. Charlton	1st		1st
1972	10-Sep	Rhodesian Grand Prix (SA)	Bulawayo	72D	1	D. Charlton	Retired	Broken rear upright	1st
1972	30-Sep	Rand Spring Trophy (SA)	Kyalami	72D	1	D. Charlton	1st		1st
1972	21-Oct	Welkom 100 (SA)	Goldfields	72D	1	D. Charlton	1st		1st
1973	06-Jan	Cape South Easter Trophy (SA)	Killarney	72D	1	D. Charlton	1st		1st
1973	27-Jan	Highveld 100 (SA)	Kyalami	72D	1	D. Charlton	1st		1st
1973	03-Mar	South African Grand Prix	Kyalami	72D	25	D. Charlton	Retired	Accident	13th
1973	31-Mar	Goldfields Autumn Trophy (SA)	Welkom	72D	1	D. Charlton	1st		1st
1973	23-Apr	Mercury 100 (SA)	Pietermaritzburg	72D	1	D. Charlton	1st		1st
1973	26-May	South Africa Republic Festival Trophy (SA)	Kyalami	72D	1	D. Charlton	1st		1st
1973	10-Jun	Bulawayo 100 (SA)	Bulawayo	72D	1	D. Charlton	4th	Pitted for new front tyres	1st
1973	01-Jul	Natal Winter Trophy (SA)	Pietermaritzburg	72D	1	D. Charlton	1st		2nd
1973	04-Aug	Rand Winter Trophy (SA)	Kyalami	72D	1	D. Charlton	1st		1st
1973	25-Aug	False Bay 100 (SA)	Killarney	72D	1	D. Charlton	1st		11th
1973	23-Sep	Rhodesian Grand Prix (SA)	Bulawayo	72D	1	D. Charlton	1st		1st
1973	06-Oct	Rand Spring Trophy (SA)	Kyalami	72D	1	D. Charlton	1st		1st
1973	20-Oct	Goldfields 100 (SA)	Welkom	72D	1	D. Charlton	Retired	Fuel pressure	1st
1974	04-May	Cape South Easter Trophy (SA)	Killarney	72E	2	E. Keizan	DNS	Crashed on warm-up lap	2nd
1974	25-May	South Africa Republic Trophy (SA)	Kyalami	72E	2	E. Keizan	2nd		3rd
1974	15-Jun	Brandkop Winter Trophy (SA)	Brandkop	72E	2	E. Keizan	2nd		1st
1974	30-Jun	Bulawayo 100 (SA)	Bulawayo	72E	2	E. Keizan	2nd		3rd
1974	13-Jul	Natal Winter Trophy (SA)	Pietermaritzburg	72E	2	E. Keizan	3rd		3rd
1974	10-Aug	Rand Winter Trophy (SA)	Kyalami	72E	2	E. Keizan	Retired	Engine	3rd
1974	31-Aug	False Bay 100 (SA)	Killarney	72E	2	E. Keizan	Retired	Gearbox	2nd
1974	15-Sep	Rhodesian Grand Prix (SA)	Donnybrook	72E	2	E. Keizan	Retired	Suspension	n/a
1974	28-Sep	Rand Spring Trophy (SA)	Kyalami	72E	2	E. Keizan	7th	Not running at finish, engine	4th
1974	19-Oct	Goldfields 100 (SA)	Welkom	72E	2	E. Keizan	DNS	Engine failure	-
1975	26-Jul	Rand Winter Trophy (SA)	Kyalami	72E	6	G. Tunmer	Retired		12th
1975	01-Sep	Natal Spring Trophy (SA)	Pietermaritzburg	72E	6	G. Tunmer	8th	NR at finish, accident	2nd
1975	04-Oct	Rand Spring Trophy (SA)	Kyalami	72E	6	G. Tunmer	3rd		4th
1975	26-Oct	Donnybrook 100 (SA, NC)	Donnybrook	72E	6	G. Tunmer	2nd		n/a

This was the long-awaited replacement for Rob Walker's venerable Lotus 49. By mid-way through 1970, the 49 was becoming such an uncompetitive proposition (in the hands of Graham Hill, at least – Fittipaldi managed to score points in one as late as Germany 1970) that Walker and his team actually skipped the Austrian Grand Prix, preferring to wait for their 72. The car was delivered much later in the season than anticipated due to the tremendous amount of redesigning required to be carried out on the initial concept. It was not until a new car (72/3) was built for Team Lotus number two driver John Miles in time for the German Grand Prix that the team could consider producing a customer car. Even this was a re-hash of the prototype chassis, 72/1, although in reality it required such a fundamental rebuild to bring it up to 72C specification that virtually nothing of the original monocoque was carried over bar the seat-back and rear bulkhead.

The car first appeared at the Oulton Park Gold Cup meeting and its debut was distinctly inauspicious, ending in an early retirement. In fact, the car was never classified in any of the races in which it competed, only finishing in one, the Canadian Grand Prix, but 23 laps down. After being withdrawn in the wake of Rindt's practice crash at Monza, the Walker car was the sole Lotus in Canada, competing with solid brake shafts as a precaution against further breakages. Its final two outings in the US and Mexican Grand Prix were equally dismal, both ending in retirement.

At the end of the 1970 season, Rob Walker threw in his lot (including sponsor Brooke Bond Oxo) with John Surtees and the 72 was deemed (probably rather foolishly in retrospect) to be surplus to the team's requirements. In August 1971 it was sold to Jo Siffert, who was rumoured to have a number of willing rent-a-drivers lined up to take part in various races that season but somehow none of the deals came off. Following the tragic death of the popular Swiss driver in October 1971, the car remained in the ownership of the Siffert family until November 1972, when it was acquired by Emerson and Wilson Fittipaldi for their expanding racing car collection. It briefly returned to the Team Lotus workshops at Hethel, where it was repainted and rebuilt using parts that made it look externally as close as possible to Emerson's World Championship-winning car.

In 1985, Adrian Hamilton acquired most of the cars in the Fittipaldi collection, including 72/4, which he sold on to computer-leasing magnate and owner of Brands Hatch group, John Foulston. By this time the car was in a pretty poor state and Foulston had to spend a considerable sum of money to get it running again, which he did. His wife Mary drove the car in several historic races before his death in a testing accident in 1987. The car was maintained for the next ten years as part of the family's collection. In December 1997, it was put forward for auction but did not sell despite a bid of £110,000 and today remains in the family's ownership **(see below)**.

Debut:	Gold Cup, Oulton Park, 1970
Final race:	Mexican Grand Prix, 1970
Race starts:	4
Grand Prix starts:	3
Race wins:	0
Grand Prix wins:	0
Other notes:	Derived from prototype 72 chassis, 72/1

The Racing Record of Chassis 72/4

Year	Date	Event	Circuit	Spec	No	Driver	Race	Notes	Practice
1970	22-Aug	Gold Cup (NC)	Oulton Park	72C	3	G. Hill	Retired	Low oil pressure	12th
1970	06-Sep	Italian Grand Prix	Monza	72C	28	G. Hill	DNS	Withdrawn	-
1970	20-Sep	Canadian Grand Prix	Mont Tremblant/St.Jovite	72C	9	G. Hill	NC	Still running but -23 laps	20th
1970	04-Oct	United States Grand Prix	Watkins Glen	72C	14	G. Hill	Retired	Clutch	10th
1970	25-Oct	Mexican Grand Prix	Autodromo Ricardo Rodriguez	72C	14	G. Hill	Retired	Overheating	8th

This is a car inextricably linked with the career of Emerson Fittipaldi, since he was the first and last person to drive it in its original incarnation. In late 1973 the car was rebuilt around a largely new tub and thereafter driven almost exclusively by Ickx.

Chassis 72/5 was built from new to 72C specification. It made its debut at the tragic Italian Grand Prix meeting at Monza in September 1970 and was due to be taken over by Jochen Rindt after being run-in by Fittipaldi on the first day of practice, Friday. However, the Brazilian new-boy had a big accident at the Parabolica due to leaving his braking too late, which saw him end up in the trees, thankfully unharmed. The mechanics were still working on the car trying to get it race-worthy on the Saturday afternoon when Rindt had his accident.

Gold Leaf Team Lotus skipped the next race, the Canadian Grand Prix, but 72/5 was repaired in time for the US Grand Prix, almost a month after Monza. What a debut it turned out to be, for Fittipaldi won the race, albeit somewhat fortuitously, safeguarding Rindt's World Championship title. The final race of 1970 in Mexico was an anti-climax by comparison, ending in retirement on the first lap.

The 1971 season was a disaster, with a string of retirements in the first part of the season and the car way off the pace. Modifications for the Monaco Grand Prix were enough for the car to be given a new designation of 72D. The performance of the car in its new spec augured well for the rest of the season but then Fittipaldi had a severe road accident which forced him to miss several races. Trimmer and Walker drove the car at Hockenheim and then Walker blotted his copybook by damaging the chassis beyond immediate repair when he crashed while practising for the Dutch Grand Prix. Emmo was back for the French race and drove to a great third place from a lowly grid position, the first sign of an improvement in form. A string of good grid positions followed, plus several good finishes, indicating that the car and team would be one to watch in 1972.

With the team's new black-and-gold colour scheme and a revised airbox, 72/5 looked even more purposeful than before. A dream start when Emerson was leading the season-opening Argentine Grand Prix was spoilt when the rear suspension broke. A second place followed in the South African Grand Prix and then Emerson scored his and the car's second victory in the non-Championship Race of Champions. His team-mate Dave Walker then took over 72/5 for the Spanish and Monaco Grand Prix rounds, qualifying and finishing down the order but Fittipaldi was back behind the wheel of his faithful favourite to score a second and a win in two non-Championship races at Oulton Park and Vallelunga. With 72/7 now his regular car, 72/5 was relegated to the role of spare until the Austrian Grand

Prix in mid-August, where the Brazilian scored a significant win from pole to put him in a strong position for the Championship. Before that, there was the lucrative business of the Rothmans 50,000 Formula Libre race (with a first prize of £50,000 to the winner) to be dealt with and 72/5 came up trumps once again, carrying Emerson to victory.

Its finest hour was probably in the Italian Grand Prix of that year. When 72/7 was damaged beyond repair in an accident on the way to the race, 72/5 (which had been kept just across the border in case of any legal difficulties with the Italian authorities arising from Rindt's 1970 crash) was pressed into service once more. It did not let him down, and Fittipaldi drove into the record books as the youngest-ever World Champion. The car was the spare in Canada, and then retired from the US Grand Prix in a somewhat ignominious end to a tremendous season.

The introduction of mandatory deformable structures was scheduled for part-way through the 1973 season. While Fittipaldi took 72/7 as his race car to the 'fly-away' races in Argentina, Brazil and South Africa, 72/5 was readied as the first of the deformable structure cars, along with the other spare, 72/6, for Ronnie Peterson. Re-designated 72E to reflect the modifications made, it was driven by the Brazilian in the Race of Champions and the International Trophy, retiring in both races. Although he had the now-deformable structure 72/7 at his disposal for the Spanish Grand Prix, Emerson chose to stick with 72/5 and scored a historic 50th Grand Prix victory for Lotus (see right). For Belgium, Monaco and Sweden, 72/5 was relegated to the role of spare again but returned for the French Grand Prix, where it was eliminated in a collision with the newly emerging star of Formula 1, Jody Scheckter. It was rebuilt in time for the British Grand Prix, where Fittipaldi was forced to retire.

In practice for the Dutch Grand Prix, the left front wheel collapsed and Fittipaldi crashed at high speed, severely damaging the car. Miraculously, he suffered only heavy bruising and no broken bones but the team was left with a substantial rebuild to undertake.

The replacement tub incorporated salvageable parts such as the rear bulkhead and engine mounts onto which were fitted the surviving ancillary components. Some of the discarded parts can still be found languishing in the Classic Team Lotus store-room. The rebuilt 72/5 made its debut in the hands of new signing Jacky Ickx in the 1974 Argentine Grand Prix but retired. An encouraging third place in Brazil was followed by a morale-boosting wet-weather victory for the Rainmaster in the Race of Champions but this was to be the high point of a year blighted by the problems associated with the development of the 76, the 72's intended replacement. A third place in the British Grand Prix was

Debut:	Italian Grand Prix, 1970 (DNS)
Final race:	US Grand Prix, 1975
Race starts:	45
Grand Prix starts:	43
Race wins:	8
Grand Prix wins:	4
Other notes:	Substantial rebuild after '73 Dutch GP practice crash

the best result in a year which culminated with a lowly 13th place in Canada and a crash in the final round, the US Grand Prix at Watkins Glen.

By 1975, the Lotus 72 in any of its various forms was past its sell-by date and 72/5 was no exception. For most races, Ickx languished towards the back of the grid in the car and struggled to achieve a decent result. Several modifications were tried throughout the year, starting with the Race of Champions, where steel cable replaced the solid steel links from the torsion bars to the suspension at the rear. After the sister car experienced a broken cable in practice, the car reverted to standard set-up for the race but the fitting was perfected in time for the International Trophy and it ran in this format until the British Grand Prix.

Rising Formula Atlantic star Jim Crawford was given a one-off outing in 72/5 for the International Trophy but managed to shunt it and damage it beyond repair for that weekend's race, having already crashed the car heavily in private testing the week prior to the race when a rear tyre came off an experimentally-wide rim. Ickx drove 72/5 in six more Grand Prix before departing from the team by mutual agreement. For the French Grand Prix, the chassis was given a 5-inch longer wheelbase by virtue of placing an oil tank between the rear bulkhead and the engine. These modifications were considered sufficiently significant for the chassis type to be re-designated 72F.

Following Ickx's departure, 72/5 was used to give opportunities to young British talent – something of a

poisoned chalice for those concerned given its lack of competitiveness. Brian Henton drove it into the sleepers in the rain-hit British Grand Prix at Silverstone, while Crawford had another chance in the car at Monza in the Italian Grand Prix. Finally, Henton gave it a swansong in the US Grand Prix, coming home 12th and ending a career which had started five years before with victory in the very same race.

Since then, the car has been in the ownership of the Chapman family. It was restored during 2000 and 2001 from the tub up by Classic Team Lotus, with original Chief Mechanic Eddie Dennis heading up the team and made its return to racing at the 2001 Silverstone International Historic Festival **(see next page)**.

The Racing Record of Chassis 72/5

Year	Date	Event	Circuit	Spec	No.	Driver	Race	Notes	Practice
1970	06-Sep	Italian Grand Prix	Monza	72C	26	E. Fittipaldi	DNS	Practice accident	-
1970	04-Oct	United States Grand Prix	Watkins Glen	72C	24	E. Fittipaldi	1st		3rd
1970	25-Oct	Mexican Grand Prix	Autodromo Ricardo Rodriguez	72C	24	E. Fittipaldi	Retired	Engine on lap 1	18th
1971	24-Jan	Argentine Grand Prix (NC)	Buenos Aires Autodrome	72C	2	E. Fittipaldi	Retired	No oil pressure, withdrawn from Heat 2	4th
1971	06-Mar	South African Grand Prix	Kyalami	72C	2	E. Fittipaldi	Retired	Engine	5th
1971	21-Mar	Race of Champions (NC)	Brands Hatch	72C	8	T. Trimmer	Retired	Electrical fuel pump	14th
1971	28-Mar	Questor Grand Prix (NC)	Ontario Motor Speedway	72C	2	E. Fittipaldi	Retired	Throttle problems	9th
1971	09-Apr	Rothmans International Trophy (NC)	Oulton Park	72C	10	E. Fittipaldi	7th	13 laps down after stop to repair transistor box	7th
1971	18-Apr	Spanish Grand Prix	Montjuich Park	72C	2	E. Fittipaldi	Retired	Broken rear suspension cross member	14th
1971	23-May	Monaco Grand Prix	Monte Carlo	72D	1	E. Fittipaldi	5th		17th
1971	13-Jun	Jochen Rindt Memorial Trophy (NC)	Hockenheim	72D	7	D. Walker	9th		11th
1971	20-Jun	Dutch Grand Prix	Zandvoort	72D	12	D. Walker	DNS	Accident in Friday practice - car damaged beyond repair	-
1971	04-Jul	French Grand Prix	Paul Ricard	72D	1	E. Fittipaldi	3rd		17th
1971	17-Jul	British Grand Prix	Silverstone	72D	1	E. Fittipaldi	3rd		4th
1971	01-Aug	German Grand Prix	Nürburgring	72D	8	E. Fittipaldi	Retired	Loss of oil	8th
1971	15-Aug	Austrian Grand Prix	Österreichring	72D	2	E. Fittipaldi	2nd		6th
1971	19-Sep	Canadian Grand Prix	Mosport Park	72D	2	E. Fittipaldi	7th		4th
1971	03-Oct	United States Grand Prix	Watkins Glen	72D	2	E. Fittipaldi	19th	10 laps down	2nd
1971	24-Oct	Rothmans Victory Race (NC)	Brands Hatch	72D	8	E. Fittipaldi	2nd		3rd
1972	23-Jan	Argentine Grand Prix	Buenos Aires Autodrome	72D	11	E. Fittipaldi	Retired	Rear suspension failure	5th
1972	04-Mar	South African Grand Prix	Kyalami	72D	8	E. Fittipaldi	2nd		3rd
1972	19-Mar	Race of Champions (NC)	Brands Hatch	72D	57	E. Fittipaldi	1st		1st
1972	01-May	Spanish Grand Prix	Jarama	72D	21	D. Walker	9th	Not running at finish - ran out of petrol	24th
1972	14-May	Monaco Grand Prix	Monte Carlo	72D	9	D. Walker	14th		14th
1972	29-May	Rothmans International Gold Cup (NC)	Oulton Park	72D	44	E. Fittipaldi	2nd		3rd
1972	04-Jun	Belgian Grand Prix	Nivelles	72D	32T	E. Fittipaldi	-	Spare	-
1972	18-Jun	Gran Premio d'ella Republica Italiana (NC)	Vallelunga	72D	1	E. Fittipaldi	1st		1st
1972	02-Jul	French Grand Prix	Clermont-Ferrand	72D	1T	E. Fittipaldi	-	Spare	-
1972	15-Jul	British Grand Prix	Brands Hatch	72D	40	E. Fittipaldi	-	Spare	-
1972	30-Jul	German Grand Prix	Nürburgring	72D	2T	E. Fittipaldi	-	Spare	-
1972	13-Aug	Austrian Grand Prix	Österreichring	72D	31	E. Fittipaldi	1st		1st

continued over page

continued from previous page

Year	Date	Event	Circuit	Spec	No.	Driver	Race	Notes	Practice
1972	28-Aug	Rothmans 50,000 (NC)	Brands Hatch	72D	5	E. Fittipaldi	1st		1st
1972	10-Sep	Italian Grand Prix	Monza	72D	6	E. Fittipaldi	1st		6th
1972	24-Sep	Canadian Grand Prix	Mosport Park	72D	5T	E. Fittipaldi	-	Spare	-
1972	08-Oct	United States Grand Prix	Watkins Glen	72D	10	E. Fittipaldi	Retired	Rear-end vibration, shredded tyres	9th
1973	18-Mar	Race of Champions (NC)	Brands Hatch	72E	64	E. Fittipaldi	Retired	Metering unit	7th
1973	08-Apr	International Trophy (NC)	Silverstone	72E	1	E. Fittipaldi	Retired	Broken flywheel	1st
1973	29-Apr	Spanish Grand Prix	Montjuich Park	72E	1	E. Fittipaldi	1st		7th
1973	20-May	Belgian Grand Prix	Zolder	72E	1T	E. Fittipaldi	-	Spare	-
1973	03-Jun	Monaco Grand Prix	Monte Carlo	72E	1T	E. Fittipaldi	-	Spare	-
1973	17-Jun	Swedish Grand Prix	Anderstorp	72E	1T	E. Fittipaldi	-	Spare	-
1973	01-Jul	French Grand Prix	Paul Ricard	72E	1	E. Fittipaldi	Retired	Accident	3rd
1973	14-Jul	British Grand Prix	Silverstone	72E	1	E. Fittipaldi	Retired	Drive-shaft failure	5th
1973	29-Jul	Dutch Grand Prix	Zandvoort	72E	1	E. Fittipaldi	-	Badly damaged in practice accident	-
1974	13-Jan	Argentine Grand Prix	Buenos Aires Autodrome	72E	2	J. Ickx	Retired	Transmission	7th
1974	27-Jan	Brazilian Grand Prix	Interlagos	72E	2	J. Ickx	3rd		5th
1974	17-Mar	Race of Champions (NC)	Brands Hatch	72E	2	J. Ickx	1st		11th
1974	26-May	Monaco Grand Prix	Monte Carlo	72E	2	J. Ickx	Retired	Gearbox	19th
1974	09-Jun	Swedish Grand Prix	Anderstorp	72E	2	J. Ickx	Retired	Oil pressure	7th
1974	23-Jun	Dutch Grand Prix	Zandvoort	72E	2	J. Ickx	9th		18th
1974	07-Jul	French Grand Prix	Dijon	72E	2	J. Ickx	5th		13th
1974	20-Jul	British Grand Prix	Brands Hatch	72E	2	J. Ickx	3rd		12th
1974	04-Aug	German Grand Prix	Nurburgring	72E	2	J. Ickx	5th		9th
1974	18-Aug	Austrian Grand Prix	Osterreichring	72E	2	J. Ickx	-	Spare	-
1974	22-Sep	Canadian Grand Prix	Mosport Park	72E	2	J. Ickx	13th		21st
1974	06-Oct	United States Grand Prix	Watkins Glen	72E	2	J. Ickx	Retired	Accident	16th
1975	12-Jan	Argentine Grand Prix	Buenos Aires Autodrome	72E	6	J. Ickx	8th		18th
1975	26-Jan	Brazilian Grand Prix	Interlagos	72E	6	J. Ickx	9th		12th
1975	01-Mar	South African Grand Prix	Kyalami	72E	6	J. Ickx	12th		21st
1975	16-Mar	Race of Champions (NC)	Brands Hatch	72E	6	J. Ickx	4th		4th
1975	12-Apr	International Trophy (NC)	Silverstone	72E	6	J. Crawford	DNS	Accident in practice, car too badly damaged to race	20th
1975	27-Apr	Spanish Grand Prix	Montjuich Park	72E	6	J. Ickx	2nd		16th
1975	11-May	Monaco Grand Prix	Monte Carlo	72E	6	J. Ickx	8th		14th
1975	25-May	Belgian Grand Prix	Zolder	72E	6	J. Ickx	Retired	Front brake-shaft failure	16th
1975	08-Jun	Swedish Grand Prix	Anderstorp	72E	6	J. Ickx	15th		18th
1975	22-Jun	Dutch Grand Prix	Zandvoort	72E	6	J. Ickx	Retired	Engine	21st
1975	06-Jul	French Grand Prix	Paul Ricard	72F	6	J. Ickx	Retired	Broken brake-shaft joint	19th
1975	19-Jul	British Grand Prix	Silverstone	72F	15	B. Henton	16th		21st
1975	07-Sep	Italian Grand Prix	Monza	72F	6	J. Crawford	13th		25th
1975	05-Oct	United States Grand Prix	Watkins Glen	72F	6	B. Henton	12th		19th

uilt new to 72D specification mid-way through 1971, this car was constructed to replace 72/3 as the regular chassis for Reine Wisell and made its debut at that year's German Grand Prix. For 1972, it was repainted in the striking black-and-gold livery of sponsor John Player Special and became the regular car of number two driver, Dave Walker. The gritty Australian made ten starts in it, half of which ended in retirement, a not uncommon occurrence for Lotus number two's. His only major accident in the car came in practice for the International Trophy. Otherwise, he qualified well down the order and his best result was a fifth in the non-Championship Brazilian Grand Prix. For the last two races of 1972, in Canada and the United States, Wisell was back behind the wheel but he fared little better, qualifying poorly and posting a retirement and a lowly finish.

For 1973, 72/6 was updated to 72E specification, with the deformable structures around the tub. With a new car (72/8) having been built for new team driver Ronnie Peterson, 72/6 was initially relegated to the role of the Swede's spare but he must have expressed a preference for it because from the Swedish Grand Prix onward it became his regular race car. The work to convert 72/6 to deformable structure specification was completed back at the factory (the same was done to 72/5) while the race team were competing in Argentina, Brazil and South Africa in the first three World Championship rounds.

The car made its first appearance in its new guise at the Race of Champions, where Peterson retired with gearbox failure. On its next appearance at the International Trophy meeting, he shunted the car so badly that it could not be repaired in time for the race. It was repaired in time to be taken to the Belgian Grand Prix as a spare but was pressed into service for the race after Peterson crashed both 72/8

and 72/6 in the warm-up, the latter being the easiest to repair in the time available. To end a disastrous weekend, SuperSwede crashed the car once again in the race. However, things really started to come together after this, Ronnie finishing third at Monaco to score his first Grand Prix podium for the team. Thereafter, if the car lasted to the finish, he was never out of the top two, scoring victories in France, Austria, Italy and the United States and coming home second in Sweden and Britain.

At the end of 1973, 72/6 and 72/7 were sold by Team Lotus to Team Gunston in South Africa, to be driven in the South African Drivers' Championship. The driver for 72/6 was Ian Scheckter, younger brother of Jody. After a steady drive to 13th in his first outing in the car at the South African Grand Prix, Scheckter really got into the groove, scoring four pole positions and five wins, ending the season with a run of four straight victories. However, arch-rival Charlton had started the season with a run of five straight wins and took another mid-season, so Scheckter finished the year as Championship runner-up. The car had proved both fast and reliable, only failing to finish twice, and Scheckter had showed himself to be an extremely quick and competent driver.

Scheckter moved to Lexington Racing for 1975 and his place driving 72/6 for Team Gunston was taken by Eddie Keizan. Although he never qualified outside the top four in the South African Drivers' Championship races, Keizan's season was blighted by retirements. The year was just about summed up by the final race of the year (and, indeed the car's last-ever race), when he broke a driveshaft on the warming-up lap. When he did finish, Keizan was always high up the order. His best result was a 2nd at the Roy Hesketh circuit in Pietermaritzburg but a win eluded him.

At the end of the 1975 season, the car became ineligible

for the South African Drivers' Championship, which was switching to Formula Atlantic rules, and so went to the Rembrandt Tobacco Company's museum at Heidelberg. It stayed there until 1982, when it was repatriated by the British collector David McLaughlin. He had found out about it in 1980 and called the museum every two months offering to buy it until they eventually accepted his offer. However, he got a shock when the car was shipped to the UK, for the museum had mistakenly sent 72/3, with race number 6 (Guy Tunmer's SADC race number in 1975, for this was the car he finished the season in), rather than chassis number 72/6! After McLaughlin refused to do a swap of chassis plates, the correct chassis was eventually sent to him and 72/3 returned to South Africa.

The car was race-prepared (rather than restored, as it was in good condition) and re-liveried in John Player Special colours (see next page). McLaughlin subsequently raced it regularly in historic races in the 1980s and early 1990s. The car still makes occasional appearances, both in FORCE Classic Grand Prix series races and other historic events such as the Goodwood Festival of Speed where it was driven by ex Lotus F1 driver Johnny Herbert, and the 2002 Monaco Grand Prix Historique, by Minardi Formula One driver Alex Yoong.

Debut:	German Grand Prix, 1971
Final race:	Donnybrook 100, 1975
Race starts:	50
Grand Prix starts:	26
Race wins:	9
Grand Prix wins:	4
Other notes:	

The Racing Record of Chassis 72/6

YYear	Date	Event	Circuit	Spec	No.	Driver	Race	Notes	Practice
1971	01-Aug	German Grand Prix	Nürburgring	72D	9	R. Wisell	8th		17th
1971	15-Aug	Austrian Grand Prix	Österreichring	72D	3	R. Wisell	4th		9th
1971	19-Sep	Canadian Grand Prix	Mosport Park	72D	3	R. Wisell	5th		7th
1971	03-Oct	United States Grand Prix	Watkins Glen	72D	3	R. Wisell	Retired	Accident	9th
1972	23-Jan	Argentine Grand Prix	Buenos Aires Autodrome	72D	12	D. Walker	Retired	Disqualified	21st
1972	04-Mar	South African Grand Prix	Kyalami	72D	9	D. Walker	10th		19th
1972	19-Mar	Race of Champions (NC)	Brands Hatch	72D	58	D. Walker	9th		10th
1972	30-Mar	Brazil Grand Prix (NC)	Interlagos	72D	2	D. Walker	5th		5th
1972	23-Apr	International Trophy (NC)	Silverstone	72D	2	D. Walker	DNS	Accident in practice	8th
1972	29-May	Gold Cup (NC)	Oulton Park	72D	45	D. Walker	Retired	Gearbox	4th
1972	04-Jun	Belgian Grand Prix	Nivelles	72D	33	D. Walker	14th		12th
1972	02-Jul	French Grand Prix	Clermont-Ferrand	72D	6	D. Walker	18th	NR at finish, gearbox/CWP	22nd
1972	15-Jul	British Grand Prix	Brands Hatch	72D	9	D. Walker	Retired	Suspension	15th

continued over page

Chassis 72/6

continued from previous page

Year	Date	Event	Circuit	Spec	No.	Driver	Race	Notes	Practice
1972	30-Jul	German Grand Prix	Nürburgring	72D	25	D. Walker	Retired	Split oil tank	23rd
1972	13-Aug	Austrian Grand Prix	Österreichring	72D	21	D. Walker	Retired	Engine	19th
1972	24-Sep	Canadian Grand Prix	Mosport Park	72D	6	R. Wisell	Retired	Engine	16th
1972	08-Oct	United States Grand Prix	Watkins Glen	72D	12	R. Wisell	10th		16th
1973	18-Mar	Race of Champions (NC)	Brands Hatch	72E	65	R. Peterson	Retired	Gearbox	6th
1973	08-Apr	International Trophy (NC)	Silverstone	72E	2	R. Peterson	-	Accident in pre-race testing	-
1973	20-May	Belgian Grand Prix	Zolder	72E	2	R. Peterson	Retired	Accident	1st
1973	03-Jun	Monaco Grand Prix	Monte Carlo	72E	2	R. Peterson	3rd		2nd
1973	17-Jun	Swedish Grand Prix	Anderstorp	72E	2	R. Peterson	2nd		1st
1973	01-Jul	French Grand Prix	Paul Ricard	72E	2	R. Peterson	1st		5th
1973	14-Jul	British Grand Prix	Silverstone	72E	2	R. Peterson	2nd		1st
1973	29-Jul	Dutch Grand Prix	Zandvoort	72E	2	R. Peterson	Retired	Engine/gearbox failure	1st
1973	04-Aug	German Grand Prix	Nürburgring	72E	2	R. Peterson	Retired	Distributor	2nd
1973	19-Aug	Austrian Grand Prix	Österreichring	72E	2	R. Peterson	1st		2nd
1973	09-Sep	Italian Grand Prix	Monza	72E	2	R. Peterson	1st		1st
1973	23-Sep	Canadian Grand Prix	Mosport Park	72E	2	R. Peterson	Retired	Puncture	1st
1973	07-Oct	United States Grand Prix	Watkins Glen	72E	2	R. Peterson	1st		1st
1974	30-Mar	South African Grand Prix	Kyalami	72E	29	I. Scheckter	13th		22nd
1974	13-Apr	Mercury 100 (SA)	Pietermaritzburg	72E	6	I. Scheckter	2nd		1st
1974	04-May	Cape South Easter Trophy (SA)	Killarney	72E	6	I. Scheckter	5th	NR at finish - transmission	13th
1974	25-May	South Africa Republic Trophy (SA)	Kyalami	72E	6	I. Scheckter	3rd		2nd
1974	15-Jun	Brandkop Winter Trophy (SA)	Brandkop	72E	6	I. Scheckter	3rd		4th
1974	30-Jun	Bulawayo 100 (SA, NC)	Bulawayo	72E	6	I. Scheckter	3rd		2nd
1974	13-Jul	Natal Winter Trophy (SA)	Pietermaritzburg	72E	6	I. Scheckter	1st		1st
1974	10-Aug	Rand Winter Trophy (SA)	Kyalami	72E	6	I. Scheckter	Retired	Fuel pressure valve	1st
1974	31-Aug	False Bay 100 (SA)	Killarney	72E	6	I. Scheckter	1st		3rd
1974	15-Sep	Rhodesian Grand Prix (SA, NC)	Donnybrook	72E	6	I. Scheckter	1st		n/a
1974	28-Sep	Rand Spring Trophy (SA)	Kyalami	72E	6	I. Scheckter	1st		1st
1974	19-Oct	Goldfields 100 (SA)	Welkom	72E	6	I. Scheckter	1st		2nd
1975	08-Feb	Cape South Easter Trophy (SA)	Killarney	72E	5	E. Keizan	Retired	Fuel pump	2nd
1975	01-Mar	South African Grand Prix	Kyalami	72E	33	E. Keizan	13th		22nd
1975	22-Mar	Goldfields 100 (SA)	Welkom	72E	5	E. Keizan	Retired	Sticking throttle	3rd
1975	29-Mar	Mercury 100 (SA)	Pietermaritzburg	72E	5	E. Keizan	3rd		3rd
1975	03-May	Brandkop Winter Trophy (SA)	Brandkop	72E	5	E. Keizan	Retired	Fuel pressure	3rd
1975	31-May	South Africa Republic Trophy (SA)	Kyalami	72E	5	E. Keizan	Retired	Puncture	3rd
1975	05-Jul	False Bay 100 (SA)	Killarney	72E	5	E. Keizan	4th	NR at finish, spun on last lap	4th
1975	26-Jul	Rand Winter Trophy (SA)	Kyalami	72E	5	E. Keizan	3rd		3rd
1975	01-Sep	Natal Spring Trophy (SA)	Pietermaritzburg	72E	5	E. Keizan	2nd		4th
1975	04-Oct	Rand Spring Trophy (SA)	Kyalami	72E	5	E. Keizan	DNS	Broken d/shaft, warm-up lap	3rd
1975	26-Oct	Donnybrook 100 (SA, NC)	Donnybrook	72E	5	E. Keizan	Retired	Blown engine	n/a

Constructed during the winter of 1971/72, chassis 72/7 was built new to 72D specification for Emerson Fittipaldi to use as his main race car during the 1972 season, taking over from 72/5 which he used in the first few races of the year. It made its first appearance at the non-Championship Brazilian Grand Prix in front of Fittipaldi's home crowd at Interlagos. Everything was going well and he was leading the race comfortably until the rear suspension failed with only a handful of laps to go, pitching the car into a lurid spin. Fortunately, Emerson didn't hit anything but his race was run. He experienced further suspension troubles in his next race with 72/7, the International Trophy. However, this time, luck was on his side and he ran out the winner after Mike Hailwood, who had passed Fittipaldi as a result of his handling problems, was forced to retire.

The Brazilian's winning streak continued into the next part of the Grand Prix season, with a popular victory at Jarama in the Spanish Grand Prix. A third place at Monaco was followed by another win in the Belgian Grand Prix, a second in France and then a sponsor- and team-pleasing triumph on 'home' (or adopted home, in the case of Fittipaldi) territory.

Things started to go slightly wrong from this point on, with a cracked gearbox casing causing a spectacular fire in the German Grand Prix, fortunately without significant damage to the car. Then, on the way to the Italian Grand Prix, 72/7 was badly damaged when the Team Lotus transporter overturned due to a tyre blow out on the Autostrada and could not be repaired in time for the race. Now the World Champion, following his victory in the Italian Grand Prix at the wheel of 72/5, Fittipaldi returned to the seat of 72/7 for the Canadian Grand Prix but endured a variety of problems in the race, including losing second and third gears and then having a nose fin rotate, which upset the handling. For the final race of the year, Dave Walker took over the car but retired after qualifying well down the order.

In 1973, 72/7 was again Fittipaldi's regular car, although he did have two short spells back in 72/5. He had made a superb start to the year, winning the Argentine and Brazilian Grand Prix and finishing third in South Africa. However, the car needed to be converted to comply with the new deformable structure regulations, which were being introduced at the Spanish Grand Prix, so Emerson drove 72/5 in the Race of Champions, International Trophy and Spanish Grand Prix.

Back in 72/7, now in 72E specification, a third and a second place in Belgium and Monaco kept him in the lead of the World Championship, but his title aspirations were dented by retirement in Sweden and then another retirement at the Dutch Grand Prix caused by the foot injuries he sustained in the practice crash which wrote off 72/5. A lowly grid position in Germany left him with a lot of work to do in the race and he could only manage one point for sixth. Another retirement in Austria when running well (see left) virtually ended his title hopes and these were finished when team-mate Peterson finished ahead of him in the Italian Grand Prix. Fittipaldi saw out the rest of the season at the wheel of 72/7, finishing second in Canada and sixth in the US Grand Prix.

In December 1973, 72/7 was sold to Team Gunston along with 72/6. Paddy Driver was the man nominated to get behind the wheel. After retiring from the South African Grand Prix, Driver started seven rounds of the South African Drivers' Championship plus two non-Championship races. He was consistent rather than blindingly fast, usually finishing third or fourth behind his team-mate Ian Scheckter and Dave Charlton and his best result was a second place in the season-closing Goldfields 100 at Kyalami.

For 1975, the rapid Guy Tunmer was recruited to drive 72/7. After a second place in the opening race of the South African Drivers' Championship, he finished 11th in his home Grand Prix. A second place at Welkom was followed by a retirement caused by a broken valve at Roy Hesketh. The team was suffering from an acute engine shortage, and this resulted in Tunmer having to switch to a Chevron Formula 2 car for the next race at Brandkop while the team awaited new DFVs. A third place at the end of May in the Republic Trophy at Kyalami was followed by a long-awaited first victory in the False Bay 100 at Killarney.

Just when things seemed to be coming good, disaster struck in practice for the Rand Winter Trophy at Kyalami, Tunmer crashing at high speed and damaging 72/7 beyond immediate repair. It was so bad that the decision was taken to send the tub back to Team Lotus in England rather than to try and effect a repair in South Africa. According to the Team Lotus invoice issued at the time, work carried out included the replacement of the side skins and undertray and also a duct panel. By the time the repaired tub was shipped back to South Africa, the season was long finished and the car was obsolete, since 1975 was the last year that Formula 1 cars were eligible to compete in the SADC. However, the tub was built up again into a complete car, using spares from the Team Gunston stores, since all the undamaged 72E components from 72/7 had been transplanted to 72/3.

Several ex-Gunston mechanics have contended that the car crashed was 72/6 and not 72/7, with one mechanic who stripped the car down after the accident stating that he personally removed the chassis plate prior to its return to

Debut:	Brazil Grand Prix, 1972
Final race:	False Bay 100, 1975
Race starts:	39
Grand Prix starts:	22
Race wins:	7
Grand Prix wins:	5
Other notes:	

Hethel and, indeed, he still possesses the plate today. However, detailed examination of photographic evidence which reveals individual characteristics specific to each car suggests this was not the case and that 72/6 was raced by Eddie Keizan right through to the end of the 1975 season, something which is also confirmed by Chief Mechanic

Eddie Pinto's engineering records. The only plausible explanation for the confusion is that the car that Tunmer crashed carried the chassis plate (which was mounted on the dash on these cars) for 72/6 but was actually 72/7, although nobody who worked for the team can provide an explanation as to how or why this might have occurred.

The car returned to take its place alongside 72/3 and 72/6 in Rembrandt Tobacco's Heidelberg Museum, where it remained until it was acquired in 1976 by a British collector, who retains ownership of the car today.

The Racing Record of Chassis 72/7

Year	Date	Event	Circuit	Spec	No.	Driver	Race	Notes	Practice
1972	30-Mar	Brazilian Grand Prix (NC)	Interlagos	72D	1	E. Fittipaldi	7th	NR suspension	1st
1972	23-Apr	International Trophy (NC)	Silverstone	72D	1	E. Fittipaldi	1st		1st
1972	01-May	Spanish Grand Prix	Jarama	72D	5	E. Fittipaldi	1st		3rd
1972	14-May	Monaco Grand Prix	Monte Carlo	72D	8	E. Fittipaldi	3rd		1st
1972	04-Jun	Belgian Grand Prix	Nivelles	72D	32	E. Fittipaldi	1st		1st
1972	02-Jul	French Grand Prix	Clermont-Ferrand	72D	1	E. Fittipaldi	2nd		8th
1972	15-Jul	British Grand Prix	Brands Hatch	72D	8	E. Fittipaldi	1st		2nd
1972	30-Jul	German Grand Prix	Nürburgring	72D	2	E. Fittipaldi	Retired	Cracked gearbox casing, fire	3rd
1972	13-Aug	Austrian Grand Prix	Österreichring	72D	20	E. Fittipaldi	-	Spare	-
1972	10-Sep	Italian Grand Prix	Monza	72D	-	E. Fittipaldi	-	Damaged on way to race	-
1972	24-Sep	Canadian Grand Prix	Mosport Park	72D	5	E. Fittipaldi	11th		4th
1972	08-Oct	United States Grand Prix	Watkins Glen	72D	11	D. Walker	Retired	Engine lost oil	30th
1972	22-Oct	John Player Challenge Trophy (NC)	Brands Hatch	72D	1	E. Fittipaldi	Retired	Oil pressure	1st
1973	28-Jan	Argentine Grand Prix	Buenos Aires Autodrome	72D	2	E. Fittipaldi	1st		2nd
1973	11-Feb	Brazilian Grand Prix	Interlagos	72D	1	E. Fittipaldi	1st		2nd
1973	03-Mar	South African Grand Prix	Kyalami	72D	1	E. Fittipaldi	3rd		2nd
1973	29-Apr	Spanish Grand Prix	Montjuich Park	72E	1	E. Fittipaldi	-	Spare	-
1973	20-May	Belgian Grand Prix	Zolder	72E	1	E. Fittipaldi	3rd		9th
1973	03-Jun	Monaco Grand Prix	Monte Carlo	72E	1	E. Fittipaldi	2nd		5th
1973	17-Jun	Swedish Grand Prix	Anderstorp	72E	1	E. Fittipaldi	Retired	Transmission	4th
1973	01-Jul	French Grand Prix	Paul Ricard	72E	1T	E. Fittipaldi	-	Spare	-
1973	14-Jul	British Grand Prix	Silverstone	72E	40	E. Fittipaldi	-	Spare	-
1973	29-Jul	Dutch Grand Prix	Zandvoort	72E	1	E. Fittipaldi	Retired	Driver retired hurt	17th
1973	04-Aug	German Grand Prix	Nürburgring	72E	1	E. Fittipaldi	6th		14th
1973	19-Aug	Austrian Grand Prix	Österreichring	72E	1	E. Fittipaldi	Retired	Broken fuel pipe	1st
1973	09-Sep	Italian Grand Prix	Monza	72E	1	E. Fittipaldi	2nd		4th
1973	23-Sep	Canadian Grand Prix	Mosport Park	72E	1	E. Fittipaldi	2nd		5th
1973	07-Oct	United States Grand Prix	Watkins Glen	72E	1	E. Fittipaldi	6th		4th
1974	30-Mar	South African Grand Prix	Kyalami	72E	30	P. Driver	Retired	Slipping clutch	26th
1974	13-Apr	Mercury 100 (SA)	Pietermaritzburg	72E	5	P. Driver	3rd		3rd
1974	04-May	Cape South Easter Trophy (SA)	Killarney	72E	5	P. Driver	3rd		4th
1974	25-May	South Africa Republic Trophy (SA)	Kyalami	72E	5	P. Driver	4th		4th
1974	15-Jun	Brandkop Winter Trophy (SA, NC)	Brandkop	72E	5	P. Driver	4th		2nd
1974	30-Jun	Bulawayo 100 (SA)	Bulawayo	72E	5	P. Driver	Retired	Engine	4th
1974	13-Jul	Natal Winter Trophy (SA)	Pietermaritzburg	72E	5	P. Driver	DNS	Engine failure in practice	-
1974	10-Aug	Rand Winter Trophy (SA)	Kyalami	72E	5	P. Driver	DNS	Crashed in practice	-
1974	31-Aug	False Bay 100 (SA)	Killarney	72E	5	P. Driver	3rd	No practice, started from back	-
1974	15-Sep	Rhodesian Grand Prix (SA, NC)	Donnybrook	72E	5	P. Driver	Retired	Gearbox	n/a
1974	28-Sep	Rand Spring Trophy (SA)	Kyalami	72E	5	P. Driver	3rd		3rd
1974	19-Oct	Goldfields 100 (SA)	Welkom	72E	5	P. Driver	2nd		3rd
1975	08-Feb	Cape South Easter Trophy (SA)	Killarney	72E	6	G. Tunmer	2nd	Did not practice, engine	9th
1975	01-Mar	South African Grand Prix	Kyalami	72E	34	G. Tunmer	11th		25th
1975	22-Mar	Goldfields 100 (SA)	Welkom	72E	6	G. Tunmer	2nd		4th
1975	29-Mar	Mercury 100 (SA)	Pietermaritzburg	72E	6	G. Tunmer	Retired	Broken valve	4th
1975	31-May	South Africa Republic Trophy (SA)	Kyalami	72E	6	G. Tunmer	3rd		7th
1975	05-Jul	False Bay 100 (SA)	Killarney	72E	6	G. Tunmer	1st		3rd
1975	26-Jul	Rand Winter Trophy (SA)	Kyalami	72E	6	G. Tunmer	DNS	Crashed heavily in practice	-

This car was built for new John Player Team Lotus recruit Ronnie Peterson to begin the 1973 season with. In fact he drove only the opening three Grand Prix in the car before switching to 72/6 which, along with 72/5, had been converted to conform to the new regulations requiring deformable structures. The conversion of 72/8 to this specification had to be hurriedly finished after SuperSwede had damaged 72/6 beyond immediate repair in unofficial practice for the International Trophy. Work that would normally have taken several weeks was completed in only one-and-a-half days in order that Peterson had a car in which he could practice. He raced 72/8 in the next World Championship round in Spain at the Montjuich Park circuit and was due to race it again at Zolder in the Belgian Grand Prix before yet another accident, this time in the morning warm-up, forced him to switch to 72/6, which he had also crashed in the morning warm-up but was less badly damaged! After this, Peterson decided that he preferred 72/6 and this became his regular race-car and 72/8 his spare.

For 1974, with 72/6 having been sold to South Africa, 72/8 became Peterson's regular race-car when he was not trying to make the temperamental Lotus 76 work properly. Despite the team's trials and tribulations with the 76, Peterson managed to mount a serious challenge for the World Championship title, winning three Grand Prix in 72/8, in Monaco, France and Italy.

Peterson continued to use 72/8 in the first two Grand Prix of the 1975 season, after which he switched to his 'new' car, the so-called 'lightweight' 72/9, and chassis 8 became his spare car. For the French Grand Prix, 72/8 appeared in a new 72F configuration, with a five-inches longer wheelbase, achieved by repositioning the oil tank between the rear bulkhead and the engine and mounting the engine on a tubular structure. In addition, so-called 'helper' coil springs were added to the front suspension to assist the torsion bar system in dealing with the car's ever-widening track. For the next race, the British Grand Prix, the torsion bar rear suspension was completely replaced by coil springs at the rear but didn't really seem to make a lot of difference as the car qualified in Jim Crawford's hands on the last row of the grid. This specification was retained for the German Grand Prix, where John Watson had a one-off drive for the team and put the wind up Peterson by outqualifying him before retiring early in the race with broken suspension.

The final documented appearance of 72/8 was in practice for the Austrian Grand Prix, where it sported modified pick-up points at the tops of the rear uprights but was otherwise unchanged. Driver Brian Henton spun on oil and damaged the car beyond repair so was unable to race. There is some disagreement as to whether this chassis may have been subsequently driven by Jim Crawford in the Italian Grand Prix at Monza, with several contemporary race reports stating that it was 72/5 and one other – written by Motor Sport's Denis Jenkinson – saying that it was indeed 72/8.

At the end of the season, the car was pensioned off and took its place on long-term loan in the Donington Grand Prix Collection, where it has remained ever since (see left & next page). In 2001, it was formally acquired from its previous owner by Tom Wheatcroft.

Debut:	Argentine Grand Prix, 1973
Final race:	German Grand Prix, 1975
Race starts:	20
Grand Prix starts:	19
Race wins:	3
Grand Prix wins:	3
Other notes:	

The Racing Record of Chassis 72/8

Year	Date	Event	Circuit	Spec	No.	Driver	Race	Notes	Practice
1973	28-Jan	Argentine Grand Prix	Buenos Aires Autodrome	72D	4	R. Peterson	Retired	Oil pressure	5th
1973	11-Feb	Brazilian Grand Prix	Interlagos	72D	2	R. Peterson	Retired	Broken rear wheel	1st
1973	03-Mar	South African Grand Prix	Kyalami	72D	2	R. Peterson	11th		4th
1973	08-Apr	International Trophy (NC)	Silverstone	72E	2	R. Peterson	2nd		2nd
1973	29-Apr	Spanish Grand Prix	Montjuich Park	72E	2	R. Peterson	Retired	Gearbox	1st
1973	20-May	Belgian Grand Prix	Zolder	72E	2	R. Peterson	-	Spare	-
1973	17-Jun	Swedish Grand Prix	Anderstorp	72E	2T	R. Peterson	-	Spare	-

continued over page

Chassis 72/8

continued from previous page

Year	Date	Event	Circuit	Spec	No.	Driver	Race	Notes	Practice
1973	01-Jul	French Grand Prix	Paul Ricard	72E	2T	R. Peterson	-	Spare	-
1973	14-Jul	British Grand Prix	Silverstone	72E	41	R. Peterson	-	Spare	-
1973	29-Jul	Dutch Grand Prix	Zandvoort	72E	-	R. Peterson	-	Spare	-
1973	04-Aug	German Grand Prix	Nürburgring	72E	2T	R. Peterson	-	Spare	-
1973	19-Aug	Austrian Grand Prix	Österreichring	72E	2T	R. Peterson	-	Spare	-
1973	09-Sep	Italian Grand Prix	Monza	72E	2T	R. Peterson	-	Spare	-
1973	23-Sep	Canadian Grand Prix	Mosport Park	72E	2T	R. Peterson	-	Spare	-
1973	07-Oct	United States Grand Prix	Watkins Glen	72E	3/2T	R. Peterson	-	Spare	-
1974	13-Jan	Argentine Grand Prix	Buenos Aires Autodrome	72E	1	R. Peterson	13th		1st
1974	27-Jan	Brazilian Grand Prix	Interlagos	72E	1	R. Peterson	6th		4th
1974	30-Mar	South African Grand Prix	Kyalami	72E	31	R. Peterson	-	Spare	-
1974	28-Apr	Spanish Grand Prix	Jarama	72E	-	-	-	Spare	-
1974	12-May	Belgian Grand Prix	Zolder	72E	1T	R. Peterson	-	Spare	-
1974	26-May	Monaco Grand Prix	Monte Carlo	72E	1	R. Peterson	1st		3rd
1974	09-Jun	Swedish Grand Prix	Anderstorp	72E	1	R. Peterson	Retired	Drive-shaft failure	5th
1974	23-Jun	Dutch Grand Prix	Zandvoort	72E	1	R. Peterson	10th		10th
1974	07-Jul	French Grand Prix	Dijon	72E	1	R. Peterson	1st		2nd
1974	20-Jul	British Grand Prix	Brands Hatch	72E	1	R. Peterson	10th		2nd
1974	04-Aug	German Grand Prix	Nürburgring	72E	1	R. Peterson	DNS	Crashed in practice	8th
1974	18-Aug	Austrian Grand Prix	Österreichring	72E	1	R. Peterson	Retired	Broken CV joint bearing cage	6th
1974	08-Sep	Italian Grand Prix	Monza	72E	1	R. Peterson	1st		7th
1974	22-Sep	Canadian Grand Prix	Mosport Park	72E	1	R. Peterson	3rd		10th
1974	06-Oct	United States Grand Prix	Watkins Glen	72E	1	R. Peterson	13th	NR at finish, loose fuel line	19th
1975	12-Jan	Argentine Grand Prix	Buenos Aires Autodrome	72E	5	R. Peterson	Retired	Engine (dropped valve)	11th
1975	26-Jan	Brazilian Grand Prix	Interlagos	72E	5	R. Peterson	15th		16th
1975	27-Apr	Spanish Grand Prix	Montjuich Park	72E	-	-	-	-	Spare
1975	11-May	Monaco Grand Prix	Monte Carlo	72E	-	-	-	Spare	-
1975	08-Jun	Swedish Grand Prix	Anderstorp	72E	5T	R. Peterson	-	Spare	-
1975	22-Jun	Dutch Grand Prix	Zandvoort	72E	-	-	-	Spare	-
1975	06-Jul	French Grand Prix	Paul Ricard	72F	5T	R. Peterson	-	Spare	-
1975	19-Jul	British Grand Prix	Silverstone	72F	6	J. Crawford	Accident		25th
1975	03-Aug	German Grand Prix	Nürburgring	72F	6	J. Watson	Retired	Broken suspension	14th
1975	17-Aug	Austrian Grand Prix	Österreichring	72F	6	B. Henton	DNS	Accident in practice	21st

The tenth 72 chassis to be constructed, 72/9 was built for Ronnie Peterson to race in 1975. Apparently, there was a clause in Peterson's contract allowing him to leave John Player Team Lotus if they did not provide him with a new car for that season, so 72/9 was presented to the un-amused Swede as his 'new' car – the much-awaited Lotus 77 would not be completed until the end of the year and would not race until 1976.

The new car made its first appearance at the South African Grand Prix, where it ran disappointingly off the pace in qualifying and race. For the next race, the Race of Champions, its rear suspension was modified to accommodate cable-actuation of the torsion bar linkage at the rear, in an effort to prevent the inside rear-wheel lifting and getting wheelspin under heavy cornering forces. However, this broke in practice and for the race the car was converted back to its original specification.

For the International Trophy four weeks later, the cable actuation was back again, with an improved fixing at the ends to try and prevent the chafing which caused the breakage at Brands Hatch. Another modification was made to the front track of the car, which was widened. The car then ran in this form until the British Grand Prix but with a conspicuous lack of success, non-starting in the International Trophy, failing to finish in Spain, Belgium and Holland, and recording a best finish of 4th in Monaco.

For the British round, the car was converted – so far as was possible taking into account regulation changes that had occurred since – back to 1973 specification, reverting to a narrow track at the front and torsion bar suspension all round actuated by steel links rather than cables. The reason was to try and identify what was causing the unpredictable handling of the cars, which was causing chronic oversteer or understeer but nothing in between. The conclusion reached by the team was that it was due to the tyres being used and whereas Firestone tyres had been developed especially for the 72 back in 1970, the reality was that by this stage cars were having to be designed to suit the tyres rather than the other way round and the 72 patently didn't suit Goodyear's tyre designs.

Retirements in Britain and Germany were followed by a brace of finishes in the points in Austria and the Swiss Grand Prix, held at Dijon in France but these were really the product of steady driving than anything else. A further retirement in Italy was followed by the car's final race – indeed the last Grand Prix for any Lotus 72 – the US Grand Prix at Watkins Glen, where it went out on a comparitive high by coming home fifth with Peterson at the wheel.

The car was subsequently retained by Team Lotus and is still owned by the Chapman family (see left).

Debut:	South African Grand Prix, 1975
Final race:	United States Grand Prix, 1975
Race starts:	14
Grand Prix starts:	12
Race wins:	0
Grand Prix wins:	0
Other notes:	

The Racing Record of Chassis 72/9

Year	Date	Event	Circuit	Spec	No.	Driver	Race	Notes	Practice
1975	01-Mar	South African Grand Prix	Kyalami	72E	5	R. Peterson	10th		8th
1975	16-Mar	Race of Champions (NC)	Brands Hatch	72E	5	R. Peterson	3rd		6th
1975	12-Apr	International Trophy (NC)	Silverstone	72E	5	R. Peterson	DNS	Blown engine in warm-up	3rd
1975	27-Apr	Spanish Grand Prix	Montjuich Park	72E	5	R. Peterson	12th	Not running at finish	12th
1975	11-May	Monaco Grand Prix	Monte Carlo	72E	5	R. Peterson	4th		4th
1975	25-May	Belgian Grand Prix	Zolder	72E	5	R. Peterson	Retired	Accident - brake failure	14th
1975	08-Jun	Swedish Grand Prix	Anderstorp	72E	5	R. Peterson	9th		9th
1975	22-Jun	Dutch Grand Prix	Zandvoort	72E	5	R. Peterson	15th	NR at finish - ran out of fuel	16th
1975	06-Jul	French Grand Prix	Paul Ricard	72E	5	R. Peterson	10th		17th
1975	19-Jul	British Grand Prix	Silverstone	72E	5	R. Peterson	Retired	Engine	16th
1975	03-Aug	German Grand Prix	Nürburgring	72E	5	R. Peterson	Retired	Clutch slip	18th
1975	17-Aug	Austrian Grand Prix	Österreichring	72E	5	R. Peterson	5th		13th
1975	24-Aug	Swiss Grand Prix (NC)	Dijon-Prenois	72E	5	R. Peterson	4th		9th
1975	07-Sep	Italian Grand Prix	Monza	72E	5	R. Peterson	Retired	Engine	11th
1975	05-Oct	United States Grand Prix	Watkins Glen	72E	5	R. Peterson	5th		14th

According to Andrew Ferguson's book Team Lotus: The Indianapolis Years, this car was built up from the repaired chassis 56/2, in which Mike Spence had crashed fatally while practising for the 1968 Indy 500. However, in the same book it also states that the Formula 1 tub was built up by the fabricators after they had finished the work of rebuilding 56/2 and 56/3, implying that it was an entirely new car.

The existence of the car first became widely known in the week before the 1970 Italian Grand Prix, although several members of the motor sport press knew about it before then but had been sworn to secrecy. However, with a Championship at stake, it did not run and the events of that tragic weekend are well-known.

The car made its first race appearance in the non-Championship Race of Champions in March 1971 and was entered for a further seven events, although it only started six of these due to engine problems in practice for the Jochen Rindt Memorial race. Its best performance was probably the International Trophy at Silverstone, the high-speed nature of the Northamptonshire circuit ideally suited to the turbine engine's characteristics. The car qualified on the front row and was only 1% slower than the pole time. Other good outings were at the British Grand Prix, when it set a time only 3% slower than pole and its final appearance, in the Preis der Nationen Formula 5000 race at Hockeheim. Again, the high-speed German circuit suited the turbine and it qualified only 2% slower than pole and ran strongly in the race to finish second.

The German event was its final outing and today the car is still in the same gold and black livery it competed in then and is still owned by the Chapman family's Classic Team Lotus. Although it is a non-runner, as the engine was returned to Pratt & Whitney when the programme ended, Classic Team Lotus hope that one day it can be restored and possibly even brought back to running order if a patron can be found to fund this work.

The Racing Record of Chassis 56B/1

Year	Date	Event	Circuit	No.	Driver	Race	Notes	Practice
1971	21-Mar	Race of Champions (NC)	Brands Hatch	6	E. Fittipaldi	Retired	Rear suspension failure	7th
1971	09-Apr	Rothmans International Trophy (NC)	Oulton Park	11	R. Wisell	Retired	Suspension damaged	9th
1971	08-May	International Trophy (NC)	Silverstone	2	E. Fittipaldi	N/C	DNF, Heat 1, 2nd Heat 2	3rd
1971	13-Jun	Jochen Rindt Memorial/Rhein-Pokalrennen (NC)	Hockenheim	9	D. Walker	DNS	Engine problems in practice	-
1971	20-Jun	Dutch Grand Prix	Zandvoort	15	D. Walker	Retired	Accident on sixth lap	22nd
1971	17-Jul	British Grand Prix	Silverstone	3	R. Wisell	13th	Not classified, 11 laps behind	19th
1971	05-Sep	Italian Grand Prix	Monza	5	E. Fittipaldi	8th	One lap behind	18th
1971	12-Sep	Preis der Nationen (NC)	Hockenheim	5	E. Fittipaldi	2nd		2nd

he first Type 76 chassis was designated JPS/9 to follow on from the most recent 72 to have been constructed, which was 72/8 (or JPS/8 if one follows the sponsor's nomenclature). However, if the numbering system used for the 72s is adopted, it is 76/1, as befits its position as the prototype car. As a further complication, the 76 was also referred to by the team as JPS Mark I, reflecting the fact that it was the first new car to be built since the John Player Special brand had become the team's title sponsor.

This car was extensively tested by Peterson and Ickx prior to its first appearance at the 1974 South African Grand Prix, with the Swede driving it at this race. As a result of the early testing done with the car, the pedal layout was changed, while the nose cone had also been moved forward.

JPS/9's debut race was short and definitely not sweet, Peterson retiring after a disastrous first-corner coming together with team-mate Ickx in JPS/10. A front-row grid position at the International Trophy was more encouraging for the Swede but more worrying was the fact that he was nearly two seconds slower than pole! Modifications for this race saw a reversion to an ordinary clutch and three-pedal layout, while the lower part of the 'bi-plane' rear wing was moved further back to try and reduce the amount of turbulent wind channelled to it. In the race, the car handled awfully before mercifully blowing an engine.

Another front row slot followed at the Spanish Grand Prix but could not be converted into a result due to engine failure as a result of chronic overheating. Here the biplane rear wing (which had been found to produce insufficient downforce) was replaced by a larger, conventional single plane wing as used on the 72s. Spongy brakes followed by a fuel leak accounted for the Swede's demise in the Belgian Grand Prix, although he had started from a reasonably competitive grid position

The inability of the 76s to last a race-distance resulted in them being rested for the next race, the Monaco Grand Prix, which Peterson promptly won, putting another nail in the new car's coffin. A testing crash in JPS/9 at Anderstorp did little to rekindle the Swede's enthusiasm for the 76 and he left his car in the paddock and concentrated on his 72. Two days after the Swedish race, JPS/9 was severely damaged in a testing accident at Zandvoort, when Peterson's rear brakes failed, the impact knocking the driver unconscious.

The car was rebuilt but did not appear again until the Austrian Grand Prix, where it had been brought up to the specification of JPS/10, with water radiators repositioned just behind the front wheels and faired in beneath a side cowling – in a bid to get heat into the front tyres - and the entire rear-end of a 72 grafted on. This was what Peterson had driven (and been impressed by) in the previous race in Germany, when he was forced to race a 'bitza' car after a practice shunt. However, the Swede reported that JPS/9 in this format felt different and again concentrated on his 72, as he did in Italy as well. In Canada, the car was Ickx's spare, Peterson having by this point in the season given up all pretence of trying to be interested in developing the car further. Its final appearance was as an unauthorised starter in the 1974 United States Grand Prix, with third driver Tim Schenken at the wheel, the Australian eventually being black-flagged for his misdemeanour.

The car remained in the ownership of the Chapman family until purchased in 2002 by the American collector Jim Bennett, who commissioned Classic Team Lotus to restore the car to its former glory. The car made its post-restoration debut at the 2002 Goodwood Festival of Speed in original Goodwood test specification, including 'bi-plane' rear wing as driven by Ronnie Peterson. The new owner intends to race it in historic events during 2003.

The Racing Record of Chassis 76/1 (JPS/9)

Year	Date	Event	Circuit	Chassis	No.	Driver	Race	Notes	Practice
1974	30-Mar	South African Grand Prix	Kyalami	76/1 (JPS/9)	1	R. Peterson	Retired	Accident damage from first-lap collision	16th
1974	07-Apr	International Trophy (NC)	Silverstone	76/1 (JPS/9)	1	R. Peterson	Retired	Engine failure after leading	2nd
1974	28-Apr	Spanish Grand Prix	Jarama	76/1 (JPS/9)	1	R. Peterson	Retired	Engine failure after leading	2nd
1974	12-May	Belgian Grand Prix	Nivelles	76/1 (JPS/9)	1	R. Peterson	Retired	Fuel leak	5th
1974	09-Jun	Swedish Grand Prix	Anderstorp	76/1 (JPS/9)	1T	R. Peterson	-	Spare	-
1974	18-Aug	Austrian Grand Prix	Österreichring	76/1 (JPS/9)	1T	R. Peterson	-	Spare	-
1974	08-Sep	Italian Grand Prix	Monza	76/1 (JPS/9)	1T	R. Peterson	-	Spare	-
1974	22-Sep	Canadian Grand Prix	Mosport Park	76/1 (JPS/9)	2T	J. Ickx	-	Spare	-
1974	06-Oct	United States Grand Prix	Watkins Glen	76/1 (JPS/9)	31	T. Schenken	Disqualified	Started race unofficially and black-flagged	DNQ

his car also made its debut in the 1974 South African Grand Prix, although unlike its sister JPS/9 it never raced with the hydraulically operated clutch due to driver Jacky Ickx not being confident about its effectiveness in a racing situation. After its first-corner accident at Kyalami, the car's next appearance at the Spanish Grand Prix was little better, due to a display of team incompetence which saw a wheel fall off in the pit lane following a tyre change and then the fire extinguisher set off by accident. By this stage, it had, like sister car JPS/9, reverted back to a 72-style single-plane rear wing in place of the ineffective 'bi-plane' original. In Belgium, spongy brakes also afflicted JPS/10 and then overheating forced its retirement. The car was taken to Monaco as a back-up but Ickx never seriously considered racing it and concentrated on his 72.

For the Dutch Grand Prix, JPS/10 was substantially revised, with the water radiators moved to just behind the front wheels and covered by a long side cowling which had been riveted on to the original structure. With yards of ugly additional water pipes, the car did not look very nice but

such a move was deemed necessary due to its inability to generate sufficient heat in its front tyres. Peterson had a go in JPS/10 in practice in France but was unable to match his pace in the 72. However, he was forced to race a 76 in Germany as a result of a heavy practice shunt in his 72. This was a hybrid car, consisting of a 76 tub and front suspension with an entire 72 rear-end grafted onto it, which involved considerable work on the part of the Team Lotus mechanics the night before the race! His fourth place paid them back in spades…

Ickx raced JPS/10 in Austria - still with its 72 rear-end - and was going well until an unfortunate accident forced his retirement. In Italy, he probably would have preferred to have reverted to his 72 as team-mate Peterson had done but there was no 72 for him to drive, so he had to race the 76, retiring with a broken throttle linkage. This was the last race appearance of JPS/10.

The car was subsequently loaned to Dave Render who competed with some success in sprint events in the mid-1970s and was later sold by Team Lotus. Its current whereabouts are unknown, although it is believed to be on the North American Continent.

The Racing Record of Chassis 76/2 (JPS/10)

Year	Date	Event	Circuit	Chassis	No.	Driver	Race	Notes	Practice
1974	30-Mar	South African Grand Prix	Kyalami	76/2 (JPS/10)	2	J. Ickx	Retired	Withdrawn by team	10th
1974	28-Apr	Spanish Grand Prix	Jarama	76/2 (JPS/10)	2	J. Ickx	Retired	Brakes	5th
1974	12-May	Belgian Grand Prix	Nivelles	76/2 (JPS/10)	2	J. Ickx	Retired	Overheating	16th
1974	26-May	Monaco Grand Prix	Monte Carlo	76/2 (JPS/10)	2T	J. Ickx	-	Spare	-
1974	23-Jun	Dutch Grand Prix	Zandvoort	76/2 (JPS/10)	2T	J. Ickx	-	Spare	-
1974	07-Jul	French Grand Prix	Dijon	76/2 (JPS/10)	1T	R. Peterson	-	Spare	-
1974	04-Aug	German Grand Prix	Nürburgring	76/2 (JPS/10)	1	R. Peterson	4th	Hybrid car with 72 rear-end after crashing 72 in practice	2nd
1974	18-Aug	Austrian Grand Prix	Österreichring	76/2 (JPS/10)	2	J. Ickx	Retired	Accident	22nd
1974	08-Sep	Italian Grand Prix	Monza	76/2 (JPS/10)	2	J. Ickx	Retired	Throttle linkage	16th

Photographers' Acknowledgements

Booen, Jerry 122

Cancelliere, Gianni 96

Catt, Ian 1, 4, 5, 18, 19, 20, 23, 31, 32, 61, 71, 83, 85, 86, 87, 88, 89, 94, 95, 99, 100, 101, 102, 103, 105, 112, 116, 118, 120, 121, 123, 125, 126, 128, 129, 131, 134, 135, 138, 143, 146, 149, 150, 152, 153, 154, 155, 156, 157, 161, 165, 166, 167, 168, 169, 173, 175, 180, 181, 184, 187, 189, 211, 212, 213, 214, 222, 227, 234, 240

Classic Team Lotus, 10, 11, 15, 19, 20, 22, 25, 26, 27, 29, 30, 31, 33, 38, 41, 54, 62, 77, 91, 97, 119, 127, 129, 150, 151, 162, 173, 186, 215

Critcher, Gary 81

Driver, Paddy 210, 202

Ferret Photographic, 39, 54, 56, 66, 68, 69, 72, 76, 93, 111, 136, 180, 188

Ford Photographic Library, 12, 13, 14, 15, 18, 21, 26, 29, 30, 32, 56, 57, 62, 63, 64, 65, 66, 67, 71, 77, 97, 91, 92, 97, 99, 103, 104, 108, 109, 112, 117, 118, 120, 121, 123, 125, 126, 128, 129, 130, 133, 134, 137, 138, 139, 141, 142, 143, 145, 146, 159, 163, 170, 174, 178, 186, 188, 190, 191, 192, 217

GP Library, The 15, 17, 21, 44, 50

Hayes, Norman 68, 93, 113, 181

Hostler, John 28

McLoughlin, John 203

Keyser, Michael 26, 55, 58

Kreisky, Brian 61, 64

L.A.T. 193, 206

Lucky Strike, 197, 199, 200, 201, 202, 205

Lyons, Pete 53, 54, 118, 153

Matthews, Tony 80

May, Stevie 75, 78, 79, 81, 84, 94, 101, 110, 115, 116, 162

Rohracher, Thomas 51

Schijatschky, Milan 41, 46, 48, 49

Schryver, Michael 44, 73, 74, 76, 96

Sims, Dave 30

Snowdon, Nigel 74

Soler-Roig, Alex 22, 23

Taylor, William 7, 8, 9, 10, 11, 13, 14, 16, 18, 24, 27, 28, 33, 34, 40, 52, 57, 59, 60, 61, 62, 63, 64, 70, 75, 77, 80, 82, 83, 84, 85, 88, 90, 91, 92, 95, 97, 98, 99, 100, 104, 105, 106, 107, 109, 11, 113, 114, 115, 117, 118, 119, 120, 122, 124, 125, 127, 128, 131, 132, 133, 134, 135, 136, 137, 139, 140, 142, 143, 145, 147, 148, 152, 156, 157, 158, 159, 160, 162, 163, 164, 166, 169, 170, 171, 172, 173, 175, 176, 177, 180, 182, 186, 187, 193, 194, 210, 216, 218, 220, 221, 224, 226, 229, 230, 231, 232, 233, 238, 239

Thedin, Joachim 130, 131, 160, 161, 162, 184, 185

Trim, Allan 178, 179, 203, 204, 207

Walton, Dave 207

Van Rensburg, Ben 154, 195, 196, 197, 199, 200, 203, 204, 205, 206, 207, 208, 209

Walitsch, Eric 32, 35, 36, 37, 43, 44, 50

Zana, Aldo 42, 45, 46, 47, 49, 50, 108

Photographer Ian Catt poses with the JPS Girls just before the 1973 British Grand Prix

Index

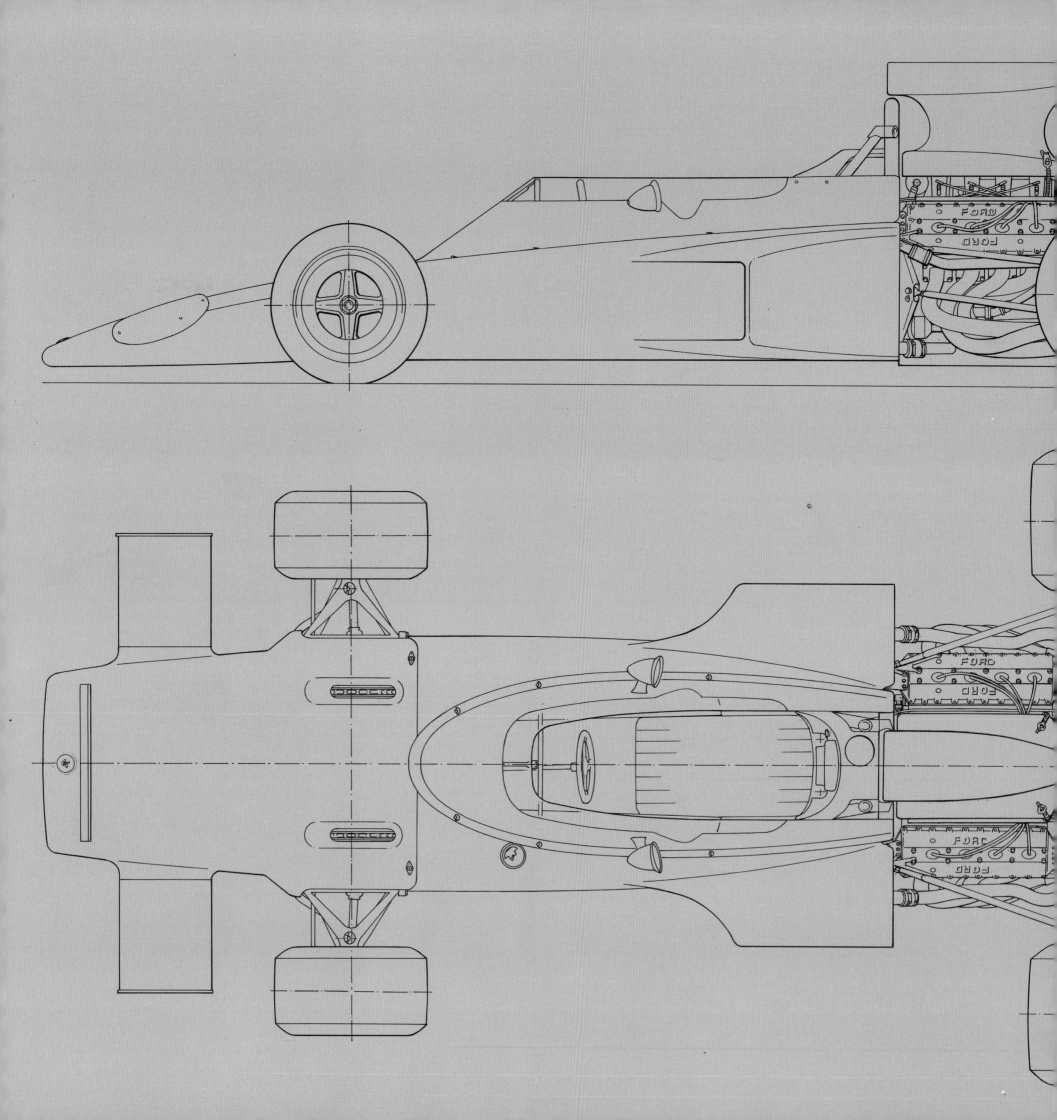